SOAP Programming
with Java™

Bill Brogden

SYBEX

San Francisco · London

Associate Publisher: Richard Mills

Acquisitions Editor: Peter Arnold

Developmental Editor: Tom Cirtin

Editor: Sally Engelfried

Production Editor: Mae Lum

Technical Editor: Piroz Mohseni

Graphic Illustrator: Tony Jonick

Electronic Publishing Specialist: Maureen Forys, Happenstance Type-O-Rama

Proofreaders: Emily Hsuan, Nelson Kim, Leslie Light, Laurie O'Connell, Yariv Rabinovitch, Nancy Riddiough

Indexer: Jerilyn Sproston

Cover Designer: Caryl Gorska, Gorska Design

Cover Photographer: D. Normark/PhotoLink, PhotoDisc

*To my wife, Rebecca, my unfailing
support through many years.*

Acknowledgments

I would like to thank the following people for their help.

As always, my wife, Rebecca, my unfailing support through many years.

My fellow LANWrights, Inc. employees Ed Tittel and Dawn Rader for their guidance and editorial expertise, respectively.

The contributors to the Apache SOAP project and developers mailing list for creating the open-source code that has been so useful in creating this book.

Finally, the wonderful people at Sybex for being a great group to work with!

Contents at a Glance

Contents

Introduction

The landscape of computing was completely changed in the last few years by a remarkable outbreak of cooperation between competitors in the software industry. As a consequence of the global nature of the Internet, and recognizing that computing no longer goes on in isolated islands of proprietary software, many important standards have been created.

One of the biggest success stories is the rapid acceptance of XML as a flexible and non-proprietary way of describing data in a form that is readable by both humans and computers. This success has encouraged industry leaders to propose SOAP (Simple Object Access Protocol) as a way of using XML for conveying not just data but also actions to be carried out on the data.

As a Java programmer, you are ideally positioned to take advantage of SOAP. Sun developers pioneered and supported the development of the basic technology of XML, so it is not surprising that some of the best tools for SOAP and XML are written in Java.

The Connectivity Revolution

Sun has been saying "the network is the computer" for years; now that vision is bearing fruit. We have a revolution in programming paradigms, from computing as something that is carried out in isolated systems to computing as a process carried out by multiple cooperating processes that may be on hardware scattered around your office or across the entire Internet.

Hardware engineers have risen to meet the connectivity challenge with cheaper and more powerful networked devices. Practically every day brings new hardware capabilities, and the great thing for us programmers is that they all can run Java programs. I would not be surprised if we end up with more Java running on mobile phones and PDAs than on desktops.

Without higher levels of organization, SOAP would not be so revolutionary. Fortunately, there are widely accepted standards that enable you to make your SOAP service available on the Web with little hassle. I am referring to the Web Services Descriptive Language (WSDL) that lets you define an interface, and the Universal Description, Discovery, and Integration (UDDI) standard, which lets you advertise the availability of your service. Of course these standards also let you find other people's SOAP services that may be able to cooperate with yours!

Implications for Programmers

It is interesting to speculate on the implications of widespread acceptance of SOAP for individual programmers and small organizations. In a public registry of SOAP services, your product has equal standing with the products of large organizations. This eliminates many of the marketing barriers that tend to keep good products from small organizations out of the public eye.

There are also interesting implications for large organizations, especially those with widely distributed operations. I think that using SOAP to improve distribution of resources inside corporate networks will be the first large-scale application in many big organizations.

Writing about SOAP

With everything in the SOAP world changing rapidly, I decided to avoid writing as if we already had the ideal API in the existing Apache SOAP project or any other existing toolkit. Instead, I have tried to emphasize the general approaches that you must use in dealing with SOAP. Naturally, the examples have to use a particular toolkit that may be superceded soon, but the general outline will remain valid.

I have also tried to avoid what seems to me to be an excessive focus in recent literature on SOAP messages traveling by HTTP and talking to web servers. Sure, that is going to be a big application area, but SOAP messages can travel by other paths as well. For that reason, I have dug into other message technology that you may not be familiar with, such as Java Message Service, JavaSpaces, JavaMail, and the Java 2 Micro Edition (J2ME) Wireless Toolkit.

About the CD-ROM

The CD contains the source code for all of the significant software used in the book, organized by chapters. In addition, it includes the source and compiled class files for the Util-Snoop program that is used in several chapters to examine the conversations between SOAP clients and servers. Several prominent vendors have consented to provide evaluation copies of programs that I think you will find interesting and useful.

Contacting the Author

I would be delighted to hear from any reader with suggestions, reports of errors in this text, or your SOAP success stories. You can reach me at wbrogden@bga.com in cyberspace. My real-space address is William Brogden, 130 Woodland Trail, Leander, TX 78641.

I will be maintaining an area on the LANWrights, Inc. website for additional SOAP resources at:

`http://www.lanw.com/books/javasoap/`

Reports of errata will be available at:

`http://www.lanw.com/books/errata/`

About the Author

William (Bill) Brogden has been working with Java since version 1.0 was released. His first big Java project was an applet that presented animated near-real-time major league baseball games. Bill is employed by LANWrights, Inc., where he has been using Java technology for online courseware. Bill has written several books about Java, including *Java Developer's Guide to Servlets and JSP* (Sybex, 2000).

In his spare time, Bill reads science fiction and trains basset hounds. He lives in the woods near Austin, Texas, with his wife Rebecca and numerous hounds.

CHAPTER 1

Understanding XML Messaging

- Messaging essentials

- Message-oriented Java APIs

- Java and XML

- The XML predecessors of SOAP

To understand why people are so excited about XML-based messaging, you must first consider the general state of messaging mechanisms in the network-connected world of distributed computing. After a review of various communication architectures, this chapter takes a look at the early history of messaging developments leading up to SOAP (Simple Object Access Protocol). Keeping track of all of the different players in this game is difficult, so I have tried to point out the most significant initiatives.

Messaging Architectures

The major distinctions you have to draw on when discussing the exchange of messages between communicating entities have to do with addressing and immediacy. With a point-to-point design, the creator of a message addresses it to exactly one recipient. With a publish/subscribe design, the creator sends the message to a third-party server. The recipients, who are subscribers to this particular kind of message, copy it from the server. Thus, the recipients in a publish/subscribe architecture are identified by their interest in a particular topic, not by their address. Figure 1.1 illustrates these different architectures.

FIGURE 1.1:

Point-to-point versus publish/subscribe

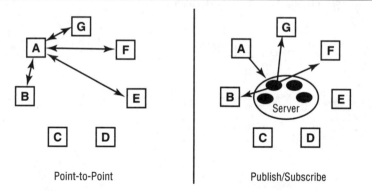

Point-to-Point   Publish/Subscribe

Immediacy has to do with the time relationship between sender and recipient. If the sender waits for an immediate response, it is a synchronous relationship. For example, in TCP/IP, the base protocol of the Internet, every message is acknowledged so that sender and recipient are synchronized. In a synchronous relationship, if the sender is waiting for an acknowledgement and none is sent, the communication has failed.

In contrast, in an asynchronous relationship, the sender transmits the message without expecting an immediate response. This provides much greater flexibility because the receiving agent can pick up the message when processing power is available. Furthermore, the system does not fail if the receiving agent is temporarily off the network. The drawback is that now the entire system depends on the server.

The Mental Shift

For many programmers, changing from an architecture in which you can expect an immediate response to calling a function to an asynchronous system requires a major mental shift. This shift is comparable to that required on going from a strictly procedural and single-threaded program to the event-oriented and multithreaded programs found on modern desktop systems and web servers.

Sometimes it just doesn't seem right that a collection of processes exchanging asynchronous messages whenever they feel like it can be as fast and as powerful as a system built around immediate response to requests. The contrast is as strong as that between "free market" and "command" economies.

However, you can expect to encounter this brand of computing more and more as you work with distributed objects. Many software architects feel that this is the only way to build resilient and failsafe systems. For a mind-bending example, consider the Jini and JavaSpaces technology for distributed systems that Sun is promoting:

```
http://java.sun.com/products/javaspaces/
```

The Spectrum of Complexity

Messaging has a spectrum of complexity ranging from simple message passing to creating and operating on remote objects. At the simple end of the spectrum, the treatment of the message is defined by the protocol in use. For example, with e-mail, the Multipurpose Internet Mail Extensions (MIME) protocol defines the treatment of the message content.

At the complex end of the spectrum, the protocol simply ensures delivery of the message. The receiving party must interpret the message content in terms of objects, methods, resources, and sequence of operations. It is at this complex end of the messaging spectrum that SOAP operates.

The Pioneer: EDI

Until relatively recently, the great bulk of electronic messages didn't go through the Internet at all, but through private networks. In spite of the fact that the format for this Electronic Data Interchange (EDI) of messages is highly industry-specific and not particularly flexible, it is still the primary means of business-to-business (B2B) data exchange. Before the rise of the Internet, communication took place on expensive leased lines or private networks. Now it is much cheaper to create a virtual private network (VPN) by sending encrypted data over the Internet, but the underlying messages still use EDI coding.

There are many industries that have an extensive investment in EDI and are going to be slow to change to Internet-based web services. Examples include hospitals, banks, and insurance companies. However, the advantages to be gained in terms of greater flexibility and lower communication costs appear to make it inevitable that even these industries will have to replace existing EDI applications.

Messaging Systems as Applications

Recent years have seen the rise of major applications for the enterprise that can be called Message-Oriented Middleware (MOM) applications. The Lotus company was one of the first to recognize that unifying the data communications for an enterprise could yield significant benefits and command a premium price. The success of the Lotus Notes application verified that corporations realized the benefits that could stem from this unification.

As the communication channels used by enterprises have expanded to include e-mail, websites, fax, voice mail, the short message service on cellular phones, personal digital assistants, and the wireless Internet, the scope of messaging systems has expanded to keep up. Lotus now talks in terms of "Unified Messaging" to encompass all of these channels.

The way in which the information resources of an organization are viewed has shifted from emphasis on the giant mainframe database to emphasis on information flow within the organization, with customers, with suppliers, and with the public. It is widely anticipated that the value of B2B transactions on the Internet will continue to exceed the value of consumer transactions.

Java Message Service

Just as JDBC (Java Database Connectivity) has become the standard interface for communication between Java programs and SQL databases, Sun hopes to make Java Message Service (JMS) the standard interface between Java programs and commercial messaging systems. The JMS package provides abstractions for message creation and delivery systems and encoding for simple data types.

Although JMS defines several types of message, an XML type is not currently one of these types; therefore, vendors of JMS-compliant messaging systems have to provide XML as a proprietary type. In view of the rapid rise in importance of SOAP it seems a safe bet that an XML type will be in the JMS package soon.

Directory Systems

An essential part of messaging systems are directories that let a potential client program locate the correct way to address a service. Getting these directory services right is not a trivial task.

The Java Naming and Directory Interface is a standard Java language extension that provides a standard interface for addressing a variety of different directory and naming systems, such as Novell NetWare NDS, CORBA Naming Service, and JMS services.

As the number of web services increases rapidly, just finding the kind of service you need requires more and more effort. A number of initiatives to create these super directory services have been undertaken. For example, IBM, Microsoft, and Sun are involved with establishing the Universal Description, Discovery, and Integration (UDDI) standard.

The objective of UDDI (see www.uddi.org) is to create a sort of web-based, universal, Yellow Pages-type directory for companies, which publishes the existence of web services in a single registry in order to promote business networking. UDDI represents one of the earliest uses of SOAP protocols.

Once you have located a service, you have to determine how that service wants to see requests formatted and how it will return results. It appears that the standard for accomplishing this will be Web Services Description Language (WSDL). Using XML formatting, a WSDL document provides all of the information needed to send a message to a SOAP-based web service and interpret the reply.

Communicating Objects

The most important of the non-XML based schemes for message passing and remote procedure calls are CORBA and DCOM. Before looking at these schemes, let me define some important terms:

Interface Definition Language (IDL)   The language used to specify the interface an object uses to communicate with the outside world.

Marshalling   The process of turning the structure of a program object into a stream of bytes is called marshalling.

Serializing   Another term for marshalling.

Unmarshalling   The process of turning a stream of bytes back into the original object structure.

Deserializing   Another term for unmarshalling.

Encoding   Turning data items into a form that can be transmitted by a particular protocol. For example, to include the binary data that makes up an image in an XML message, the bytes must be encoded as characters compatible with XML tags.

Another Pioneer: CORBA

A pioneering effort to get reliable communication of objects between disparate systems was the Common Object Request Broker Architecture (CORBA). The Object Management Group (OMG; see www.omg.org) was set up to create a protocol capable of providing communication between objects on completely different operating systems and written in different languages. An Object Request Broker (ORB) provides the interface needed for a client program to talk to a remote object.

Because the initial CORBA specification was released in 1992, it has had quite a long time for refinement compared to other technologies. Many software vendors produce CORBA-compliant products. In spite of—or perhaps because of—its maturity, CORBA is considered a difficult programming technology to master.

The OMG created a standard Interface Definition Language (IDL) that permits definition of an object's interface in a language-independent fashion. OMG also created a protocol—Internet Inter-ORB Protocol (IIOP)—for message communication over the Internet. The OMG is currently working on creating a SOAP-CORBA interface standard.

The Component Object Model

The Component Object Model (COM) is a Microsoft specification for integrating components within an application. This communication is low-level but can allow components written in different languages to interact. Distributed COM (DCOM) is a more recent development that allows components to interact over a network. The form of interaction is essentially a remote procedure call similar to Remote Method Invocation (RMI) in Java.

COM and DCOM are considered mature technologies because COM has been around since 1995. The specifications for COM and DCOM have been turned over to the Open Group for standardization efforts. Although Microsoft Windows systems are the primary users of DCOM, there is no reason it could not be extended to use on other operating systems.

Remote Method Invocation

The simplest approach in Java to communication between objects in distributed systems is provided by the RMI classes. Added to the standard Java library in JDK 1.1, and subsequently enhanced, RMI is the core technology for Java object to Java object communication.

The RMI classes allow programmers to treat a remote object as if it resides within the local application. All a programmer has to do is determine the public interface to be exposed by the remote object. The `rmic` utility program examines the interface and creates classes called the *stub* and *skeleton* classes.

The resulting architecture is shown in Figure 1.2. On the server side, the server application registers the interface with the `rmiregistry` and waits for a connection. A client application uses the `rmiregistry`, that lives on the network at a standard port, to obtain an instance of the stub class that implements the desired interface. Calls made to the stub class instance behave as if the remote object is in the local JVM address space.

The details of serializing objects, deserializing objects, and socket communication between systems are handled by the stub and skeleton classes. These classes use standard Java serialization techniques. Errors on the server side are signaled to the client by `RemoteException` objects that behave just like an exception thrown on the local system.

FIGURE 1.2:

Architecture of Java
Remote Method
Invocation

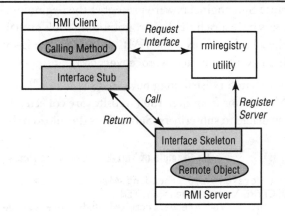

Advantages and Disadvantages of RMI

The most obvious advantages of Java RMI are ease of use and complete compatibility of data types. For programmers, all details of serialization and communication are taken care of by the RMI classes. As long as an object is serializable, it can be used in a call to a remote object method. For these reasons, RMI is the essential technology for all-Java distributed applications.

However, RMI has some disadvantages as well. Naturally, it can be used only between a Java client and a Java server. Furthermore, both sides of the communication link must have access to matching class files. Another disadvantage is that the ports used are likely to be blocked by firewalls and proxy servers. For these reasons, RMI is most successful within intranets.

RMI and IIOP

For the Java 2 Platform, Sun created tools capable of bridging the gap between Java RMI objects and CORBA-compliant objects written in other languages. If you have to communicate with remote objects in legacy systems, this standard extension may be your best choice. The RMI-IIOP package comes standard with the JDK 1.3 and subsequent versions of Java.

Java Programming and XML

The Sun engineer Jon Bosak was heavily involved in creating the first XML standard. The fascinating story of this pioneering effort can be read at:

```
http://java.sun.com/xml/birth_of_xml.html
```

Because Sun engineers were present at the beginning, it is not surprising that Java programmers have a rich field of programming tools available. Before proceeding to the tools, let's take a look at an example XML document (see Listing 1.1). This is a sample from the headline news service at www.moreover.com.

This system for distributing news items is an excellent example of publish/subscribe architecture. News items from over 1800 websites are collected by the Moreover organization and made available to subscribers. Subscribers download only the news items they are interested in.

Listing 1.1:   **An Example of XML-Encoded News Items**

```xml
<?xml version="1.0" encoding="iso-8859-1"?>
<!DOCTYPE moreovernews SYSTEM
      "http://p.moreover.com/xml_dtds/moreovernews.dtd">
<moreovernews>
 <article id="_25776592">
  <url>http://c.moreover.com/click/here.pl?x25776575</url>
  <headline_text>Nextel provides mobile Java downloads
  </headline_text>
  <source>PMN Publications</source>
  <media_type>text</media_type>
  <cluster>Java news</cluster>
  <tagline> </tagline>
  <document_url>http://www.pmn.co.uk/content.html</document_url>
  <harvest_time>Oct 10 2001 12:39AM</harvest_time>
  <access_registration> </access_registration>
  <access_status> </access_status>
 </article>
  <article id="_25774000">
  <url>http://c.moreover.com/click/here.pl?x25773993</url>
  <headline_text>MS charts new course round Java</headline_text>
  <source>ZDNet</source>
  <media_type>text</media_type>
  <cluster>Java news</cluster>
  <tagline> </tagline>
  <document_url>http://www.zdnet.com/zdnn/intweek/</document_url>
  <harvest_time>Oct 10 2001 12:01AM</harvest_time>
  <access_registration> </access_registration>
  <access_status> </access_status>
 </article>
</moreovernews>
```

The Document Object Model

The essential feature of DOM programming is that the entire document resides in memory during processing. The basic Java interfaces for DOM programming follow the architecture defined for XML by the W3C (World Wide Web Consortium) and are contained in the `org.w3c.dom` package. Every part of an XML document is represented as a Java object implementing an interface derived from the base `Node` interface. All nodes are connected in a tree structure that represents the hierarchical structure of the original document with a single `Document` object as the base.

In the case of the example XML in Listing 1.1, the base or root of the document is created by the `<moreovernews>` tag. This root has two child nodes created by the `<article>` tags and these in turn have child nodes representing the headline content tags.

Creating this structure is accomplished by creating a parser object and feeding a stream of characters representing the XML document to it. As shown in Figure 1.3, if all goes well, the result is a DOM in memory that can be searched and manipulated. Furthermore, the DOM maintains the complete hierarchical structure of the source document.

You can also create a DOM directly in memory by creating a new document node and attaching or modifying the child nodes. All of the methods for these operations are defined by the interfaces in Java's `org.w3c.dom` package.

FIGURE 1.3:
Document Object
Model processing

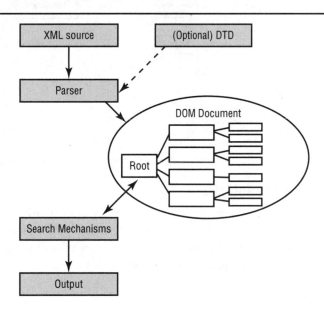

The Simplified API for XML Processing

It didn't take long for the pioneer XML programmers to discover that the DOM model can be a real pain to work with if you have really large XML data files to parse. With DOM, you are stuck with building the entire memory structure even if you are only interested in the contents of a couple of tags near the end of the file.

The solution to this is the Simplified API for XML (SAX) Processing model of processing. As shown schematically in Figure 1.4, a SAX parser scans an XML document in a single pass without looking back. Every time a tag or other significant element is recognized, the processor calls handler methods corresponding to the particular event. Generally speaking, SOAP messages will be handled with the DOM style because all of the tag content is of interest.

FIGURE 1.4:

XML processing
with SAX

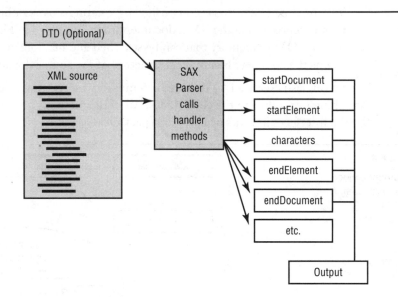

Java Parser Toolkits

It is a reflection of the rapid pace of activity in the world of Java, XML, and the Internet that there are a large number of parser toolkits available. Some of these adhere to the complete DOM or SAX specification and some have struck out on their own. Table 1.1 summarizes some of the major parser toolkits for Java.

TABLE 1.1: XML Parser Toolkits for Java

Acronym	Organization	Status	Comments
JAXP	Sun	DOM 2 and SAX 2 supported	Sun is developing this XML parser toolkit for eventual inclusion in the standard library.
XML4J	IBM	DOM 2, SAX 2 compatible	Continued development by IBM.
XERCES	Apache	The current version supports almost all of DOM 2 and SAX 2	Based on code contributed by IBM, the DOM and SAX parser is the basis for many Apache XML-related projects, such as Cocoon.
XDK	Oracle	DOM and SAX 1	XML developer's kit for Oracle systems includes a parser and XSL processor.
JDOM	www.jdom.org	working	A simplified document model optimized for ease of manipulation with Java.

XML Goodies

Because XML is extensible, it is a natural consequence that there is a great proliferation of XML-related initiatives in the programming world. Such standardization as is occurring is handled by the W3C (www.w3.org). Here are some that you need to be familiar with:

Extensible Stylesheet Language (XSL)   Similar to CSS (Cascading Stylesheets) as used for HTML formatting, but expressed in XML elements. Various toolkits have been written to automatically process XML documents by applying XSL commands. XSL can either transform your XML document to another XML form or format it as a completely different document. The W3C is attempting to formalize XSL, but the three main parts of XSL—XSLT, Xpath, and FO—have not reached the same state of development.

XSL Transformations (XSLT)   A language for transforming one XML document into another document. With XSLT, you can convert an XML document to HTML, other XML styles, or even to plain text documents. XSLT is already a W3C recommendation, and there are well developed tools for applying XSLT. The Xalan toolkit from the Apache organization is an essential part of Apache SOAP.

XSL-Formatting Objects (XSL-FO)   A scheme for advanced formatting capabilities in XSL. The Apache Xalan toolkit includes FO utilities to output a document in PDF format.

XML Linking (XLink) Language   Provides for elements that can be added to XML documents to create and describe links between pages and resources. XLink uses XML syntax to create simple one-way hyperlinks like those found in HTML, as well as more sophisticated links.

XPath   A language used by both XSL and XLink to address parts of XML documents using the hierarchy of elements.

XML-Based Messages

Many initiatives to use XML in messages are currently underway. Just keeping track of the players is quite a job. One attempt to list the major initiatives can be found at:

```
www.w3.org/2000/03/29-XML-protocol-matrix
```

Table 1.2 summarizes the initiatives discussed in this chapter.

TABLE 1.2: Summary of XML Messaging and Related Technology Initiatives

Acronym	Organization	Status	Comments
XML-RPC	UserLand	In use with many languages	XML Remote Procedure Call is a system for transmission of messages and remote procedure calls with HTTP and XML. This is the direct ancestor of SOAP.
JAXM	Sun	In early release	Java API for XML Messaging, based on the ebXML project.
SOAP	Microsoft, IBM, UserLand, DevelopMentor	Version 1.1	Simple Object Access Protocol is a system for transmission of messages and remote procedure calls and a more complex extension of XML-RPC.
WDDX	Allaire	In use since 1998	Web Distributed Data Exchange is a lightweight, XML-based data exchange technology.
RSS	O'Reilly	In active use	Rich Site Summary is a system for syndication of site content.
ebXML	OASIS, Sun, UN/CEFACT	Standard is available	Electronic Business XML is a complex set of specifications designed to enable a global electronic marketplace with XML. SOAP will be used as the messaging protocol. Due to backing by OASIS and UN/CEFACT, this is likely to become a widely used standard in competition with BizTalk.

Continued on next page

TABLE 1.2 CONTINUED: Summary of XML Messaging and Related Technology Initiatives

Acronym	Organization	Status	Comments
BizTalk	Microsoft	Available	A set of XML schema standards for business-to-business communication that is simpler than ebXML.
XAML	Bowstreet, HP, IBM, Oracle, and Sun	Proposed	Transaction Authority Markup Language is a system to define business transactions.
WSDL	IBM, Microsoft	Available	Web Services Description Language is a system for describing the interface and protocols used by a web service.
UDDI	IBM, Microsoft, Sun	Available	A web-based, universal, Yellow Pages–type directory for companies that enter their web services in a single directory.
XML encoding for SMS	W3C initiative	In draft	XML for Short Message Services is a message service used in mobile phone networks.

The Forerunner to SOAP: XML-RPC

The XML-RPC protocol was invented by Dave Winer at UserLand in 1998 and first implemented in the Frontier web server. It sends a remote procedure call using an HTTP POST request with XML 1 encoding. Using the widely supported HTTP protocol makes it possible to add XML-RPC processing to any web server that supports CGI (Common Gateway Interface) programming. Furthermore, using this standard protocol allows penetration of typical firewalls, making it easy to install an XML-RPC server without compromising security.

XML-RPC hits a happy balance between power and complexity, using a simple solution that is easy to program yet can transmit many kinds of data. The original SOAP proposal was based largely on XML-RPC.

Although SOAP has extended XML-RPC, this simpler approach is easier to implement and is still generating a lot of activity. It is by no means certain that XML-RPC will be replaced by SOAP. The home page at the www.xmlrpc.com website lists pointers to many implementations of the protocol in many languages. An example usage is retrieval of RSS (Rich Site Summary) data.

XML-RPC messages are sent with an HTML POST header and a content type of text/xml. XML encoding follows version 1 and does not use a DTD or namespaces. Listing 1.2 shows a request to a hypothetical lookup service.

Listing 1.2:   **An Example XML-RPC Request**

```
POST /RPC2 HTTP/1.0
User-Agent: Frontier/5.1.2 (WinNT)
Host: someserver.com
Content-Type: text/xml
Content-length: 181

<?xml version="1.0"?>
<methodCall>
  <methodName>lookup.getStateFromAreaCode</methodName>
   <params>
      <param> <value><int>512</int></value>
      </param>
   </params>
</methodCall>
```

The data contained in the <methodName> tag is quite flexible; it could name a Java class and method, a Perl script file to be executed, or any other resource. The order of the <param> tags inside the <params> must be consistent with the method being called.

The response format is also simple, as shown in Listing 1.3. Only a single <param> is returned if the call succeeds, but because this can be a collection of values, this limitation is not serious. If an error resulted from the attempt, the <methodResponse> will contain a <fault> tag giving both an error code and a text representation of the problem.

Listing 1.3:   **An Example of a Response to the Request**

```
HTTP/1.1 200 OK
Connection: close
Content-Length: 158
Content-Type: text/xml
Date: Fri, 17 Jan 2001 11:50:13 GMT
Server: UserLand Frontier/5.1.2-WinNT
<?xml version="1.0"?>
<methodResponse>
   <params>
      <param> <value><string>Texas</string></value>
   </param> </params>
</methodResponse>
```

Data types supported by XML-RPC are quite compatible with Java. The <int> data type is a 32-bit (4-byte) signed integer exactly corresponding to Java int values. Table 1.3 summarizes the allowed data types.

TABLE 1.3: XML-RPC Data Types

XML-RPC Data Tag	Corresponding Java Data Type
<int> or <i4>	int
<boolean>	boolean
<string>	java.lang.String
<double>	double
<dateTime.iso8601>	java.util.Date
<struct>	java.util.Hashtable
<array>	java.util.Vector
<base64>	byte array
<nil/>	null

The <struct> and <array> types can be nested so you can build quite complex structures. Because the request and response message must be parsed by XML parsers that have obvious restrictions on characters, arbitrary binary data must be encoded in a base64 character stream.

The Major Players

As you have seen, there is a lot of activity in the area of XML messages and network communication. Here is a summary of the organizations I think will play the most significant part in the ongoing revolution:

Apache   A nonprofit organization devoted to the development of open-source software. Apache has a number of projects related to Java, XML, and SOAP. Several of these projects use code contributed by IBM and Sun. Due to the very widespread use of the Apache web server, this organization has credibility in spite of a loose organization.

Microsoft   Codevelopers of UDDI, WSDL, and SOAP. Creators of the BizTalk messaging standard and .NET Web services based on XML and SOAP. Microsoft has committed to extensive use of XML in future products. Microsoft provides many XML- and SOAP-related tools, but these are not written in Java due to Microsoft's long-running lawsuits with Sun.

Sun   Developer and custodian of the Java language, active participant in XML, ebXML, and promoting web services. Intends to use the Apache version of SOAP as a lightweight messaging system in web services.

IBM   Committed to the use of Java and XML, developing many XML applications, contributed the SOAP4J code to the Apache organization to serve as the basis for Apache SOAP.

Oracle   The major supplier of database systems for Internet applications, Oracle provides extensive facilities for using XML in connection with database operations, including support for SOAP.

OASIS   The Organization for the Advancement of Structured Information Standards is a nonprofit international organization dedicated to creation of public standards, heavily involved with ebXML.

UN/CEFACT   The United Nations Centre for Trade Facilitation and Electronic Business is heavily involved with coordinating the acceptance of business communication standards all over the world.

W3C   The World Wide Web Consortium creates recommendations for standards such as XML, XSL, SOAP, and many other protocols. Widely accepted as the authority in spite of not having governmental status.

## CHAPTER 2

A Survey of SOAP

- How SOAP got started

- Who determines the standard

- What's in a SOAP message?

- How SOAP handles attachments

- Where WSDL and UDDI fit in

With the background of XML-based messaging in Java established in Chapter 1, "Understanding XML Messaging," we move on to the current state of the SOAP standard. What you'll find is that, although the basic documentation of SOAP version 1.1 is widely accepted, it does not constitute a standard. The first task of this chapter is to survey the status of SOAP as it evolves into a potential standard. From there, it examines the basic components of SOAP messages and some important SOAP-related developments.

The Status of SOAP

As of this writing, the nearest thing to a standard is the W3C Note dated May 8, 2000, entitled "Simple Object Access Protocol (SOAP) 1.1." This document was created by a group of authors from organizations involved in the Internet. The authors and their sponsoring organizations are as follows (in alphabetical order):

- Don Box, DevelopMentor
- David Ehnebuske, IBM
- Gopal Kakivaya, Microsoft
- Andrew Layman, Microsoft
- Noah Mendelsohn, Lotus Development Corp.
- Henrik Frystyk Nielsen, Microsoft
- Satish Thatte, Microsoft
- Dave Winer, UserLand Software, Inc.

The full text of the original note can be found on the Web at:

```
http://www.w3.org/TR/2000/NOTE-SOAP-20000508
```

A proposed extension to the original note, called "SOAP Messages with Attachments" was submitted to the W3C in December 2000. This proposal provides a way for a SOAP 1.1 message to be carried inside a MIME (Multipurpose Internet Mail Extensions) multipart message. The purpose of this proposal is to provide a way to transmit a SOAP message with a variety of additional data as attachments. The full text of this note can be found at:

```
http://www.w3.org/SOAP
```

As notes, these documents have no real force. They are intended to serve as a basis for the formation of a working group in the area of XML-based protocols. However, the Apache, IBM, and Microsoft groups working on SOAP implementations appear to be sticking to the frameworks outlined in the notes. Any more widely recognized standard will probably have to come from the activities of the W3C XML Protocol Working Group.

XML Protocol Working Group

In recognition of the widespread interest in using XML for messaging and remote procedure calls over the World Wide Web, the W3C created an "XP" working group in September 2000. This group includes members from all the major organizations interested in using the Web for this purpose, as well as many smaller organizations. The original plan was that a recommendation would be released in September 2001, and the working group would be terminated in April 2002. However, many questions have arisen, and as of this writing, the group is still working on drafts. The XML Protocol working group home page can be found at:

```
http://www.w3.org/2000/xp/Group/
```

The approach that the XP working group is taking is to create a "requirements document" and then evaluate the SOAP 1.1 design versus these requirements. Where SOAP is found deficient, improved solutions will be recommended. The current draft of the requirements document can be found at the working group home page.

Scope of the XP Working Group

In establishing the charter of the XP working group, the W3C recognized that a very large number of other XML- and HTTP-related standardization efforts are ongoing. Therefore, the working group is expected to confine itself to the design of the following components of an XML-based messaging protocol:

Envelope   The protocol must provide a structure that can enclose all other components for transport. The method chosen must allow for interoperation between system and extensibility. It must also allow for transfer of the message between intermediaries (that is, store and forward, and so on).

Data encoding   The protocol must define a mechanism to represent a variety of data types, including complex objects. This mechanism must be based on the XML Schema recommendations.

RPC convention   The protocol must provide a convention for representation of a remote procedure call (RPC) in the body of the message.

HTTP transport   The working group will develop a mechanism for transport of XP messages using HTTP.

In addition to designing these components, the working group is expected to give the following requirements a high priority:

Simplicity   To keep the protocol easy to understand, easy to implement, and easy to evolve, the working group is expected to strive for simplicity.

Evolvability and extensibility   The protocol must provide a design that permits extensions that do not interfere with each other.

This is rather a tall order. In recognition of this fact, the working group charter also lists areas that XP groups should not address or should consider a low priority. These are areas that are being tackled by other industry groups or are considered too complex to tackle in the time available:

Binary data   Although XML provides a handy representation of many languages that can be expressed in text, exactly how to support binary data is better addressed by other groups.

Compact encoding and compression   It is one of the design principles of XML that terseness is of minor importance. An XML representation is frequently many times larger than the basic data it marks up. Unfortunately, many potential areas of application for XP, such as wireless devices, are bandwidth sensitive. To keep things simple, compression techniques are outside the scope of the working group.

Additional transport mechanisms   The XP working group is expected to focus on HTTP as a transport mechanism and only consider others if time is available.

Metadata descriptions of services   It is envisioned that Web services using XP will be advertising their availability with some sort of metadata description. It is recognized that other groups are creating these services, such as WSDL (Web Services Description Language).

Relation of XP to Other Standards

Because there are so many activities related to XML going on in the W3C and other organizations, the XP working group specifically recognizes that other developing standards may impact the final recommendations. In particular, the XML Schema and XML Linking working groups are clearly important. Fortunately, these specifications are closer to a final recommendation than the XP specifications. The XML Schema standard is particularly important because it is the basis for the standard methods of encoding various data types in SOAP messages.

There is a good deal of cross-fertilization between the XP working group and other groups working on various XML and messaging APIs, such as ebXML and Sun's JAXM project.

Other Standards Organizations

The Internet Engineering Task Force (IETF) has activities related to message transport and XML digital signatures that are expected to be relevant to SOAP. IETF activities are summarized at www.ietf.org.

The Components of SOAP 1.1

In this discussion I will be closely following the approach used to define SOAP in the original note. The basic features of the SOAP specification can be divided into three areas:

Envelope   The protocol provides a structure (envelope) that defines what is in a message, directs the message to a specific recipient, and defines whether it is optional or mandatory.

Data encoding   The protocol defines a serialization mechanism to represent a variety of application data types.

RPC convention   The protocol defines a convention for representation of remote procedure calls and responses.

The intent of this three-part specification is to allow for maximum flexibility in implementation of each part with minimum interference with other parts. For example, the way an envelope is implemented should have no impact on the data encoding convention.

In addition to the three points just described (which define a message), a messaging system needs a *transmission method*. Although the initial examples of SOAP followed the XML-RPC path and used HTTP transmission, alternate methods of message transmission are not ruled out by the specification. The main alternatives that developers have been exploring are SMTP and Java Message Service (JMS).

Implementing SOAP in Java

The Apache implementation of SOAP in Java is organized along the same lines as the organization of a SOAP message. Thus there is an `org.apache.soap.Envelope` class that implements the methods needed to define an envelope. The major elements possible inside an envelope are the Header, Body, and Fault—each element is represented by a class in the `org.apache.soap` package.

Sun's Java API for XML Messaging (JAXM) also follows the same general approach, with classes in the `javax.xml.soap` package for Header and Body. However, it is pretty clear that it won't be possible to mix and match classes between the implementations. Changing an application from one implementation to another will be a serious undertaking.

Things Left Out of SOAP

As discussed in Chapter 1, messaging systems can get pretty complicated. The XML-RPC protocol, which served as the starting point for SOAP, is one of the simplest messaging technologies around. Although SOAP adds complexity, the designers intentionally left out some features that appear in other object-oriented messaging systems.

SOAP does not attempt to provide for distributed control of object creation, object activation, or garbage collection. SOAP also does not attempt to provide for bidirectional communication. The original SOAP 1.1 proposal does not attempt to provide for flexible attachments to SOAP messages, but this has been addressed in the "SOAP Messages with Attachments" note.

The original proposal also considers a single SOAP message at a time. Any protocol for transmission of collections of messages would have to be provided by modification of the 1.1 version of the standard.

SOAP and Namespaces

Let's look at the actual messages created in an example remote procedure call. Listing 2.1 and Listing 2.2 show the messages transmitted between client and server in the address book example provided in the 2 Apache SOAP distribution of August 2000. The server is Tomcat version 3.2 and the client is the GetAddress in the samples.addressbook package. The messages were captured by the UtilSnoop program provided on the CD.

Listing 2.1:   **Transmission of an RPC Message by HTTP**

```
POST /xml-soap/servlet/rpcrouter HTTP/1.0
Host: localhost:9000
Content-Type: text/xml
Content-Length: 450
SOAPAction: ""

<SOAP-ENV:Envelope
    xmlns:SOAP-ENV="http://schemas.xmlsoap.org/soap/envelope/"
    xmlns:xsi="http://www.w3.org/1999/XMLSchema-instance"
    xmlns:xsd="http://www.w3.org/1999/XMLSchema">
<SOAP-ENV:Body>
<ns1:getAddressFromName xmlns:ns1="urn:AddressFetcher"
    SOAP-ENV:encodingStyle="http://schemas.xmlsoap.org/soap/encoding/">
<nameToLookup xsi:type="xsd:string">John B. Good</nameToLookup>
</ns1:getAddressFromName>
</SOAP-ENV:Body>
</SOAP-ENV:Envelope>
```

The first five lines are HTTP request headers that are followed by a blank line. The meaning of these lines is discussed later in the section "Transmission with HTTP." The <SOAP:Envelope> tag pair encloses the entire remaining message. The opening tag establishes three namespaces, SOAP-ENV, xsi and xsd:

SOAP-ENV   The namespace for SOAP envelope elements

xsd   The namespace for data types defined in the XML schema standard

xsi   The namespace for data types as used in a particular instance

The namespace specific to the `AddressFetcher` class is established by the first tag inside the `<SOAP-ENV:Body>` as `ns1`. Namespaces are essential to SOAP because they prevent possible confusion with respect to different applications by providing unique identifiers. Namespace declarations appear as attributes in an element and are in force only between the opening and closing tags of that element. In Listing 2.1, the `nameToLookup` is defined to be an `xsd:string` type variable.

Unfortunately, a complete and final standardization of XML schema has not yet been achieved as of this writing. The evolving standard is not a single document but a group of interrelated documents, and there are many potential points of conflict between SOAP implementations using slightly different schema. As an example, a recent note in the Apache SOAP users mailing list described a situation in which a Microsoft server was expecting the first namespace declaration but the Apache code expected the second:

```
xmlns:xsi="http://www.w3.org/2000/08/XMLSchema-instance"
xmlns:xsi="http://www.w3.org/1999/XMLSchema-instance"
```

Now let's look at the response from the sample application, as shown in Listing 2.2. The response headers are discussed in the "Transmission with HTTP" section. Note that the remainder of the response is entirely contained with `<SOAP-ENV:Envelope>` tags just as the request was. In the body, the tag pair named for the method called, `ns1:getAddressFrom-NameResponse`, completely encloses another tag pair named `return`. The `return` tag establishes a new namespace `urn:xml-soap-address-demo` and encloses the payload of returned data, each item of which is characterized by a data type such as `xsd:int` or `xsd:string`.

Listing 2.2:   **Response from the *getAddressFromName* Method Call**

```
HTTP/1.0 200 OK
Content-Type: text/xml; charset=UTF-8
Content-Length: 902
Set-Cookie2: JSESSIONID=o51hzvqx51;Version=1;Discard;Path="/xml-soap"
Set-Cookie: JSESSIONID=o51hzvqx51;Path=/xml-soap
Servlet-Engine: Tomcat Web Server/3.2.1 (JSP 1.1; Servlet 2.2;
    Java 1.2.2; Windows NT 4.0 x86; java.vendor=Sun Microsystems Inc.)

<SOAP-ENV:Envelope
    xmlns:SOAP-ENV="http://schemas.xmlsoap.org/soap/envelope/"
    xmlns:xsi="http://www.w3.org/1999/XMLSchema-instance"
    xmlns:xsd="http://www.w3.org/1999/XMLSchema">
<SOAP-ENV:Body>
<ns1:getAddressFromNameResponse xmlns:ns1="urn:AddressFetcher"
    SOAP-ENV:encodingStyle="http://schemas.xmlsoap.org/soap/encoding/">
<return xmlns:ns2="urn:xml-soap-address-demo" xsi:type="ns2:address">
<phoneNumber xsi:type="ns2:phone">
<exchange xsi:type="xsd:string">456</exchange>
<areaCode xsi:type="xsd:int">123</areaCode>
```

```
<number xsi:type="xsd:string">7890</number>
</phoneNumber>
<zip xsi:type="xsd:int">12345</zip>
<streetNum xsi:type="xsd:int">123</streetNum>
<streetName xsi:type="xsd:string">Main Street</streetName>
<state xsi:type="xsd:string">NY</state>
<city xsi:type="xsd:string">Anytown</city>
</return>
</ns1:getAddressFromNameResponse>
</SOAP-ENV:Body>
</SOAP-ENV:Envelope>
```

More About Namespaces

A Uniform Resource Identifier (URI) is used to uniquely define a namespace in XML in lines such as the following from Listing 2.2:

```
<SOAP-ENV:Envelope
    xmlns:SOAP-ENV="http://schemas.xmlsoap.org/soap/envelope/"
```

This line establishes a namespace prefix of SOAP-ENV and identifies it with the URI of `"http://schemas.xmlsoap.org/soap/envelope/"`. Note that the element is named using the prefix that is established in the attribute. This namespace prefix is in force only up to the matching closing element.

You have already noticed the similarity between namespace declarations and addresses used to locate resources on the Web. However, don't assume that there is a real addressable document at that address. There are three terms in use here:

URI (Uniform Resource Identifier)   This is the most general term; the other two are subsets of URI.

URL (Uniform Resource Locator)   This form is used to locate a particular resource on the Web.

URN (Uniform Resource Name)   This form is used as a unique descriptor of a resource that will always be available.

The SOAP Envelope

The XML grammar rules for a SOAP Envelope are laid down in the note as follows:

- The element name is "Envelope".

- The element must be present in a SOAP message.

- The element may contain namespace declarations as well as additional attributes. If present, such additional attributes must be namespace-qualified. Similarly, the element may contain additional subelements. If present, these elements must be namespace-qualified and must follow the SOAP Body element.

The namespace for elements and attributes in the envelope is required to be like the following:

```
http://schemas.xmlsoap.org/soap/envelope/
```

Any other namespace should cause an error return. There is no provision for versioning of the envelope syntax.

The SOAP Header

The Header portion of a SOAP message is intended to be used as a flexible area for extending message content. The designers envision that the Header area might be used for message routing, authentication, transaction management, or payment information. The XML grammar rules for a SOAP Header are laid down in the note as follows:

- The element name is Header.

- The element may be present in a SOAP message. If present, the element must be the first immediate child element of a SOAP Envelope element.

- The element may contain a set of header entries, each being an immediate child element of the SOAP Header element. All immediate child elements of the SOAP Header element must be namespace-qualified.

When a SOAP message passes through intermediaries on its way to the final recipient, the intermediaries may use information in the Header to control further processing of the message. If an intermediary recognizes and processes a Header element, it must strip that element out of the Header when the message is retransmitted, as shown in Figure 2.1. Elements inside the Header can have two attributes that have special importance, the *actor* and the *mustUnderstand* attributes.

FIGURE 2.1:

Processing of a message by an actor

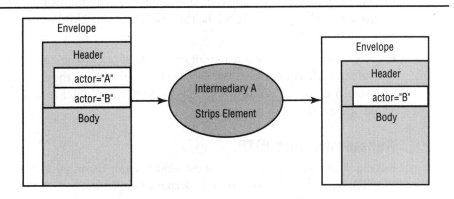

The *actor* Attribute

The actor attribute designates the recipient of a particular header element. This actor processes the header element and removes it from the total SOAP header. Figure 2.1, shown earlier, suggests how intermediary actor processes perform an operation and forward the remaining headers and SOAP body.

The SOAP *mustUnderstand* Attribute

An element inside the Header may have an attribute named mustUnderstand that indicates whether the recipient of the message must process the element correctly or can safely ignore the element. The mustUnderstand attribute has numeric values of either 1, meaning true, or 0, meaning false.

If the process by an actor with a mustUnderstand attribute of 1 fails, then a SOAP fault element must be generated as part of the return message body. The specification calls for four elements inside the fault element:

A fault code An initial set of codes is provided in the note, but it is expected that this will be expanded.

A fault string A human readable explanation.

A fault actor This designates the entity that found the fault.

A detail element This is generated only if the fault was in the body of the SOAP message.

The SOAP Body

The XML grammar rules for a SOAP Body are laid down in the note as follows:

- The element name is Body.
- The element must be present in a SOAP message and MUST be an immediate child element of a SOAP Envelope element. It must directly follow the SOAP Header element if present. Otherwise it MUST be the first immediate child element of the SOAP Envelope element.
- The element may contain a set of body entries, each being an immediate child element of the SOAP Body element. Immediate child elements of the SOAP Body element may be namespace-qualified. SOAP defines the SOAP Fault element, which is used to indicate error messages.

Transmission with HTTP

Let's look again at the HTTP request headers from Listing 2.1. The first line defines this as POST type request directed to the rpcrouter servlet in the xml-soap application of the server, and using HTTP 1. The second line gives the host and port number. In this case, I used port 9000 to send the request through the UtilSnoop application in order to trap the content of both request and response. UtilSnoop retransmitted the request to Tomcat.

```
POST /xml-soap/servlet/rpcrouter HTTP/1.0
Host: localhost:9000
Content-Type: text/xml
Content-Length: 450
SOAPAction: ""
```

The declaration of the content type as "text/xml" is required for HTTP messages containing a SOAP Envelope. The SOAPAction: Header is required in a SOAP request message. It can be used to indicate the intent of the request, or, as in this case, an empty string indicates that the request URI indicates the intent. The SOAPAction: line can also be empty, but it must appear. The purpose of the SOAPAction: Header is to enable servers to filter and direct SOAP messages.

SOAP HTTP Responses

Let's look again at the headers in the response from Listing 2.2. The first line is the usual HTTP status code, which in this case indicates that the message was received and processed. If an error occurs while processing the request, a 500 code indicating an internal server error would appear. As with the request, the content type of "text/xml" is required.

```
HTTP/1.0 200 OK
Content-Type: text/xml; charset=UTF-8
Content-Length: 902
Set-Cookie2: JSESSIONID=o51hzvqx51;Version=1;Discard;Path="/xml-soap"
Set-Cookie: JSESSIONID=o51hzvqx51;Path=/xml-soap
Servlet-Engine: Tomcat Web Server/3.2.1 (JSP 1.1; Servlet 2.2; Java
        1.2.2; Windows NT 4.0 x86; java.vendor=Sun Microsystems Inc.)
```

The Set-Cookie lines give the session id generated for the transaction in both "original" Netscape cookie style and the RFC 2109 style (Set-Cookie2:). In an application requiring an exchange of multiple messages, this session id could serve as a unique identifier.

SOAP Messages with Attachments

The SOAP messages with attachments proposal has been published as a W3C Note at http://www.w3.org/TR/SOAP-attachments. In this scheme, the MIME multipart message format is used to bundle a complete standard SOAP message with additional data in a "SOAP message package." The SOAP message, occupying the first position in the package, can incorporate references to the other parts of the message using a naming convention described in the note. SOAP message packages can be transmitted by HTTP, SMTP, or any other message protocol.

The example given in the W3C Note will serve to demonstrate the kind of situation for which a SOAP message package could be used. This example is the submission of an insurance claim to a SOAP-enabled processing application. The basic SOAP remote procedure call message is accompanied by a TIFF format image of a signed insurance claim form. The SOAP message gives processing instructions and includes a reference to the claim form image.

WSDL, UDDI, and SOAP

Web Services Description Language (WSDL) is an XML-based markup language for describing Web services such as SOAP. This system is currently under development by IBM, Microsoft, and other industry leaders. The basic idea is that a WSDL description can give enough detail to enable automated or semi-automated creation of programs to access Web services such as SOAP servers.

WSDL is considered an essential part of the industry initiative called Universal Description, Discovery, and Integration (UDDI). The purpose of UDDI is to provide a way for businesses to create descriptions of available online services. If this all works out, a person trying to locate a Web service to fill a particular need would be able to perform the following steps:

1. Look up potential services in a UDDI directory.

2. Use WSDL to uncover the interfaces needed to access the service.

3. Use the interface description to create SOAP messages that access the service and return the desired results.

Sun Microsystems and SOAP

As interest in SOAP as a universal XML-based messaging and remote procedure call mechanism grew during 2000, I could not help but notice that Sun Microsystems was not saying anything about it. This seemed odd because Java developers at Sun have been in the forefront of XML applications.

As discussed in Chapter 1, the main XML business messaging–related project at Sun, ebXML (electronic business XML), has received widespread acceptance. The UN/CEFACT and OASIS organizations released a finished standard for ebXML in June 2001. The main objection to the use of SOAP in this standard had been a requirement for arbitrary attachments to ebXML messages, a capability that was not present in SOAP 1.1.

The publication of the "SOAP Messages with Attachments" note by the W3C has removed this objection. As a result, OASIS and UN/CEFACT have announced that these organizations are committed to the use of SOAP as the basic standard for XML messaging in ebXML. Due to the involvement of the UN, it appears that ebXML will have international acceptance as a framework for business-to-business communication.

Java API for XML Messaging

Sun's official Java API for XML Messaging (JAXM) is currently working its way through the Java community process. As of this writing, version 0.92 of the specification has been released as "Public Review Draft 1," accompanied by binary versions of the proposed packages. JAXM will support SOAP 1.1 and the proposed SOAP with attachments standard. The current status of this project should be found at:

```
http://java.sun.com/xml/jaxm/index.html
```

The proposed API goes beyond support for SOAP protocol messaging as used in ebXML, by defining "Messaging Profiles." SOAP 1.1 would be defined in one of these profiles, but other profiles for other messaging standards can be defined. Thus JAXM is intended to be a generalized API capable of being used with a variety of standards for required header information. This design is rather similar to the way the Java API for XML Parsers (JAXP) is intended to be used as a generalized approach to working with various XML parsers. The "factory" design pattern is heavily used in both APIs.

An unusual feature distinguishing JAXM from other SOAP implementations is that the JAXM is intended to work in the environment of Java 2.3 servlet or J2EE 1.3 containers, not as a free-standing application. Because these use the most recent servlet APIs, JAXM will mainly be used by developers on the cutting edge of Java technology.

Tracking the Status of SOAP

As with many Internet-related technologies, many books on SOAP are out of date the minute they are printed. I suggest that you check the following Web resources to keep up with the changes:

```
http://soap.weblogs.com/
http://msdn.microsoft.com/soap/
http://www.w3.org/2000/xp/
http://www.w3.org/TR/
```

CHAPTER 3

A SOAP Server Example

- Setting up a SOAP server

- SOAP in a Tomcat server environment

- Additional tools you need

- Deploying your first SOAP service

- How a SOAP service works

- Things that may go wrong

To give you a feel for what goes on in a typical SOAP application, this chapter follows the installation of the Apache SOAP 2.2 package on a Tomcat server. This approach uses a servlet to process a SOAP request and generate a response. If you don't already have SOAP running on a web server, just follow along and you'll have one up and running by the end of this chapter.

NOTE   Because the Apache SOAP project is still evolving, some details may change between when this chapter is written and when you read this. The basics should remain the same, however, because they depend on the SOAP standard.

Installing the Tomcat Server

Although Sun experimented with supporting a Java-based web server and servlet engine for a while, they finally turned over development of the reference implementation of the Java Servlet API and JavaServer Pages API to the Apache organization. Apache is a real hotbed of development of Internet- and XML-related projects. The Tomcat server provides the current reference implementation of servlet and JSP technology. Tomcat is part of the overall Jakarta project whose primary website can be found at:

```
http://jakarta.apache.org/
```

The goal of the Jakarta project, as stated at that site, is as follows:

> *The goal of the Jakarta project is to provide commercial-quality server solutions based on the Java platform that are developed in an open and cooperative fashion.*

The Tomcat server has been recognized as a major accomplishment. For example, the editors of *JavaWorld* selected Jakarta Tomcat 3.2 as that magazine's Most Innovative Java Product of 2001.

This chapter works with the next generation of Tomcat, version 4.0, because it implements the Java Servlet API 2.3 and JavaServer Pages API 1.2, the latest and greatest at this writing. In this chapter I am using Apache SOAP version 2.2. This version has the advantage of compatibility with Sun's JAXP (Java API for XML Processing) package, version 1.1.

Installing Tomcat

Although you can download the complete source code for Tomcat from the Apache site and compile it yourself, that is not necessary. Just download the Zip file for the compiled package and unpack the compressed file to a convenient directory. Source code is available as a separate download. As of this writing, the Tomcat 4.0 package including source takes about 38MB of disk space.

The directory structure created by unpacking the zipped file as of Tomcat version 4.0 is shown in Table 3.1. Note that the logs and work directories are created when Tomcat is first executed. Some details of this structure may change with future versions.

TABLE 3.1: Tomcat Directory Structure

Directory	Subdirectory	Used For
bin		Batch or shell script files to execute various functions
common		
	lib	Common library jar files
conf		Configuration files
webapps	Root/docs	HTML-formatted documentation
jasper		JSP compiler
lib		All applications can use class and jar files stored here
logs		Tomcat logs are written here by default
server		
	lib	Library files used only by the Tomcat server
webapps		All web applications are here
	examples	The example applications provided with Tomcat
	manager	Tomcat management
	Root	Web pages corresponding to "/"
work		JSP compiler uses this directory

Setting Environment Variables

Certain environment variables must be set before Tomcat can be executed. Here are the variables required in the version 4.0 beta 5 I am using here. CATALINA_HOME is used instead of TOMCAT_HOME to allow developers to have both Tomcat 3.2 and 4 on the same system. This may change when Tomcat 4.0 becomes the official release.

JAVA_HOME   Points to the base directory for your SDK installation, such as c:\jdk1.3.

CATALINA_HOME   Points to the base directory for your Tomcat 4.0 installation, such as c:\tomcat4.

PATH   Your path variable should include the bin directory of your Java SDK installation.

NOTE   On Windows 98 installations, the default memory space allocated for MS-DOS prompt windows is not sufficient to contain the variables that Tomcat's startup procedure adds to the environment. To fix this, open an MS-DOS prompt window and right-click the title bar. Open the Properties dialog and go to the Memory tab. Set the initial environment variable to 4096.

Running Tomcat

Tomcat is started by executing the *startup* batch or shell script file found in the `bin` subdirectory. This batch file checks that the `CATALINA_HOME` path is defined and calls the `catalina` batch file (or shell script) that sets up environment variables and executes the Java interpreter to start the server.

By default, the Tomcat web server listens for browser connections at port 8080, so you should address your browser as follows to see the startup page:

```
http://localhost:8080/
```

NOTE   In the remainder of this chapter, I use URLs that assume your Tomcat server is addressed as `localhost` on port 8080.

The page presented is the `index.html` file located in the following directory, where *$CATALINA_HOME* stands for the base directory of your Tomcat installation:

```
$CATALINA_HOME/webapps/ROOT/index.html
```

Before proceeding with SOAP installation, you should try at least one servlet example and one JSP example to verify that everything is working. You should also familiarize yourself with the Javadoc format documentation of the servlet and JSP-related packages that the Tomcat installation conveniently provides.

The servlet examples are designed to demonstrate many of the handy capabilities of the Java Servlet API. If you are not already familiar with servlet programming, you should execute each of these examples and also examine the source code provided.

When you first try one of the JSP examples, there is a perceptible delay while the JSP page is translated into servlet code and the servlet code is compiled. After a JSP is compiled, it behaves just like a servlet. The `snoop` JSP example is useful because it shows how much information is transmitted with a request from your browser.

Web Applications in Tomcat

Every programmer working with Java Servlets or JavaServer Pages should have copies of the official Sun API documents for the APIs. In PDF format, these documents only take up a few megabytes on your hard drive and are easy to use. In particular, the Servlet API lays down the law about how web applications must be laid out in terms of the directories and configuration files used. These documents can be downloaded from the following locations:

```
http://java.sun.com/products/jsp
http://java.sun.com/products/servlet
```

As shown in Table 3.1, the standard Tomcat installation has a `webapps` directory that contains all web application files in a standard installation. The `ROOT` subdirectory corresponds to the `"/"` web server URL root. The `examples` subdirectory corresponds to the relative URL `"/examples/"` and so forth. All of the resources under the `examples` subdirectory are part of the `examples` web application. All of the resources of this application, such as image, html, and JSP files can be addressed by a web browser, except the resources in the WEB-INF subdirectory.

When creating your own web application, create a directory for it as a subdirectory of the `webapps` directory. Study the `examples` directory as a model for organizing your web application.

The WEB-INF Subdirectory

Java class files and other resources required by the servlets and JSP in a web application must be organized under the WEB-INF subdirectory for the application. The server is forbidden to allow direct access to these resources by a web service client, such as a browser.

Following the rules laid down in the Java Servlets API, the configuration of a web application is controlled by a file named `web.xml`. For example, the `examples` application is controlled by the file:

```
$CATALINA_HOME/webapps/examples/WEB-INF/web.xml
```

You should take a look at this `web.xml` file now using any convenient text editor. Note that the initial lines, as shown in the following code, follow XML conventions, naming the root element of the document as `web-app` and citing a public DTD.

```
<?xml version="1.0" encoding="ISO-8859-1"?>

<!DOCTYPE web-app
    PUBLIC "-//Sun Microsystems, Inc.//DTD Web Application 2.3//EN"
    "http://java.sun.com/j2ee/dtds/web-app_2_3.dtd">

<web-app>
```

The standard `web.xml` file provides a complete system for describing the components of a web application, including servlet names, classes, aliases, and initialization parameters. For example, here is the `web.xml` entry for the `rpcrouter` servlet:

```
<servlet>
  <servlet-name>rpcrouter</servlet-name>
  <display-name>Apache-SOAP RPC Router</display-name>
```

```
<description>no description</description>
<servlet-class>org.apache.soap.server.http.RPCRouterServlet
</servlet-class>
<init-param>
  <param-name>faultListener</param-name>
  <param-value>org.apache.soap.server.DOMFaultListener
  </param-value>
</init-param>
</servlet>
```

There is also a `web.xml` file in the Tomcat `conf` subdirectory. This `web.xml` file establishes defaults for a number of web server parameters and initialization parameters for the servlets that handle basic Tomcat functions.

Class and JAR Files

The Java class files used by servlets and JSP must be stored under the `classes` subdirectory of `WEB-INF` if they are in the form of individual class files or under the `lib` subdirectory of `WEB-INF` if they are in Java ARchive (JAR) files. Individual class files must be in a directory structure that reflects the package they belong to. For example, the `JspCalendar.class` file, part of the `examples` web application and declared as belonging to the `cal` package, lives in this directory:

```
$CATALINA_HOME\webapps\examples\WEB-INF\classes\cal
```

Web Application Independence

It is important to note that web applications behave independently. That is, a web application acts as if it is the only application installed on a server. Servlets installed in Application A can't make use of any resources, such as JAR files, in Application B, and vice-versa. If you want to make a Java library available to more than one web application, you must make it available to all by putting it in the classpath. See the section "Classpath Conventions" later in this chapter for details.

Web Application Installation and the WAR File

By making web applications independent, Sun has also made it easy to install, update, and remove web applications without interfering with other applications running on the same server. An entire application with all of its html, graphics, Java class, and other resource files can be packaged as a single Web Application Resource (WAR) file.

The format of this file is that of a JAR or Zip-compressed collection of files. The trick to using this simple format for distribution is the way a compatible server handles a WAR file. When Tomcat sees a WAR file that does not have a corresponding application directory, it expands the compressed file into the complete set of application files. You will see this in action when you install SOAP.

Tomcat Server Configuration

As previously discussed, web application configuration follows rules laid down in the Java Servlet API. This API does not attempt to define how configuration of the web server is accomplished; this is left up to the individual vendor. Tomcat uses a mixture of text files in the conf subdirectory to handle a variety of details:

server.xml   This file contains the parameters that configure the server. For example, a <Connector> tag defines the port that the server listens to for HTTP connections. This file must be well formed XML, but there is no DTD to validate it because it is anticipated that there may be additions and changes. Comments in the file are the primary documentation, and there is additional documentation reachable from the Tomcat startup page.

web_23.dtd   An example of the DTD used by the web.xml files in the Java Servlet API version 2.3 as used by Tomcat 4.0. This is not actually read by Tomcat.

web_22.dtd   An example of the DTD used by the web.xml files in the Java Servlet API version 2.2 as used in Tomcat 3.2.

tld_12.dtd   An example of the DTD used by the JSP tag library descriptor file for the JSP 1.2 API as used in Tomcat 4.0.

tld_11.dtd   An example of the DTD used by the JSP tag library descriptor file for the JSP 1.1 API as used in Tomcat 3.2.

web.xml   Default settings used by all web applications unless overridden by the application's web.xml.

tomcat-users.xml   This file defines user "roles" and passwords for use when security options are turned on.

catalina.policy   This file contains security policy definitions that are enforced if Tomcat is started with the security option on. The Java SDK comes with a policytool program to assist in editing this file.

Installing a SOAP Web Application

At a minimum, the SOAP package you download from the Apache organization website at xml.apache.org contains some documentation, example SOAP client programs, and the soap.war file. If your Tomcat installation contains an earlier version of Apache SOAP, including the soap directory itself, you must remove all traces of that installation before proceeding.

With your Tomcat server not running, copy the soap.war file to the Tomcat webapps directory where Tomcat finds and expands it on startup. Also, modify the server.xml file in the conf directory by adding the following context information for the soap application context following the "Tomcat Root Context" entry:

```
<Context path="/soap" docBase="soap" debug="1" reloadable="true">
</Context>
```

This tag establishes the web application context as follows:

path   The physical directory relative to the webapps directory root.

docBase   The relative URL the web server uses for this application.

debug   Establishes a level of debugging output, with 0 being the minimum.

reloadable   When true, the servlet engine checks for a new version of the servlet class file before responding to a request. If the new version exists, the old servlet is destroyed and a new object created with the new code.

Consult the Tomcat documentation files for more details on other possible parameters in a web application Context.

What the WAR File Installs

Now start Tomcat. When Tomcat finds that there is a WAR file that does not have a corresponding application directory, it creates a SOAP application directory and all of the required subdirectories with their resources. You should find that subdirectories named admin, META-INF, and WEB-INF have been created. Following the Java Servlet API requirements, all of the class files required to run the examples, and the web.xml file that controls the use of them, are in the WEB-INF directory.

Take a look at the web.xml file for the soap application. There are servlet name entries for rpcrouter and messagerouter. At this point, it may not be ready to run because SOAP requires other Java packages that are not normally included in the SDK distribution. What are now called "optional packages" used to be known as "standard extensions." Whatever they are called, Java has a formal Java Extension Mechanism for naming these packages and locating them where the JVM can find them.

If, for some reason, Tomcat does not automatically expand the WAR file, you can use any Zip-compatible utility to expand it in the webapps directory. Be sure to use the option that preserves directory structure.

Additional Libraries Needed

To make full use of Apache SOAP, you must get the mail and activation library jar files:

```
http://java.sun.com/products/javamail/
http://java.sun.com/products/beans/glasgow/jaf.html
```

* ie

...\ tomcat \ webapps \ soap \ ↙ soap.war

harlem: c:\Java\editable-classpath.txt = CLASSPATH

Because these are standard extensions, you can place `mail.jar` and `activation.jar` in the `JAVA_HOME\jre\lib\ext` directory and they will be found automatically when you start Tomcat.

The `mail.jar` extensions implement the Java Mail API and are used when processing SOAP messages with attachments. The `activation.jar` file provides the API for the Java-Beans Activation Framework. This standard extension API provides convenient methods for dealing with arbitrary data objects.

An XML Parser Library

Naturally, you must have an XML parser library installed on your system. Until recently, conflicts between different XML parser packages have caused a lot of trouble for programmers experimenting with SOAP. Because SOAP requires the namespace support in DOM 2 and SAX level 2, if your system has an earlier parser on the classpath, you can get some very strange error messages.

Fortunately, this type of problem has been largely alleviated by the arrival of Sun's JAXP 1.1 package. This package is expected to become part of the standard Java SDK so you might as well get used to using it. You can download the package and read more about the design philosophy behind it at:

```
http://java.sun.com/xml/
```

The Apache organization's Xerces parser is also compatible with the JAXP package. Consult the `xml.apache.org` website for the latest versions.

Testing the Installation

With all of these support libraries installed, it is time to test the main server classes that Apache SOAP installs. Assuming you installed Tomcat on port 8080, point your browser to:

```
http://localhost:8080/soap/servlet/rpcrouter
```

The response should be something like the following message, indicating that the rpcrouter servlet is correctly installed:

```
SOAP RPC Router
Sorry, I don't speak via HTTP GET- you have to use HTTP POST to talk to me.
```

Likewise, if you point your browser to the following address:

```
http://localhost:8080/soap/servlet/messagerouter
```

The browser should display something like the following message indicating that the messagerouter servlet is correctly installed:

```
SOAP Message Router
Sorry, I don't speak via HTTP GET- you have to use HTTP POST to talk to me.
```

The rpcrouter servlet is used to demonstrate remote procedure calls (RPCs), in which the output of a Java method is returned. The messagerouter servlet is used to demonstrate a more general approach to XML messaging.

You should also verify that the Apache SOAP administration utilities are running correctly by pointing your browser to the following address:

```
http://localhost:8080/soap/admin/index.html
```

A page giving several administration choices on the left side should be shown. These choices are as follows:

List   This lists all deployed services. Clicking any item displays the properties of the service.

Deploy   This displays a form called the Service Deployment Descriptor Template that you can fill in to deploy a new service. (Don't worry, there is an easier way to deploy a service.)

Undeploy   This displays a list of deployed services. Selecting one removes it from the system.

Deploying a Server Application

Your installation of Apache SOAP includes a samples directory with examples that act as clients to services dispatched by the rpcrouter and messagerouter servlets. These sample applications are all run from the command line. Because the sample applications all use classes in the Apache SOAP library, you must modify your classpath to include the soap.jar file. Here is the command I use to set the classpath for running the sample clients from the sample directories:

```
SET CLASSPATH=.;../..;path_to_soap_lib\soap.jar
```

There are two ways to deploy an Apache SOAP service: by filling in a form through the Apache administration page as just discussed, or by executing the ServiceManagerClient utility with the **deploy** command and the name of an XML-formatted file containing the deployment information. Each of the sample directories contains .cmd (for Windows) and .sh (for Unix) files that execute the utility and deploy the sample service. Here is an example command line:

```
java org.apache.soap.server.ServiceManagerClient
    http://localhost:8080/soap/servlet/rpcrouter deploy
    DeploymentDescriptor.xml
```

I'll delve into the mysteries of the deployment descriptor later. Right now, let's get the AddressBook example deployed so you can actually see SOAP in action.

Deploying the *AddressBook* Service

In the soap\samples\addressbook directory is a testit.cmd file that contains a sequence of commands that deploys the AddressBook service, tests retrieval of built-in data, adds more data, tests that, and finally undeploys the service. This file is shown in Listing 3.1. Note that for presentation here, the longer lines have been wrapped.

If your server is at a different URL, be sure to change the references in the file. While logged in to the soap\samples\addressbook directory, execute the testit file from a command line and observe the results.

Listing 3.1:   **The *testit.cmd* File**

```
@echo off
echo This test assumes a server URL of
    http://localhost:8080/soap/servlet/rpcrouter
echo Deploying the addressbook service...
java org.apache.soap.server.ServiceManagerClient
    http://localhost:8080/soap/servlet/rpcrouter deploy
    DeploymentDescriptor.xml
echo .
echo Verify that it's there
java org.apache.soap.server.ServiceManagerClient
    http://localhost:8080/soap/servlet/rpcrouter list
echo .
echo Getting info for "Mr Good"
java samples.addressbook.GetAddress
    http://localhost:8080/soap/servlet/rpcrouter "John B. Good"
echo .
echo Adding "John Doe"
java samples.addressbook.PutAddress
    http://localhost:8080/soap/servlet/rpcrouter "John Doe" 123
    "Main Street" AnyTown SS 12345 800 555 1212
echo .
echo Query "Mr Doe" to make sure it was added
java samples.addressbook.GetAddress
    http://localhost:8080/soap/servlet/rpcrouter "John Doe"
echo .
echo Adding an XML file of listings
java samples.addressbook.PutListings
    http://localhost:8080/soap/servlet/rpcrouter sample_listings.xml
echo .
echo Get everyone!
java samples.addressbook.GetAllListings
    http://localhost:8080/soap/servlet/rpcrouter
```

```
echo .
echo Undeploy it now
java org.apache.soap.server.ServiceManagerClient
   http://localhost:8080/soap/servlet/rpcrouter undeploy
   urn:AddressFetcher
echo .
echo Verify that it's gone
java org.apache.soap.server.ServiceManagerClient
   http://localhost:8080/soap/servlet/rpcrouter list
```

If this file of commands does not run all the way through, consult the "Troubleshooting Server-Side SOAP" section for possible causes.

To deploy the service and leave it deployed, save a revised version of testit.cmd with the undeploy command line edited out. If you call this file deploy.cmd and execute it, the service will be deployed and stay resident.

Now send your browser to the administration page at:

```
http://localhost:8080/soap/admin/index.html
```

Select the list option and you should see an entry for urn:AddressFetcher. Click this item to display the characteristics of this service. Figure 3.1 shows the display I got. Due to the length of some of the entries, you must scroll around the page.

FIGURE 3.1:

The Apache SOAP Admin display for the *AddressBook* service

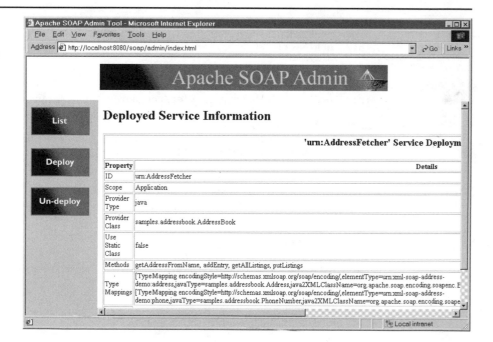

What Deployment Created

Somewhere in the server's SOAP web application directory structure is a file that contains information on SOAP services the system is now aware of. In version 2.2 of Apache SOAP, this file is named `DeployedServices.ds`, and it contains a serialized Java `Hashtable` representing all of the current services. This mechanism may change in later versions.

The `AddressBook` service installation did not create any database of addresses. Therefore, if you restart Tomcat, only the example addresses built into the code will be there. In general, SOAP has nothing to say about how services maintain their data.

Running the Address Client

Now let's try running one of the client classes that uses the `AddressBook` service. This assumes that you have run the revised version of `testit.cmd` with the `undeploy` command line edited out, so that the service is deployed. With Tomcat running and the CLASSPATH set as just discussed, execute the following command from the command line (the command has been word-wrapped to fit on the page, but it should all be on one line):

```
java samples.addressbook.GetAddress
    http://localhost:8080/soap/servlet/rpcrouter "John B. Good"
```

Note that because John B. Good contains spaces, the phrase must be enclosed in quotes. You should get back the example address as translated by `GetAddress`:

```
123 Main Street
Anytown, NY 12345
(123) 456-7890
```

If `GetAddress` does not execute, check your CLASSPATH setting. If you get an error message from the server, go to the "Troubleshooting Server-Side SOAP" section. If you refer to Listing 2.2, which contains the full text of the response, you can see that the `GetAddress` class had to deal with a complex SOAP message to abstract and format that address. I discuss typical client operations in later chapters.

Now try the same query with a name that is not in the example data:

```
F:\ApacheXML\SOAP\soap-2_2\samples\addressbook>java
    samples.addressbook.GetAddress

    http://localhost:8080/soap/servlet/rpcrouter "John Doe"
```

You should receive the message:

```
I don't know.
```

How Deployment Works

Apache SOAP can get the information to deploy a service in two ways: from the online Apache SOAP Admin manager, which processes form data entered by a user, or with the `deploy` function of the `rpcrouter` servlet, which processes data sent by the `ServiceManagerClient` application. This application uses information from a deployment descriptor file such as that shown in Listing 3.2.

Listing 3.2:   **The Deployment Descriptor for the *AddressFetcher* Service**

```
<isd:service xmlns:isd="http://xml.apache.org/xml-soap/deployment"
     id="urn:AddressFetcher">
<isd:provider type="java"
  scope="Application"
  methods="getAddressFromName addEntry getAllListings putListings">
  <isd:java class="samples.addressbook.AddressBook" static="false"/>
</isd:provider>
<isd:faultListener>org.apache.soap.server.DOMFaultListener
</isd:faultListener>

<isd:mappings>
  <isd:map encodingStyle="http://schemas.xmlsoap.org/soap/encoding/"
     xmlns:x="urn:xml-soap-address-demo" qname="x:address"
     javaType="samples.addressbook.Address"
     java2XMLClassName=
       "org.apache.soap.encoding.soapenc.BeanSerializer"
     xml2JavaClassName=
       "org.apache.soap.encoding.soapenc.BeanSerializer"/>
  <isd:map encodingStyle="http://schemas.xmlsoap.org/soap/encoding/"
     xmlns:x="urn:xml-soap-address-demo" qname="x:phone"
     javaType="samples.addressbook.PhoneNumber"
     java2XMLClassName=
       "org.apache.soap.encoding.soapenc.BeanSerializer"
     xml2JavaClassName=
       "org.apache.soap.encoding.soapenc.BeanSerializer"/>
</isd:mappings>
</isd:service>
```

Let's look in detail at the information in the deployment descriptor file, on a tag-by-tag basis. A more expanded form of this discussion can be found in the Apache SOAP user's guide documentation.

isd:service   This tag defines the `isd` namespace and gives the name of the service as `"urn:AddressFetcher"` in the `id` attribute. The `isd` namespace is in force until the closing `isd:service` tag. Optional attributes in this tag (not illustrated in the example) are

> ***type* attribute**   If the service is message-oriented instead of being a RPC, use `type="message"`.

> ***checkMustUnderstands* attribute**   This attribute may have the value true or false. If true, the server must be able to throw a fault if the SOAP message has headers marked as `MustUnderstand`.

***isd:provider scope* attribute**   The `scope` attribute corresponds to the `scope` term used in Java servlets and JSP for various objects. In particular, it corresponds to the usage of scope in JSP `useBean` tags. In the SOAP server case, it refers to the object that the server creates to respond to requests directed to the `urn:AddressFetcher` service. Selecting the `scope` has important consequences for service design. The possible values for `scope` are

Application   Once created, the object is available to all requests until the server is stopped. Because the `urn:AddressFetcher` service has application scope, each request can add data to the object and subsequent requests will see the changed data.

Session   A new copy of the object is created for each session. This means that if a session maintaining mechanism is in place, subsequent requests from the same client will see the same object. The SOAP 1.1 standard does not require session maintaining capability, but subsequent standards may change this.

Request   The object lives only for the duration of the request. Note that although page scope has meaning for JSP pages, it is meaningless for SOAP.

***isd:provider methods* attribute**   This is a list of names of methods that the service implements separated by spaces.

***isd:provider type* attribute**   This designates the language to be used. Apache SOAP can execute various scripting languages, a capability I am not going to get into at this time. Because the type is `"java"`, the `isd:provider` tag has a child tag named `isd:java`. This tag carries two attributes:

***isd:java class* attribute**   The fully qualified name of the Java class that implements the service.

***isd:java static* attribute**   This attribute can be either false or true, but all of the Apache SOAP samples use false.

isd:faultlistener   This designates the Java class that processes `SOAPFaultEvent` events. When an exception or other error occurs in a SOAP service, an attempt is made to return a valid SOAP message containing information about the cause of the problem. A fault listener is responsible for composing extra information about the cause of the problem.

isd:mappings   This optional tag encloses one or more `isd:map` tags that define how to serialize specific Java types not included in the set of basic type serializers provided with Apache SOAP. An optional attribute named `defaultMappingRegistry` can be named in this tag if you want to override the normal default Registry.

isd:map   Each map tag contains attributes describing how a Java type is converted from Java to XML and back.

Mapping and the SOAP Mapping Registry

Each type of variable that is transmitted to a server by a SOAP message must be translated from XML to a Java primitive or reference variable and, in turn, variables returned by the RPC must be encoded from Java into XML. Selecting the right method to accomplish a conversion is accomplished by "type mapping" data. This data lives in a registry, which is an object of the type org.apache.soap.encoding.SOAPMappingRegistry by default.

The SOAPMappingRegistry class has a large set of predefined type mappings, so for many cases you won't have to define special conversions. As of Apache SOAP 2.2, these predefined type mappings include:

- Java primitive types, such as int, float, boolean, byte, and so on, and their corresponding wrapper classes

- Java arrays

- java.lang.String

- java.util.Date

- java.util.GregorianCalendar

- java.util.Vector

- java.util.Hashtable

- java.util.Map (requires SDK 1.2 or later)

- java.math.BigDecimal

- javax.mail.internet.MimeBodyPart

- java.io.InputStream

- javax.activation.DataSource

- javax.activation.DataHandler

- org.apache.soap.util.xml.QName

- org.apache.soap.rpc.Parameter

- java.lang.Object (a deserializer for null objects only)

As you can see, this is a pretty impressive list, so why does the address server define extra map tags such as the following?

```
<isd:map encodingStyle="http://schemas.xmlsoap.org/soap/encoding/"
    xmlns:x="urn:xml-soap-address-demo" qname="x:phone"
    javaType="samples.addressbook.PhoneNumber"
    java2XMLClassName=
      "org.apache.soap.encoding.soapenc.BeanSerializer"
    xml2JavaClassName=
      "org.apache.soap.encoding.soapenc.BeanSerializer"/>
```

This mapping illustrates one of the serializers that Apache SOAP provides but which is not built into the SOAPMappingRegistry class. The BeanSerializer class uses introspection to provide serialization for Java classes that implement the JavaBean convention of get and set methods for all variables that must be serialized.

The preceding example map declaration says that the Java object that appears in a SOAP message to the AddressFetcher server with the name phone can be handled by the standard BeanSerializer class for conversion both from XML to Java and from Java to XML. The bean serializer creates a object of the samples.addressbook.PhoneNumber type using the no-arguments constructor and then sets the object variables using the matching set methods.

The Actual Deploy Request

Recall that the command to deploy the service looks like this:

```
java org.apache.soap.server.ServiceManagerClient
    http://localhost:8080/soap/servlet/rpcrouter deploy
    DeploymentDescriptor.xml
```

ServiceManagerClient is a class in the org.apache.soap.server package that turns a deployment descriptor into a message directed to the deploy method of the service manager.

I used the UtilSnoop program to capture the SOAP message sent to the rcprouter servlet when the command just shown is executed. The complete message is shown in Listing 3.3 with long lines wrapped to fit the page and some additional indenting supplied to aid readability. What a monster! Aren't you glad that Apache SOAP supplies the ServiceManager-Client to handle this?

Listing 3.3:   **The SOAP Message That Deploys the Address Service**

```
<?xml version='1.0' encoding='UTF-8'?>
<SOAP-ENV:Envelope
    xmlns:SOAP-ENV="http://schemas.xmlsoap.org/soap/envelope/"
    xmlns:xsi="http://www.w3.org/1999/ XMLSchema-instance"
    xmlns:xsd="http://www.w3.org/1999/XMLSchema">
<SOAP-ENV:Body>
<ns1:deploy xmlns:ns1="urn:xml-soap-service-management-service"
 SOAP-ENV:encodingStyle="http://schemas.xmlsoap.org/soap/encoding/">
<descriptor xmlns:ns2="http://xml.apache.org/xml-soap"
xsi:type="ns2:DeploymentDescriptor">
<faultListener xmlns:ns3="http://schemas.xmlsoap.org/soap/encoding/"
xsi:type="ns3:Array" ns3:arrayType="xsd:string[1]">
    <item xsi:type="xsd:string"
    >org.apache.soap.server.DOMFaultListener</item>
</faultListener>
<providerClass xsi:type="xsd:string"
    >samples.addressbook.AddressBook</providerClass>
```

```xml
<serviceType xsi:type="xsd:int">0</serviceType>
<serviceClass xsi:type="xsd:string" xsi:null="true"/>
<methods xmlns:ns4="http://schemas.xmlsoap.org/soap/encoding/"
xsi:type="ns4:Array" ns4:arrayType="xsd:string[4]">
<item xsi:type="xsd:string">getAddressFromName</item>
<item xsi:type="xsd:string">addEntry</item>
<item xsi:type="xsd:string">getAllListings</item>
<item xsi:type="xsd:string">putListings</item>
</methods>
<providerType xsi:type="xsd:byte">0</providerType>
<scriptLanguage xsi:type="xsd:string" xsi:null="true"/>
<mappings xmlns:ns5="http://schemas.xmlsoap.org/soap/encoding/"
   xsi:type="ns5:Array" ns5:arrayType="ns2:TypeMapping[2]">
<item xsi:type="ns2:TypeMapping">
  <encodingStyle xsi:type="xsd:string"
     >http://schemas.xmlsoap.org/soap/encoding/</encodingStyle>
  <elementType-ns xsi:type="xsd:string"
     >urn:xml-soap-address-demo</elementType-ns>
  <elementType-lp xsi:type="xsd:string"
     >address</elementType-lp>
  <javaType xsi:type="xsd:string"
     >samples.addressbook.Address</javaType>
  <xml2JavaClassName xsi:type="xsd:string"
     >org.apache.soap.encoding.soapenc.BeanSerializer
  </xml2JavaClassName>
  <java2XMLClassName xsi:type="xsd:string"
     >org.apache.soap.encoding.soapenc.BeanSerializer
  </java2XMLClassName>
</item>
<item xsi:type="ns2:TypeMapping">
  <encodingStyle xsi:type="xsd:string"
     >http://schemas.xmlsoap.org/soap/encoding/</encodingStyle>
  <elementType-ns xsi:type="xsd:string"
     >urn:xml-soap-address-demo</elementType-ns>
  <elementType-lp xsi:type="xsd:string"
     >phone</elementType-lp>
  <javaType xsi:type="xsd:string"
     >samples.addressbook.PhoneNumber</javaType>
  <xml2JavaClassName xsi:type="xsd:string"
     >org.apache.soap.encoding.soapenc.BeanSerializer
  </xml2JavaClassName>
  <java2XMLClassName xsi:type="xsd:string"
     >org.apache.soap.encoding.soapenc.BeanSerializer
  </java2XMLClassName>
</item>
</mappings>
<checkMustUnderstands xsi:type="xsd:boolean"
   >false</checkMustUnderstands>
<defaultSMRClass xsi:type="xsd:string" xsi:null="true"/>
<ID xsi:type="xsd:string">urn:AddressFetcher</ID>
<props xsi:type="ns2:Map" xsi:null="true"/>
```

```
<isStatic xsi:type="xsd:boolean">false</isStatic>
<scriptFilenameOrString xsi:type="xsd:string" xsi:null="true"/>
<scope xsi:type="xsd:int">2</scope>
</descriptor>
</ns1:deploy>
</SOAP-ENV:Body>
</SOAP-ENV:Envelope>
```

The deploy service turns the message into a DeploymentDescriptor object containing all of the information describing a deployed service. It is this object that is used to locate the correct class to perform a service and translate the input to it. In the present version of Apache SOAP, this object is written out as a serialized Hashtable to the DeploymentDescriptor.ds file.

How *AddressBook* Works

Let's follow the steps that the rpcrouter servlet takes to handle a message directed to the service that was just installed. Here is how the GetAddress client is used to send the query message. Note that, as usual, this single-line command has been word-wrapped to fit this page:

```
java samples.addressbook.GetAddress http://localhost:9000/soap/servlet/rpcrouter
"John B. Good"
```

The actual HTTP transmission to the rpcrouter servlet is shown in Listing 3.4. Recall that the message type getAddressFromName was defined in the deployment descriptor isd:provider tag as shown in Listing 3.2.

Listing 3.4:   **The Complete Transmission to the *AddressFetcher* Service**

```
POST /soap/servlet/rpcrouter HTTP/1.0
Host: localhost
Content-Type: text/xml; charset=utf-8
Content-Length: 492
SOAPAction: ""

<?xml version='1.0' encoding='UTF-8'?>
<SOAP-ENV:Envelope
    xmlns:SOAP-ENV="http://schemas.xmlsoap.org/soap/envelope/"
    xmlns:xsi="http://www.w3.org/1999/XMLSchema-instance"
    xmlns:xsd="http://www.w3.org/1999/XMLSchema">
<SOAP-ENV:Body>
<ns1:getAddressFromName xmlns:ns1="urn:AddressFetcher"
 SOAP-ENV:encodingStyle="http://schemas.xmlsoap.org/soap/encoding/">
  <nameToLookup xsi:type="xsd:string">John B. Good</nameToLookup>
</ns1:getAddressFromName>
</SOAP-ENV:Body>
</SOAP-ENV:Envelope>
```

Because the HTTP transmission is a POST, it is the `doPost` method in the `rpcrouter` servlet that gets the request. Just like any other any other servlet derived from `javax.servlet.http.HttpServlet`, the entire information from the client request comes in with a `HttpServletRequest` object, and the entire response goes through a `HttpServlet-Response` object.

As you may recall from the `web.xml` declarations, the class handling `rpcrouter` is `RPCRouterServlet` in the `org.apache.soap.server.http` package. I am not going to go into detail of the handling of the request because implementation details may change. Instead, I follow the general processing steps in terms of the functionality of objects involved:

1. The first step is to parse out the entire SOAP envelope. The `doPost` method creates an XML parser and uses several utility classes to create a `Call` object from the `HttpServletRequest` input.

   A `Call` object is the general object used to represent a RPC in both server and client processing. The `Call` class is in the `org.apache.soap.rpc` package.

2. The next step is to use the `targetID` string from the `Call` object to locate the corresponding `DeploymentDescriptor`. In this case, this string has the value `"getAddressFromName"` so the `DeploymentDescriptor` is the one that was established by deploying the address server. If the target service is not known, an exception is thrown resulting in an error message being returned to the client.

3. Using more utility classes, an object of the required class is located. Depending on the scope declared in the `DeploymentDescriptor`, the utilities may provide a new object or one that was created earlier. In our example, the service has application scope and the implementing object of the `samples.addressbook.AddressBook` class may have been created earlier.

4. Actual deserializing of parameters and execution of the target method is carried out by the `RPCRouter` utility class using reflection. It is important to note that the order of parameters in the SOAP request message must match the order in the actual method, although in this case the method takes only a single name, `String`.

5. The value returned by the method is encoded into a `Response` object. The class used is `Response` in the `org.apache.soap.rpc` package. Although Java methods can return only a single value, that value can be an array, custom object, `Hashtable`, or other collection, so there really is no limit on the returned data. In the case of the `AddressBook` server, the `getAddressFromName` is declared as returning an object of the `Address` class from the `samples.addressbook` package.

6. The Response is used to build a SOAP envelope that is finally transmitted back to the client.

Listing 3.5 shows the complete response text, with some lines reformatted for readability and to fit the page. Note that the content of the SOAP body is a tag named `getAddress-FromNameResponse`, a name created by concatenation of the method called with `Response`.

Listing 3.5:   The Complete Response

```
HTTP/1.0 200 OK
Content-Type: text/xml; charset=utf-8
Content-Length: 946
Date: Thu, 05 Jul 2001 16:50:38 GMT
Server: Apache Tomcat/4.0-b5 (HTTP/1.1 Connector)
Set-Cookie: JSESSIONID=E2A72237428486B3A28127C5E72992C6;Path=/soap

<?xml version='1.0' encoding='UTF-8'?>
<SOAP-ENV:Envelope
    xmlns:SOAP-ENV="http://schemas.xmlsoap.org/soap/envelope/"
    xmlns:xsi="http://www.w3.org/1999/ XMLSchema-instance"
    xmlns:xsd="http://www.w3.org/1999/XMLSchema">
<SOAP-ENV:Body>
<ns1:getAddressFromNameResponse
    xmlns:ns1="urn:AddressFetcher" SOAP-ENV:encodingStyle=
        "http://schemas.xmlsoap.org/soap/encoding/">
<return xmlns:ns2="urn:xml-soap-address-demo"
    xsi:type="ns2:address">
<phoneNumber xsi:type="ns2:phone">
<exchange xsi:type="xsd:string">456</exchange>
<areaCode xsi:type="xsd:int">123</areaCode>
<number xsi:type="xsd:string">7890</number>
</phoneNumber>
<zip xsi:type="xsd:int">12345</zip>
<streetNum xsi:type="xsd:int">123</streetNum>
<streetName xsi:type="xsd:string">Main Street</streetName>
<state xsi:type="xsd:string">NY</state>
<city xsi:type="xsd:string">Anytown</city>
</return>
</ns1:getAddressFromNameResponse>

</SOAP-ENV:Body>
</SOAP-ENV:Envelope>
```

Troubleshooting Server-Side SOAP

The old saying "you can always tell the pioneers—they are the ones with the arrows in their backs" is certainly true for programmers trying to get SOAP running. In this section, I attempt to save you countless hours of debugging by relating some of the problems that others have experienced. The main Apache SOAP list of Frequently Asked Questions (FAQ) is maintained at:

```
http://xml.apache.org//soap/faq/index.html
```

CLASSPATH Problems

A large fraction of the problems that Java programmers experience when trying to get a Java SOAP application running seems to be related to the CLASSPATH used by the Java Virtual Machine (JVM) to locate class code. To see why this is, let's look at Java's conventions for the use of the CLASSPATH environment variable.

CLASSPATH Conventions

Historically speaking, the Java CLASSPATH has been a source of endless confusion, frustration, and wasted time to Java programmers. Sun has attempted to reduce the confusion by making some aspects of class location automatic. As detailed in the tooldocs section of the Java SDK documentation, the Java Virtual Machine attempts to load classes in *this order*:

1. **Bootstrap classes**   These are the standard library classes, such as those in the java .lang package, that are typically found in the files rt.jar and i18n.jar. The convention is that these files are in the \jre\lib directory of the Java SDK installation. The JVM finds this directory by navigating from the JAVA_HOME directory where the java.exe program is found.

2. **Extension classes**   Also known as standard extensions, these classes are in packages beginning with javax. An example would be the e-mail related classes in the mail.jar file or the XML parser classes in jaxp.jar and crimson.jar. By convention, these are found in the \jre\lib\ext directory of the Java SDK installation.

3. **User application classes**   These are the specific classes required to run an application such as Tomcat itself or your custom servlet. The -classpath command line option or the CLASSPATH environment variable is used to locate user application classes.

With this order in mind, you can see how certain types of problem arise. If you have an older XML parser in your standard extensions directory, it does not matter that your CLASSPATH lists a new version of the parser; it will never be found, and you will get strange error messages. I would hate to tell you how many days I wasted tracking this one down.

You also have to consider the web application conventions as described in the Java Servlet API. As discussed earlier in the chapter under the heading "Class and JAR Files," a servlet such as rpcrouter automatically has access to classes and JAR files under the WEB-INF directory belonging to the SOAP web application.

However, any other web application will not have access to class and jar files in the SOAP WEB-INF directory, nor will SOAP services have access to class and jar files in other web applications. This absolute separation is designed into the servlet API so that a web application can be moved to any server without dependence on other applications. Sometimes this means you will have multiple copies of jar files.

Setting CLASSPATH

Unfortunately, setting the classpath used by a servlet container is not the subject of standardization. The installation documentation that comes with Apache SOAP describes how to handle some of the common servers. If you examine the batch files used to start Tomcat, you will find that extensive manipulation of classpath and related environment variables occurs. If necessary, you can insert specific paths that you want Tomcat to have available in these batch files.

XML Parser Problems

XML parser incompatibility is the most frequent cause of difficulty in getting a SOAP server running. SOAP requires a parser compatible with DOM level 2 and SAX 2 because namespaces are heavily used. When Apache SOAP 2.2 was first released, a large number of people had problems because they were using the Xerces version 1.3.1 XML parser package. This parser version failed to handle namespaces correctly and caused mysterious errors.

Many people have had problems due to earlier parser versions that may have been installed by other programs. Versions of Sun's web server development kit from before development was turned over to the Apache organization have caused lots of trouble. I feel that your best bet is to clear old parsers out of your system and stick to the latest Sun JAXP package.

Mystery Errors

In this category, I am putting error messages that appear to make no sense or sound completely impossible. You might see these when trying to run one of the SOAP samples or one of your own clients.

Unsupported response content type   Your SOAP client may show this due to errors that prevent the server from generating an XML-formatted response. The server error message has a content type of text/html but the SOAP client is expecting text/xml. The real cause of the error has nothing to do with this error report from the client; you must examine the actual message content with one of the snoop utilities (see the "Snooping on Messages" section later in this chapter).

Connection refused   You can get this if something is wrong with the URL specified for the server or if the server is not actually running. Using the wrong port number is a possible cause, particularly if you have been debugging with one of the snoop utilities.

Unable to resolve target   Normally this means that the service class can not be found. Possible causes include a misspelled method in a request or an error in constructing the service class object. You should use the SOAP administration utility service listing to verify that the service is deployed and that the names that the service uses correspond with your client usage.

Debugging Tools

Because the Tomcat server is entirely written in Java, you can start the entire server through a debugger. This is pretty tricky because you must supply the command-line parameters that are normally set up by the batch files. Look at the startup batch files for clues on how to do this and for the name of the class that actually has the normal Java `main` method. In my current copy of Tomcat, this is:

```
org.apache.catalina.startup.Bootstrap
```

Certain Java Integrated Development Environments (IDEs) provide built-in support for running Tomcat in the debugger.

Snooping On Messages

A surprising number of SOAP problems can be solved by looking at the text of the messages sent between client and server. The SOAP distribution provides a utility named `TcpTunnel-Gui` in the `org.apache.soap.util.net` package for capturing these messages, and I have written the `UtilSnoop` utility that performs a similar function.

The basic idea of these utilities is to interpose the utility between the client and server. Instead of having the client connect directly with the SOAP server, the client connects with the utility on a different port. The utility relays the request data stream to the server on the normal port while keeping a copy of every character sent. The returned response data is treated the same way.

The `UtilSnoop` utility is provided on the CD accompanying this book and updated versions will be available at

```
http://www.lanw.com/books/javasoap/
```

CHAPTER 4

The Significance of WSDL and UDDI

- Web services must advertise

- Universal Description, Discovery, and Integration (UDDI)

- Electronic business XML

- How a web service describes itself

- Automated WSDL tools

Not only are there a lot of proposed ways to perform remote procedure calls (RPCs) and send messages with XML (XML-RPC, SOAP, and so on), there are also a lot of proposed ways to talk about the kind of message you can send. What I am referring to is sometimes called *metadata*—information about information. In this case, metadata refers to information that describes available web services and how to connect to them. This is an area with a lot of ongoing research in various corporations and standards bodies so I don't expect the material in this chapter to have a very long shelf life, but it can get you started.

High-Level Descriptions

At the highest level of abstraction, you find the conventions that businesses use to describe and publicize information about services so that potential customers can locate them. Think in terms of a telephone book with yellow pages for web services, except that instead of printed ads in random format, this yellow pages–equivalent consists of electronic ads in standard formats.

The high-level protocol you are most likely to run into is UDDI (Universal Description, Discovery, and Integration). This proposed standard, first publicly released in November 2000, is heavily supported by both IBM and Microsoft. Conceptually, it is integrated with WSDL (Web Services Description Language) and SOAP. However, UDDI has not been submitted to any Internet standards agency. Extensive information is maintained at the www.uddi.org website.

Other major players, such as Sun, OASIS (Organization for the Advancement of Structured Information Systems), and the U.N. (yes, the United Nations) have been developing a standard known as ebXML, which I will also be exploring.

UDDI

The UDDI initiative is intended to promote ease of discovery of Internet-based services through central registry facilities. It recognizes that the wide range of designs of corporate websites prevent any sort of web search engine from doing a good job of locating services. The kind of keyword-based searches that a search engine can perform just don't give enough resolution, as anybody who has tried to deal with a search result of several thousand hits can testify.

XML is the key technology that goes beyond keywords and makes UDDI possible. When using UDDI, a business provides XML-formatted information in three areas:

Contact points   Also termed "white pages" by analogy with phone books, this is real-world information such as physical addresses, corporate phone numbers, and so on.

Industry classification This is similar to the yellow pages because standard industry classification schemes are used. A tremendous amount of work has gone into the industry classification schemes used by government agencies and industry associations. By preserving these conventions, UDDI makes transition to the Internet easier.

Web service discovery UDDI documentation calls this information "green pages." Here you find the technical information needed to automate the creation of connections to services and use of the service methods.

UDDI Registries

Rather than requiring a potential user to interrogate possible web service sites individually, UDDI calls for a distributed registry of data, the idea being that once you have registered your information at one site, it will automatically be propagated to other sites. IBM and Microsoft have been the primary creators of the UDDI specification, so it is not surprising they have created the initial registry sites as well. Additionally, Hewlett-Packard is expected to have a registry online by the time this book reaches print. Right now, the primary public registries may be located through the following sites:

```
http://www-3.ibm.com/services/uddi/
http://uddi.microsoft.com
```

A website offering a facility for searching UDDI registries can be found at:

```
http://www.soapclient.com/uddisearch.html
```

At this stage of development, these registries are not that useful to the general computing public because using them requires detailed knowledge of industry classification codes.

UDDI Technical Information

Technical information about a web service, such as the location of a WSDL document, is held in what UDDI refers to as a `bindingTemplate`, which in turn contains one or more `tModel` data structures. A `tModel` contains a name, a description, and URL locations of detailed specifications, such as a WSDL document. Keeping only a reference to the detailed specifications instead of the specifications themselves in a UDDI repository makes it easier for businesses to update services without having to modify repository data.

What About ebXML?

Not exactly in competition with UDDI, the ebXML (Electronic Business XML) standard is the product of a very wide ranging design effort by OASIS and UN/CEFACT, a United Nations group for facilitation of worldwide commerce. The intent of ebXML is to define a data exchange standard for business-to-business (B2B) trade. The basic idea has been accepted by international organizations representing hundreds of thousands of manufacturers and retailers around the world.

At one time, during the evolution of these various standards, it appeared that ebXML was going to create its own implementation of XML-based messaging. Fortunately for Java developers, SOAP was formally adopted by ebXML as the standard protocol for messages. However, just to keep things interesting, ebXML defines some extensions within the confines of SOAP.

Here are some of the major sites for the ebXML standard and the organizations involved with creating the standard:

```
http://www.ebxml.org
http://www.oasis-open.org
http://www.unece.org/cefact/UN/CEFACT
```

EbXML provides for the creation of a registry of businesses and for querying that registry, so it would appear to create a parallel system to UDDI. However, ebXML covers a much wider range of business operations beyond what we currently think of as web services. The ebXML working groups appear to acknowledge that UDDI access to ebXML registries of online businesses and business services will be highly desirable. Generally speaking, the implementation of UDDI with real online registries is considerably ahead of the implementation of ebXML.

Web Services Description Language (WSDL)

The current standard for Web Services Description Language (WSDL) is a W3C note dated March 15, 2001, maintained at www.w3.org/TR/wsdl. This note characterizes WSDL as an XML format for describing network services as a set of "endpoints" that operate on "messages." Certain parts of a WSDL document describe the messages and operations abstractly, and these abstract concepts are bound to concrete details of protocols and formats. The degree of abstraction is needed to allow WSDL to describe a wide variety of possible web services. The SOAP service is what is discussed here.

The example I will be using here is for a SOAP service created by a consulting company named LemurLabs (thanks, guys!). The service is called FortuneService because it serves up random "fortune cookie" messages. FortuneService is described at the following website:

```
http://www.lemurlabs.com/projects/soap/
```

Overview of WSDL

WSDL can be mind-boggling if you try to take the total complexity in all at once (the W3C note is over 30 pages.) I am going to sneak up on the total picture gradually. First, let's consider the primary tags.

The root tag of a WSDL description of a service is a `definitions` tag. Attributes of this tag are used to name the document and define the namespaces to be used. The direct child elements that can be found inside this root tag include:

documentation   You can include a `documentation` element inside any of the other element. This can contain arbitrary text and other elements, "mixed" content in XML Schema terms.

types   A `types` element encloses definitions of data types used in the messages exchanged.

message   Each `message` element gives an abstract definition of one message, either to or from the service.

portType   A `portType` element encloses abstract definitions of operations supported by endpoints.

binding   A `binding` element gives a concrete description that associates a protocol with abstract entities such as `message` and `portType`.

service   A `service` groups a set of related ports that were defined in the `portType` element.

These elements and their contents and functions are discussed in greater detail in the following sections.

Problems with Schema Versions

There are currently several versions of XML Schema to which a WSDL file may refer. For example, in the FortuneService WSDL examined in this chapter, the following line declares that the document follows the 1999 XML schema definitions:

```
xmlns:xsd = "http://www.w3.org/1999/XMLSchema"
```

As of this writing, the most recent schema definition by the W3C, which is used in any WSDL documents I have encountered, is cited this way:

```
xmlns:xsd="http://www.w3.org/2001/XMLSchema"
```
XML Spy 2004

However, I have also encountered the following in a few WSDL documents:

```
xmlns:xsd="http://www.w3.org/2000/10/XMLSchema"
```

It seems likely that the W3C schema definition will eventually be the standard that everybody uses, so if you have a choice, stick with that one.

Attributes of the *definitions* Element

In the `definitions` tag example in Listing 4.1, note that the `name` attribute is supplied as a convenient way to describe the document rather than to create any part of the address. The main use of attributes is to define various namespaces that the remainder of the document will use.

Listing 4.1: **The *definitions* Element for *FortuneService***

```
<definitions
  name = "FortuneService"
  targetNamespace =
"http://www.lemurlabs.com/projects/soap/fortune/FortuneService.wsdl"
xmlns:tns=
"http://www.lemurlabs.com/projects/soap/fortune/FortuneService.wsdl"
xmlns:xsd = "http://www.w3.org/1999/XMLSchema"
xmlns:soap = "http://schemas.xmlsoap.org/wsdl/soap/"
xmlns = "http://schemas.xmlsoap.org/wsdl/">
```

types

The types tag encloses descriptions of the data types in use by the service. Typically, the simple types will be those defined by XML Schema that are automatically assumed, so it is only the complex types that must be described here. Listing 4.2 shows how the types tag used in FortuneService defines an array of strings. Other types used in this service are simple strings so they don't have to be defined.

Listing 4.2: **The *types* Tag Used in *FortuneService***

```
<types>
<schema targetNamespace =
  "http://www.lemurlabs.com/projects/soap/fortune/FortuneService.xsd"
  xmlns = "http://www.w3.org/1999/XMLSchema">
 <complexType name = "ArrayOfString" base = "soap:Array">
  <sequence>
  <element name = "item" type = "xsd:string"/>
  </sequence>
 </complexType>
</schema>
</types>
```

message

A definition may have multiple message tags, each representing a single data transmission, either Request or Response. Each message has a name attribute declaring a name that is unique within the WSDL document. This name will be used in further definitions. A message tag may be empty if the service does not take an input, or if the return from a method is void. The following example of an empty message tag from FortuneService describes a call to a method that does not take any input:

```
<message name = "getAnyFortuneRequest"/>
```

When describing an RPC to a Java method, there is a part tag for each argument. The order in which part tags appear must be the order of arguments in the method signature. The following defines the message returned by the server in response to a getAnyFortune= Request message. The type of "xsd:string" is one of the standard schema types.

```
<message name = "getAnyFortuneResponse">
   <part name = "return" type = "xsd:string"/>
</message>
```

The convention for naming usage for messages appends Request or Response to the operation name to make the message purpose obvious. It is not clear how extensively this convention is being followed.

portType

The following shows the opening portType tag in the FortuneService WSDL. Within the portType there is one operation tag for each function exposed by the SOAP service. An operation corresponds to a specific Request/Response sequence such as a single RPC call and response. The operation tag relates the names of the input and output messages (from the message tags) to the name of the function being called.

```
<portType name = "FortunePortType">
  <operation name = "getAnyFortune">
   <input message = "tns:getAnyFortuneRequest" name="getAnyFortune"/>
   <output message = "tns:getAnyFortuneResponse"
      name="getAnyFortuneResponse"/>
  </operation>
```

When a web service is one-way message passing, the operation will have only an input message defined. In typical Java usage, a portType will correspond to a single Java class or interface, and the operations will correspond to the various method call parameters and return values.

binding

A binding connects a portType to a particular protocol. A portType can have any number of protocol bindings, but I am only going to discuss SOAP. Note that other web service protocols would use different tags in the binding element.

In Listing 4.3, note that the type attribute in the binding tag uses the name established in the portType tag. The input and output tags establish the fact that the SOAP body will be used to transport the message. The WSDL note defines some example terminology in a SOAP binding, but the exact usage does not seem to be completely standardized.

Listing 4.3:   The *binding* for the *getAnyFortune* Operation

```
<binding name = "FortuneBinding" type = "tns:FortunePortType">
  <soap:binding style = "rpc"
    transport = "http://schemas.xmlsoap.org/soap/http"/>
  <operation name = "getAnyFortune">
   <soap:operation/>
   <input>
     <soap:body use = "encoded"
        namespace = "urn:lemurlabs-Fortune"
        encodingStyle = "http://schemas.xmlsoap.org/soap/encoding/"/>
   </input>
   <output>
     <soap:body use = "encoded" namespace = "urn:lemurlabs-Fortune"
        encodingStyle = "http://schemas.xmlsoap.org/soap/encoding/"/>
   </output>
  </operation>
```

service and *port*

Inside the service tag are one or more port tags. Each port associates a binding to a real address. In WSDL terminology, the location attribute in the following example defines an "endpoint" for the service. Note that a WSDL document may have more than one service tag, but each must be distinguished by a unique name.

```
<service name = "FortuneService">
   <documentation>Returns XML-formatted fortunes</documentation>
   <port name = "FortunePort" binding = "tns:FortuneBinding">
     <soap:address
        location = "http://www.lemurlabs.com:80/rpcrouter"/>
   </port>
</service>
```

Interpreting a WSDL Description

The complete WSDL example for the LemurLabs FortuneService is shown in Listing 4.4, with long lines word-wrapped. In theory, a WSDL document gives all of the information necessary to access the service, so let's see how far we can get. Look for the following elements as you peruse Listing 4.4:

Data types   Looking at the types tag, you can conclude that in addition to the default XML schema types, messages may also include an array of strings.

Messages   There are three sets of Request/Response messages using data types of either string or ArrayOfString.

portType* and *operation   There is one portType with three operation elements. These define three operations corresponding to the sets of messages.

binding   The binding tag shows that the portType uses SOAP protocol.

service   The service tag gives a real-world address corresponding to the SOAP binding.

Listing 4.4:   **The Complete WSDL for the *FortuneService***

```
<?xml version = "1.0"?>
<definitions name = "FortuneService" targetNamespace =
"http://www.lemurlabs.com/projects/soap/fortune/FortuneService.wsdl"
xmlns:tns=
"http://www.lemurlabs.com/projects/soap/fortune/FortuneService.wsdl"
xmlns:xsd = "http://www.w3.org/1999/XMLSchema"
xmlns:soap = "http://schemas.xmlsoap.org/wsdl/soap/"
xmlns = "http://schemas.xmlsoap.org/wsdl/">
<types>
<schema targetNamespace =
  "http://www.lemurlabs.com/projects/soap/fortune/FortuneService.xsd"
  xmlns = "http://www.w3.org/1999/XMLSchema">
 <complexType name = "ArrayOfString" base = "soap:Array">
  <sequence>
  <element name = "item" type = "xsd:string"/>
  </sequence>
 </complexType>
</schema>
</types>
<message name = "getAnyFortuneRequest"/>
<message name = "getAnyFortuneResponse">
   <part name = "return" type = "xsd:string"/>
</message>
<message name = "getDictionaryNameListRequest"/>
<message name = "getDictionaryNameListResponse">
   <part name = "return" type = "tns:ArrayOfString"/>
</message>
<message name = "getFortuneByDictionaryRequest">
   <part name = "dictionaryName" type="xsd:string"/>
</message>
<message name = "getFortuneByDictionaryResponse">
   <part name = "return" type="xsd:string"/>
</message>
<portType name = "FortunePortType">
 <operation name = "getAnyFortune">
  <input message = "tns:getAnyFortuneRequest" name="getAnyFortune"/>
  <output message = "tns:getAnyFortuneResponse"
    name="getAnyFortuneResponse"/>
 </operation>
 <operation name = "getDictionaryNameList">
  <input message = "tns:getDictionaryNameListRequest"
    name="getDictionaryNameList"/>
  <output message = "tns:getDictionaryNameListResponse"
```

```
        name="getDictionaryNameListResponse"/>
  </operation>
  <operation name = "getFortuneByDictionary">
   <input message = "tns:getFortuneByDictionaryRequest"
     name="getFortuneByDictionary"/>
   <output message = "tns:getFortuneByDictionaryResponse"
     name="getFortuneByDictionaryResponse" />
  </operation>
 </portType>
 <binding name = "FortuneBinding" type = "tns:FortunePortType">
  <soap:binding style = "rpc"
    transport = "http://schemas.xmlsoap.org/soap/http"/>
  <operation name = "getAnyFortune">
  <soap:operation/>
   <input>
   <soap:body use = "encoded"
       namespace = "urn:lemurlabs-Fortune"
       encodingStyle = "http://schemas.xmlsoap.org/soap/encoding/"/>
   </input>
   <output>
   <soap:body use = "encoded" namespace = "urn:lemurlabs-Fortune"
      encodingStyle = "http://schemas.xmlsoap.org/soap/encoding/"/>
   </output>
  </operation>
  <operation name = "getDictionaryNameList">
   <soap:operation/>
     <input>
       <soap:body use = "encoded"
        namespace = "urn:lemurlabs-Fortune"
       encodingStyle = "http://schemas.xmlsoap.org/soap/encoding/"/>
     </input>
     <output>
       <soap:body use = "encoded" namespace = "urn:lemurlabs-Fortune"
        encodingStyle = "http://schemas.xmlsoap.org/soap/encoding/"/>
     </output>
   </operation>
   <operation name = "getFortuneByDictionary">
     <soap:operation/>
   <input>
    <soap:body use = "encoded" namespace = "urn:lemurlabs-Fortune"
       encodingStyle = "http://schemas.xmlsoap.org/soap/encoding/"/>
   </input>
   <output>
      <soap:body use = "encoded" namespace = "urn:lemurlabs-Fortune"
       encodingStyle = "http://schemas.xmlsoap.org/soap/encoding/"/>
   </output>
   </operation>
  </binding>
  <service name = "FortuneService">
    <documentation>Returns XML-formatted fortunes</documentation>
    <port name = "FortunePort" binding = "tns:FortuneBinding">
      <soap:address
```

```
        location = "http://www.lemurlabs.com:80/rpcrouter"/>
    </port>
  </service>
</definitions>
```

Automated WSDL

After reading all those details, I am sure you will be glad to learn that you will seldom have to edit a WSDL description directly. As of this writing, the utility of WSDL has become apparent to many developers and Java tools for working with WSDL are under development. For example, the Apache organization follow-on to Apache SOAP, the "Axis" project, has WSDL support as one of the requirements. You can track the progress of the Axis project at the following site:

```
http://xml.apache.org/axis/
```

As a demonstration of what is possible, let's look at a new Java web service framework called Glue. Glue is a product of a company called The Mind Electric. It includes facilities for SOAP, WSDL, and UDDI. More information and downloads are available at:

```
http://www.themindelectric.com
```

Creating WSDL from a Java Class

To create an example of generating a WSDL document from a Java class, I used a utility in the Glue package. This utility can look at the compiled class and Java source code and create WSDL.

As an example, I am using the following Java source code. It simply defines an interface with two methods. Note that a package is declared and that there is a Java comment in the code.

```
package com.lanw.pubs ;

public interface PublicationData {

// isbn must not have punctuation or spaces
 public String getTitle( String isbn );

 public String[] getAuthors( String isbn );

}
```

In addition to the name of the class to be read, the Glue java2wsdl utility requires only a URL for the endpoint and a URN for the service. These are given on the command line like this (note that the long line has been wrapped):

```
java2wsdl com.lanw.pubs.PublicationData
    -e http://localhost:8080/glue -u urn:pubs
```

The generated WSDL is shown in Listing 4.5. Due to the extremely long lines created in some tags, I have cut some lines arbitrarily. Note that the utility has generated message names using the Request and Response naming convention plus a number. Another nice touch is that the Java comment has been turned into a documentation tag.

Listing 4.5: **The Generated WSDL Document for *PublicationsData***

```
<?xml version='1.0' encoding='UTF-8'?>
<definitions name='com.lanw.pubs.PublicationData'
  targetNamespace='http://www.themindelectric.com/wsdl/com.lanw.pubs.
  PublicationData/'
xmlns:tns='http://www.themindelectric.com/wsdl/com.lanw.pubs.
  PublicationData/' xmlns:electric='http://www.themindelectric.com/'
  xmlns:soap='http://schemas.xmlsoap.org/wsdl/soap/'
  xmlns:xsd='http://www.w3.org/2001/XMLSchema'
  xmlns:soapenc='http://schemas.xmlsoap.org/soap/encoding/'
  xmlns:wsdl='http://schemas.xmlsoap.org/wsdl/'
  xmlns='http://schemas.xmlsoap.org/wsdl/'>
  <types>
   <schema xmlns='http://www.w3.org/2001/XMLSchema'
     xmlns:tns='http://www.themindelectric.com/schema/'
     targetNamespace='http://www.themindelectric.com/schema/'>
       <complexType name='ArrayOfstring'>
         <complexContent>
           <restriction base='soapenc:Array'>
             <attribute
               ref='soapenc:arrayType' wsdl:arrayType='string[]'/>
           </restriction>
         </complexContent>
       </complexType>
   </schema>
  </types>
  <message name='getAuthorsRequest2'>
   <part name='isbn' type='xsd:string'/>
  </message>
  <message name='getTitleResponse1'>
   <part name='Result' type='xsd:string'/>
  </message>
  <message name='getAuthorsResponse2'>
   <part name='Result'
     xmlns:ns1='http://www.themindelectric.com/schema/'
     type='ns1:ArrayOfstring'/>
  </message>
  <message name='getTitleRequest1'>
   <part name='isbn' type='xsd:string'/>
  </message>
  <portType name='com.lanw.pubs.PublicationDataPortType'>
   <operation name='getTitle' parameterOrder='isbn'>
     <documentation>isbn must not have punctuation or
       spaces</documentation>
```

```
      <input message='tns:getTitleRequest1'/>
      <output message='tns:getTitleResponse1'/>
    </operation>
    <operation name='getAuthors' parameterOrder='isbn'>
      <input message='tns:getAuthorsRequest2'/>
      <output message='tns:getAuthorsResponse2'/>
    </operation>
  </portType>
  <binding name='com.lanw.pubs.PublicationDataBinding'
    type='tns:com.lanw.pubs.PublicationDataPortType'>
    <soap:binding style='rpc'
      transport='http://schemas.xmlsoap.org/soap/http'/>
    <operation name='getAuthors'>
      <soap:operation soapAction='urn:pubs#getAuthors'/>
      <input>
        <soap:body use='encoded'
        namespace='http://tempuri.org/com.lanw.pubs.PublicationData'
        encodingStyle='http://schemas.xmlsoap.org/soap/encoding/'/>
      </input>
      <output>
        <soap:body use='encoded'
        namespace='http://tempuri.org/com.lanw.pubs.PublicationData'
        encodingStyle='http://schemas.xmlsoap.org/soap/encoding/'/>
      </output>
    </operation>
    <operation name='getTitle'>
      <soap:operation soapAction='urn:pubs#getTitle'/>
      <input>
        <soap:body use='encoded'
        namespace='http://tempuri.org/com.lanw.pubs.PublicationData'
        encodingStyle='http://schemas.xmlsoap.org/soap/encoding/'/>
      </input>
      <output>
        <soap:body use='encoded'
        namespace='http://tempuri.org/com.lanw.pubs.PublicationData'
        encodingStyle='http://schemas.xmlsoap.org/soap/encoding/'/>
      </output>
    </operation>
  </binding>
  <service name='com.lanw.pubs.PublicationDataService'>
    <port name='com.lanw.pubs.PublicationDataPort'
        binding='tns:com.lanw.pubs.PublicationDataBinding'>
      <soap:address location='http://localhost:8080/glue'/>
    </port>
  </service>
</definitions>
```

Whew! No wonder everybody is interested in automatic WSDL generation.

Future Web Services

As the computer industry reorients itself to a world built around a fluid and ever-changing sea of competing web services, it is obvious that directory systems such as those I have discussed will become increasingly important. The WSDL-UDDI approach, although strongly supported by industry leaders, may not be the final word.

Java programmers creating web services should plan to support WSDL and UDDI now, but keep an eye out for alternatives.

CHAPTER 5

How SOAP Encodes Data

- What the standards say about encoding

- How XML Schemas fit in the SOAP picture

- Examples with simple variables

- Examples with complex variables and binary data

- How to write your own encoder for Apache SOAP

- Why JavaBeans are convenient for SOAP

This book has already provided examples of SOAP messages encoding simple data values. Now let's look at the rules the SOAP standard prescribes for encoding. Because it is tied closely to XML Schema, this is one of the least controversial aspects of the SOAP standard. Additionally, this chapter explores some Apache SOAP innovations that encode Java objects.

The SOAP Specifications

As of this writing, the basic SOAP 1.1 Note of May 2000 has been supplemented by the SOAP 1.2 Working Draft of July 9, 2001, produced by the XML Protocol (XP) working group. In regard to data encoding, the main aspect that has changed between the two specification releases is that XML Schema specifications have been refined. To keep up with the latest releases by the XML Protocol working group, visit the following site:

```
http://www.w3.org/2000/xp/Group/
```

Schema Evolution

The original SOAP 1.1 Note used the 1999 draft version of XML Schema as the basis for data encoding. The XML Schema specifications have now reached the status of a W3C Recommendation, released May 2, 2001. Based on that release, the XP working group was able to update the SOAP 1.2 Working Draft (WD) with many corrections and changes.

As SOAP developers have tried to keep up with the various stages of refinement in XML Schema, three versions have been used. The URIs for these versions are

```
http://www.w3.org/1999/XMLSchema
http://www.w3.org/2000/10/XMLSchema
http://www.w3.org/2001/XMLSchema
```

> **NOTE**   Because various SOAP messages cite any one of these three URIs, there has been a lot of incompatibility among SOAP implementations. While writing this chapter, I used a version of Apache SOAP that still uses the 1999 schema citation. It is likely that most SOAP versions will be using the 2001 URI by the time this book is published.

Some Terminology

Here are short descriptions of some of the terms essential to the following discussion. Some of these definitions seem circular, but that's the way the specification is written. Later examples should make things a little clearer.

Independent element   An XML element at the top level of the body of a SOAP message.

Embedded element   An XML element, not an independent element.

Value   A string containing a single chunk of data or a compound value.

Simple value   A value without named parts.

Compound value   An aggregation of other values, for example, a Java object.

Accessor   A name or index used to address part of a compound value. If a name, this is the name of the XML element.

Single-reference   If a particular data item is to be used only once within a SOAP message, it is considered a single-reference value.

Multireference   If the data item is actually or potentially referenced by more than one accessor, it is a multireference value.

Qname   A name qualified with a namespace in the format *namespace:name*.

General Encoding Rules

The very general XML Schema rules have to be restricted for SOAP. The following paraphrases the main parts of the SOAP 1.2 WD document, Section 5, on serialization rules:

- All values are represented as XML element content as opposed to element attributes.

- For each element containing a value, there must be a provision for determining the type of the value by one of the following:

  - The element has an attribute of the `xsi:type`.

  - The element is contained in an array of a defined type.

  - The name of the element can be used to determine a type via a schema.

- The element content representing simple values must be character data without subelements. Simple values must be of a type listed in the XML schemas specification or be based on a type found there by using XML schemas mechanisms.

- A compound value element contains a sequence of elements, each having an element name that acts as an accessor.

- A multireference value is encoded as an independent element containing an attribute named `id`. This value can be accessed elsewhere in the message by using an empty element (no closing tag) with an `href` attribute that refers to the `id` of the independent element.

- Arrays are compound values and must have a type that incorporates `Array`.

I demonstrate all of these rules with example SOAP messages in the remainder of this chapter.

Values versus Types

Think of types as the class of values, for instance, the types string, integer, or date. Think of values as instances of types. I also speak of a *simple type*, meaning the class of a simple value, and *compound type*, meaning the class of a compound value.

Simple versus Compound Data Values

Another critical nomenclature distinction required is between simple and compound data values. Simple data values, such as an integer or string, do not have subparts. Compound data values are an aggregation of multiple values. The individual values in a compound type may be accessed by name or index number. The name or index number is called the *accessor* of that value. For example, the name po-number could be the accessor of part of a purchase order object (a compound value).

If a compound value uses only an index number to distinguish between members, it is called an *array*. If it only uses an accessor name to distinguish between members, it is called a *struct*. Apache SOAP provides methods for encoding common Java objects as compound data values.

Simple Data Types

There seems to be general agreement about the kinds of simple data types you must support for any message passing or remote procedure call (RPC) system. Therefore, there aren't any real surprises here. However, there are a lot of names for essentially the same thing. The Apache SOAP implementation recognizes only a subset of these alternate names; this subset is defined in the org.apache.soap.Constants class.

Simple Numeric Types

Table 5.1 shows the XML Schema integer numeric types, with examples and comments. The Supported column is checked if that name appears in Apache SOAP version 2.2 as a member of the 2001 schema built-in types. Comments in this table such as "derived from integer" refer to the way XML Schema definitions are stated.

TABLE 5.1: Integer Numeric Data Types

Name	Examples	Supported	Comments
Byte	−128, 47	x	A signed byte value
unsignedByte	0, 255		Derived from unsignedShort
Short	−3, 256	x	Signed 16-bit integer
unsignedShort	0, 65535		Unsigned 16-bit integer
Int	−3, 42	x	Signed 32-bit integer
integer	−3, 46		Same as int

TABLE 5.1 CONTINUED: Integer Numeric Data Types

Name	Examples	Supported	Comments
positiveInteger	0, 32000		Derived from integer
negativeInteger	−128, −42		Derived from integer
nonNegativeInteger	0, 4, 1024		Derived from integer
nonPostiveInteger	−43, −1, 0		Derived from integer
unsignedInt	0, 255		Derived from integer
Long	−1, 123456	x	Signed 64-bit integer
unsignedLong	0, 123456		

Table 5.2 shows the two floating point data types defined in SOAP and supported by Apache SOAP. In addition to the expected decimal notation, there is an exponential notation and three abbreviations. Exponential notation uses an *e* or *E* followed by an integer value that may have a sign.

There are five special values defined in XML Schema: negative infinity, positive infinity, negative zero, positive zero, and Not a Number (NaN). Java does not recognize negative zero or positive zero as special values; other than that, the SOAP usage matches Java primitive usage. See the Java class documentation for the use of these special values.

TABLE 5.2: Floating Point Data Types

Name	Examples	Supported	Comments
Float	0, −INF, −1E4, −0, 0, 12.78e−2, 12, INF, NaN	x	Conforming to IEEE 754 for 32-bit single precision floating point number. Note the use of short abbreviations for positive and negative infinity and Not a Number (NaN).
double	−INF, −1E4, −0, 0, 12.78E−2, 12, INF, NaN	x	Conforming to IEEE 754 for 64-bit double precision floating point numbers.

A Note About the Examples

All the sample methods in this chapter are in the `Chap05Exercise` class in the `com.lanw.soap` package. The source code and deployment descriptor files are included on the CD. The deployment descriptor for this service, which I call `Exercise`, is shown in Listing 5.1.

Listing 5.1:   **The Deployment Descriptor Used for Examples in This Chapter**

```
<isd:service xmlns:isd="http://xml.apache.org/xml-soap/deployment"
             id="urn:Exercise">
 <isd:provider type="java"
   scope="Application"
   methods="getIntegerType getBytes getDateNow myBirthday doXor
       conCat loadDOM getNthElement getUniqueValues">
   <isd:java class="com.lanw.soap.Chap05Exercise" static="false"/>
 </isd:provider>

 <isd:faultListener>org.apache.soap.server.DOMFaultListener
 </isd:faultListener>
 <isd:mappings>
   <isd:map encodingStyle="http://xml.apache.org/xml-soap/literalxml"
     xmlns:x="urn:ExercisePubs" qname="x:book-element"
     javaType="org.w3c.dom.Element"
     java2XMLClassName=
       "org.apache.soap.encoding.literalxml.XMLParameterSerializer"
     xml2JavaClassName=
       "org.apache.soap.encoding.literalxml.XMLParameterSerializer"
     />
 </isd:mappings>
</isd:service>
```

Example of Numeric Coding

To see how Apache SOAP encodes a simple integer, I wrote a simple service that responds to an RPC through the Apache SOAP `rpcrouter` servlet and returns a constant integer:

```
public int getIntegerType(){
    return 42 ;
}
```

The SOAP message to the service is very simple because it does not take any input:

```
<?xml version='1.0' encoding='UTF-8'?>
<SOAP-ENV:Envelope xmlns:SOAP-ENV="http://schemas.xmlsoap.org/soap/envelope/"
  xmlns:xsi="http://www.w3.org/2001/XMLSchema-instance"
  xmlns:xsd="http://www.w3.org/2001/XMLSchema">
<SOAP-ENV:Body>
<ns1:getIntegerType xmlns:ns1="urn:Exercise"
  SOAP-ENV:encodingStyle="http://schemas.xmlsoap.org/soap/encoding/">
</ns1:getIntegerType>
</SOAP-ENV:Body>
</SOAP-ENV:Envelope>
```

The service response, as formulated by the Apache SOAP `rpcrouter` service, is as follows:

```
<?xml version='1.0' encoding='UTF-8'?>
<SOAP-ENV:Envelope
```

```
  xmlns:SOAP-ENV="http://schemas.xmlsoap.org/soap/envelope/"
  xmlns:xsi="http://www.w3.org/1999/XMLSchema-instance"
  xmlns:xsd="http://www.w3.org/1999/XMLSchema">
<SOAP-ENV:Body>
<ns1:getIntegerTypeResponse xmlns:ns1="urn:Exercise"
   SOAP-ENV:encodingStyle="http://schemas.xmlsoap.org/soap/encoding/">
<return xsi:type="xsd:int">42</return>
</ns1:getIntegerTypeResponse>

</SOAP-ENV:Body>
</SOAP-ENV:Envelope>
```

Interpreting the return tag attributes, you see that xsi:type, which means the instance type, is "xsd:int" (the type established by the XML Schema), so the value 42 can be interpreted as a 32-bit integer, according to Table 5.1. The SOAP-ENV:encodingStyle attribute establishes the encoding that a program interpreting this response would use, which, in this case, is the standard SOAP encoding.

Simple Date Types

Table 5.3 shows XML Schema types related to date and time. As of this writing, Apache SOAP has built-in support only for date and dateTime. Earlier versions of Apache SOAP used the timeInstant name for what is now named dateTime. The naming conventions and formats for these primitive data types are based on the ISO 8601 standard, with some deviations.

TABLE 5.3: Schema Types for Date and Time

Name	Examples	Supported	Comments
Time	13:30:00.000, 13:30:00.00–05:00		The –05:00 means 5 hours behind Coordinated Universal time
dateTime	1999-05-031T13::00.00–05:00	x	Year, month, day, time
duration	P2Y3M4DT9H20M11.4S		Duration in years, months, days, hours, minutes, and seconds
Date	1939-10-17	x	Year-Month-Day
gMonth	--10--		October; the g stands for Gregorian calendar
gYear	1939		
gYearMonth	1939-10		1939, October
gDay	---17		17th day, any year or month
gMonthDay	--05-31		May 31, any year

To demonstrate how Apache SOAP handles dates, I wrote the following simple method that returns a `java.util.Date` object:

```
public Date getDateNow(){
    return new Date();
}
```

Here is an example of the encoded response returned by a beta version of Apache SOAP 2.2:

```
<ns1:getDateNowResponse xmlns:ns1="urn:Exercise"
SOAP-ENV:encodingStyle="http://schemas.xmlsoap.org/soap/encoding/">
<return xsi:type="xsd:timeInstant">2001-07-22T18:59:53Z</return>
</ns1:getDateNowResponse>
```

NOTE   This encoding has not caught up with the SOAP 1.2 and XML 2001 Schema and still uses the `timeInstant` name. Undoubtedly, by the time this book is printed, Apache SOAP will be compliant with the most recent schema.

The `Date` class in `java.util`, which was the only date-related class in Java 1.0, has many deficiencies, so Java 1.1 introduced the `Calendar` and `GregorianCalendar` classes. Apache SOAP automatically encodes a `GregorianCalendar` object as an XML Schema `date`, as seen in the following return from the `myBirthday` method in the `Exercise` class, where the encoding is in the familiar `yyyy-mm-dd` format.

```
<return xsi:type="xsd:date">1939-10-17</return>
```

This results in the contrary-to-expectation situation that a `Date` object becomes a `dateTime` type and a `GregorianCalendar` object becomes encoded as an `xsd:date` type.

Boolean Data

Boolean values are naturally returned as either a `true` or `false` string. As an example of that usage and to set things up for a subsequent demonstration of literal XML encoding, I wrote the following method. Note that `doc` is declared as an `org.w3c.dom.Document` reference.

```
public boolean loadDOM( String s ){
    File f = new File( s ) ;
    System.out.println("loadDOM from: " + f.getAbsolutePath() );
    try {
      DocumentBuilderFactory dbf =
            DocumentBuilderFactory.newInstance();
      dbf.setValidating( false );
      DocumentBuilder db = dbf.newDocumentBuilder();
      doc = db.parse( f );
      return true ;
    }catch(Exception e){
      e.printStackTrace();
      return false ;
    }
}
```

On successful operation, the returned value is encoded as follows:

```
<return xsi:type="xsd:boolean">true</return>
```

Binary Data and Byte Arrays

With all of the special character meanings that XML assigns, binary data can't be transmitted directly. Arbitrary binary data can be encoded two ways: `hexBinary` and `base64Binary`. The `hexBinary` approach uses pairs of characters to represent 8-bit bytes. The digits 0–9 and letters A–F or a–f are used in the familiar notation. For example, the four ASCII characters in "Java" become eight hex digits "4a617661".

Encoding with `base64Binary` follows the MIME approach. The 24 bits contained in 3 bytes are encoded in 4 characters by means of bit shifting and substitution rules. You can find the encoding algorithm used in the `Base64.java` class in the `org.apache.soap.encoding.soapenc` package. Six bits at a time are turned into a character using these rules:

- Values 0 through 25 become characters A through Z

- Values 26 through 51 become characters a through z

- Values 52 through 61 become characters 0 through 9

- Value 62 becomes the plus character (+)

- Value 63 becomes the forward slash character (/)

If the byte array size is not evenly divisible by 3, the special equal sign (=) character is used to fill out the set of four resulting characters. Thus an arbitrary stream of bytes can be turned into a stream of characters compatible with XML. Using `base64Binary` is obviously more efficient for binary data larger than a few bytes, but `hexBinary` has the advantage of being relatively easy for humans to interpret.

The default encoder used by Apache SOAP is `base64Binary`. Here is an example of the return of a `byte[]`—note the trailing `"=="` that fills out the string to a multiple of four characters. The line that contains the encoded `byte[]` has been broken arbitrarily here. In contrast to the way MIME messages in `base64` have to be broken into small lines, SOAP `base64Binary` text can be any length.

```
<ns1:doXorResponse xmlns:ns1="urn:Exercise"
  SOAP-ENV:encodingStyle="http://schemas.xmlsoap.org/soap/encoding/">
<return xmlns:ns2="http://schemas.xmlsoap.org/soap/encoding/"
xsi:type="ns2:base64">BSkpPmhYXBQ3XFRyIiMlOkJXFCxSEToOITEmEVdCJl==
</return>
</ns1:doXorResponse>
```

Compound Types

A good example of a compound type is provided by the `AddressBook` service from the Apache SOAP sample applications. As you can see in Listing 5.2, the return element contains a hierarchy of elements within it. In this case, the creation of this compound type was accomplished by serializing the data in a Java object using Apache SOAP's JavaBeans serialization capability.

Listing 5.2:   **Returning the Compound Type Used in the *AddressBook* Example**

```
<?xml version='1.0' encoding='UTF-8'?>
<SOAP-ENV:Envelope
  xmlns:SOAP-ENV="http://schemas.xmlsoap.org/soap/envelope/"
  xmlns:xsi="http://www.w3.org/1999/XMLSchema-instance"
  xmlns:xsd="http://www.w3.org/1999/XMLSchema">
<SOAP-ENV:Body>
<ns1:getAddressFromNameResponse
  xmlns:ns1="urn:AddressFetcher"
  SOAP-ENV:encodingStyle="http://schemas.xmlsoap.org/soap/encoding/">
<return xmlns:ns2="urn:xml-soap-address-demo"
    xsi:type="ns2:address">
<phoneNumber xsi:type="ns2:phone">
  <exchange xsi:type="xsd:string">456</exchange>
  <areaCode xsi:type="xsd:int">123</areaCode>
  <number xsi:type="xsd:string">7890</number>
</phoneNumber>
<zip xsi:type="xsd:int">12345</zip>
<streetNum xsi:type="xsd:int">123</streetNum>
<streetName xsi:type="xsd:string">Main Street</streetName>
<state xsi:type="xsd:string">NY</state>
<city xsi:type="xsd:string">Anytown</city>
</return>
</ns1:getAddressFromNameResponse>

</SOAP-ENV:Body>
</SOAP-ENV:Envelope>
```

Arrays

Arrays are compound values whose members are all of the same type and distinguished by their position in the array. Listing 5.3 shows the encoded return from the getUniqueValues method in the Exercise service. This method returns an array of strings representing the unique values of a particular element in an XML document.

This particular example lists book titles. Most of the title string elements have been removed from the listing to save space. Listing 5.3 illustrates the following SOAP array encoding requirements.

Encoding type   The xsi:type must use the word "Array", seen in the return element of Listing 5.3 as "ns2:Array".

Array type   There must be an `arrayType` attribute giving the type of the array elements and the count of elements. In Listing 5.3, this attribute value is `"xsd:string[73]"`.

Although it is not a SOAP encoding requirement, Apache SOAP includes a type indicating attribute in each of the array elements.

Listing 5.3:   **Apache SOAP Encoding of an Array of Strings**

```
<ns1:getUniqueValuesResponse
  xmlns:ns1="urn:Exercise"
  SOAP-ENV:encodingStyle="http://schemas.xmlsoap.org/soap/encoding/">
<return xmlns:ns2="http://schemas.xmlsoap.org/soap/encoding/"
    xsi:type="ns2:Array" ns2:arrayType="xsd:string[73]">
<item xsi:type="xsd:string">
  CNE Advanced NetWare 5 Admin. Exam Cram</item>
<item xsi:type="xsd:string">
  CNE NetWare 4.11 to NetWare 5 Update Exam Cram</item>
.............
<item xsi:type="xsd:string">XML for Dummies, 2nd Edition</item>
</return>
</ns1:getUniqueValuesResponse>
```

Encoding of arrays with more than one dimension and for sparse arrays is provided for in the SOAP Specification, Section 5.1.8. However, I do not have any examples demonstrating this.

Multiple References

In the encoding examples presented thus far, the data values transmitted have been quite compact. If a message required the same value in two locations, it is no big deal to repeat the entire value. However, with applications that may require bulky or complex values, repeating values would cause excessive bulk and cause for error. Fortunately, SOAP provides for multi-reference simple and compound values.

Any independent value can be given an identifier that is unique within the message, and this identifier can be used any number of times within the message. SOAP follows the XML 1.0 convention of using an attribute named `id` that is of the XML Schema type `ID`.

To demonstrate this, I added a `conCat` method to the `Exercise` class. This method takes two strings and returns the concatenation of the inputs. An RPC message to the `conCat` method is shown in Listing 5.4. Note that where you would expect to find the two input strings, there are two empty elements with `href` attributes. Following the `ns1:conCat` element is the complete definition of the string values, each with a unique `id` attribute.

Listing 5.4:   **A SOAP Message Using Multireference Notation**

```
<?xml version='1.0' encoding='UTF-8'?>
<SOAP-ENV:Envelope xmlns:SOAP-ENV="http://schemas.xmlsoap.org/soap/envelope/"
  xmlns:xsi="http://www.w3.org/2001/XMLSchema-instance"
  xmlns:xsd="http://www.w3.org/2001/XMLSchema">
<SOAP-ENV:Body xmlns:ns1="urn:Exercise">
<ns1:conCat
   SOAP-ENV:encodingStyle="http://schemas.xmlsoap.org/soap/encoding/">
  <stra href="#nam" />
  <strb href="#ins" />
</ns1:conCat>
<ns1:insult id="ins" xsi:type="xsd:string" xmlns:ns2="urn:paramA"
   > is a jerk.</ns1:insult>
<ns1:namstr id="nam" xsi:type="xsd:string"
   >My brother in law</ns1:namstr>
</SOAP-ENV:Body>
</SOAP-ENV:Envelope>
```

When the RPC call is executed, the string values input to the method are those indicated by the `id` attribute. When the message shown in Listing 5.4 is sent, the returned value is, as expected:

```
<return xsi:type="xsd:string">My brother in law is a jerk.</return>
```

The `href` notation can be used to refer to elements of arrays, as long as the array is an independent element. The `href` attribute is further qualified by a `position` attribute. For example, the following would refer to the element at position 2 (where 0 is the first element) in an array having the attribute `id="array-1"`.

```
<ns1:someName href="#array-1" ns1:position="[2]" />
```

Apache SOAP Special Encoding

I have been working with standard encoding established by XML schema and SOAP 1.2 documentation up to this point. Apache SOAP incorporates some useful encoding types not mentioned in XML Schema because they are not supported in other languages. For example, the default `SOAPMappingRegistry` includes encoding classes for Java `Vector`, `Hashtable`, `Map`, and `BigDecimal` objects.

Useful classes not in the default mapping registry include encoding classes for XML Elements and JavaBeans objects. Furthermore, Apache SOAP provides interface definitions that allow you to write your own serializing classes.

Literal XML Encoding

Probably the most useful of the extra encoding types provides for serialization of XML data as long as the data can be represented as an org.w3c.dom.Element object. For an example, I created a method that takes a String and an int and returns an Element.

```
public org.w3c.dom.Element getNthElement(String s, int n){
    NodeList theNL =
        doc.getDocumentElement().getElementsByTagName( s );
    return (Element) theNL.item(n);
}
```

For the Apache SOAP rpcrouter to encode the Element returned from this method, I had to include a special mapping in the deployment descriptor shown in Listing 5.1. The following shows how an RPC call to this method is expressed. Note the SOAP-ENV:encodingStyle attribute that tells the rpcrouter to use the literalxml mapping provided in the deployment descriptor.

```
<ns1:getNthElement xmlns:ns1="urn:Exercise"
  SOAP-ENV:encodingStyle="http://xml.apache.org/xml-soap/literalxml">
<elementName xsi:type="xsd:string"
   SOAP-ENV:encodingStyle="http://schemas.xmlsoap.org/soap/encoding/"
   >Book</elementName>
<eN xsi:type="xsd:int"
  SOAP-ENV:encodingStyle="http://schemas.xmlsoap.org/soap/encoding/"
      >10</eN>
</ns1:getNthElement>
```

Note that because the method call sets an encoding style of literalxml, each element's defining parameters must provide an attribute setting the default SOAP encoding for that element. This makes for a bulky message but allows you to mix default and specialized encodings in the same message. Listing 5.5 shows the returned value, which is the complete XML representation of the retrieved element.

Listing 5.5:   **A SOAP Message Incorporating an Encoded *Element* Object**

```
<?xml version='1.0' encoding='UTF-8'?>
<SOAP-ENV:Envelope
    xmlns:SOAP-ENV="http://schemas.xmlsoap.org/soap/envelope/"
    xmlns:xsi="http://www.w3.org/1999/XMLSchema-instance"
    xmlns:xsd="http://www.w3.org/1999/XMLSchema">
<SOAP-ENV:Body>
<ns1:getNthElementResponse xmlns:ns1="urn:Exercise"
  SOAP-ENV:encodingStyle="http://xml.apache.org/xml-soap/literalxml">
<return>
<Book isbn="0-7821-2809-2">
    <Title>Java Developer's Guide to Servlets and JSP</Title>
    <Errata code="jdgjsp"/>
```

```
        <Author>Bill Brogden</Author>
        <Publisher>Sybex</Publisher>
        <Topic>Java,servlets,JSP,XML,Tomcat,debugging,JDBC</Topic>
        <Edition edition="1"/>
        <Size pp="411"/>
    </Book>
    </return>
    </ns1:getNthElementResponse>
```

Apache SOAP does not provide for encoding an entire XML document, but you can get the root element and encode that.

The Bean Serializer

As you may recall from Chapter 3, the addressbook sample application provided with Apache SOAP uses a BeanSerializer class to encode parameters held in a JavaBeans object into a SOAP message. The same class is used to extract the parameters and reconstruct the JavaBeans object. This is a very powerful technique that makes it easy to send and receive complex data as long as you can create a class that supports the bean conventions to carry the data.

Listing 5.6 shows a SOAP message generated by the PutAddress class in the Apache SOAP addressbook sample application. The listing has been reformatted by splitting some lines and adding indentation to emphasize the structure. This message calls the addEntry method in the AddressFetcher service with a serialized Address class bean. Note that the Address object includes a PhoneNumber bean.

Listing 5.6: **A Message Incorporating Serialized Beans**

```
<?xml version='1.0' encoding='UTF-8'?>
<SOAP-ENV:Envelope
  xmlns:SOAP-ENV="http://schemas.xmlsoap.org/soap/envelope/"
  xmlns:xsi="http://www.w3.org/1999/XMLSchema-instance"
  xmlns:xsd="http://www.w3.org/1999/XMLSchema">
<SOAP-ENV:Body>
<ns1:addEntry xmlns:ns1="urn:AddressFetcher"
  SOAP-ENV:encodingStyle="http://schemas.xmlsoap.org/soap/encoding/">
<nameToRegister xsi:type="xsd:string">John Doe</nameToRegister>
<address xmlns:ns2="urn:xml-soap-address-demo" xsi:type="ns2:address">
    <phoneNumber xsi:type="ns2:phone">
        <exchange xsi:type="xsd:string">555</exchange>
        <areaCode xsi:type="xsd:int">800</areaCode>
        <number xsi:type="xsd:string">1212</number>
    </phoneNumber>
    <zip xsi:type="xsd:int">12345</zip>
```

```
    <streetNum xsi:type="xsd:int">123</streetNum>
    <streetName xsi:type="xsd:string">Main Street</streetName>
    <state xsi:type="xsd:string">SS</state>
    <city xsi:type="xsd:string">AnyTown</city>
  </address>
 </ns1:addEntry>
 </SOAP-ENV:Body>
 </SOAP-ENV:Envelope>
```

To use the `BeanSerializer`, all that is required of your class design is that it fulfill the basic JavaBeans requirements. Those of you who have programmed JavaServer Pages applications with the `jsp:useBean` tag will recognize these:

Constructor   There must be a public no-arguments constructor.

Setter methods   Each property (variable) to be serialized must have a matching public setting method setXXX, where XXX represents the name of the property.

Getter methods   Each property to be serialized must also have a matching public getter method.

Method naming   The naming convention relating variable names to setter and getter method names is as follows: the variable name must start with a lowercase letter. The setter method name is created by taking the variable name, changing the first letter to uppercase, and combining it with the prefix "set". Likewise the getter is created using the prefix "get".

Order independence   The order in which getter and setter methods are called must not be significant to the values fetched or set.

Serialization uses only the simplest aspects of the complete JavaBeans specification. Java-Beans can get much more complex than this, but the previous are all that are required for the `BeanSerializer` to work. For the latest JavaBeans specification, visit the `http://java.sun`.com/beans/docs/ website.

Behind the *BeanSerializer*

The key to the `BeanSerializer` functions is information about the `bean` object obtained through the use of the `Introspector` class in the `java.beans` package. The `Introspector` works with a fully qualified Java class name, `samples.addressbook.PhoneNumber` in the case of the example in Listing 5.6. `Introspector` first looks for a class named `PhoneNumberBean-Info` in that package, in case the programmer has provided additional information in that form. If, as in the `addressbook` sample, an additional information class is not found, `Introspector` can still examine `PhoneNumber` directly.

The end result is an object implementing the `BeanInfo` interface that encapsulates information about all properties of the class for which getter and setter methods exist. The `Phone-Number` class example has the following methods:

```
public void setAreaCode( int code )
public int getAreaCode();
```

The information derived from the `BeanInfo` allows the `BeanSerializer` to write the following tag deriving the `areaCode` name from the `getAreaCode` method name and the encoding type from the method signature.

```
<areaCode xsi:type="xsd:int">800</areaCode>
```

When rebuilding a `PhoneNumber` object using the SOAP message, the `BeanSerializer` creates a new `PhoneNumber` using the no-arguments constructor, then sets the properties by locating the setter methods that match the XML element names.

Custom Serializers

If you can't transmit a particular Java object with the default encodings or the specialized encodings provided by Apache SOAP, you can always write your own custom classes. All you have to do is implement the `Serializer` and `Deserializer` interfaces as defined in the `org.apache.soap.util.xml` package. Provide a mapping that associates your data class with the encoding classes in the deployment descriptor as shown in Listing 5.1, and you are in business.

Here is the code for the `Serializer` interface declaration:

```
public interface Serializer {
  public void marshall(
      String inScopeEncStyle,
      Class javaType,
      Object src,
      Object context,
      Writer sink,
      NSStack nsStack,
      XMLJavaMappingRegistry xjmr,
      SOAPContext ctx)
          throws IllegalArgumentException, IOException;
}
```

Essentially, a `Serializer` takes a source object and writes it to a "sink" output stream, while keeping track of namespaces. Study the examples in the `org.apache.soap.encoding.soapenc` package to see how a typical implementation of this interface works. The main complexity is introduced by the need to keep track of namespaces.

A `Deserializer` has to take an XML element from a SOAP message, locate the matching Java class, and create an `org.apache.soap.util.Bean` object. This `Bean`, not to be confused with a JavaBeans object, is simply a container for the object constructed from the XML data plus a `Class` object indicating the type. Here is the definition of the `Bean` class:

```
public class Bean {
  // type of this bean
  public Class type;

  public Object value;

  public Bean (Class type, Object value) {
    this.type = type;
    this.value = value;
  }
}
```

Here is the declaration of the `Deserializer` interface:

```
public interface Deserializer {
  public Bean unmarshall(
    String inScopeEncStyle,
    QName elementType,
    Node src,
    XMLJavaMappingRegistry xjmr,
    SOAPContext ctx)
    throws IllegalArgumentException;
}
```

Listing 5.7 shows an example implementation of `Deserializer` from the Apache SOAP 2.2 distribution. This works by extracting the `String` representation of a `double` value from the XML node, parsing it, and creating a `Bean` to contain the value.

The most interesting point here is found in the `return` statement where a new `Bean` is constructed. The `double.class` is a constant `Class` object representing double primitive values. The compiler that treats `double.class` as a reference to the `Class` object is stored as the static `TYPE` variable in the `java.lang.Double` class. Because the object containing the value is a `java.lang.Double`, it is the `Class` object that determines whether this value is to be interpreted as an object or a primitive.

Listing 5.7:   **Source Code for the *DoubleDeserializer* Class**

```
package org.apache.soap.encoding.soapenc;

import java.io.*;
import org.w3c.dom.*;
import org.apache.soap.util.xml.*;
```

```
import org.apache.soap.*;
import org.apache.soap.util.*;
import org.apache.soap.rpc.*;

public class DoubleDeserializer implements Deserializer {
  public Bean unmarshall(String inScopeEncStyle, QName elementType,
                         Node src, XMLJavaMappingRegistry xjmr,
                         SOAPContext ctx)
      throws IllegalArgumentException {
    Element root = (Element)src;
    String value = DOMUtils.getChildCharacterData(root);
    return new Bean(double.class, FPDeserUtil.newDouble(value));
  }
}
```

The SOAP specification provides straightforward encoding methods based on XML Schema to encode all of the simple data types commonly used in Java programs. Apache SOAP adds easy-to-use methods for transmitting many common Java objects with a consistent system that is easily extended.

CHAPTER 6

Creating a SOAP Server Application

- Handling a SOAP message envelope

- The differences between RPC and other message handlers

- How a server reports problems

- A complete example service

- A bare-bones SOAP service

This chapter examines what is required to create a SOAP server application based on the requirements of the SOAP specifications. The Apache SOAP architecture for both remote procedure calls and messaging is examined to illustrate the principles. In conclusion, this chapter details the required steps for creating a modest server application.

SOAP Server Architecture

It is unfortunate that most discussions of SOAP concentrate on remote procedure call (RPC) applications using HTTP. This tends to obscure that the basic component of SOAP is a single XML message that can be transported by a variety of mechanisms and may or may not require a return message. There is also a tendency to concentrate on examples in which a client talks directly to a server. As discussed in Chapter 2, "A Survey of SOAP," the protocol provides for a SOAP message passing through any number of intermediary handlers.

Let's consider some of the usage scenarios or use cases from the W3C working group on XML Protocols (XP) requirements document. The current version of this document can be found at:

```
http://www.w3.org/TR/xmlp-reqs/
```

These usage scenarios are intended to provide examples of situations in which XML messaging might be applicable.

Fire-and-forget to single receiver   In this case, the sender creates a SOAP message and sends it to a receiver but does not expect any form of response. For example, a remote weather station reporting readings every hour.

Fire-and-forget to multiple receivers   In this case, the SOAP message is sent by a system that repeats or duplicates the message to multiple receivers, also known as "publish/subscribe" messaging. For example, stock price updates to multiple websites.

Request-response   In general, a request that expects a response of some sort. For example, a purchase order request to which the response might be an order confirmation or simply a bid.

Remote procedure call   A more specific case of request-response in which the request supplies parameters to a known method and expects a response from that method. An example would be a request for a stock quote.

Request with acknowledgment   Message delivery that reports whether delivery was accomplished without error. High value messages such as an order to buy or sell a stock would fall in this category.

Request with encrypted payload In which the entire body of the SOAP message is encrypted using previously agreed upon key and method. It seems likely that encryption will be adopted for all high-value messages such as the stock purchase example.

Extended conversations In which a series of messages are exchanged, with both parties keeping track of the state of the conversation. An example would be negotiation of an auction price.

Delivering the SOAP Message

A complete SOAP message is always enclosed in a SOAP envelope. The delivery mechanism, whether it is HTTP, e-mail, or a messaging system, only has to get the envelope to the right handler. Figure 6.1 shows a conceptual model of a SOAP envelope.

The term *SOAP block* first appeared in the SOAP 1.2 Working Draft document of July 2001. A SOAP block is an XML structure that logically defines a single computational unit as far as some SOAP processing mechanism is concerned. Blocks in the SOAP header are called header blocks; those in the SOAP body are called body blocks.

FIGURE 6.1:

The SOAP envelope

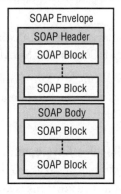

A SOAP envelope may or may not have a SOAP header, but it will always have a SOAP body element. As you will recall from Chapter 2, SOAP header elements (blocks) may be processed by intermediaries that handle a SOAP message.

What Is a SOAP Node?

Another term formalized in the SOAP 1.2 Working Draft document is *SOAP node*. Essentially, a SOAP node is a software entity that processes a SOAP message. A SOAP node is not to be confused with an `org.w3c.dom.Node`, which is the fundamental element of an XML document in a document object model.

Processing the Envelope

The first step in processing an envelope is checking the namespace. A SOAP application must respond with a `VersionMismatch` faultcode if the envelope namespace is not recognized. This namespace takes the place of any other sort of version control, such as the major version dot minor version numbers used with XML, HTML, and other standards. The SOAP 1.2 Working Draft specification gives a required namespace as illustrated in the following `Envelope` tag:

```
<env:Envelope xmlns:env="http://www.w3.org.2001/06/soap-envelope">
```

At present, there are a number of other namespaces in use. For example, Apache SOAP 2.2 uses an entirely different namespace, as seen in the following. You can only hope that a common namespace will be widely accepted, or there will be a lot of `VersionMismatch` messages flying around.

```
<SOAP-ENV:Envelope
    xmlns:SOAP-ENV="http://schemas.xmlsoap.org/soap/envelope/"
    xmlns:xsi="http://www.w3.org/1999/XMLSchema-instance"
    xmlns:xsd="http://www.w3.org/1999/XMLSchema">
```

Although a SOAP envelope is always an XML document, there are restrictions on the XML content:

DTD   A SOAP message must not contain a Document Type Declaration. However, note that there is an XML Schema for SOAP under development.

Processing instructions   A SOAP message must not contain processing instructions. This restriction has probably been created in the interest of keeping a message as self-contained as possible.

How Apache SOAP Handles Envelopes

The Apache SOAP `RPCRouterServlet` constructs an `Envelope` object in the `doPost()` method from the `request` input stream. This is accomplished by a rather complex set of calls, starting with the servlet `doPost()` method. Here is a summary of the sequence of method calls:

```
org.apache.soap.server.http.RPCRouterServlet.doPost()
```

which calls the static method:

```
org.apache.soap.server.http.ServerHttpUtils.readEnvelopeFromRequest()
```

which in turn calls

```
org.apache.soap.server.ServerUtils.readEnvelopeFromInputStream()
```

which in turn constructs an

```
org.apache.soap.transport.TransportMessage
```

The `TransportMessage` constructor reads the input stream into a byte array in order to check the message length against the content-length from the HTTP header. If the constructor does not throw an exception, the `ServerUtils` `readEnvelopeFromInputStream()` method then calls the `TransportMessage` `read()` method. The `read()` method interprets the byte array with the aim of adding data to a SOAPContext object that was originally created in the `doPost()` method and creating a String containing the envelope.

The `TransportMessage` `read()` method can also determine if the message has one or more attachments. If attachments are present, the data is used to create a `MimeMultipart` object for each part. The `MimeMultipart` class is in the `javax.mail.internet` package. If attachments are not present, the SOAP envelope ends up as a `MimeMultipart` object constructed from the input byte array. Finally, the `read()` method returns a `String` containing the envelope. But you still have not parsed the envelope as XML.

Now, back to `ServerUtils`. The `readEnvelopeFromInputStream()` method finally calls the `unmarshall()` method in `TransportMessage`, which uses a parser created all the way back in `RPCRouterServlet`, to parse the envelope text and return an `Envelope` object to `Server-HTTPUtils`, which finally returns it to `RPCRouterServlet`.

Whew! Now the servlet has an `Envelope` object representing the SOAP request, and any attachments are in the `SOAPContext` object. The `Envelope` contains a `Body` object, and, if a SOAP header was present in the request, a `Header` object.

This is the point at which RPC handling and message handling diverge.

Executing an RPC with an *Envelope*

The next thing `RPCRouterServlet` does with the `Envelope` is to create a `Call` object by calling the `static` `extractCallFromEnvelope()` method in `RPCRouter`. This method looks at the first `Element` in the body and gets a `String` representing the target method. This `String` is used to look up a `DeploymentDescriptor` for the target method. If a `DeploymentDescriptor` is found, a `Call` object is constructed by locating and decoding all of the method parameters.

Typically, Apache SOAP knows to use an object of the `RPCJavaProvider` class based on the `isd:provider` tag in the deployment descriptor. The function of the provider is to locate the class called for and finally to call the required method with `SOAPContext` objects representing the request and response.

If nothing goes wrong, the response `SOAPContext` is used to create a `TransportMessage` object, which formats the content for the output stream back to the client.

Message Processing with an *Envelope* Object

Apache SOAP provides a message-processing example that uses the `MessageRouterServlet` class in the `org.apache.soap.server.http` package on the server. This example represents purchase order processing. Parsing of the incoming SOAP data proceeds as with the RPC servlet until an `Envelope` object is constructed.

Instead of extracting a `Call` object from the `Envelope`, the entire `Envelope` is passed to the target processor. Thus message processing is a much more general approach than RPC. For example, if you were implementing a SOAP intermediary processor that examined header blocks for authentication or decryption, your methods would be called via `MessageRouterServlet`.

As with RPC processing, the target class is designated in the deployment descriptor for the service as shown in the following for the purchase order processor example:

```
<isd:service xmlns:isd="http://xml.apache.org/xml-soap/deployment"
             id="urn:po-processor" type="message">
  <isd:provider type="java"
      scope="Application"
      methods="purchaseOrder bustedRequest XXX">
    <isd:java class="samples.messaging.POProcessor" static="false"/>
  </isd:provider>
  <isd:faultListener>org.apache.soap.server.DOMFaultListener
  </isd:faultListener>
</isd:service>
```

Here is the entire `purchaseOrder()` method:

```
public void purchaseOrder (Envelope env, SOAPContext reqCtx,
        SOAPContext resCtx)
        throws MessagingException, IOException {
  resCtx.setRootPart(
     "OK thanks, got the PO; we'll contact you when ready.",
     "text/xml");
  }
```

In the example, the `purchaseOrder()` method in the `POProcessor` class responds by attaching a text message to the response but doesn't do anything with the `Envelope`. A real-world example would presumably process the `Envelope` somehow. The response is plain unformatted text as shown in the response message:

```
HTTP/1.0 200 OK
Content-Type: text/xml
Content-Length: 52
Date: Wed, 15 Aug 2001 12:31:11 GMT
Server: Apache Tomcat/4.0-b6 (HTTP/1.1 Connector)
Set-Cookie: JSESSIONID=46E1C4E7401990B4D434E09845B04028;Path=/soap

OK thanks, got the PO; we'll contact you when ready.
```

SOAP Messages with Attachments

Apache SOAP provides a simple example of sending an attachment to a SOAP server. As discussed previously, the read() method in the TransportMessage class can determine if the message has one or more attachments. Any attachment is parsed and the content used to build a MimeBodyPart. Attachments are made available to your custom code as javax.activation .DataHandler objects that act as containers for the actual bytes transmitted as attachments.

Listing 6.1 shows the text of a SOAP message with a single attachment consisting of four characters: "bar!". The first Content-Type line has been split for presentation. Let's look at the parts that compose this message.

The initial headers declare that the Content-Type is "multipart/related" and give the text string that serves as a boundary marker, plus a unique text string used as a "start" ID. The boundary string marks the start of a "part". The Content-Length gives the total number of bytes following the blank line that ends the initial headers. This total includes all of the part headers as well as the part contents.

Listing 6.1:   A MIME Multipart Message to a SOAP Server

```
POST /soap/servlet/rpcrouter HTTP/1.0
Host: localhost
Content-Type: multipart/related;
    boundary="----=_Part_0_6060112.997889230734"; type="text/xml";
    start="5813833.997889230921.apache-soap.brogden"
Content-Length: 876
SOAPAction: ""

------=_Part_0_6060112.997889230734
Content-Type: text/xml; charset=utf-8
Content-Transfer-Encoding: 8bit
Content-ID: <5813833.997889230921.apache-soap.brogden>
Content-Length: 468

<?xml version='1.0' encoding='UTF-8'?>
<SOAP-ENV:Envelope xmlns:SOAP-ENV="http://schemas.xmlsoap.org/soap/envelope/"
xmlns:xsi="http://www.w3.org/1999/XMLSchema-instance"
xmlns:xsd="http://www.w3.org/1999/XMLSchema">
<SOAP-ENV:Body>
<ns1:sendFile xmlns:ns1="urn:mimetest" SOAP-
ENV:encodingStyle="http://schemas.xmlsoap.org/soap/encoding/">
<addedfile href ="cid:6340152.997889230718.apache-soap.brogden"/>
</ns1:sendFile>
</SOAP-ENV:Body>
</SOAP-ENV:Envelope>

------=_Part_0_6060112.997889230734
```

```
Content-Type: text/plain
Content-Transfer-Encoding: 7bit
Content-ID: <6340152.997889230718.apache-soap.brogden>
Content-Length: 4

bar!
------=_Part_0_6060112.997889230734--
```

The first MIME part consists of a set of headers followed by a SOAP message. Note that among the headers is a Content-ID header that gives the "start" ID string. The SOAP message Body names the sendFile() method as the target, with the input parameter named addedfile, which is given using an href attribute with a code starting with cid. This is the multireference format discussed in Chapter 5, "How SOAP Encodes Data."

The second MIME part in this example consists of a set of headers including the Content-ID value that identifies this content as the addedfile input to the SOAP method.

WARNING   A limitation of the Apache SOAP approach to message attachments is that the entire message must be held in memory before any processing starts. This requirement could overwhelm a server handling many clients at the same time.

Server Fault Codes

If a SOAP server is unable to complete a request, it must respond with a SOAP fault message. This message is encoded as an entry in the body of a SOAP message following rules described in the SOAP specifications. In SOAP applications using RPCs, this is the message returned to the client instead of the expected method call results. Exactly what happens to the message in other application architectures, such as the "fire and forget" applications suggested earlier, is up to the application designer.

An example encoded SOAP fault is shown in Listing 6.2. Note that many of the long lines have been split to fit the page and that many boring lines of the actual stack trace have been cut out.

Listing 6.2:   **A SOAP Fault Response**

```
<?xml version='1.0' encoding='UTF-8'?>
<SOAP-ENV:Envelope
    xmlns:SOAP-ENV="http://schemas.xmlsoap.org/soap/envelope/"
    xmlns:xsi="http://www.w3.org/1999/XMLSchema-instance"
    xmlns:xsd="http://www.w3.org/1999/XMLSchema">
<SOAP-ENV:Body>
<SOAP-ENV:Fault>
```

```
<faultcode>SOAP-ENV:Server</faultcode>
<faultstring>java.lang.IllegalArgumentException: No Serializer
    found to serialize a 'org.w3c.dom.Element' using encoding style
    'http://schemas.xmlsoap.org/soap/encoding/'.
</faultstring>
<faultactor>/soap/servlet/rpcrouter</faultactor>
<detail>
<stackTrace>[SOAPException: faultCode=SOAP-ENV:Server;
    msg=java.lang.IllegalArgumentException: No Serializer found to
    serialize a 'org.w3c.dom.Element' using encoding style
    'http://schemas.xmlsoap.org/soap/encoding/'.]
  at org.apache.soap.providers.RPCJavaProvider.invoke(
    RPCJavaProvider.java:138)
  at org.apache.soap.server.http.RPCRouterServlet.doPost(
    RPCRouterServlet.java:287)
..........
  at java.lang.Thread.run(Thread.java:484)
</stackTrace>
</detail>
</SOAP-ENV:Fault>
</SOAP-ENV:Body>
</SOAP-ENV:Envelope>
```

There are several important points to note in this listing:

Namespace   The `Fault` encoding uses the SOAP envelope namespace. This is required by the specification.

Faultcode   The `SOAP-ENV:Server` value is one of the four faultcode values defined by the specification.

Faultstring   This is intended to be a human-readable explanation rather than a machine-processed message.

Faultactor   The SOAP node causing the fault is named here.

detail   The `detail` element carries application-specific error information, in this case, a stack trace obtained when the `IllegalArgumentException` was caught.

The Defined Faultcodes

The SOAP 1.2 Specification defines four faultcode values that have particular implications, as follows:

VersionMismatch   The namespace for the SOAP envelope was not valid. Namespace checking is the only form of version control in SOAP.

mustUnderstand   One of the `Header` elements that had the attribute `mustUnderstand` with a value of "1" or "true" could not be processed.

Client Something about the way the client message was formed was incorrect for this service.

Server The server was unable to process the message.

The specification allows for extending the faultcode set by adding a dot and an additional identifier to one of the four base names. For example, you might create a faultcode like this:

```
<faultcode>SOAP-ENV:Server.DatabaseNotAvailable</faultcode>
```

How Apache SOAP Handles Faults

You will not be surprised to learn that Apache SOAP uses a `Fault` class (in the `org.apache.soap` package) that encapsulates all of the data required to generate a `Fault` message. This class is used both in creating `Fault` elements on servers and in interpreting them on clients.

Apache SOAP does not generate a `Fault` immediately at the source of a problem. Instead, it throws a `SOAPException` that is caught, for example, in the `doPost()` method of `RPCRouter-Servlet`, and used to build a `Fault` object. This `Fault` object is then used to generate the response message.

As you may recall from Chapter 3, "A SOAP Server Example," the deployment descriptor for a service contains a `faultListener` element, such as the following entry in the address-book deployment descriptor:

```
<isd:faultListener>org.apache.soap.server.DOMFaultListener
</isd:faultListener>
```

This particular listener creates the `detail` element, but in general a fault listener can be used both to furnish more information about a fault and to log the error event.

Service Architecture

Although most present SOAP applications take the form of remote procedure calls, it is a good idea to consider other sorts of XML message processing when creating a SOAP application. After all, the RPC convention is simply that the message from client to server is always followed by a results message from server to client.

When designing a SOAP service architecture, it seems like a good idea to keep in mind all of the possible transport mechanisms and service support architectures that might be needed. Fortunately, XML and Java provide the abstractions that will let us create a flexible architecture.

Figure 6.2 suggests some of the alternate transport mechanisms by which a SOAP envelope might arrive at a server and some of the application support that might be required. The goal of the transport mechanisms is to get a SOAP envelope to the SOAP server. Thanks to the abstraction provided by XML, the SOAP server can be independent of the actual transport mechanism. The way Apache SOAP is organized tends to obscure this independence.

As suggested by Figure 6.2, application support could take many forms. You can use a Java interface to insulate the SOAP server from the details of working with these support resources. With the proper design of an interface, you can switch between various types of application backends without any change to the SOAP server.

FIGURE 6.2:

A generalized SOAP architecture

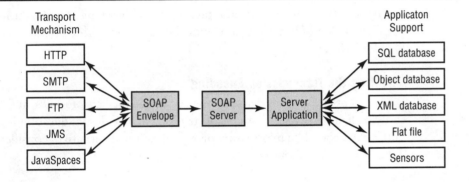

The Publications Example

It is not very original, but I decided to create a publications database for the server example. My company has to keep track of a number of books in various stages of creation before publication, and after publication the company needs to track errata. We would also like to eventually include citations for magazine articles and presentations.

The public services to support include requests for:

- List of titles
- List of topics
- List of authors
- Publication information by ISBN number or similar characteristic code
- Publication lists for a specific topic
- Publication lists for a specific author

The services required for in-house use include the following:

- Count of publications
- Date of last database modification
- Being able to remove a publication
- Being able to insert a publication

Design for Flexibility

Although my most immediate need is for keeping track of books, there are other materials that might need to be made available in the future. Furthermore, it is likely that users of the system may come up with additional requirements. All of these considerations suggest starting with an XML representation of publications.

One advantage of an XML representation is that it easily handles fields that are not always present, such as pointers to book cover images. XML also makes it easy to experiment with adding new elements. However, representing publications as XML during development does not lock me out of later using a relational database or object-oriented database for use with a SOAP service.

Selecting the Transmission Encoding

It seemed pretty obvious that the services such as the lists of topics, authors, and titles could easily be handled as SOAP arrays of strings. The real design question is how to handle transmitting the complete information on a publication. Alternatives considered are shown in Table 6.1 and are discussed further following the table.

TABLE 6.1: Evaluating Alternative Encodings for Publications Data

Approach	Method Call Count	Comments
simple String	very large	Flexible, handled by standard encoding, but the client has to make many calls to assemble complete information. Many wasted calls for sparse information.
array of Strings	reasonable	Handled by standard encoding and suitable for simple display. However, the returned data is not suitable for further processing because the items are not labeled.
Bean encoding	reasonable	Handled by standard encoding but would work best with Java on both ends. Use of the bean on the client would require distributing the class files to all interested parties. Not good for sparse information.
Literal XML encoding	reasonable	Handled by Apache SOAP literal XML encoding. Disadvantage is the requirement for building a document to return multiple elements.
Custom serializer/deserializer to XML	reasonable	Great flexibility but configuring the server may be more difficult.

Conceptually, the simplest thing to do would be to have one SOAP method per element in the publication representation, each one returning a string. Encoding the data can be handled by standard SOAP methods. However, this has several disadvantages:

Slow   Every data item has to be requested in a separate call. Furthermore, requests for data that does not exist for a particular publication are wasteful of time and server resources.

Not flexible   Every modification of the database requires writing new methods and revising the SOAP server.

The server could return formatted strings in an array; for instance, HTML-formatted strings designed to look good in a browser. However, this approach is not flexible; the client would have a hard time picking specific data out of the strings.

Another alternative would be to create a Java class in the JavaBeans style to represent each kind of publication. The Apache SOAP bean serialization mechanism can easily handle simple beans as seen in the addressbook sample in Chapter 5, Listing 5.2. Using bean encoding would be particularly handy if the client wanted to use the data in a JSP page or similar Java application. Disadvantages of the bean approach include:

- Every database change requires a modification to the bean code and, if clients use beans, would require distribution of the bean class for every revision.

- Because a bean would have to provide for every field, special handling for default fields would have to be provided for publications without a complete set of data.

Apache SOAP provides the convenient literal XML encoding mechanism to encode an XML org.w3c.dom.Element object. An example was shown in Chapter 5, Listing 5.5. Although the result is similar to what a bean serialization would produce, this approach has the advantage of only encoding fields for which data actually exists, so less-than-complete database entries are handled efficiently. Literal XML encoding is particularly attractive in that nothing in the SOAP server has to be changed if the XML representation of a publication is modified. A further advantage of using the literal XML serialization is that clients can easily process the data with XSL or other tools.

The Server Application Interface

Based on all of these considerations, I decided to use a combination of default Apache SOAP encoding and literal XML encoding for the SOAP service. The interface shown in Listing 6.3 is used to provide the RPC interface for the SOAP server.

Listing 6.3:   Source for the *PubsInterface* Interface

```
package com.lanw.soapsrvr ;

import java.util.* ;
import org.w3c.dom.Element ;

public interface PubsInterface {

  int getPubCount() ; // total all publications
  String getModDate() ; // from date of modification

  Element getByCode( String code ) ;
  Element getByTopic( String topic );
  Element getByAuthor( String author );
  String[] getAllTitles() ;
  String[] getAllAuthors() ;
  String[] getAllTopics() ;
  boolean removePublication( String code, String password );
  boolean addPublication( Element pub, String password );
}
```

With this interface designed, development of the actual methods exposed for SOAP remote procedure calls proceeded rapidly.

The Deployment Descriptor

Listing 6.4 shows the deployment descriptor for my Publications service, with some long lines split for presentation. Note the isd:map element that associates org.w3c.dom.Element objects with the literalxml encoding style.

Listing 6.4:   The *Publications* Deployment Descriptor

```
<isd:service xmlns:isd="http://xml.apache.org/xml-soap/deployment"
        id="urn:Publications">
 <isd:provider type="java"
   scope="Application"
   methods="getPubCount getModDate getByCode getByTopic getByAuthor
       getByTitle getAllTitles getAllAuthors getAllTopics
       removePublication addPublication">
 <isd:java class="com.lanw.soapsrvr.PubsServer" static="false"/>
 </isd:provider>
 <isd:faultListener>org.apache.soap.server.DOMFaultListener
 </isd:faultListener>
 <isd:mappings>
   <isd:map encodingStyle="http://xml.apache.org/xml-soap/literalxml"
     xmlns:x="urn:Ch06Pubs" qname="x:book-element"
     javaType="org.w3c.dom.Element"
     java2XMLClassName=
```

```
        "org.apache.soap.encoding.literalxml.XMLParameterSerializer"
    xml2JavaClassName=
        "org.apache.soap.encoding.literalxml.XMLParameterSerializer"
    />
  </isd:mappings>
</isd:service>
```

Example Server Methods

Because the server is based on a particular interface, individual server methods turn out to be very simple. All a method has to do is ensure that an object implementing PubsInterface is resident, as shown in the following:

```
public Element getByCode( String code )throws SOAPException {
    PubsInterface p = getDataSource();
    return p.getByCode( code );
}
```

To switch between different versions of the database code, all you have to do is change the getDataSource() method.

Creating XML Element Objects

Sun's JAXP package provides convenient methods for creating an XML document from a variety of sources. This is illustrated in Listing 6.5, in which an array of char is used as input. In this listing, the variable dbf is a DocumentBuilderFactory that was created in the constructor for the class. A DocumentBuilderFactory essentially creates a parser with capabilities that are customized according to various settings. The following shows how the Document-BuilderFactory was created for this application:

```
dbf = DocumentBuilderFactory.newInstance();
dbf.setValidating( false );
dbf.setNamespaceAware( false );
dbf.setIgnoringElementContentWhitespace( false );
```

Note that because DocumentBuilderFactory is not guaranteed to be thread safe, a synchronized block must be used for the code that obtains a new DocumentBuilder, as shown in Listing 6.5.

Listing 6.5:   **A Method to Create an *org.w3c.dom.Document* Object**

```
Document buildFromChar( char[] cc ){
  DocumentBuilder db = null ;
  try {
     synchronized( dbf ){
        db = dbf.newDocumentBuilder();
     }
```

```
        InputSource is = new InputSource( new CharArrayReader(cc));
        return db.parse( is );
    }catch( ParserConfigurationException pce){
        System.out.println("Parser: " + pce );
    }catch(SAXParseException spe ){
        System.out.print( spe );
    }catch( Exception se ){
        System.out.println("createDocument threw " + se );
        se.printStackTrace( System.out );
    }
    return null ;
}
```

Apache SOAP's literal XML encoding can only handle an `Element`; however, it is easy to obtain the root element of a `Document`, as shown in Listing 6.6. This is the method used to create a single `Element` from a list of `Element`s that resulted from a database search.

Listing 6.6: **Creating an *Element* to Contain a List of *Element*s**

```
private Element elementListToElement( List el ){
    Element ee = null ;
    StringBuffer sb = new StringBuffer("<booklist>\r\n");
    for( int i = 0 ; i < el.size() ; i++ ){
      ee = (Element)el.get(i) ;
      sb.append( ee.toString() );
    }
    sb.append("</booklist>\r\n");
    Document dd = buildFromChar( sb.toString().toCharArray() );
    if( dd == null ) return null ;
    return dd.getDocumentElement() ;
}
```

Roll Your Own Server

The Apache SOAP and AXIS toolkits are intended to provide complete and highly flexible general-purpose SOAP servers. However, if your application only requires handling of a few message types, why not think about building your own special-purpose server? There are plenty of XML processing resources to choose from.

XML Parsers for SOAP

The main requirement to keep in mind when selecting an XML parser toolkit is that SOAP requires recognition and processing of namespaces. This implies a parser that is compatible with the DOM level 2 and SAX level 2 specification. However, as discussed earlier, DTD and entity processing are not required; therefore, only portions of XML parser toolkits such as JAXP and Apache Xerces are actually used.

Here are some of the XML parser toolkits currently available:

Electric XML   This is an extremely compact library from www.themindelectric.com, currently in the final stages of beta testing. Part of the speed and compactness is accomplished by not implementing the org.w3c.dom interfaces. This parser is used in the Glue SOAP server and web application development environment. If you had to implement a SOAP client or server in a small memory footprint, this might be a good choice because the size of the jar file is only 56K.

JAXP   An acronym for Java API for XML Processing, this is Sun's official set of XML parsing extensions. It is anticipated that JAXP will become part of the standard Java SDK distribution. Apache SOAP and the Tomcat web server are compatible with JAXP.

JDOM   A toolkit that emphasizes ease of use and a close match to typical Java programming practice, instead of using the org.w3c.dom and org.xml.sax interfaces. This toolkit, which can be found at www.jdom.org, requires a separate parser library such as the JAXP or Xerces parsers.

Xerces   Probably the most advanced XML parser, this package is a product of the Apache organization and until recently was required to work with Apache SOAP.

A Bare Bones Server

Suppose you need a SOAP server to handle a single type of request and respond with a simple message. An example might be some sort of environmental monitor producing readings that are potentially important to a number of clients. For this clearly defined and limited purpose, a complete general-purpose server such as Apache SOAP is not necessary.

Here are the steps that a minimal SOAP server would have to accomplish, assuming that the message transport is taken care of by some unspecified protocol:

1. The transport mechanism provides a byte stream containing the raw request.
2. A parser turns the byte stream into an XML DOM document. If a parsing error occurs, the server sends a Client SOAP fault message. Because this is a minimal server, this message is simply a preset string of characters.
3. Taking the DOM object, the server examines the namespace of the SOAP envelope. If this is not compatible with the allowed namespaces, the server sends a VersionMismatch SOAP fault message.
4. The server checks the target of the envelope body block. If this is not the expected value, the server sends a Client SOAP fault message. This can include a short explanation of how the service should be addressed.

5. If the service requires an input parameter, the server extracts it from the body. Any error should cause a Client SOAP fault message to be sent.

6. The server locates the current value(s) of the parameter(s) to be returned. Any error at this point, such as malfunctioning sensors, should cause a Server SOAP fault message to be sent.

7. Preset strings representing the SOAP envelope are combined with the current value(s) and sent to the transport mechanism.

Note that in this sequence of events, the only use of XML is to ensure that the received message is in a valid format and to extract any parameters. All message creation by the server is done by combining preset strings.

Using SOAP Servers

Although the Apache SOAP examples tend to concentrate on SOAP servers in an HTTP request-response situation, you should avoid thinking about servers only in that context. The general steps described in this chapter will be required in any SOAP server configuration.

CHAPTER 7

SOAP Client Architecture with HTTP

- How Apache SOAP constructs a Call object

- Error handling on SOAP clients

- How a client serializes data

- The essentials of client-side debugging

- Common client-side problems

- A client to work with the server example

M ost SOAP development has been directed at remote procedure call (RPC) style messages sent over HTTP. Due to the widespread support for HTTP in networks, firewalls, proxy servers, and Java libraries, it is likely that HTTP messaging will remain the most
popular use for SOAP in the next few years. This chapter discusses the framework that
Apache SOAP provides and develops an example client application.

Apache SOAP Client Framework

Classes that can be used on both the client and server are a feature of the design of Apache
SOAP. The advantage of this approach is that design changes affecting both client and server
can be made in the same place. This section examines how Apache classes are used on a
SOAP client.

RPC Client Architecture

As mentioned in Chapter 6, "Creating a SOAP Server Application," after the rpcrouter servlet
parses a SOAP message into an Envelope object, it constructs an org.apache.soap.rpc.Call
object to contain all of the call information. This Call object is then used by the server to execute the appropriate method call.

The Call class is also an essential part of an RPC client. Listing 7.1 shows the client-side
code for creation of a Call object using the no-arguments constructor, with separate method
calls to add the target URI and other parameters.

Listing 7.1:   **Example of Client Use of a *Call* Object**

```
private Element getElement( String method, String param )
    throws Exception {
  URL url = new URL( protocol, pubsHost, port, pubsURL );
  Call call = new Call();
  //
  call.setTargetObjectURI("urn:Publications");
  call.setMethodName(method);
  call.setEncodingStyleURI(Constants.NS_URI_LITERAL_XML);
  if( param != null ){
    Vector params = new Vector();
    params.addElement(new Parameter("param", String.class,
                      param, Constants.NS_URI_SOAP_ENC ));
    call.setParams(params);
  }
  // Invoke the call.
  Response resp;
  try {
    resp = call.invoke(url, "");
  } catch (SOAPException e) {
```

```
        System.err.println("Caught client SOAPException (" +
                           e.getFaultCode() + "): " +
                           e.getMessage());
        if( e.getTargetException() != null ){
            // alternately we could throw e.getTargetException() ;
            // and let the caller take care of it.
            e.getTargetException().printStackTrace( System.err );
        }
        return null ;
    }
    if (!resp.generatedFault()) {
      Parameter ret = resp.getReturnValue();
      Element bookEl = (Element)ret.getValue();
      // option for debugging
   //   System.out.println(DOM2Writer.nodeToString(bookEl));
      return bookEl ;
    }
    // if here, response contains a fault
    printFault( resp, System.err );
    return null ;
}
```

Listing 7.2 shows a SOAP message generated by the getElement method where the method variable is getByCode and the param variable is 1-5888-0139-X. Note that this example does not contain a <SOAP-ENV:Header> element.

Listing 7.2:   **SOAP Message Generated by the *getElement* Method**

```
<?xml version='1.0' encoding='UTF-8'?>
<SOAP-ENV:Envelope
    xmlns:SOAP-ENV="http://schemas.xmlsoap.org/soap/envelope/"
    xmlns:xsi="http://www.w3.org/1999/XMLSchema-instance"
    xmlns:xsd="http://www.w3.org/1999/XMLSchema">
<SOAP-ENV:Body>
<ns1:getByCode
 xmlns:ns1="urn:Publications"
 SOAP-ENV:encodingStyle="http://xml.apache.org/xml-soap/literalxml">
<param xsi:type="xsd:string"
 SOAP-ENV:encodingStyle="http://schemas.xmlsoap.org/soap/encoding/"
 >1-5888-0139-X</param>
</ns1:getByCode>
</SOAP-ENV:Body>
</SOAP-ENV:Envelope>
```

Note that the encoding style in the ns1:getByCode tag is literal xml, which defines the default encoding for the RPC return type and input parameters. However, in this case, I want to send a String parameter so the param tag declares a different encoding to override the default.

The *Call* Class

The Call class extends the RPCMessage class, which is also the base for the Response class. The Response class is used by both client and server to represent the response from an RPC method call.

The important member variables of RPCMessage that are inherited by Call are

- A String with the URI for the target object.

- A String with the method name.

- A String with the encoding style.

- A Vector to contain Parameter objects if any input parameters are used by the method.

- A Header object if the message requires <SOAP-ENV:Header> elements.

- A SoapContext object. The SoapContext class is used to hold the parts of a MIME multipart message and to hold arbitrary objects that may be used in operations involving a SOAP message. The SOAPContext method setProperty is used to store an arbitrary object that another method can retrieve from the SOAPContext with getProperty. Note that these stored objects do not alter the message parts.

Let's examine the sequence of events that occurs when the following statement is executed:

```
resp = call.invoke(url, ""); // note resp is a Response
```

1. The buildEnvelope method in the RPCMessage class constructs an Envelope object.

2. A SOAPHTTPConnection object is used to send the Envelope. This object is responsible for the HTTP headers, including any cookie header values that might contain session information. In the absence of any specified SOAP action value, the SOAPAction header looks like this:

```
SOAPAction: ""
```

Other header items could include a cookie identifying a session, basic authentication, or proxy authorization data. The headers and message content are used to create a TransportMessage object, the class that Apache SOAP uses for transport-type independent encapsulation of a SOAP message.

3. Actual creation of a connection to the server, transmission of the TransportMessage contents by HTTP Post request, and receipt of the response is accomplished by the static post method in the HTTPUtils class in the org.apache.soap.util.net package. The response is enclosed in another TransportMessage object.

4. The response results come back to the Call object as a SOAPContext object and a String containing the SOAP envelope. If there has been no error, the String is parsed into an

XML Document object. Exceptions thrown during parsing cause the creation and throwing of a SOAPException object, which contains information from the actual exception.

5. Finally, if all has gone well, a Response object is built from the parsed Document and the SOAPContext. This Response object is the returned result of all that work. This Response may contain the expected RPC result object, or it may contain a Fault object from which the client should extract error information.

That takes care of what the Call object does. Referring to Listing 7.1, you can see that if there is no Fault associated with the Response object, you can proceed with extracting the actual object returned by the RPC call with this code:

```
if (!resp.generatedFault()) {
    Parameter ret = resp.getReturnValue();
    Element bookEl = (Element)ret.getValue();
    return bookEl ;   // the normal return from getElement
}
```

SOAPException and Fault Handling

It is important to note that when a client sees a SOAPException, it is due to a problem occurring on the client side. Exceptions thrown on the SOAP server are supposed to result in the generation of a SOAP Fault element in the returned SOAP message body. Examples of client-side problems include an inability to connect to the server and problems with parsing the returned message content.

As discussed in Chapter 6, the SOAP 1.2 Specification defines four fault types that a server must be able to generate: VersionMismatch, MustUnderstand, Client, and Server. Apache SOAP supplies a Fault class in the org.apache.soap package to encapsulate fault details.

Recall that a deployment descriptor for a SOAP service has to declare a fault listener as in the following:

```
<isd:faultListener>org.apache.soap.server.DOMFaultListener
</isd:faultListener>
```

When a Fault element is generated in a server response, it must contain elements named faultcode and faultstring. Depending on the circumstances, elements named faultactor and detail may also be provided. Filling in the content of the details element and possibly other elements is the responsibility of the faultListener class designated in the deployment descriptor.

The detail element is intended to carry only error information related to the SOAP body processing, as opposed to error related to header processing. The detail element may contain multiple detail entries. Listing 7.3 shows an example of code to extract and output the various parts of a SOAP fault message.

Listing 7.3:   **A Method to Output Fault Details**

```
private void printFault( Response resp, PrintStream out ){
    Fault fault = resp.getFault();
    out.println("Generated fault: " );
    out.println(" Fault Code   = " + fault.getFaultCode());
    out.println(" Fault String = " + fault.getFaultString());
    out.println(" Fault Actor = " + fault.getFaultActorURI());
    Vector de = fault.getDetailEntries();
    if( de != null && de.size() > 0 ){
      out.println( de.size() + " detail entries found");
      Enumeration ee = de.elements();
      while( ee.hasMoreElements() ){
        out.println( ee.nextElement().toString() );
      }
    }
}
```

The *Parameter* Class

The `org.apache.soap.rpc.Parameter` class is a simple data holder for four pieces of information that characterize either an input to an RPC call or a returned value. These pieces of information are as follows:

Name   A `String` giving the name used for the variable in the SOAP message

Class   A `Class` object for the type of the variable

Object   A reference to the actual data object

Encoding style   A `String` giving the encoding style, typically a URI

Thus the following code fragment from Listing 7.1 creates a `Parameter` holding information on a `String` input:

```
new Parameter("param", String.class,
      param, Constants.NS_URI_SOAP_ENC
```

When this gets encoded in the SOAP message it becomes

```
<param xsi:type="xsd:string"
 SOAP-ENV:encodingStyle="http://schemas.xmlsoap.org/soap/encoding/"
 >1-5888-0139-X</param>
```

If the method being invoked requires more than one parameter, the corresponding `Parameter` objects must be created and added to the `params` `Vector` in the order the method expects. There is no way to designate parameters out of order.

Controlling HTTP Headers

The SOAPHTTPConnection class in the org.apache.soap.transport.http package provides for several functions unique to HTTP headers. Listing 7.4 shows the start of the getElement method of Listing 7.1 as modified to preserve a SOAPHTTPConnection object between calls. Note that SOAPHTTPConnection implements the SOAPTransport interface so the setSOAP-Transport method in the Call object is used. An instance variable for the SOAPHTTP-Connection has been added to the code:

```
SOAPHTTPConnection str ;
```

Listing 7.4:   **The *getElement* Method Modified to Preserve Cookie Data**

```
private Element getElement( String method, String param )
  throws Exception {
    URL url = new URL( protocol, pubsHost, port, pubsURL );
    if( str == null ){
        str = new SOAPHTTPConnection();
        str.setMaintainSession( true );
    }
    Call call = new Call();
    call.setSOAPTransport( str );
```

Cookie Headers

When the maintainSession flag is set to true, headers received in a response from the SOAP server are examined for Cookie and Cookie2 header lines. (The reason there are two kinds of cookies is related to the history of HTTP and browsers, with Cookie2 headers providing more options.) If found, these values are saved and used for the next outgoing request headers. As long as the SOAPHTTPConnection object is preserved, the cookie headers will be sent as in the following:

```
POST /soap/servlet/rpcrouter HTTP/1.0
Host: localhost
Content-Type: text/xml; charset=utf-8
Content-Length: 409
SOAPAction: ""
Cookie: JSESSIONID=2852A5F5E643747398473653B1E38460
```

Starting with SOAP 2.2, the maintainSession flag is true by default. In earlier versions, maintainSession was false, and cookies were not preserved.

Additional *SOAPHTTPTransport* Header Functions

Here are some more of the methods in the SOAPHTTPConnection class that set HTTP headers (the usage is self-explanatory):

- setProxyHost(String host)

- setProxyPort(int port)
- setProxyUserName(String uname)
- setProxyUserPassword(String pword)

Code using these methods could look like this:

```
SOAPHTTPConnection conn = new SOAPHTTPConnection();
    conn.setProxyHost("proxy");
    conn.setProxyPort(8080);
    conn.setProxyUserName("username");
    conn.setProxyPassword("password");
```

The following methods can be used to set headers for HTTP basic authentication:

- setUserName(String uname)
- setPassword(String pwd)

Setting Socket Parameters

The setTimeout method sets a timeout on the socket that is created to send the SOAP message. This socket is created in the HTTPUtils class post method. If the time expires before the socket is closed, a client-side InterruptedException is generated.

The default socket sending buffer size, as set in HTTPUtils, is 512 bytes. If you know that your messages will always be a particular size, some improvement in efficiency can be achieved by setting a buffer size to match:

- setTimeout(int t), where t is in milliseconds
- setOutputBufferSize(int sz)

The *SOAPMappingRegistry* Class

By default, a Call object uses an instance of the SOAPMappingRegistry class (in the org .apache.soap.encoding package) to relate types to serialization and deserialization methods. As created, a SOAPMappingRegistry object has preset entries for about 20 standard variable types, including the literal XML style that the example in Listing 7.2 calls for in this line:

```
call.setEncodingStyleURI(Constants.NS_URI_LITERAL_XML);
```

If a SOAP client has to use a custom serialization method, the Call object has to be modified with a SOAPMappingRegistry that has entries for the custom types. For example, in the Apache SOAP addressbook sample code, you find the following:

```
SOAPMappingRegistry smr = new SOAPMappingRegistry();
BeanSerializer beanSer = new BeanSerializer();
smr.mapTypes(Constants.NS_URI_SOAP_ENC,
                new QName("urn:xml-soap-address-demo", "address"),
```

```
                      Address.class, beanSer, beanSer);
    smr.mapTypes(Constants.NS_URI_SOAP_ENC,
                      new QName("urn:xml-soap-address-demo", "phone"),
                      PhoneNumber.class, beanSer, beanSer);
    Call call = new Call();
    call.setSOAPMappingRegistry(smr);
```

Due to all of the default mappings, the SOAPMappingRegistry class has a very complex constructor. Because a new one is created for every Call, constructing a Call is expensive in CPU time and memory. In an application requiring frequent SOAP requests, a pool of Call objects similar to a pool of database connection objects would probably improve efficiency.

Client Side Debugging

As with many client/server applications, there are a lot of places for bugs to lurk in a SOAP application. Bugs seem to be more likely to show when you are working on the client side, even if the problem is really on the server. Sometimes it is hard to decide where the bug actually lives.

Watching the Messages

It is extremely handy to be able to see the text content of SOAP messages as transmitted by HTTP. Apache SOAP 2.2 includes the TcpTunnel and TcpTunnelGui classes that can be used to watch the messages. I have created a more elaborate Java application for this purpose called UtilSnoop. Appendix C contains full instructions for the utility. Upgrades developed after the book is published will be posted at:

    http://www.lanw.com/books/javasoap/

Using the Exception Information

When you first see a page-long stack trace returned by a client, you may be tempted to panic. Don't worry, you won't have to dig through every single line, just scan for certain key phrases in certain key areas. For example, I was just looking at an error message that started with this:

```
[SOAPException: faultCode=SOAP-ENV:Server;
  msg=java.lang.IllegalArgumentException: No Serializer found to
  serialize a 'org.w3c.dom.Element' using encoding style
  'http://schemas.xmlsoap.org/soap/encoding/'.] at
org.apache.soap.providers.RPCJavaProvider.invoke(
  RPCJavaProvider.java:138) at
org.apache.soap.server.http.RPCRouterServlet.doPost(
  RPCRouterServlet.java:287) at
  javax.servlet.http.HttpServlet.service(HttpServlet.java:760)
```

The message continued for another 34 lines; however, the key information is in the first few lines. The first thing to look for in a SOAPException message is the faultcode. See the discussion in the section "Illegal Argument" for the cause of this particular error.

Some Common Problems

The SOAP users mailing list has had a lot of messages related to problems that seem to turn up frequently. The following sections address the probable causes.

Namespace Support In XML Parsers

You may see an error message like one of these:

```
java.lang.NoSuchMethodError at org.apache.soap.util.xml.QName
org.w3c.dom.Node: method getNamespaceURI() not found
java.lang.AbstractMethodError at org.apache.soap.util.xml.QName
```

The probable cause is the presence on your system of an XML parser library that does not support DOM level 2 namespaces. Apache SOAP 2.2 uses Sun's JAXP 1.1 parser package. This is the first JAXP package to support namespaces, so if you have used an earlier version, your system may still have library jar files with the old classes.

Because of the way the JVM locates classes, jar files in the standard extensions directory, JAVA_HOME/jre/lib/ext, will be found before jar files you name in your classpath are found. Look for the tooldocs directory in your SDK documentation and read the findingclasses .html file to understand how this works.

Unsupported Response Content Type

You will see something like this reported by your client if the SOAP message does not get all the way to the rpcrouter or other SOAP service:

```
SOAPException= SOAP-ENV:Protocol, Unsupported response content
type "text/html", must be: "text/xml".
Response was: <head><title>Error: 400</title></head>
<h1>Error: 400</h1>
<h2>Location: /soap/servlet/rpcrouter</h2>
<b>Content type must be: 'text/xml'.</b><br></body>
```

In this case, the web server has generated an error message in straight HTML, but the client was expecting a Content-Type: text/xml header. The error number 400 is the HTTP status code for "Bad Request," which indicates that the request did not have a syntax understood by the server.

Illegal Argument

This exception is likely to show up if your input parameters and returned data type are not of the same encoding style:

```
java.lang.IllegalArgumentException: No Serializer found to
    serialize a 'org.w3c.dom.Element' using encoding style '
http://schemas.xmlsoap.org/soap/encoding/'.
```

This was due to an RPC to a method returning an `Element` with the style of the request set as follows:

```
SOAP-ENV:encodingStyle="http://schemas.xmlsoap.org/soap/encoding/"
```

The correct form of the request is shown in Listing 7.2.

Connection Refused

The most likely cause is that your client program specified a different port from the one the server is watching. This can easily happen if you are switching back and forth between servers or using the `UtilSnoop` program. An alternative explanation is that the server has stopped working. The error report looks like this:

```
SOAPException : Error opening socket:connection refused
```

A Client for the Publications Server

Many of the Apache SOAP sample applications put the entire client in a single class, such as the `GetAddress` class in the `addressbook` sample. This is done to illustrate call creation in a single compact class, not because it is a good design idea.

In creating a client for the publications server, I have various potential uses in mind so it seems reasonable to put the client code in a class that simply performs a SOAP request. This class can be tested independently and then used in a servlet, JSP, or whatever other application occurs to me.

The publication server has four types of data return that this client will have to deal with:

- An XML DOM `Element` object
- An array of `String` objects
- A single `String` object
- A single `Integer` object

Each type of returned data requires a slightly different interpretation of the `Parameter` returned in the `Response`, so I ended up with four different private methods to do the SOAP message sending and receiving, with public methods that set up the parameters for the private ones.

Listing 7.5 shows the start of the GetPubsData class, including the instance variables and constructor. The constructor takes a java.util.Properties object that specifies the variables needed to create a connection to the SOAP server. Note that one of the instance variables is a SOAPHTTPConnection object that can be used to preserve cookie data between multiple queries.

Listing 7.5:   **Start of the *GetPubsData* Client Code**

```
package com.lanw.clients ;

import java.io.*;
import java.util.*;
import java.net.*;
import org.w3c.dom.*;
import org.apache.soap.util.xml.*;
import org.apache.soap.*;
import org.apache.soap.encoding.*;
import org.apache.soap.encoding.soapenc.*;
import org.apache.soap.rpc.*;
import org.apache.soap.transport.http.* ;

public class GetPubsData
{
  public String protocol = "http" ;
  public String pubsHost = "localhost" ;
  public int    port = 9000 ; // for use with UtilSnoop
  public String pubsURL = "/soap/servlet/rpcrouter" ;
  SOAPHTTPConnection str ; // implements SOAPTransport interface
          // used to maintain session during life of a GetPubsData

    // constructor expects a properties
  public GetPubsData( Properties p ){
    String tmp = p.getProperty("host");
    if( tmp != null ) pubsHost = tmp ;
    tmp = p.getProperty("pubsurl");
    if( tmp != null ) pubsURL = tmp ;
    tmp = p.getProperty("port");
    if( tmp != null ){
      try { port = Integer.parseInt( tmp );
      }catch(NumberFormatException e){
        System.err.println("GetPubsData: " + e );
      }
    }
  }
```

The group of methods shown in Listing 7.6 expects the server to return a DOM Element. The private getElement method does all the work, using a method name and parameter supplied by the public methods such as getByCode.

Listing 7.6: **Methods Returning a DOM Element or Null**

```java
public Element getByCode(String code) throws Exception
{ return getElement( "getByCode", code );
}

public Element getByTitle(String title) throws Exception
{ return getElement( "getByTitle", title );
}

public Element getByTopic(String topic) throws Exception
{ return getElement( "getByTopic", topic );
}

public Element getByAuthor(String author) throws Exception
{ return getElement( "getByAuthor", author );
}

private Element getElement( String method, String param ) throws Exception {
  URL url = new URL( protocol, pubsHost, port, pubsURL );
  if( str == null ){
      str = new SOAPHTTPConnection();
      // setTimeout and other SOAPHTTPConnection calls go here
      str.setMaintainSession( true );
  }
  Call call = new Call();
  call.setSOAPTransport( str );
  //
  call.setTargetObjectURI("urn:Publications");
  call.setMethodName(method);
  call.setEncodingStyleURI(Constants.NS_URI_LITERAL_XML);
  if( param != null ){
    Vector params = new Vector();
    params.addElement(new Parameter("param", String.class,
                        param, Constants.NS_URI_SOAP_ENC ));
    call.setParams(params);
  }
  // Invoke the call.
  Response resp;
  try {
    resp = call.invoke(url, "");
  } catch (SOAPException e) {
    System.err.println("Caught client SOAPException (" +
                    e.getFaultCode() + "): " +
                    e.getMessage());
    if( e.getTargetException() != null ){
      e.getTargetException().printStackTrace( System.err );
    }
    return null ;
  }
  if (!resp.generatedFault()) {
```

```
      Parameter ret = resp.getReturnValue();
      Element bookEl = (Element)ret.getValue();
      // option for debugging
//    System.out.println(DOM2Writer.nodeToString(bookEl));
      return bookEl ;
    }
    // if here, response contains a fault
    printFault( resp, System.err );
    return null ;
  }
```

The group of methods that returns a `String` array, shown in Listing 7.7, is organized in a similar fashion. The public methods specify a SOAP method name, and the `getStrings` method does the work.

Listing 7.7:   Methods Returning a *String* Array or Null

```
public String[] getAllTitles() throws Exception {
  return getStrings("getAllTitles");
}

public String[] getAllAuthors() throws Exception {
  return getStrings("getAllAuthors");
}

public String[] getAllTopics() throws Exception {
  return getStrings("getAllTopics");
}

private String[] getStrings( String method ) throws Exception {
  URL url = new URL( protocol, pubsHost, port, pubsURL );
  if( str == null ){
      str = new SOAPHTTPConnection();
      str.setMaintainSession( true );
  }
  Call call = new Call();
  call.setSOAPTransport( str );
  call.setTargetObjectURI("urn:Publications");
  call.setMethodName(method);
  call.setEncodingStyleURI( Constants.NS_URI_SOAP_ENC );
  // Invoke the call.
  Response resp;
  try {
    resp = call.invoke(url, "");
  } catch (SOAPException e) {
    System.err.println("Caught client SOAPException (" +
                       e.getFaultCode() + "): " +
                       e.getMessage());
    if( e.getTargetException() != null ){
```

```
      e.getTargetException().printStackTrace( System.err );
    }
    return null ;
  }
  if (!resp.generatedFault()) {
    Parameter ret = resp.getReturnValue();
    String[] strings = (String[])ret.getValue();
    // option for debugging
//   System.out.println(DOM2Writer.nodeToString(bookEl));
    return strings ;
  }
  // if here, response contains a fault
  printFault( resp, System.err );
  return null ;
}
```

There is only one method that gets a single String returned, but, as shown in Listing 7.8, I used the same approach of a private general method and a public specific method that supplies the SOAP method name.

Listing 7.8: **The *getModDate* Method Returns a *String***

```
public String getModDate() throws Exception {
  return getSingleString("getModDate");
}

private String getSingleString( String methodName )
      throws Exception {
  URL url = new URL( protocol, pubsHost, port, pubsURL );
  if( str == null ){
    str = new SOAPHTTPConnection();
    str.setMaintainSession( true );
  }
  Call call = new Call();
  call.setSOAPTransport( str );
  call.setTargetObjectURI("urn:Publications");
  call.setMethodName( methodName );
  call.setEncodingStyleURI( Constants.NS_URI_SOAP_ENC );
  // Invoke the call.
  Response resp;
  try {
    resp = call.invoke(url, "");
  } catch (SOAPException e) {
    System.err.println("Caught client SOAPException (" +
                        e.getFaultCode() + "): " +
                        e.getMessage());
    if( e.getTargetException() != null ){
      e.getTargetException().printStackTrace( System.err );
    }
```

```
      return null ;
    }
    if (!resp.generatedFault()) {
      Parameter ret = resp.getReturnValue();
      String val = (String)ret.getValue();
      return val ;
    }
    // if here, response contains a fault
    printFault( resp, System.err );
    return null ;
  }
```

Code for the method that expects an Integer object is similar to the code for a single String. However, as shown in Listing 7.9, in the event of the SOAP call failing to return an Integer, the code must provide for returning a special error value.

Listing 7.9:   The *getPubCount* Method Expects SOAP to Return an *Integer* Object

```
    // return count in db or -1 if error
  public int getPubCount( ) throws Exception {
    Integer ret = getInteger("getPubCount") ;
    if( ret == null ){
      return -1 ;
    }
    return ret.intValue();
}

private Integer getInteger( String method ) throws Exception {
    URL url = new URL( protocol, pubsHost, port, pubsURL );
    if( str == null ){
        str = new SOAPHTTPConnection();
        str.setMaintainSession( true );
    }
    Call call = new Call();
    call.setSOAPTransport( str );
    call.setTargetObjectURI("urn:Publications");
    call.setMethodName(method);
    call.setEncodingStyleURI( Constants.NS_URI_SOAP_ENC );
    // Invoke the call.
    Response resp;
    try {
      resp = call.invoke(url, "");
    } catch (SOAPException e) {
      System.err.println("Caught client SOAPException (" +
                        e.getFaultCode() + "): " +
                        e.getMessage());
      if( e.getTargetException() != null ){
        e.getTargetException().printStackTrace( System.err );
      }
```

```
        return null ;
      }
    if (!resp.generatedFault()) {
      Parameter ret = resp.getReturnValue();
      Integer val = (Integer)ret.getValue();
      // option for debugging
   //   System.out.println(DOM2Writer.nodeToString(bookEl));
      return val ;
    }
    // if here, response contains a fault
  printFault( resp, System.err );
  return null ;
}
```

Finally, there are the two utility methods shown in Listing 7.10. The printFault method provides a convenient way to output the contents of a SOAP fault message, and the dumpHeaders method creates a String containing the header information stored in the SOAPHTTPConnection object.

Listing 7.10: **Last of the *GetPubsData* Class Code**

```
private void printFault( Response resp, PrintStream out ){
    Fault fault = resp.getFault();
    out.println("Generated fault: " );
    out.println ("  Fault Code   = " + fault.getFaultCode());
    out.println ("  Fault String = " + fault.getFaultString());
}


    // for debugging, dump all HTTP headers
    // from   SOAPHTTPConnection str
public String dumpHeaders(){
  StringBuffer sb = new StringBuffer("SOAPHTTPConnection headers");
  sb.append( "\r\n" );
  if( str == null ){ sb.append("object is null");
  }
  else {
    sb.append("Maintain Session is: " + str.getMaintainSession() +
        "\r\n");
    Hashtable ht = str.getHeaders();
    Enumeration keys = ht.keys();
    while( keys.hasMoreElements() ){
        String key = (String)keys.nextElement();
        sb.append( key + " = " + ht.get( key ) );
        sb.append("\r\n");
    }
  }
  return sb.toString();
}
```

Testing and Debugging

To test the GetPubsData class, I wrote a simple utility executed from the command line. Listing 7.11 shows part of this class. (There is an instance method to test each GetPubsData method, but only one example is shown here.)

Listing 7.11:　　　**Program to Test the *GetPubsData* Class**

```
package com.lanw.clients ;
import java.io.* ;
import org.w3c.dom.*;
import java.util.* ;
import org.apache.soap.* ;

public class TestC {

 static Properties prop ;
 static {
    prop = new Properties();
    prop.put("host", "localhost");
    prop.put("pubsurl", "/soap/servlet/rpcrouter");
    prop.put("port","8080");
 }

 public static void main(String[] args){
   try {
     TestC tc = new TestC( args ) ;
     tc.getByCode("0-7821-2827-0");
     tc.getHeaders();
   }catch(SOAPException se ){
     System.out.println("SOAPException faultCode: " +
         se.getFaultCode());
     System.out.println("SOAPException message: " + se.getMessage());
     Throwable t = se.getRootException();
     if( t != null ){
         t.printStackTrace( System.out );
     }
   }catch(Exception e){
      e.printStackTrace( System.out );
   }
 }

 // instance variable
 GetPubsData getPubs ;

 // Constructor
 TestC( ) {
    System.out.println("TestC constructor: "  ) ;
```

```
    getPubs = new GetPubsData( prop ) ;
  }

  public void getHeaders(){
    System.out.println("Headers: " + getPubs.dumpHeaders() );
  }

  public void getByCode(String s ) throws Exception {
    Element se = getPubs.getByCode( s );
    System.out.println("by code " + se );
  }
  // class continues with
  // one test method per GetPubsData method
}
```

Listing 7.12 shows the output from running the test program. Note that long lines have been reformatted to fit this page.

Listing 7.12: **Output from Test Execution**

```
TestC constructor:
by code <Book isbn="0-7821-2827-0">
    <Title>Java Developer's Guide to E-Commerce with XML and JSP
    </Title>
    <Errata code="jdgxml" />
    <DatePublished month="null" year="2001" />
    <Publisher>Sybex</Publisher>
    <BriefDescription>The book is intended to introduce a Java
        developer to the use of XML, using example applications
        typical of eCommerce. We cover both the DOM and SAX
        approaches to programming applications in XML.
    </BriefDescription>
    <Edition edition="1" />
    <Press />
    <Series>Java Developer's Guide</Series>
    <Size pp="441" />
    <Cover img="null" />
    <Author>Bill Brogden,Chris Minnick</Author>
    <Topic>Java,XML,eCommerce,JSP,servlets</Topic>
  </Book>
Headers: SOAPHTTPConnection headers
Maintain Session is: true
Date = Wed, 29 Aug 2001 03:07:11 GMT
Server = Apache Tomcat/4.0-b6 (HTTP/1.1 Connector)
Set-Cookie = JSESSIONID=85B200E6020353F791B53471A123D203;Path=/soap
```

I was pleasantly surprised to see how nicely the JAXP 1.1 `Element` class `toString` method, as used in the emphasized line in Listing 7.11, formatted the output. Previous versions have not been so elegant.

Building SOAP Clients

Many of the Apache SOAP classes, such as `Call`, are used on both the server and client ends of a SOAP application. This elegant design greatly reduces the number of classes you need to learn about.

CHAPTER 8

SOAP Architecture Using Messages

- Point-to-Point vs. Publish-Subscribe messaging

- The principles of Java Message Service

- Working SOAP examples with Java Message Service

- The JavaSpaces architecture

- The advantages of JavaSpaces over Java Message Service

- Getting JavaSpaces running on your system

- Working SOAP examples with JavaSpaces

I t is important to stress that SOAP is quite flexible with transport mechanisms, which is what makes it such an attractive technology. Having covered the HTTP-based architecture in the previous chapters, this chapter reviews two message transport mechanisms, Java Messaging and JavaSpaces, with extensive example code for each.

Messaging Systems in General

Messaging systems came into being with the first networks, and a variety of messages are exchanged over computer networks. Naturally, one thinks first of the ubiquitous e-mail; however, many other types of valuable data are moved over networks, making messaging systems very important in enterprise-level computing, even without e-mail.

There has been a recent trend to recognize messaging systems as a separate class of application, frequently called Message-Oriented Middleware (MOM). A MOM system takes responsibility for transmitting application messages over a network and provides support for load balancing, fault tolerance, and transactions. Basically, there are two models for messaging: point-to-point and publish/subscribe.

The Point-to-Point Model

In this model, a message is transmitted from a sender to a single recipient. As shown in Figure 8.1, once the sender, client A, dispatches a message to a local router, the message can travel directly to the recipient, client B, or be relayed through additional routers to client C. Once the sender has succeeded in getting the message to the router, the sender's work is done.

The router holds the message in a message *queue*, which may or may not be backed up to permanent storage. Each queue has a unique name. A given queue can be associated with one recipient or multiple recipients, but the router ensures that each message goes only to a single recipient. You might use multiple recipients for load-balancing jobs between multiple worker processes.

FIGURE 8.1:

Point-to-point message transmission

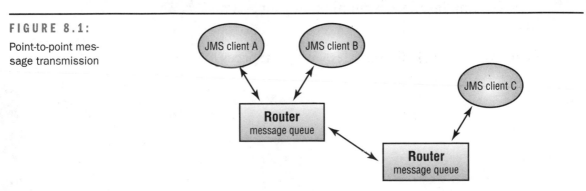

The Publish/Subscribe Model

In a point-to-point system, a message is sent to a named queue where it is held until it's retrieved by a specific receiver. In the publish/subscribe model, a message is sent by a message producer, or publisher, to a *topic*, and copies are sent to all of the topic's subscribers. This architecture is depicted in Figure 8.2 with a single router, but the message distribution system could involve many router applications.

FIGURE 8.2:

The publish/subscribe architecture

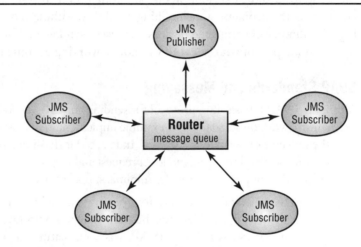

Advantages

Because of the services a MOM system provides, messaging offers some advantages over the client-server or remote procedure call (RPC) architectures:

Asynchronous   With MOM, the sender and receiver of a message do not have to be working, be connected, and have available CPU cycles at the same time.

Fault tolerance   MOM software can route around network problems, adjust to network loads, and resend messages in the event of errors.

Ignore network architecture   Applications using MOM can totally ignore all of the complexities of the network architecture past the initial entry point.

Security   MOM systems can enforce security precautions independently from the applications.

Disadvantages

An obvious disadvantage for MOM systems is speed. Message transmission through an intermediary server can never be as fast as direct client-server or RPC connectivity. Another possible disadvantage is the added complexity of maintaining yet another application in the form of the message server, with the attendant storage, network traffic, and processing power requirements.

Reliability Requirements

As the number of separate components in enterprise networks grows, messaging becomes more and more attractive, despite the disadvantages. The rush to wireless connectivity and the trend toward the distribution of computing power into smaller and simpler devices emphasizes the problem of maintaining reliability. Although device reliability keeps increasing, the number of connected devices increases even faster. Therefore, it is a good probability that some part of your network will not be working at some point along the way.

SOAP Standards and Messaging

Although SOAP is basically a protocol for sending an XML-encoded message via any transport mechanism, work on standards and example implementations has not been evenly distributed over the universe of possible SOAP uses. In fact, so far the standardization effort has emphasized HTTP transport and the RPC model of request and response. The Apache SOAP implementation reflects this emphasis; it provides minimal support for various messaging architectures.

Fortunately, the suitability of Java for creating messaging services has been apparent from the very start. There are two approaches to messaging with Java APIs: Java Message Service (JMS) API and JavaSpaces. The JMS API has been mature since 1998 and has numerous commercial implementations. The more innovative JavaSpaces API has been developed in connection with Sun's Jini initiative and does not have as many commercial implementations.

Java Message Service

Creation of the JMS API was accomplished by Sun in close cooperation with industry vendors of MOM software. Although the initial intent was simply to create an API for messaging, the increasing industry interest in messaging as an alternative to Remote Method Invocation (RMI) resulted in a much more complete API than originally planned. The current reference version of JMS can be downloaded from the following site:

```
http://java.sun.com/products/jms/
```

Message Characteristics

The most important element in the JMS API is the `javax.jms.Message` interface, which defines all of the basic characteristics of `Message` objects. This interface defines a huge number of methods, but for the purposes of this chapter, the most important variables that a message has in addition to payload are delivery mode, time-to-live, and priority.

Delivery Mode

The DeliveryMode interface defines two integer constants:

PERSISTENT   Messages with this mode must be saved to a storage medium when received by the JMS provider. After the message expiration time has elapsed, it may be discarded, which is the default value for delivery mode.

NON_PERSISTENT   The JMS provider is not required to save the message; it is simply delivered to currently active clients.

Time-to-Live

When a JMS provider receives a Message, the time-to-live (TTL) value attached to it is added to the current system time to create an expiration date. The TTL value is specified in milliseconds and can be set by the method that transmits the message. By default, messages have an infinite TTL and never expire.

Priority

The JMS API provides for 10 levels of priority, from 0, the lowest, to 9. The default priority is 4 and is provided as a constant DEFAULT_PRIORITY in the Message interface.

Types of JMS Messages

Naturally, each message sent by JMS has a corresponding Java class. The JMS API defines a base Message interface and five derived interfaces. Each vendor provides a concrete implementation of the interfaces. The actual content of a JMS message is very similar to a SOAP message: there is a header for routing and identifying messages, a set of properties to be used by the receiving application, and a message body. (I'll cover only message body content here, but the message properties can also be useful.)

The TextMessage interface is ideal for sending an XML message, and in fact, the API designers had XML in mind specifically. Essentially, it carries a single Java String object. Other JMS message classes are as follows:

BytesMessage   This class provides methods that let you write a message to a byte-oriented stream similar to the DataOutputStream class in the java.io package. The resulting content is a byte array.

MapMessage   This class lets you write name-value pairs where the value can be a Java primitive or object.

ObjectMessage   This is the form to use when sending a serialized Java object.

StreamMessage   This class is similar to the BytesMessage class but is slightly simpler.

The SwiftMQ Implementation

The SwiftMQ implementation of JMS 1.0.2 that I use here is a creation of IIT GmbH, of Bremen, Germany. This is a pure Java implementation that requires Java SDK 1.2 or higher. The free download distribution package may be obtained from the site at:

```
http://www.swiftmq.com/
```

The rather compact download of about 3MB contains everything you need to get started with JMS, including:

- Support for both point-to-point and publish/subscribe messaging.
- A Java Naming and Directory Interface (JNDI) implementation as a JMS service. If you already have a JNDI installed, perhaps as part of a J2EE package, see the SwiftMQ documentation for instructions on using it.
- JNDI API documentation in Javadoc format.
- Two JMS implementations, one of which is a compact version for small systems such as hand-held devices.
- JMS administration programs.
- JMS API documentation in Javadoc format.
- JMS sample applications.
- Support for a variety of router networking topologies.

SwiftMQ provides add-on functionality in modules called "swiftlets." For example, the JNDI implementation and a SMTP mailer are both swiftlet modules.

Setting Up SwiftMQ for SOAP Examples

In the following, I assume that you have already installed the SwiftMQ distribution and that you are using a Windows system. Equivalent commands are available on Unix systems.

1. To start the router, execute the `smqr1.bat` batch file from the `swiftmq\scripts\win32` directory in a new command prompt window. This starts router1, and you should see various startup messages.

2. To start the Explorer administrator, execute the `explorer.bat` file in another command prompt window.

3. Choose the Connect option from the Connection menu.

4. When the `router1` entry appears, open it and expand the Queue Manager Swiftlet entry.

5. Select the Queues item, right-click it, and choose the Create a New Entity option from the pop-up menu. Note that to get this menu, the Queues item must show as selected when you right-click it.

6. In the new Queue dialog, name the queue `eventlog` and leave the other parameters at their defaults.

7. Open the Topic Manager Swiftlet entry and expand it.

8. Select the Topics item, right-click it, and choose the Create a New Entity option from the pop-up menu.

9. In the new topic dialog, name the topic `policychange`.

10. Select the router1 item, right-click it, and choose the Save This Router Configuration option from the pop-up menu.

That accomplishes the configuration of the messaging system. You must have `router1` running for all of the following experiments with JMS.

A Point-to-Point SOAP Messaging Example

The following example application is a simple centralized event logging system. For the purposes of this exercise, I assume that there are multiple applications throughout an unspecified network that must log messages with a central facility. To keep this example as simple as possible, the SOAP message contains only a single `String`.

Sending a SOAP Message with JMS

The `SStest` class is used to generate some SOAP messages and send them to the router queue. The messages are created by combining strings with the basic XML framework of a message, plus data generated on the fly. Listing 8.1 shows the initialization data for the `SStest` class.

The `timeout` parameter for the property named `smqpURL` sets the amount of time allowed for JNDI to return an `InitialContext` object. If the named queue is not available, a `NameNot-FoundException` is thrown. The `javax.naming` package provides a large number of very specific exceptions for various JNDI problems.

Listing 8.1:   **Static Initialization of the _SStest_ Class That Generates Message Text**

```
package com.lanw.clients ;
import java.util.* ;
public class SStest{
 public static Properties prop ;
 static {
   prop = new Properties() ;
   prop.put( "smqpURL", "smqp://localhost:4001/timeout=15000" );
    // the Context Provider URL
   prop.put( "qcfName", "plainsocket@router1" );
    // the QueueConnectionFactory
```

```
    prop.put( "queueName", "eventlog@router1" );
      // the Queue Name
    }
    static String[] msgStart = {
"<?xml version='1.0' encoding='UTF-8'?>",
"<SOAP-ENV:Envelope ",
"xmlns:SOAP-ENV=\"http://schemas.xmlsoap.org/soap/envelope/\"",
"xmlns:xsi=\"http://www.w3.org/1999/XMLSchema-instance\"",
"xmlns:xsd=\"http://www.w3.org/1999/XMLSchema\">",
"<SOAP-ENV:Body><ns1:addEntry xmlns:ns1=\"urn:EventLogger\"" ,
"SOAP-ENV:encodingStyle=\"" +
"http://schemas.xmlsoap.org/soap/encoding/\">" ,
"<event xsi:type=\"xsd:string\">"
    } ;
    static String[] msgEnd = {
      "</event>",
      "</ns1:addEntry>",
      "</SOAP-ENV:Body>",
      "</SOAP-ENV:Envelope>"
    } ;
```

The main method of the SStest class is shown in Listing 8.2. When executed, this method creates a new SoapSender object initialized to send to the eventlog queue. Then it calls the createConnection method, creates and sends two example messages, and calls closeConnection. Note that I have provided for timing the various parts of the program.

Listing 8.2:　　　　　**The *main* Method of the *SStest* Class**

```
public static void main(String[] args)
{
  try {
    String qN = (String)prop.getProperty("queueName");
    SoapSender ss = new SoapSender(qN, prop );
    long start = System.currentTimeMillis();
    ss.createConnection();
    long mark = System.currentTimeMillis();
    System.out.println("Time to create connection " +
         (mark - start));
    start = mark ;
    for(int i = 0 ; i < 2 ; i++ ){
      ss.sendMsg( createMsg( i ) );
      mark = System.currentTimeMillis();
      System.out.println("Send time: " + ( mark - start ));
      start = mark ;
    }
    ss.closeConnection();
    System.out.println("Time to close connection " +
       (mark - start));
  }catch(Exception e ){
```

```
      e.printStackTrace( System.out );
    }
  }

  static String createMsg( int n ){
    StringBuffer sb = new StringBuffer( 1000 );
    for( int i = 0 ; i <  msgStart.length ; i++ ){
      sb.append( msgStart[i] ); sb.append("\r\n");
     }
    if( (n & 0x01) == 0 ){ sb.append( "User x logged on");
    }
    else { sb.append("User x logged off");
    }
    for( int i = 0 ; i < msgEnd.length ;i++ ){
      sb.append( msgEnd[i] ); sb.append("\r\n");
    }
    return sb.toString();
  }
}
```

The SoapSender class has been designed to be a complete mechanism for sending text messages to a given queue. As shown in Listing 8.3, the constructor takes a String giving the name of the queue and a Properties object containing various initialization parameters.

The constructor locates the router and creates a connection factory using JNDI lookup facilities. In Listing 8.3, the String named initContextFacImpl names the class that SwiftMQ provides to implement the InitialContext for this implementation of JNDI; if you are using a different version of JNDI, a different class name would be required. The InitialContext and Context classes are in the javax.naming package.

Listing 8.3:   **Instance Variables and Constructor of the *SoapSender* Class**

```
package com.lanw.clients ;

import javax.jms.*;
import javax.naming.*;
import java.util.*;

public class SoapSender
{
  static String initContextFacImpl =
      "com.swiftmq.jndi.InitialContextFactoryImpl";
  //
  Queue queue ; // the queue identity in JMS terms
  QueueConnectionFactory conFac ;
  QueueConnection connection ;
  QueueSession session ;
  QueueSender sender ;
```

```
public SoapSender(String qName, Properties prop )
        throws Exception {
  Hashtable env = new Hashtable();
  // this is javax.naming.Context
  env.put(Context.INITIAL_CONTEXT_FACTORY,initContextFacImpl);
  env.put(Context.PROVIDER_URL,prop.get("smqpURL"));
  System.out.println("try to create InitialContext");
  //
  InitialContext ctx = new InitialContext(env);
  System.out.println("Try to lookup " + prop.get("qcfName") );
  conFac = (QueueConnectionFactory)ctx.lookup(
            (String)prop.get("qcfName"));
  System.out.println("Connection Factory created");
  queue = (Queue)ctx.lookup( qName );
  System.out.println("Queue is: " + queue );
  ctx.close(); // must close because it uses a JMS connection
}
```

A SoapSender object is associated with a router address and a queue. To send one or more messages, a connection to the router and message session must be established. There are two important parameters used when creating a session: a flag that indicates whether or not the message is *transacted* and an integer giving the message acknowledgement type.

Use the transacted style for guaranteed delivery—it provides for typical transaction commitment and rollback functions. If the session does not use the transacted style, you have your choice of message acknowledgment methods, as indicated by constants in the Session class. In Listing 8.4, I am using the AUTO_ACKNOWLEDGE approach, in which the message receiver acknowledges the receipt of a message only when the entire message has been received and processed.

Creating a connection is a time consuming operation. Applications that must send a lot of messages should probably keep an open connection, or use a connection pool similar to that used for database connections with JDBC.

The example uses the setDeliveryMode method to set the delivery mode as PERSISTENT—this means that the router writes the message to disk storage as soon as it is received. Even if the router has to be restarted, the messages will not be lost. Other methods that QueueSender inherits from MessageProducer provide for setting priority and time-to-live parameters that will be applied to all messages sent by this instance of QueueSender.

Listing 8.4:   The Methods That Create a Connection and Send a Message

```
public void createConnection()throws Exception {
  connection = conFac.createQueueConnection();
  // flag = transacted, int = ack mode
  session = connection.createQueueSession(false,
    Session.AUTO_ACKNOWLEDGE);
  sender = session.createSender(queue);
```

```
      // see MessageProducer - NON_PERSISTENT means lost message
      // can be tolerated
      // PERSISTENT means store to disk immediately
      sender.setDeliveryMode(DeliveryMode.PERSISTENT);
   }

   // createConnection must be called before this
   public void sendMsg(String msg) throws Exception {
      TextMessage txMsg = session.createTextMessage();
      txMsg.setText( msg );
      System.out.println("Sending "+ msg );
      sender.send( txMsg);
   }

   public void closeConnection() throws Exception {
      sender.close();
      session.close();
      connection.close();
      sender = null ; session = null ; connection = null ;
      System.out.println("\nFinished.");
   }
}
```

For me, the greatest surprise in developing the message sender was that it takes several seconds to create a connection, whereas actual message transmission takes only a few milliseconds.

Receiving a SOAP Message with JMS

I created the SoapJMSlistener class for receiving and dispatching SOAP messages. The SoapJMSlistener class implements the MessageListener interface in the javax.jms package. A MessageListener has an onMessage method that gets called when a complete message is available for processing. This method is responsible for directing the SOAP message to the EventLogger class, which is the target of the message in this example.

A class implementing the QueueConnection interface is responsible for actually implementing a socket, listening for messages from the router, and calling the MessageListener using a dedicated Thread. The Connection interface is the parent of both QueueConnection and the TopicConnection interfaces that are used in the publish/subscribe examples.

The *JMStest* Program

Before describing SoapJMSlistener, let's take a look at the test program that sets up the example. Listing 8.5 shows this JMStest program. Note that there are two static variables: a Properties object and the ddStr String that contains XML in the form of a deployment descriptor for the EventLogger class and addEntry method.

Apache SOAP 2.2 does not provide as much support for message applications as it does for RPC applications. To make use of what it does provide, the JMStest program creates a DeploymentDescriptor object from the XML contained in the ddStr String and puts it in the Properties object. Once the SoapJMSlistener is created, the JMStest program simply waits for a keystroke and then terminates.

Listing 8.5: **The *JMStest* Program**

```
package com.lanw.soapsrvr ;

import org.apache.soap.server.* ;
import java.io.* ;
import java.util.* ;

import java.util.* ;

public class JMStest {
 static Properties prop ;
 static {
  prop = new Properties() ;
  prop.put( "smqpURL", "smqp://localhost:4001/timeout=15000" );
   // Context Provider URL - 15 second timeout
  prop.put( "qcfName", "plainsocket@router1" );
   // QueueConnectionFactory
  prop.put( "queueName", "eventlog@router1" );
   // Queue Name
 }
 static String ddStr = "<isd:service xmlns:isd=" +
  "\"http://xml.apache.org/xml-soap/deployment\" " +
  "id=\"urn:EventLogger\">" +
  "<isd:provider type=\"java\" scope=\"Application\" " +
  "methods=\"addEntry\">" +
  "<isd:java class=\"com.lanw.soapsrvr.LogEntries\" " +
  "static=\"false\"/>" +
  "</isd:provider>" +
  "<isd:faultListener>org.apache.soap.server.DOMFaultListener" +
  "</isd:faultListener></isd:service>" ;
 public static void main(String[] args ){
   try {
     StringReader rdr = new StringReader( ddStr );
     DeploymentDescriptor dd = DeploymentDescriptor.fromXML( rdr );
     prop.put("dd", dd );
     System.out.println("DeploymentDescriptor is\r\n" +
               dd.toString() );
     SoapJMSlistener sjms =
            SoapJMSlistener.JMSlistenerFactory( prop );
     System.out.println("Created new SoapJMSlistener");
     int ch = System.in.read();
     System.exit(0);
   }catch(Exception e){
     e.printStackTrace( System.out );
   }
 }
}
```

The *SoapJMSlistener* Class

Listing 8.6 shows the package and import statements for SoapJMSlistener and the static String naming the SwiftMQ class that is used to create the JNDI InitialContext.

Listing 8.6:   The Start of the *SoapJMSlistener* Class

```
package com.lanw.soapsrvr ;

import org.w3c.dom.* ;
import javax.xml.parsers.* ;

import org.apache.soap.* ;
import org.apache.soap.util.* ;
import org.apache.soap.rpc.* ;
import org.apache.soap.server.* ;
import org.apache.soap.transport.* ;

import javax.jms.*;
import javax.naming.* ;
import java.io.* ;
import java.util.*;

public class SoapJMSlistener implements javax.jms.MessageListener {
  // the class name for SwiftMQ implementation of JMS
  static String initContextFacImpl =
    "com.swiftmq.jndi.InitialContextFactoryImpl";
```

Rather than using a public constructor for SoapJMSlistener, I decided to use a "factory" design pattern, as shown in Listing 8.7. This approach is not essential, but I felt it has more potential for expansion.

Listing 8.7:   The *JMSlistenerFactory* Method

```
public static SoapJMSlistener JMSlistenerFactory(Properties prop)
  throws Exception {
  DeploymentDescriptor dd = (DeploymentDescriptor)prop.get("dd");
  Hashtable env = new Hashtable();
      // this is javax.naming.Context
  env.put(Context.INITIAL_CONTEXT_FACTORY,initContextFacImpl);
  env.put(Context.PROVIDER_URL,prop.get("smqpURL"));
  System.out.println("try to create InitialContext");
    //
  InitialContext ctx = new InitialContext(env);
  System.out.println("Try to lookup " + prop.get("qcfName") );
  QueueConnectionFactory qFac =
    (QueueConnectionFactory)ctx.lookup((String)prop.get("qcfName"));
  System.out.println("Connection Factory created");
    //
  Queue queue = (Queue)ctx.lookup( prop.getProperty("queueName") );
  QueueConnection qCnct = qFac.createQueueConnection();
```

```
//  false means not transacted, AUTO_ACKNOWLEDGE means that when
//  the message has been processed, the server is sent an
//  Acknowledge msg so the next message will be sent
QueueSession qSession = qCnct.createQueueSession(false,
            Session.AUTO_ACKNOWLEDGE);
QueueReceiver qRec = qSession.createReceiver(queue);
SoapJMSlistener lis = new SoapJMSlistener( queue, dd );
lis.setConnection( qCnct );
lis.setReceiver( qRec ); //  qRec.setMessageListener(textListener);
lis.start();
ctx.close();
return lis ;
}
```

As shown in Listing 8.8, the constructor takes a JMS `Queue` object and an Apache SOAP `DeploymentDescriptor`. The `Queue` object essentially encapsulates the identity of the queue to which this `SoapJMSlistener` listens.

The constructor creates a `DocumentBuilderFactory` that will be used later to create a `DocumentBuilder` to parse the SOAP envelope in a message.

Listing 8.8:   **The Instance Variables and Constructor for *SoapJMSlistener***

```
// instance variables
QueueConnection qConnection ;
QueueReceiver qReceiver ;
Queue qID ;

DocumentBuilderFactory docBF ;
DeploymentDescriptor dd ;
Object targetObj ;
int errCt ;

  // the constructor
private SoapJMSlistener( Queue q, DeploymentDescriptor d )
      throws Exception {
   qID = q ; dd = d ;
   docBF = DocumentBuilderFactory.newInstance();
   docBF.setIgnoringComments( true );
   docBF.setValidating( false ) ; // no DTD for this xml
   System.out.println("Created SoapJMSlistener for " + qID );
   String providerClass = dd.getProviderClass();
   if( dd.getScope() == DeploymentDescriptor.SCOPE_APPLICATION ){
     Class targetClass = Class.forName( providerClass );
     targetObj = targetClass.newInstance();
   }
   /* uncomment to aid debugging
   System.out.println("provider class is: " + dd.getProviderClass()
     + " scope is " + dd.getScope() + " " + targetObj );
   */
}
```

Listing 8.9 shows various utility methods, including the methods used to attach Queue-Connection and QueueReceiver objects to a SoapJMSlistener object. Note that it is the set-Receiver method that attaches the object as a MessageListener to the QueueReceiver object.

The start method simply calls the QueueConnection start method, which starts a Thread to receive messages. The finalize method ensures that the QueueConnection is closed to conserve system resources.

The onMessage method receives a completed message from the QueueReceiver object. It simply extracts the String contents and calls the processMsg method. Note that in this simple example, all exceptions simply cause output to the System.out print stream. A real messaging application would provide a more detailed error logging facility.

Listing 8.9:   Some Instance Methods in the *SoapJMSlistener* Class

```java
// instance methods
void setConnection( QueueConnection qc ){ qConnection = qc ; }
void setReceiver( QueueReceiver qr ) throws JMSException {
  qReceiver = qr ;
  qReceiver.setMessageListener( this );
}

void start() throws JMSException {
  qConnection.start();
}

public void finalize() throws Exception {
  System.out.println("SoapJMSlistener.finalize");
  if( qConnection != null ){
    qConnection.close();
  }
}

 // implementation of the MessageListener
public void onMessage(Message message) {
  TextMessage    txtMsg = (TextMessage) message;
  try {
    String msg = txtMsg.getText();
    processMsg( msg );
  } catch (JMSException je) {
    System.out.println("Messaging Exception in onMessage(): " +
        je.toString());
    errCt++ ;
  } catch (Exception e ){
    e.printStackTrace( System.out );
  }
}
```

The processMsg method shown in Listing 8.10 gets the String containing the SOAP message and uses the Apache SOAP TransportMessage class to unmarshall the String and create an org.apache.soap.Envelope object. This is the same Envelope object used in an RPC application, but further processing is completely different from the way the RpcRouterServlet uses it.

The Body in the Envelope is used to get the Element that represents the SOAP target method call. After you extract the method name, the MessageRouter class is used to determine if this is a valid method in the DeploymentDescriptor. If the call is valid, MessageRouter is used to invoke the method.

Listing 8.10:   **The *processMsg* Method in *SoapJMSlistener***

```
private void processMsg(String msg ) throws Exception {
  SOAPContext ctx = new SOAPContext(); // request ctx
  SOAPContext respCtx = new SOAPContext(); // in case we need it
  TransportMessage trMsg = new TransportMessage(msg,ctx,null );
  trMsg.setContentType("text/xml");
  javax.xml.parsers.DocumentBuilder xdb =
          docBF.newDocumentBuilder();
  Envelope ev = trMsg.unmarshall( xdb );
  Body body = ev.getBody();
  Vector bodyEntries = body.getBodyEntries();
  Element mainEntry = (Element)bodyEntries.elementAt( 0 );
  /* uncomment for debugging information
   String uri = mainEntry.getNamespaceURI();
   System.out.println("NamespaceURI is " + uri );
   System.out.println("Provider type: " + dd.getProviderType());
   System.out.println("message Name: " + mainEntry.getLocalName());
  */
  String msgName = mainEntry.getLocalName();
  if( MessageRouter.validMessage( dd, msgName )){
     MessageRouter.invoke( dd, ev, targetObj, msgName,
           ctx, respCtx );
  }
  else {
     throw new SOAPException( Constants.FAULT_CODE_CLIENT,
         msgName + " Not a valid message name");
  }
}
```

The MessageRouter convention requires all target methods to have the signature:

```
method( Envelope env, SOAPContext reqCtx, SOAPContext respCtx)
```

This leaves all processing of the SOAP message up to the target method but provides the SOAPContext objects to hold general request and response information. For this simple example using the LogEntries class, I am not using any of these capabilities.

The *LogEntries* Class

For this example, the LogEntries class simply keeps a specified number of the most recent log messages in a Vector. Listing 8.11 shows the start of the code, including instance variables, the constructor, and the toString method.

Listing 8.11:   The Start of the *LogEntries* Class Source Code

```java
package com.lanw.soapsrvr ;

import java.util.* ;
import org.w3c.dom.* ;
import org.apache.soap.* ;
import org.apache.soap.rpc.SOAPContext ;

public class LogEntries{

  static int maxEntries = 20 ;
  Vector recent ;
  int count ;
  String lineSep = System.getProperty("line.separator");

  LogEntries(){
    recent = new Vector();
  }
  public String toString(){
    StringBuffer sb = new StringBuffer("Recent entries");
    sb.append( lineSep );
    synchronized( recent ){
      Enumeration e = recent.elements();
      while( e.hasMoreElements() ){
        sb.append( e.nextElement().toString() ) ;
        sb.append( lineSep );
      }
    } // end synchronized
    return sb.toString() ;
  }
```

The addEntry method shown in Listing 8.12 gets the SOAP message in the form of an Envelope object. It simply extracts the text of the event tag and saves the resulting String. Note that if the tag is not found or is empty, a SOAPException is thrown, which indicates a client fault.

Listing 8.12:   The *addEntry* Method

```java
// this method signature is required for
//  Apache SOAP message service dispatch
public void addEntry( Envelope env, SOAPContext reqCtx,
    SOAPContext respCtx)  throws SOAPException {
```

```
            Body body = env.getBody();
            Vector bodyEntries = body.getBodyEntries();
            Element root = (Element) bodyEntries.elementAt(0);
            NodeList nlist = root.getElementsByTagName( "event" );
            if( nlist.getLength() == 0 ) {
                throw new SOAPException(Constants.FAULT_CODE_CLIENT,
                     "No event supplied");
            }
            Element e = (Element)nlist.item(0);
            Node node = e.getFirstChild();
            if( node == null ){ // only possibility is an empty tag
              throw new SOAPException(Constants.FAULT_CODE_CLIENT,
                   "Incorrect event format supplied");
            }
            String s = node.getNodeValue().trim();
            System.out.println("Got event: " + s );
            while( recent.size() > maxEntries ){
                recent.removeElementAt(0);
            }
            recent.addElement( s );
            count++ ;
        }
    }
```

Publish/Subscribe Messaging

For the publish/subscribe example, I assumed that numerous applications throughout an enterprise must be aware of certain business policies. New policies and changed policies are published by a central server and picked up by subscribing applications. The topic to be published is named policychange; setting up this topic with the message server was discussed previously in the section "Setting Up SwiftMQ for SOAP Examples."

The SOAP Publisher Example

Listings 8.13 and 8.14 show the PStest program used to demonstrate an example of a simple SOAP message publisher. As with the point-to-point example, a static Properties object is used to hold the initialization data, and a static String array provides the basic SOAP skeleton.

Listing 8.13:   Start of the Source Code for an Example Message Publisher

```
package com.lanw.clients ;
import java.util.* ;
public class PStest{

 public static Properties prop ;

 static {
  prop = new Properties() ;
```

```
  prop.put( "smqpURL", "smqp://localhost:4001/timeout=15000" );
   // Context Provider URL
  prop.put( "tcfName", "plainsocket@router1" );
   // TopicConnectionFactory name
  prop.put( "topicName", "policychange" );
   // topic Name is "policychange@router1"
}
static String[] msgStart = {
  "<?xml version='1.0' encoding='UTF-8'?>",
"<SOAP-ENV:Envelope xmlns:SOAP-
  ENV=\"http://schemas.xmlsoap.org/soap/envelope/\"",
"xmlns:xsi=\"http://www.w3.org/1999/XMLSchema-instance\"",
"xmlns:xsd=\"http://www.w3.org/1999/XMLSchema\">",
"<SOAP-ENV:Body><ns1:setPolicy xmlns:ns1=\"urn:EventLogger\"" ,
"SOAP-ENV:encodingStyle=\"" +
        " http://schemas.xmlsoap.org/soap/encoding/\">",
"<policy xsi:type=\"xsd:string\">"
} ;
static String[] msgEnd = {
  "</event>",
  "</ns1:addEntry>",
  "</SOAP-ENV:Body>",
  "</SOAP-ENV:Envelope>"
} ;
```

The test program main method, shown in Listing 8.14, creates a PublishSender object and uses it to send three messages to the topic. As with the point-to-point example, the SOAP message is created by combining static text that defines the SOAP Envelope with a single String variable. I have included some timing statements to get an idea of which process is most time consuming.

Listing 8.14:   **The *main* Method of the Publishing Test Program**

```
public static void main(String[] args)
{
  try {
    String tN = (String)prop.getProperty("topicName");
    long start = System.currentTimeMillis();
    PublishSender ps = new PublishSender(tN, prop );
    ps.createSession();
    long mark = System.currentTimeMillis();
    System.out.println("Time to create connection " + (mark - start));
    start = mark ;
    for(int i = 0 ; i < 3 ; i++ ){
      ps.sendMsg( createMsg( i ) );
      mark = System.currentTimeMillis();
      System.out.println("Send time: " + ( mark - start ));
      start = mark ;
    }
```

```
    ps.closeConnection();
    System.out.println("Time to close connection " + (mark - start));
  }catch(Exception e ){
    e.printStackTrace( System.out );
  }
 }

 static String createMsg( int n ){
   StringBuffer sb = new StringBuffer( 1000 );
   for( int i = 0 ; i <  msgStart.length ; i++ ){
     sb.append( msgStart[i] ); sb.append("\r\n");
   }
   sb.append("Some Policy Change Data " + n );
   for( int i = 0 ; i < msgEnd.length ;i++ ){
     sb.append( msgEnd[i] ); sb.append("\r\n");
   }
   return sb.toString();
 }
}
```

The PublishSender class is a general purpose class for publication to a particular topic established in the constructor. As shown in Listing 8.15, the constructor creates an InitialContext that is used to get a TopicConnectionFactory based on the parameter named tcfName. That factory, in turn, is used to get a TopicConnection. In this case, I used the version of create-TopicConnection that does not specify user name and password, so the default user identity is assumed.

The InitialContext is also used to get an object implementing the Topic interface using the name passed to the constructor. A Topic object represents the identity of the topic, just as a Queue object represents the identity of a point-to-point message queue.

Listing 8.15: **The Start of the *PublishSender* Class Source Code**

```
package com.lanw.clients ;

import javax.jms.*;
import javax.naming.*;
import java.util.*;

public class PublishSender
{
  static String initContextFacImpl =
    "com.swiftmq.jndi.InitialContextFactoryImpl";

  //
  String topName ;
  Topic topic ; // the topic identity in JMS terms
  TopicConnectionFactory topFac ;
```

```
TopicConnection connection ;
TopicSession session ;
TopicPublisher publisher ;

public PublishSender(String name, Properties prop )
    throws Exception {
 topName = name ;
 Hashtable env = new Hashtable();
  // the constants are in the javax.naming.Context class
 env.put(Context.INITIAL_CONTEXT_FACTORY,initContextFacImpl);
 env.put(Context.PROVIDER_URL,prop.get("smqpURL"));
 System.out.println("try to create InitialContext");
 //
 InitialContext ctx = new InitialContext(env);
 System.out.println("Try to lookup " + prop.get("tcfName") );
 topFac = (TopicConnectionFactory)ctx.lookup(
        (String)prop.get("tcfName"));
 System.out.println("Create TopicConnection from factory "
        + topFac );
 connection = topFac.createTopicConnection();
  // note that an alternative uses username and password
 System.out.println("Connection created " + connection +
   " try to create topic " + topName );
 topic = (Topic) ctx.lookup( topName );
 System.out.println("Topic created " + topic );
 ctx.close(); // must close because it uses a JMS connection
 }
```

Now that we have a TopicConnection and a Topic, the next step is to get a TopicSession and use that to create a TopicPublisher. This operation is shown in the createSession method in Listing 8.16. It is the TopicPublisher that is actually used for message transmission, as shown in the sendMsg method. A new TopicPublisher starts a new sequence of messages. In point-to-point messaging, the equivalent to TopicPublisher is QueueSender.

The length of time that messages are retained by the JMS router is determined by the publisher of the message. The TopicPublisher interface extends the MessageProducer interface, where you find the method setTimeToLive. The sendMsg method shown uses the publish method that provides a default delivery mode, time-to-live, and priority. The default value for time-to-live is 0, implying that the message never expires.

Listing 8.16:   **Methods for Managing a *PublishSender* Object**

```
public void createSession()throws Exception {
    // flag = transacted, int = ack mode
  session = connection.createTopicSession(false,
          Session.AUTO_ACKNOWLEDGE);
  publisher = session.createPublisher( topic );
  System.out.println("publisher time to live: " +
```

```
      publisher.getTimeToLive() );

}

   // createConnection must be called first
   public void sendMsg(String msg) throws Exception {
     // Send the messages to the queue
     TextMessage txMsg = session.createTextMessage();
     txMsg.setText( msg );
     System.out.println("Publishing "+ msg );
     publisher.publish( txMsg);
   }

   public void closeConnection() throws Exception {
     publisher.close();
     session.close();
     connection.close();
     publisher = null ; session = null ; connection = null ;
     System.out.println("\nFinished.");
   }
}
```

Just to keep things confusing, when you execute the publication test, you will see a message like the following, which mentions a keepaliveInterval parameter. This is not the message time-to-live, but a timeout for the TopicConnection socket.

```
Create TopicConnection from factory [ConnectionFactoryImpl,
   socketFactoryClass=com.swiftmq.net.PlainSocketFactory,
   hostname=172.16.1.3, port=4001, keepaliveInterval=60000]
```

As with the point-to-point example, creating the initial connection is by far the most time consuming operation. In one test, creating the connection took 5.5 seconds, whereas sending individual messages took from 60 to 110 milliseconds.

The SOAP Subscriber Example

Listing 8.17 shows the test program on the subscriber side. It simply creates three SoapJMSsubscriber objects, each with a unique clientID name.

Listing 8.17:   **The *SubTest* Subscriber Test Program**

```
package com.lanw.soapsrvr ;
import java.util.*;

public class SubTest {

   static Properties prop ;
   static {
    prop = new Properties() ;
```

```
      prop.put( "smqpURL", "smqp://localhost:4001/timeout=15000" );
        // Context Provider URL
      prop.put( "tcfName", "plainsocket@router1" );
       // TopicConnectionFactory
      prop.put( "topicName", "policychange" );
    }
  public static void main(String[] args)
  {
    try {
      String tName = (String)prop.getProperty("topicName");
      String id = "unique_id1" ; // no spaces allowed
      prop.put("clientID", id );
      SoapJMSsubscriber sub1 = new SoapJMSsubscriber(
          tName, prop );
      id = "unique_id2" ; // no spaces allowed
      prop.put("clientID", id );
      SoapJMSsubscriber sub2 = new SoapJMSsubscriber(
          tName, prop );
      id = "unique_id3" ; // no spaces allowed
      prop.put("clientID", id );
      SoapJMSsubscriber sub3 = new SoapJMSsubscriber(
          tName, prop );

    }catch(Exception e){
      e.printStackTrace( System.out );
    }
  }
}
```

The SoapJMSsubscriber code is shown in Listing 8.18. Note that in this example, the object implementing the TopicSubscriber interface is created as a "durable" topic subscriber. This implies that the topic messages will be received even if the subscriber is not active when the message is published.

Note that this does not imply that the subscriber will get messages published to this topic before the TopicConnection is created. After the TopicConnection has been created, it may be stopped and started repeatedly to control the load on the subscriber. As long as the Topic-Connection exists, all durable messages sent while the TopicConnection is stopped will be received when it is started again. This behavior is in contrast to the JavaSpaces messaging architecture.

Listing 8.18:   The *SoapJMSsubscriber* Source Code

```
package com.lanw.soapsrvr ;

import javax.jms.*;
import javax.naming.*;
```

```java
import java.util.*;

public class SoapJMSsubscriber implements MessageListener {

  static String initContextFacImpl =
    "com.swiftmq.jndi.InitialContextFactoryImpl";

   // instance variables
     String topicName ;
     String clientID ;
  Topic topic ; // the topic identity in JMS terms

  TopicSession tSession ;
  TopicPublisher publisher ;

  public SoapJMSsubscriber (String tName, Properties prop )
         throws Exception {
    Hashtable env = new Hashtable();
       // this is javax.naming.Context
    env.put(Context.INITIAL_CONTEXT_FACTORY,initContextFacImpl);
    env.put(Context.PROVIDER_URL,prop.get("smqpURL"));
    System.out.println("try to create InitialContext");
    InitialContext ctx = new InitialContext(env);
    System.out.println("Try to lookup " + prop.get("tcfName") );
    TopicConnectionFactory topFac = (TopicConnectionFactory)
         ctx.lookup((String)prop.get("tcfName"));
    System.out.println("TopicConnection Factory created " +
      "try to create Topic from " + tName );
    topic = (Topic) ctx.lookup( tName );
    System.out.println("Topic created: " + topic );
    ctx.close(); // must close because it uses a JMS connection
    TopicConnection tConnect = topFac.createTopicConnection();
      // we now have a open TopicConnection to  the router
    tSession = tConnect.createTopicSession( false,
         Session.AUTO_ACKNOWLEDGE );
     /* A durable subscriber will get all messages, even those that
       were published while the subscriber was down. To accomplish
       this, the subsName must be unique
       */
    clientID = prop.getProperty("clientID");
    TopicSubscriber tSubs = tSession.createDurableSubscriber(
       topic, subsName  );
    topicName = topic.toString() ;
    System.out.println("Topic is: " + topic );
    tSubs.setMessageListener( this );
    tConnect.start();
  }

  public void onMessage( Message msg ){
    TextMessage tMsg = (TextMessage) msg ;
    try {
```

```
        String s = tMsg.getText();
        System.out.println("client " + clientID + " got Msg, size " + s.length() );
      }catch( JMSException je ){
      }
    }
  }
}
```

A `TopicConnection` is always created in an inactive or stopped mode; it cannot send or receive messages until specifically started. A subscribing application can stop and restart the `TopicConnection` if necessary.

Timing Results

As with the point-to-point example, the main time consuming operation is the creation of the initial connection to the messaging server. In one test run, creating the connection took about 5.5 seconds, whereas sending a single message took between 100 and 150 milliseconds.

JavaSpaces

The JavaSpaces API is based on an academic research project called Linda at Yale University that got started in about 1982. Researchers from that project have been instrumental in the JavaSpaces project at Sun, which has been closely associated with Sun's Jini distributed computing initiative. Another major "spaces" initiative, also in Java, is IBM's TSpaces project. For more information about TSpaces, see:

```
http://www.almaden.ibm.com/cs/TSpaces/
```

In theory, the basic data structure in a space is called a *tuple*. This is essentially a collection of fields, where each field contains a typed value. Values can be primitive types or complex types such as an array, Java objects, or Java classes. Everything in a space is a tuple. In a JavaSpace, a tuple is represented as a Java object with a collection of public values.

An essential feature of space architecture is the use of associative addressing. This means that entries are located according to their content, rather than any sort of index or a single valued locator such as a topic in JMS. Thus, rather than getting messages by subscribing to a simple topic such as `policychange`, as in my earlier example, an application based on a spaces architecture might request entries by matching multiple values like this:

```
type = policychange
department = marketing
product-line = software
```

The intent of JavaSpaces is to provide a simple unified mechanism for distributed computing. Computing entities can exchange messages, share data, and distribute objects by means of a shared space in a very loosely coupled architecture. This shared space is managed by a Java-Spaces server. For Sun's JavaSpaces Technology Kit and API documents, visit the following site:

```
http://java.sun.com/products/javaspaces/
```

Operations in a JavaSpaces Space

Figure 8.3 summarizes the operations that can be conducted on a space. It is traditional to represent a space in diagrams like this as a cloud to emphasize the absence of any ordering imposed by the space.

FIGURE 8.3:

A JavaSpace diagram showing processes and operations

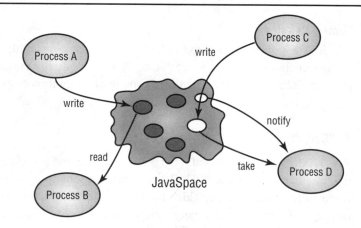

The basic operations in a space managed by JavaSpaces are extremely simple:

write   A process writes a Java object into the space.

read   A process gets a copy of a selected object in the space. Selection is accomplished by providing a template object to the space server.

take   A process removes a selected object.

notify   A process gets an event when an object matching a particular template is written into the space.

A single JavaSpaces server can manage a number of separate spaces, each identified by a unique name.

Selection by Template

The revolutionary concept embodied in spaces is selection of entries by means of a template. In JavaSpaces, the template for retrieval of objects of type A is simply another object of type A with instance variables set to values that control retrieval. The rules are very simple:

• Only entries with the same type as the template are eligible for selection.

- If the template has a variable set to `null`, any value for that variable will be accepted.

- All template variables that have a reference will be checked versus the matching candidate entry variable using the `equals` method. If all match, the entry will be selected.

It is important to note that selection by template does not provide for any sort of selection by a range of values the way a JDBC-compliant database does.

Persistent versus Nonpersistent Storage

When choosing a messaging system for SOAP messages, you must balance your requirements for persistent and safe storage of messages versus your requirements for speed and simplicity. Both JMS and JavaSpaces servers can be set up for simple and fast nonpersistent storage of messages or for persistent storage.

The JavaSpaces approach offers greater control over long-term storage. One advantage is that because the retrieval mechanism does not depend on preassigned topics, new applications can be written to access entries long after the program that wrote them is no longer connected to the system.

What's Different About Spaces?

It is reasonable to ask "what's the big deal" about JavaSpaces—at first glance, it looks like a slight extension from JMS messaging. Here are the differences:

Truly asynchronous   When an entry is written, a process does not have to be a subscriber to read it.

Controlled persistence   The lease concept used by JavaSpaces is considerably more flexible than the simple time-to-live used by JMS. For example, a lease can be renewed or cancelled.

Associative lookup   The flexibility of template matching goes far beyond the simple topic selection of JMS. Essentially, a space functions like a simple object database.

Object storage   JavaSpaces applications are not limited to the simple variable types of JMS. Because a complete Java object is stored and retrieved, applications can execute operations directly on retrieved objects.

Event notification   Processes may be notified when an entry matching a particular template has been written.

Applicability to SOAP Messages

It seems to me that JavaSpaces technology is a very good match for SOAP messaging. For example, each of the message processing functions that are indicated in SOAP headers could be carried out by Java processes watching a space. Given the following header on a message to be processed:

```
<SOAP-ENV:Header>
 <a:Authenticate xmlns:a="AuthenticateURI"
   mustUnderstand="true">username,password
 </a:Authenticate>
</SOAP-ENV:Header>
```

The entry object placed in the space could have the following values:

needsAuthentication A `Boolean` with the value `true`.

authenticated A `Boolean` with the value `null`.

soapMsg A `String` containing the full SOAP message.

The authentication process would simply read entries where `needsAuthentication` has the value of `true`, process the entry, and rewrite it with changed values.

Some SOAP applications naturally seem to match JavaSpaces capabilities; for example, distributed processing of complex calculations. Suppose your SOAP service processes credit applications received over an enterprise-wide network, and the load is more than any single machine can handle. You can solve this with a pool of systems on a network, all connected to a JavaSpaces server.

The initial application in the form of a SOAP message could be placed in a space with `Boolean` variables indicating the type of processing needed set to `true`. Any available machine can take the entry and perform the needed calculations. This automatically balances the load and makes it easy to add new processing power without taking the system down.

As a further improvement, processing could be broken down into smaller steps, each handled by a specialized application. For example, one application might specialize in lookups in a particular database.

Getting Started with JavaSpaces

It takes a lot of work to get a JavaSpaces system running at the present state of development, but when that initial obstacle is overcome, writing programs to use the system is quite simple. The first step is to locate the needed software packages.

The first version of JavaSpaces was available as a separate download, but now the packages are closely associated with Sun's larger Jini technology for distributed computing. You can get Jini as part of a subscription to Sun's Developer Essentials CD subscription program or download the Jini package from:

```
http://www.sun.com/jini/
```

Here is a summary of the steps to go through to get JavaSpaces running. All will be discussed in detail, but this list will give you an idea of where you are going:

1. Create a policy file. Java provides for very fine-grained control over what applications are going to do. However, for the purposes of development, the simplest thing to do is to allow everything. You should be able to find a file named `policy.all` in the Jini distribution.

2. Decide where you want to keep the log files. Several of the utilities that must be installed keep extensive logs and temporary files.

3. Start a HTTP server that has specific jar files in the root directory. JavaSpaces depends on a web server to provide class files over the network.

4. Start an RMI activation daemon, which is a utility that activates and manages the other needed services.

5. Start the Jini lookup service utility.

6. If your JavaSpaces applications use transactions, start a Transaction Manager.

7. Start the JavaSpaces service.

8. To verify that everything is working, run the space browser utility.

The commands to start these services are generally quite complicated. You should set up batch or shell command files for each of them. The examples in this chapter contain paths related to my specific system configuration; naturally, you must substitute your own values.

The *Policy* File

The `policy.all` file contains the following:

```
grant {
    permission java.security.AllPermission "", "";
};
```

This essentially lets any class do anything, so it is not something you would want to leave on a production system. You will be passing a path to this file to the RMI Activation Daemon so it can be placed anywhere on your system. Further discussion of Java security and permission granting is beyond the scope of this book.

The Log Files

Paying attention to the following note is essential to a frustration free experience with Java-Spaces technology.

NOTE   The utilities to be started require that the log directory you specify does not exist when the utility starts. Starting with a new directory presumably ensures that there are no files left over from previous runs to confuse things. This is a bit of a pain when frequently stopping and starting the utilities during development. Plan to delete the previous log directory before starting.

The HTTP Server

The server is used to provide Java class files to the many distributed applications in a Jini or JavaSpaces environment. You must provide a URL that points to specific jar files for the various utilities. The Jini installation lib directory contains small jar files containing only the class files used by typical JavaSpaces applications. For example, there are two jar files named reggie that are used by the Jini lookup service. The reggie.jar file contains the full set of classes, whereas the reggie-dl.jar file contains a minimum set and is less than a quarter of the size of the full set. Many classes appear in more than one jar file because the format of the command line used to start the utilities only allows one URL. Here are the files from the lib directory that you will need to copy to the HTTP server root directory:

outrigger-dl.jar   JavaSpaces classes

mahalo-dl.jar   Transaction Manager classes

reggie-dl.jar   Lookup service support

space-examples-dl.jar   JavaSpaces utilities classes used for sample programs

The RMI Activation Daemon

The Remote Method Invocation (RMI) service must be running before any of the other utilities on all computers accessing a JavaSpaces space. It provides for automatically creating remote objects when requested by a client and providing a reference to that object for use in RMI calls. It is also responsible for enforcing a security policy.

The rmid program is part of the standard Java SDK. Here is the command to start the service using the default port of 1098 and specifying a policy file and a log directory:

```
rmid -J-Djava.security.policy=C:\tools\policy.all
    -log C:\temp\Logs\logRMID
```

Note that although the rmid instructions for earlier versions of Java do not call for setting a policy in the command line, it is necessary from Java 1.2 on.

The Jini Lookup Service

In version 1.0 of JavaSpaces, you had the option of using either the rmiregistry program or Jini for lookup services. The current version requires the use of Jini lookup service, known familiarly as "reggie." Reggie runs from an executable jar file. When the command line shown is executed, a startup Java program parses the command-line parameters, registers the lookup service with the RMI Activation Daemon (RMID), and then exits.

At this point, the service can be activated but not actually be running. The RMID handles creating a JVM to run the service when it is first requested. Because of this approach, when you issue the following command in an MS-DOS command prompt window, there will be a pause and some disk activity, and then the command will return. This is not the result of some anonymous unreported error; it is normal behavior. In the event of an error, you may get messages in this command window or in the command window in which RMID is running.

The following shows the command split on separate lines for easier reading; the actual command is all on one line.

```
java -jar
    G:\jini1_1\lib\reggie.jar
    http://localhost:8080/reggie-dl.jar
    C:\tools\jmspolicy.txt
    C:\temp\Logs\logREGGIE
    public
```

Following the complete path to the reggie.jar file is the URL that gives the HTTP server location for the client class files. Next is the location of the policy file that controls what the lookup service is allowed to do. Following that is the directory for the service to use for logs and temporary files.

If you get the highly annoying error message that the directory already exists, you must kill the RMID program, erase any log directories, and try again.

The Transaction Manager

If you are using transactions in a JavaSpaces server, the next utility to start is the Jini Transaction Manager server. Here is the command line that registers the service with RMID so that it can be activated and started when needed. As with the reggie startup sequence, the command returns when registration is finished.

```
java -jar
    -Djava.security.policy=C:\tools\jmspolicy.txt
    -Dcom.sun.jini.mahalo.managerName=TransactionManager
    G:\jini1_1\lib\mahalo.jar
    http://localhost:8080/mahalo-dl.jar
    C:\tools\jmspolicy.txt C:\temp\Logs\logTM
```

The JavaSpaces Server

Now that the HTTP server, RMID, lookup, and Transaction Manager services are running, it's time to start the JavaSpaces server. Here is an example command to start a persistent JavaSpaces server:

```
java -jar
    -Djava.security.policy=C:\tools\jmspolicy.txt
    -Dcom.sun.jini.outrigger.spaceName=JavaSpaces
    G:\jini1_1\lib\outrigger.jar
    http://localhost:8080/outrigger-dl.jar
    C:\tools\jmspolicy.txt
    C:\temp\Logs\logJS
    public
```

The `java.security.policy` line sets the permissions for the temporary program that registers the service. The second mention of the policy file sets the permissions for the service itself.

The line that sets `spaceName=JavaSpaces` defines the name of the space with which to work. If you needed additional named spaces, they would be defined here as a list of comma-separated names.

The `outrigger.jar` file contains the classes to create a persistent space; you would use `transient-outrigger.jar` to create a transient space. The difference is that entries in a transient space do not survive shutting down and restarting the JavaSpaces service. The URL gives a network location of a HTTP server that can supply class jar files to clients.

The final parameter, `public`, specifies the name of the Jini group of which this service will be a part.

Example SOAP Message in a Space

Now that you have a JavaSpaces server running, the hard part is over. This section shows a minimum set of functions to write and read space entries containing a SOAP message.

The *JSpaceSoapMsg* Class

First, let's look at the object to be managed in a space. All that is required for a custom object is that it implement the `net.jini.core.entry.Entry` interface. This is simply a marker interface that contains no methods.

The `Entry` class implements the `java.io.Serializable` interface, which is also just a marker interface that indicates objects of this class can be serialized for transmission between Java applications. All members of the class must also be serializable, or an exception will be thrown the first time you try to write the object into the space.

Listing 8.19 shows the `JSpaceSoapMsg` class to be used in the demonstration programs. The intent here is that the SOAP message will be stored as one `String` and a topic name will be stored as another. A real application could use a much more complex object with more public variables and methods.

Listing 8.19:   **The *JSpaceSoapMsg* Class**

```
package com.lanw.clients ;

import net.jini.core.entry.Entry; // note, Entry extends Serializable

public class JSpaceSoapMsg implements Entry {
  public String soapmsg ;
  public String topic ;
```

```
    // no args constructor is required
  public JSpaceSoapMsg() {
  }

  public JSpaceSoapMsg( String msg, String tp ){
    soapmsg = msg ; topic = tp ;
  }
}
```

Writing into a Space

The program to write a single entry into a space is shown in Listing 8.20. The call to SpaceUtil.getSpace gets a JavaSpace reference for the default space named JavaSpace.

Listing 8.20:   **The *JSpaceTest* Program That Writes an Entry**

```
package com.lanw.clients ;

import java.io.* ;
import java.util.* ;
import net.jini.space.JavaSpace;

public class JSpaceTest {
public static void main(String[] args ){
  try {
    long start = System.currentTimeMillis();
    JavaSpace jsp = SpaceUtil.getSpace();
    long end = System.currentTimeMillis();
    System.out.println("Got Jsp= " + jsp + " in " +
        (end - start) + " milliseconds" );
    start = end ;
    JSpaceSoapMsg msg = new JSpaceSoapMsg( createMsg(0),
        "policychange" );
    jsp.write( msg, null, 60000 );
    end = System.currentTimeMillis();
    System.out.println("Msg written to space in " +
        (end - start) + " milliseconds");
    int ch = System.in.read();
    System.exit(0);
  }catch(Exception e){
    e.printStackTrace( System.out );
  }
}

  static String[] msgStart = {
  "<?xml version='1.0' encoding='UTF-8'?>",
"<SOAP-ENV:Envelope ",
"xmlns:SOAP-ENV=\"http://schemas.xmlsoap.org/soap/envelope/\"",
"xmlns:xsi=\"http://www.w3.org/1999/XMLSchema-instance\"",
"xmlns:xsd=\"http://www.w3.org/1999/XMLSchema\">",
```

```
"<SOAP-ENV:Body><ns1:addEntry xmlns:ns1=\"urn:EventLogger\"" ,
"SOAP-ENV:encodingStyle=\"" +
"http://schemas.xmlsoap.org/soap/encoding/\">" ,
"<policychange xsi:type=\"xsd:string\">"
} ;
static String[] msgEnd = {
  "</policychange>",
  "</ns1:addEntry>",
  "</SOAP-ENV:Body>",
  "</SOAP-ENV:Envelope>"
} ;

static String createMsg( int n ){
  StringBuffer sb = new StringBuffer( 1000 );
  for( int i = 0 ; i < msgStart.length ; i++ ){
    sb.append( msgStart[i] ); sb.append("\r\n");
   }
  sb.append("disallow credit userID=" + n );
  for( int i = 0 ; i < msgEnd.length ;i++ ){
    sb.append( msgEnd[i] ); sb.append("\r\n");
  }
  return sb.toString();
 }
}
```

Utility methods to acquire a JavaSpace reference are shown in Listing 8.21. The getSpace method depends on the Locator and Finder classes. These classes were created as utilities for the book *JavaSpaces Principles, Patterns and Practice* by Eric Freeman, Susanne Hupfer, and Ken Arnold (Addison-Wesley, 1999). They have been deprecated in the Jini 1.1 release but are still much more convenient than the alternatives and are included in the release, so I used them in this example. By the time this is published, there may be more convenient methods to obtain a JavaSpace reference.

Listing 8.21:   **The *SpaceUtil* Class**

```
package com.lanw.clients ;

import java.rmi.*;
import net.jini.space.JavaSpace;
import net.jini.core.discovery.LookupLocator ;

import com.sun.jini.mahout.binder.RefHolder;
import com.sun.jini.mahout.Locator;
import com.sun.jini.outrigger.Finder;

public class SpaceUtil {

  public static JavaSpace getSpace(String name) {
```

```
try {
 if (System.getProperty("com.sun.jini.use.registry") == null)
 {
   System.err.println("Use DiscoveryLocator to locate " + name);
   Locator locator =
         new com.sun.jini.outrigger.DiscoveryLocator();
   Finder finder =
         new com.sun.jini.outrigger.LookupFinder();
   return (JavaSpace)finder.find(locator, name);
 } else {
   RefHolder rh = (RefHolder)Naming.lookup(name);
   return (JavaSpace)rh.proxy();
 }
} catch (Exception e) {
   System.err.println(e.getMessage());
   e.printStackTrace( System.err );
}
   return null;
}

public static JavaSpace getSpace() {
   return getSpace("JavaSpaces");
}
}
```

Running the JSpaceTest program requires a rather long command line to define a number of variables. I prefer to run the program from a batch file. The following shows the complete command, with line breaks inserted to fit on the page:

```
java -Djava.security.manager
 -Djava.security.policy=C:\tools\jmspolicy.txt
 -Doutrigger.spacename=JavaSpaces
 -Dcom.sun.jini.lookup.groups=public
 -Djava.rmi.server.codebase=http://localhost:8080/
space-examples-dl.jar
 -cp .; G:\jini1_1\lib\space-examples.jar
 com.lanw.clients.JSpaceTest
```

Timing Results
The time to get a JavaSpace reference averaged about 1700 milliseconds (or 1.7 seconds) and the time to write the entry about 110 milliseconds. This compares favorably with the JMS publishing times.

Reading from a Space
Listing 8.22 shows an example of reading a JSpaceSoapMsg object from a space. Selecting a message is done by means of the template object, which is simply a JSpaceSoapMsg object that has a value set for the topic String but has null for the soapmsg variable. The JavaSpace

returns a copy of any entry that has the same class and topic variable contents as the template object.

Note that the call to read includes a 60,000 millisecond "lease" time. If no entry satisfying the template requirement appears in that time, the read method returns null. A lease time of zero will cause an immediate return, with or without an object.

Listing 8.22:   **The *JSpaceProcess* Program to Read a *JSpaceSoapMsg***

```
package com.lanw.soapsrvr ;

import com.lanw.clients.* ;
import java.io.* ;
import java.util.* ;
import java.rmi.* ;
import net.jini.space.JavaSpace;

public class JSpaceProcess {

  public static void main(String[] args){
    try {
      JavaSpace jsp = SpaceUtil.getSpace();
      System.out.println("Got Jsp= " + jsp );
      JSpaceSoapMsg msgTemplate = new JSpaceSoapMsg();
      msgTemplate.topic = "policychange" ;
      JSpaceSoapMsg msg = (JSpaceSoapMsg) jsp.read( msgTemplate,
          null, 60000 );
      System.out.println("JSpace read got " + msg );
      int ch = System.in.read();
      System.exit(0);
    }catch(Exception e){
      e.printStackTrace( System.out );
    }
  }
}
```

Here is the command line for executing the JSpaceProcess program:

```
java -Djava.security.manager
  -Djava.security.policy=C:\tools\jmspolicy.txt
  -Doutrigger.spacename=JavaSpaces
  -Dcom.sun.jini.lookup.groups=public
  -Djava.rmi.server.codebase=http://localhost:8080/space-examples-dl.jar
  -cp .;G:\jini1_1\lib\space-examples.jar
  com.lanw.soapsrvr.JSpaceProcess
```

Further processing of the SOAP message contents would be similar to that shown in the JMS examples.

An Alternative Based on Events

The example shown in Listing 8.22 is based on a style of programming based on the JavaSpace read method waiting for a message to appear. JavaSpaces also supports an event-oriented style in which an application registers as a listener for a particular template.

Listing 8.23 shows an example of a listener being notified. Note that a separate reading step would be required if you wanted to get the message contents.

Listing 8.23:   **The *JSpaceListener* Class**

```java
package com.lanw.soapsrvr ;

import com.lanw.clients.* ;
import java.io.* ;
import java.util.* ;
import java.rmi.* ;
import net.jini.space.JavaSpace;
import net.jini.core.event.* ;

public class JSpaceListener implements RemoteEventListener, Serializable {

  public static void main(String[] args){
    try {

      JavaSpace jsp = SpaceUtil.getSpace();
      System.out.println("Got Jsp= " + jsp );
      JSpaceSoapMsg msgTemplate = new JSpaceSoapMsg();
      msgTemplate.topic = "policychange" ;
      JSpaceListener jsListen = new JSpaceListener();
      jsListen.setNotification( jsp, msgTemplate );
      System.out.println("Template written to space");
      int ch = System.in.read();
      System.exit(0);
    }catch(Exception e){
      e.printStackTrace( System.out );
    }

  }

  // instance variables

  public JSpaceListener(){
  }

  public void setNotification( JavaSpace sp, JSpaceSoapMsg msg ){
    try {
    sp.notify( msg, // template
               null, // transaction if any
               this, // listener
```

```
           60000, // lease in msec
           null   // handback
             );
    }catch( Exception te ){ // may get TransactionException
      te.printStackTrace( System.out );
    }
  }

  public void notify( RemoteEvent evt ){
    long id = evt.getID();
    long seq = evt.getSequenceNumber();
    java.rmi.MarshalledObject obj = evt.getRegistrationObject();
    System.out.println( id + " " + seq + " " + obj );
  }
}
```

Alternate SOAP Message Transport

It seems to me that the SOAP community has been over-emphasizing RPC applications with HTTP as the transport mechanism. With the excellent Java tools available for other transport methods, you should not feel constrained to use HTTP and servlets. There are plenty of uses for SOAP messages in private networks, away from the Internet using JMS or JavaSpaces.

CHAPTER 9

SOAP over E-mail

- Why I am not using the Apache e-mail example

- Sun's JavaMail API architecture

- An example e-mail SOAP server

- An example e-mail SOAP client

Electronic mail is the most used Internet function in most people's lives. As discussed in the previous chapter, messaging systems offer some advantages when creating SOAP services. In particular, electronic mail has an existing huge network of servers with store and forward capability. It is well adapted to asynchronous utilization, portable wireless systems, and multiple media types.

SOAP and E-mail So Far

As I write this, very little seems to have been done with using e-mail to transmit SOAP messages. The initial SOAP note and following W3C documents have recognized that transporting SOAP messages by SMTP (Simple Mail Transfer Protocol) is possible but have not attempted to nail down the details. The XML Protocol working group seems to recognize the necessity of providing some guidance, but they are still arguing over many details.

An example of an unsettled question is how the MIME type for a SOAP message should be expressed. The Apache SOAP package currently uses text/xml everywhere, but the XML Media Types working group appears to prefer application/xml or application/soap+xml.

The Apache SOAP 2.2 package provides a bare-bones approach to SOAP over SMTP by means of the SMTP2SOAPBridge class. On the server side, this creates a separate Java application that polls a mail server occasionally. All mail messages received by this application are simply reformatted as HTTP requests and posted to the web server. Responses are reformatted as mail messages and sent back.

On the client side, the SOAPSMTPConnection class in the org.apache.soap.transport.smtp package implements the SOAPTransport interface and can be used to dispatch a SOAP message as SMTP mail. An example of this is provided in the GetQuoteSMTP class in the samples .stockquote package.

Both server and client examples make use of classes in an IBM-specific mail library and are not based on the JavaMail standard. This undoubtedly reflects the origin of the Apache SOAP project in code contributed by IBM but is not very general.

E-mail Standards

Before we jump into the JavaMail API, I want to provide you with some references to the various standards that are related to Internet e-mail. These standards are to be found in various RFC (Request For Comments) documents such as those in the following list, which shows the document number, title, and release date:

RFC822   "Standard for the format of ARPA Internet Text Messages," released in 1982.

RFC2045   "Multipurpose Internet Mail Extensions (MIME), Part One: Format of Internet Message Bodies," released in 1996.

RFC2046 "Multipurpose Internet Mail Extensions (MIME), Part Two: Media Types," released in 1996.

RFC2387 "The MIME Multipart/Related Content Type," released in 1998.

RFC2554 "SMTP Service Extension for Authentication," released in 1999.

A convenient source for RFC documents is the following site:

```
http://www.faqs.org/rfcs/
```

The JavaMail API

The intent of the JavaMail API is to provide a complete general framework of interfaces and abstract classes suitable for creating a mail system. In addition, concrete subclasses are provided, but these are not necessarily complete in all respects. It appears that Sun expects commercial implementers of the API to provide improvements and extensions.

As Sun's concept of the Java platform has evolved to include the Java 2 Enterprise Edition APIs for the support of large-scale enterprise systems, the JavaMail API has also evolved. Many of Sun's industry partners have cooperated in the creation of the latest release, which is version 1.2 of the JavaMail API.

For downloads of the current implementation, API documentation and other reference material, a good starting point can be found at:

```
http://java.sun.com/products/javamail/index.html
```

The JavaMail API is intended to meet the needs of a wide variety of developers. In this chapter, I am using just the simplest capabilities to send and receive SOAP messages. However, the design of the API is so general that it could be used to create a complete SOAP application system supporting complex features and custom data types.

The JavaMail API is not intended to provide everything needed to create a complete mail server. However, it could serve as a starting point in case you are designing a Java-based mail server. The JavaMail download package contains a document, `providers.pdf`, that explains more about how mail service providers can work with the JavaMail interfaces to provide expanded services.

JavaMail Architecture

The abstract classes in the API define methods to support mail-handling functions that all mail systems need. These classes are in the `javax.mail` package. These abstract layer classes are supplemented by concrete implementations that can handle basic mail protocols and functions.

Applications are expected to use JavaBeans-style components to provide custom methods for interacting with mail content. The JavaBeans Activation Framework (JAF) is used to provide a consistent way to relate message content types to data handling classes. The JAF will be discussed after I cover the classes representing the basic parts of a mail system.

The *Part* Interface and the *Message* Class

A mail message must be represented by a class that extends the abstract `javax.mail.Message` class. The `Message` class implements the `Part` interface, which defines the get and set methods for attributes considered to be common to all mail messages. The other class implementing the `Part` interface is `BodyPart`. The `BodyPart` class is used as a base for representing the components of multipart mail messages.

The most commonly used concrete message class is `MimeMessage`, which represents a MIME style e-mail message.

Generally speaking, a message contains two parts: a set of header attributes and a body. An application creating a new message starts with an empty object, for example, a `MimeMessage` object, and then sets the header attributes and body content. A message must have a `Content-Type` header, following the MIME specification in RFC 2045.

In the JavaMail grand design, an application working with a message gains access to the header attributes by using methods in the `Parts` interface and gains access to the body of the message by using a DataHandler specific to the content type of the message. The `DataHandler` class is discussed later under the section "The JavaBeans Activation Framework."

Multipart mail messages can be created using the `MimeMultipart` class. This class allows construction of SOAP messages with attachments. The content type of such a message is `Multipart` and each part has its own header and body.

The Role of Sessions

A `javax.mail.Session` object handles the details of communicating with the mail server and message management applications. `Session` objects are created using a `Properties` object containing values for protocols and other configuration information.

As you may recall, the `java.util.Properties` class is an extension of `Hashtable` and permits storage of objects indexed by keys. There is a very convenient constructor for `Properties` that takes an existing `Properties` object and uses its values as defaults. This means that the properties needed to create a `Session` can be created by combining default values, for instance, the URL of the mail server, with values for a specific application, such as the user ID.

Message Management

Facilities for holding messages are provided by the Store and Folder classes. A Store object holds a hierarchy of Folder objects that in turn contain messages. Both Store and Folder are abstract classes; there are separate subclasses for dealing with different mail protocols. The information in a Session is used to create a Store object that knows how to handle the protocol for dealing with a particular mail server.

A Store object contains a "root" folder that is accessed like this:

```
Folder f = store.getDefaultFolder();
```

This default Folder contains named Folders corresponding to the organization of the user's data on the mail server. For most Internet mail servers, this is a single "INBOX" Folder, but other organizations are possible. This open-ended design is typical of the Java-Mail API, which tries to avoid locking the application designer into particular limitations.

The JavaBeans Activation Framework

The JavaMail API depends on the JAF to relate the MIME type of a message to the classes and functions that can operate on the content of the message. The JAF provides for creating instances of classes as needed and for discovering the possible operations the classes can carry out. A full explanation of JAF capabilities is far beyond the scope of this chapter, but it appears to me that creating a SOAP application based on electronic mail would be simplified by making use of JAF. Documentation on how JAF fits into the JavaBeans specifications can be found at:

```
http://java.sun.com/products/javabeans/glasgow/
```

Figure 9.1 shows an overview of the JAF architecture as described in the Sun documentation. Here is a quick survey of the function of these components.

DataSource   An object implementing the DataSource interface provides access to some arbitrary collection of data through four methods. In the example, Listings 9.1and 9.2 show a class implementing the interface for an XML document.

DataHandler   An object of the DataHandler class presents a consistent interface for manipulating the data to an application.

CommandMap   An object implementing this interface acts like a registry of JavaBeans-style components related to the data types they can handle.

CommandObject   A JavaBeans-style component must implement this interface to relate the names of various operations to the DataHandler data.

DataContentHandler   This interface defines additional capabilities to the DataHandler.

In the example code, I am making use of only the DataSource interface and DataHandler class.

Review of the JavaMail Package Organization

The JavaMail API consists of four packages, all in the javax or standard extension group of APIs. Here is a general survey of these packages.

The *javax.mail* Package

The javax.mail package contains the basic interfaces, abstract classes, and concrete classes that define a basic system for creating, sending, and receiving mail. For many applications, the javax.mail and javax.mail.internet packages are all you need.

The *javax.mail.event* Package

This package contains classes for events and interfaces for listeners following the typical Java event and listener pattern. These enable an application to be notified when a variety of events affecting a mail system occur. Folder, Store, Message, and Transport objects can generate events when various changes occur. These classes facilitate creating an application that uses mail for messaging.

The *javax.mail.internet* Package

This package contains the MimeMessage class and many other classes related specifically to Internet e-mail. Note that Sun intends that the JavaMail API should cover all sorts of mail applications, not just those implemented over the Internet, which explains why the Internet-specific classes are in a separate package.

The *javax.mail.search* Package

This package contains a large number of utility classes useful in searching and categorizing messages. For example, the SubjectTerm class supports searching for substring patterns in message subject fields. The intent appears to be to provide an extensible framework that allows application designers to add new searchable attributes to messages.

A JavaMail SOAP Example

To run these examples, you must install the JavaMail and Java Activation Framework libraries. The JavaMail download from Sun contains several jar files, but the only one you need to install is mail.jar. The others contain more compact subsets of the full library.

The jar file for the JAF is called (no surprise!) activation.jar. A download package with the jar file and extensive documentation of the JAF can be found at:

    http://java.sun.com/beans/glasgow/jaf.html

Because the JAF classes are standard extensions, it is sufficient to place the mail.jar and activation.jar file with other standard extensions in the /jre/lib/ext subdirectory of your Java SDK installation.

A *DataSource* for SOAP

To experiment with the JavaMail approach of having a DataSource for a particular MIME type, I created the SoapXmlDataSource class. The start of the source code, shown in Listing 9.1, shows the alternate constructors. The first constructor accepts an XML document and writes it to a ByteArrayOutputStream. The second constructor shown accepts a String, presumably containing a complete SOAP message, and saves a reference.

The third constructor, with no arguments, is used when the content of the DataSource is to be set by writing to the OutputStream obtained from a call to getOutputStream.

Listing 9.1:   **Constructors for the *SoapXmlDataSource* Class**

```
package com.lanw.clients ;

import javax.activation.* ;
import java.util.* ;
import org.w3c.dom.*;
import javax.xml.transform.* ;
import javax.xml.transform.dom.DOMSource ;
import javax.xml.transform.stream.StreamResult ;
import java.io.*;

public class SoapXmlDataSource implements DataSource {

  private String src ;
  private ByteArrayOutputStream baos ;

  public SoapXmlDataSource( Document doc ){
    try {
      TransformerFactory tfac = TransformerFactory.newInstance();
      Transformer trans = tfac.newTransformer();
```

```
      DOMSource source = new DOMSource( doc );
      baos = new ByteArrayOutputStream();
      StreamResult result = new StreamResult( baos );
      trans.transform( source, result );
    }catch(Exception e){
        System.err.println( e.toString());
        throw new IllegalArgumentException("Document could not be transformed");
    }
  }
  public SoapXmlDataSource( String s ){ src = s ; }
  public SoapXmlDataSource(){
    System.out.println("no args SoapXmlDataSource constructor");
  }
```

The DataSource interface requires the methods shown in Listing 9.2. These methods basically allow you to read data from the DataSource, write data to it, ascertain its name, and get its MIME type. The getInputStream method returns an InputStream that can read the String from the constructor that uses a String, or an InputStream derived from the Byte-ArrayOutputStream named baos. The baos variable can be created in the constructor that takes a Document object or in the getOutputStream method.

Listing 9.2:   **The Methods in *SoapXmlDataSource* Implementing the *DataSource* Interface**

```
// this is the MIME type
public String getContentType(){ return "application/soap+xml" ;}

public InputStream getInputStream(){
  if( src != null ){
    return new ByteArrayInputStream( src.getBytes() );
  }
  if( baos != null ){
    System.out.println("getInputStream from baos");
    return new ByteArrayInputStream( baos.toByteArray() );
  }
  return null ;
}

public String getName() { return "SoapXmlDataSource" ;
}

public OutputStream getOutputStream(){
  baos = new ByteArrayOutputStream();
  return baos ;
}

  }
```

Creating and Sending Mail

I created the TestSoapSend class to experiment with sending mail messages. At the start of the class, as shown in Listing 9.3, I define a bunch of static variables, including a Properties object named defProp. The Properties object is used to create a Session so values defining the protocols, mail server, and user are required. Note that the mail.transport.protocol property defines the protocol used by the mail server to which the message is sent. When running this code on your own system, you will naturally have to substitute your own values in the Properties.

For testing purposes, I am sending mail to myself, and the SOAP message is simply created from a String.

Listing 9.3:   **Start of the *TestSoapSend* Class**

```
package com.lanw.clients ;
import java.io.* ;
import java.util.* ;
import javax.mail.* ;
import javax.mail.internet.* ;
import javax.activation.* ;
import javax.xml.parsers.*;
import org.xml.sax.*;
import org.xml.sax.helpers.*;
import org.w3c.dom.*;

public class TestSoapSend {

 static Properties defProp = new Properties() ;

 static {
   defProp.put( "mail.store.protocol", "POP3" );
   defProp.put( "mail.transport.protocol", "SMTP" );
   defProp.put( "mail.host", "outgoing.mpinet.net" );
   defProp.put( "mail.user", "wbrogden" );
   defProp.put( "mail.from", "wbrogden@mpinet.net" );
   defProp.put( "mail.debug", "false" );
 }

 static String to = "wbrogden@mpinet.net" ;
 static String from = "wbrogden@mpinet.net" ;
 static String subject = "SOAP response";

 // to keep the example short, I am faking the message with a constant
 static String content =
 "<?xml version='1.0' encoding='UTF-8'?>\r\n" +
 "<SOAP-ENV:Envelope\r\n" +
 " xmlns:SOAP-ENV=\"http://schemas.xmlsoap.org/soap/envelope/\"\r\n" +
 " xmlns:xsi=\"http://www.w3.org/1999/XMLSchema-instance\"\r\n" +
```

```
" xmlns:xsd=\"http://www.w3.org/1999/XMLSchema\">\r\n" +
" <SOAP-ENV:Body>\r\n" +
"<ns1:getByCode xmlns:ns1=\"urn:Publications\" \r\n" +
"SOAP-ENV:encodingStyle=\"http://xml.apache.org/xml-soap/literalxml\">\r\n" +
"<param xsi:type=\"xsd:string\"\r\n" +
" SOAP-ENV:encodingStyle=\"http://schemas.xmlsoap.org/soap/encoding/\">" +
"1-5888-0139-X</param>\r\n" +
"</ns1:getByCode>\r\n" +
"</SOAP-ENV:Body>\r\n" +
"</SOAP-ENV:Envelope>\r\n" ;
```

The main method, as shown in Listing 9.4, creates a Session using the defProp Properties object. Next, a DataSource is created from the example Document object. Note that I could have also created the DataSource from a String as shown in the commented-out code.

Next, I get a MimeMessage by calling createMessage using the Session and DataSource objects. Finally, I call the Transport class send method, which takes care of all of the protocol details as specified by the Session object and actually transmits the message to the mail server.

Listing 9.4: **The *main* Method**

```
public static void main(String[] args){
  try {
    Session session = Session.getDefaultInstance( defProp );
    System.out.println( session.toString() );
    Document doc = buildMsgDoc( content );
    DataSource dsrc = new SoapXmlDataSource( doc );
    /* alternate version using a String constructor looks like this
       DataSource dsrc = new SoapXmlDataSource( content );
    */
    MimeMessage msg = createMessage( session, to, from, subject, dsrc );
    Transport.send( msg );
    // dumpMessge( msg ); // option for debugging
  }catch(Exception e ){
    e.printStackTrace( System.out );
  }
  System.exit(0);
}
```

Listing 9.5 shows the buildMsgDoc method, which uses the standard DocumentBuilder techniques from the JAXP API to build a Document object.

Listing 9.5: **This Method Creates an XML Document for Testing**

```
static Document buildMsgDoc( String msg ) throws Exception {
  DocumentBuilderFactory dbf = DocumentBuilderFactory.newInstance();
  dbf.setValidating( false );
  dbf.setNamespaceAware( false );
```

```
    dbf.setIgnoringElementContentWhitespace( false );
    DocumentBuilder db = dbf.newDocumentBuilder();
    Reader rs = new StringReader( msg );
    return db.parse( new InputSource( rs ) );
}
```

The `createMessage` method shown in Listing 9.6 creates a new `MimeMessage` and fills out the header attributes. Note that the recipients are specified by an array of `InternetAddress` objects. In this case, there is only one recipient, but the message could be sent to many. Next, it creates a `DataHandler` based on the `DataSource` and attaches it to the message.

When the message is sent, the `DataSource` is the source of the body of the message. As opposed to setting the body contents as a `String`, this indirect approach saves memory resources. The `DataSource` could be attached to a file or could perform some database operation to produce the `InputStream` that creates the message body.

Listing 9.6:　　　**The *createMessage* Method**

```
static MimeMessage createMessage( Session session,String to,
    String from, String subject, DataSource src )
    throws AddressException, MessagingException {
MimeMessage msg = new MimeMessage( session );
msg.setFrom( new InternetAddress( from ) );
InternetAddress[] adr = new InternetAddress[1] ;
adr[0] = new InternetAddress( to ) ;
msg.setRecipients( Message.RecipientType.TO, adr );
msg.setSubject( subject ) ;
msg.setSentDate( new Date() );
DataHandler dh = new DataHandler( src );
msg.setDataHandler( dh );
return msg ;
}
```

Finally, in Listing 9.7, I use some utility methods to debug the class.

Listing 9.7:　　　**The Remaining Methods in the *TestSoapSend* Class**

```
static void dumpMessage( Message m ) throws MessagingException, IOException {
    Address[] a = m.getFrom();
    if( a != null && a.length > 0) dumpAddress( a, "FROM: ");
    a = m.getAllRecipients();
    if( a != null && a.length > 0 ) dumpAddress( a, "RECIPIENTS: ");
    System.out.println("Content type is: " + m.getContentType() );
    System.out.println("start getContent:" + m.getContent().toString() );
    System.out.println("end getContent output:");
}

static void dumpAddress( Address[] a, String msg ){
    for( int i = 0 ; i < a.length ; i++ ){
```

```
        System.out.println( msg + a[i].toString() );
      }
    }
  }
```

Here is an example of output from the `dumpMessage` method for a message with only one recipient, dumped after the message has been transmitted:

```
:FROM: wbrogden@mpinet.net
RECIPIENTS: wbrogden@mpinet.net
Content type is: application/soap+xml
getInputStream from baos
start getContent:java.io.ByteArrayInputStream@37c60d
end getContent output:
```

Receiving the Mail Message

To test the JavaMail API for receiving a SOAP message, I wrote the `TestSoapRead` class. Listing 9.8 shows the start of the class, including the definition of the properties that are used to create a `Session`. Note that the property named `mail.store.protocol` defines the protocol used by the mail server from which I will be reading. The `mailURL String` contains the user ID and password used when the mail server is contacted. When running this code, you must substitute your own ID and password.

Listing 9.8:   The Start of the *TestSoapRead* Class

```
package com.lanw.clients ;
import java.io.* ;
import java.util.* ;
import javax.mail.* ;
import javax.activation.* ;
import org.xml.sax.*;
import org.xml.sax.helpers.*;
import org.w3c.dom.*;
import javax.xml.parsers.*;

public class TestSoapRead {

  static Properties defProp = new Properties() ;

  static {
    defProp.put( "mail.store.protocol", "POP3" );
    defProp.put( "mail.transport.protocol", "SMTP" );
    defProp.put( "mail.host", "incoming.mpinet.net" );
    defProp.put( "mail.user", "wbrogden" );
    defProp.put( "mail.from", "wbrogden@mpinet.net" );
    defProp.put( "mail.debug", "false" );
  } // setting mail.debug to true will cause extensive progress
```

```
// reports

// format is  protocol://userid:password@mailserver.for.incoming
static String mailURL = "pop3://wbrogden:XX@incoming.mpinet.net" ;
static boolean delFlag = true ; // delete after reading if true
```

The `main` method, shown in Listing 9.9, carries out the following steps. First, a `Session` based on the `Properties` is created. Next, the `mailURL` `String` is used to create a `URLName`. The `URLName` class provides basic parsing functions that can handle a variety of URL schemes. The `Session` and the `URLName` are used to get a `Store` that represents messages stored at the mail server.

The `connect` method call establishes an Internet connection to the mail server. Next, I get the default `Folder` from the `Store`. Because, in this case, I am talking to a simple mail server, there is only one named `Folder`, representing the "INBOX". This `Folder` is opened in `READ_WRITE` mode because we want to be able to delete messages after reading them. Calling `getMessages` returns a `Message` array, which may be empty.

Listing 9.9:   **The *main* Method in *TestSoapRead***

```
public static void main(String[] args){
 try {
  Session session = Session.getDefaultInstance( defProp );
  System.out.println( session.toString() );
  URLName urlName = new URLName( mailURL );
  Store store = session.getStore( urlName );
  System.out.println( "Store is " + store.toString() );
  store.connect();
  System.out.println("store connected " );
  Folder folder = store.getDefaultFolder();
  System.out.println("try to open default folder" );
  if( folder == null ){
    System.out.println("Unable to obtain default folder");
    System.exit(1) ;
  }
  folder = folder.getFolder("INBOX");
  folder.open(Folder.READ_WRITE);   // write required to delete msg
  Message[] msg = getMessages( folder );
  if( msg != null ){
    for( int i = 0 ; i < msg.length ; i++ ){
      String tmp = msg[i].getContentType() ;
      if( "application/soap+xml".equals( tmp )){
        dumpSoapMessage( msg[i] );
        msg[i].setFlag( Flags.Flag.DELETED ,delFlag );
      }
      else { dumpMessage( msg[i] ); // don't delete unknown type
      }
    }
  }
}
```

```
    folder.close(true) ; // must remain open during operations
    store.close();
  }catch(Exception e ){
    e.printStackTrace( System.out );
  }
  System.exit(0);
}
```

For each Message in the array, I check the content type String. If the type is recognized as the type I am using for SOAP messages, the dumpSoapMessage method is called. SOAP messages get the DELETED flag set according to the static delFlag variable. Messages are only marked as deleted at this point; actual deletion on the server can only occur when the Store is closed. Unrecognized types go to the dumpMessage method.

After all Message objects have been examined, I close the Folder and then the Store. The boolean flag in the folder.close method call indicates that messages tagged as deleted should be removed from the server. The Folder takes care of communicating the instruction to delete to the server.

The dumpSoapMessage method shown in Listing 9.10 starts by extracting the "from" and "to" addresses and printing the results. Next the Message getContent method is called. Because, in this case, I have not registered a DataHandler for the application/soap+xml content type, the Object returned is an InputStream that gives access to the body content.

I tried setting the message DataHandler to a DataHandler using the SoapXmlDataSource class, but I ran into a problem. It seems that the default POP3 message implementation provided with the JavaMail API does not support the necessary methods.

However, the InputStream object can easily be fed to a parser and the Document recovered, so there is no need for the DataHandler approach. In the dumpSoapMessage method, the XML Document object is extracted but not processed. In a real application, further processing would proceed along the lines shown in Chapter 8, "SOAP Architecture Using Messages." If a response in SOAP or other format is generated, the from address String would be used to mail the reply.

Note that a Message may also carry a "reply to" address, so a SOAP application could work by processing a message from one address and sending the results to another. The reply could carry any form of information.

Listing 9.10:   **The *dumpSoapMessage* Interprets a SOAP Message**

```
// content type known to be application/soap+xml
static void dumpSoapMessage( Message m ) throws Exception {
  Address[] a = m.getFrom();
  String from = null ;
```

```
        if( a != null && a.length > 0){
            from = a[0].toString() ;
        }
        a = m.getAllRecipients();
        if( a != null && a.length > 0 ) dumpAddress( a, "RECIPIENTS: ");
        Object obj = m.getContent();
        if( obj instanceof InputStream ){
          DocumentBuilderFactory dbf =
                DocumentBuilderFactory.newInstance();
          dbf.setValidating( false );
          dbf.setNamespaceAware( false );
          dbf.setIgnoringElementContentWhitespace( false );
          DocumentBuilder db = dbf.newDocumentBuilder();
          Document doc = db.parse( new InputSource( (InputStream)obj ) );
          System.out.println("Document recovered " + doc );
        }
        else {
          System.out.println("start getContent:" + m.getContent().toString() );
          System.out.println("end getContent output:");
        }
    }
```

Listing 9.11 shows a simple method for dumping information on messages that don't have the content type I am using for SOAP messages. Also shown is a simple method to output the contents of an array of Address objects.

Listing 9.11:   The *dumpMessage* Method for Unknown Message Types

```
// unknown message type
static void dumpMessage( Message m ) throws MessagingException, IOException {
  Address[] a = m.getFrom();
  if( a != null && a.length > 0) dumpAddress( a, "FROM: ");
  a = m.getAllRecipients();
  if( a != null && a.length > 0 ) dumpAddress( a, "RECIPIENTS: ");
  System.out.println("Content type is: " + m.getContentType() );
  System.out.println("start getContent:" + m.getContent().toString() );
  System.out.println("end getContent output:");
}

static void dumpAddress( Address[] a, String msg ){
  for( int i = 0 ; i < a.length ; i++ ){
    System.out.println( msg + a[i].toString() );
  }
}
```

Listing 9.12 shows the method used to get the contents of messages in an open folder. The important thing to note here is the use of the FetchProfile object. Executing the following statement creates an array of Message objects that don't have any content:

```
msgs = folder.getMessages();
```

The FetchProfile controls exactly what parts of the message are retrieved from the mail server. In this example, it is set to retrieve all content, but it might be more efficient when dealing with potentially long messages to start by fetching only the CONTENT_INFO. You could then create a new array containing only the messages with SOAP content and retrieve the full message in a separate step.

Listing 9.12:   **The Method to Get the Contents of Messages in a Folder**

```
// folder is INBOX
  static Message[] getMessages( Folder folder ) throws MessagingException {
   int msgCt = folder.getMessageCount();
   System.out.println("INBOX folder has " + msgCt );
   Message[] msgs = null ;
   if( msgCt > 0 ){
     msgs = folder.getMessages();  // unpopulated Message objects
     FetchProfile fetch = new FetchProfile();
     fetch.add( FetchProfile.Item.CONTENT_INFO );
     fetch.add( FetchProfile.Item.ENVELOPE );
     fetch.add( FetchProfile.Item.FLAGS );
     folder.fetch( msgs, fetch ); // this gets actual data
   }
   return msgs ;
 }

}
```

The Potential for SOAP and E-mail

It appears to me that electronic mail offers great possibilities for creating SOAP applications. Using the capabilities of the JavaMail API, SOAP messaging could generate a wide variety of useful messages in a form already widely accepted by users.

CHAPTER 10

SOAP and .NET

- Why .NET is a revolution in web services

- What Microsoft's .NET My Services tries to accomplish

- How .NET can make money

- Compatibility problems between .NET and Apache SOAP

- What Microsoft's competition is up to

It is common knowledge in the computing industry that Microsoft was a little slow in picking up on the significance of the rise of the Internet. However, once that realization occurred, the giant organization was able to move rapidly. As computing and communication power spread far beyond the desktop to many forms of communicating devices, Microsoft came to realize that "the network is the computer"—but you already knew that. Along with the other major computing industry powers, Microsoft is expecting to find future profitability in the area of web services.

In a major reorganization touching many Microsoft products, a new vision has been articulated. As this is being written, this vision is still a little blurry, but you can be very sure that XML and SOAP will play a big part in it. In this chapter, I examine what is presently known about Microsoft's approach to web services and what the competition is doing, and I also consider the potential for problems when mixing Apache SOAP with Microsoft implementations.

The .NET Vision

Microsoft's effort is generally described as the .NET (or dotNET) initiative. The key point in this reorganization is its recognition of the change in user's computing activities away from being centered on particular hardware on the desktop. The new architecture for computing will be user-centric. The user's need for access to particular data and services will be satisfied by a variety of hardware and connectivity solutions.

There are many parts to the .NET initiative, some simple rebranding of existing products and some major redesigns and totally new products. The Visual Basic language, an extremely successful component-oriented application development language is now Visual Basic.NET, and the C# (pronounced C sharp) language has been created as a replacement for C++. Both of these languages feature extensive XML support.

The part of the .NET initiative related to web service architecture was called Hailstorm in the early stages. Now that it has reached the stage of beta release to developers, it is called My Services. Let's look at the problems My Services are expected to solve.

The Problems

In the early days of the personal computer, the user's experience was typically centered on a single desktop machine. Even as networks of desktop machines became more common in homes and offices, the emphasis was still on the desktop.

However, the rapid changes in technology for consumer electronics has brought highly capable computing power to portable objects such as your PalmPilot and cell phone. Computing power is rapidly appearing in places that would have been considered science fiction only a few years ago, as TV set attachments, in your cars, and even in your appliances. A short list of the problems these changes create includes:

Lack of consistency of access   When every device and service you use has a different interface, you waste time and energy trying to remember how to do things.

Proprietary data formats   There are many causes for the use of proprietary formats, among them are attempts to lock users into a particular project, attempts to attract customers by adding features, and use of inherited formats from legacy systems.

Isolation of information   Sometimes there is simply no way to move data from one application to another. For example:

> Phone number information can't be shared between your cell phone and your PalmPilot.

> For every online store you shop at, your street address has to be entered again.

> Your calendar service does not know you just booked an airline flight.

Difficulty in establishing your identity securely   When each web service you use requires an ID and password, the difficulty of remembering all of those passwords becomes annoying. If you simplify by using the same password all the time, you run an increased risk that the password will be discovered.

The .NET My Services Solution

The idea with the .NET My Services architecture is that, based on your identity information safely stored in the Passport user authentication system, a variety of web services will be able to cooperate and exchange information. In theory, this sharing of your personal information will always be under your control.

A key feature of .NET My Services is that all services will use industry standard and nonproprietary XML SOAP messages for information exchange. In addition to the XML, WSDL, UDDI, and SOAP standards, Microsoft has proposed additional standards to clarify and extend the existing SOAP specifications. Here is a quick survey of these additional proposals.

Web Services: Routing

Although items in the SOAP `Header` tag area appear to imply an order of processing by intermediaries in a "SOAP message path," and diagrams of the use of headers enforce this implication, there is currently nothing in the SOAP Specification that requires a particular order. This proposal eliminates this deficiency for both one-way and request-response message patterns. The proposed routing specification makes it possible to describe the complete message path for a SOAP message and to describe which parts of a SOAP message are intended for what SOAP receiver in the message path. The detailed specification can be found at:

```
http://msdn.microsoft.com/ws/2001/10/Routing/
```

Web Services: Referral

The proposed Referral Specification would supplement the Routing Specification by describing how a SOAP intermediary can be allowed to dynamically alter the routing information. An obvious use for rerouting a message would be to provide for load-balancing or adapting to changes in a server site configuration, such as changes in firewall characteristics. The proposal details can be found at:

```
http://msdn.microsoft.com/ws/2001/10/Referral/
```

Web Services: Security

The SOAP Specification does not currently address any form of message security. Surely the vision of widespread use of web services for all forms of important and valuable information will not come true unless users have confidence that the process is safe. This specification addresses three aspects of security: credentials, integrity, and confidentiality. The details of the proposed specification can be found at:

```
http://msdn.microsoft.com/ws/2001/10/Security/
```

Credentials

The function of credentials is to ensure that a message originates from the source it says it comes from. The proposed specification does not address the technology for generating credentials, only how a credentials tag can be used to transmit them.

Integrity

The problem of ensuring the integrity of SOAP messages is complicated by the fact that SOAP intermediaries may legally alter part or all of the message, thus one cannot depend on a simple signature for the entire message. This proposal provides for multiple signatures for various parts of a message that may be generated by SOAP intermediaries as they process it. This proposal extends a related proposal for XML signatures, which can be found at the W3C site:

```
http://www.w3.org/TR/xmldsig-core/
```

Confidentiality

The fact that the SOAP messages shown so far in this book are easily read and interpreted is great for developers but a glaring security flaw. Obviously, for a production system used for valuable information, it must be impossible, or at least extremely difficult, to interpret an intercepted message. The proposed encryption scheme is based on one that the W3C is currently working on. The current status of this recommendation for XML message encryption can be found at:

```
http://www.w3.org/TR/xmlenc-core/
```

Web Services License Language

Microsoft's Web Services License Language (WS-License) proposal simply suggests a namespace and tag scheme for extending the credentials proposal discussed earlier specifically to handle digital licenses.

```
http://msdn.microsoft.com/ws/2001/10/License/
```

Microsoft Passport

The purpose of the Passport system is to provide a single Internet identity that is accepted at many Internet sites. With the minimum Passport service, authentication of a user to a site is handled indirectly through Microsoft's Passport server system. Your single Passport ID and password get you into multiple sites, but the only site that handles the actual login password is Passport. Passport is already in widespread use.

If you shop online using a credit card, Passport provides an option for including an "electronic wallet" plus your billing and shipping address. All of this information is supposedly preserved by the best security practices. Convincing users that the information is safe is probably Microsoft's biggest obstacle to wider use of the system.

The Proposed My Services

Now let's look at what Microsoft expects will be commercially useful web services. Microsoft press releases in October 2001 suggest that the initial set of My Services will include the following:

Profile   Your name and address, optionally supplemented with personal information such as your birthday, picture, and special date

Contacts   Your address book/contacts list

Locations   Where you can be found in the physical and electronic world

Alerts   Management of your subscriptions to news services and other alert sources

Presence   Your contact status, such as whether you are online for alerts and chats

Inbox   Electronic mail and voice mail

Calendar   Scheduling and task management functions

Documents   Raw document storage

ApplicationSettings   Your preferred settings for various applications

FavoriteWebSites   Bookmarks for your favorite web resources

Wallet   Electronic banking information and transaction records

Devices   Information on your various electronic devices

Lists   Support for general-purpose list making

Categories   Support for general-purpose filing of lists

Note that these are not all Microsoft services. The idea is that vendors of web services will write to the My Services APIs and fit their products into the whole scheme. Microsoft wants to host these services within the My Services framework and, presumably, draw fees at a certain point in the process.

Who Will Use My Services?

It seems to me that the most likely candidates for early adopters of My Services are business users who travel frequently. Instead of having to carefully synchronize laptop, PalmPilot, and desktop documents and applications, you would depend on My Services to provide a synchronized view to all of your data. An organization that whole-heartedly adopted My Services would expect to gain considerable benefit from better coordination of a widely dispersed workforce.

This implies that it will be developers of business applications who will be most likely to develop applications for the My Services API. However, the most prominent developers of business services are organizations such as IBM, who have their own schemes for integrating web services. Given IBM's extensive experience with integrating business communication with the first successful business communication product, Lotus Notes, Microsoft will be up against tough competition.

Show Me the Money

Exactly who pays how much for what when adopting My Services seems to be rather unclear at the moment. The Passport authentication system for individual users is already being adopted by commercial sites, but this is only a small part of the .NET initiative. Presently, users do not bear the costs associated with a Passport identity; the commercial sites involved pay such expenses.

It is clear, however, that in addition to selling services, Microsoft will be licensing technology and selling tools to potential developers. The tool you are most likely to come in contact with is the .NET version of Microsoft's famous Visual Studio development environment.

The .NET Tools

The .NET initiative is thoroughly integrated into Microsoft's business applications such as the Microsoft Transaction Server, Microsoft Message Queue, and Microsoft SQL Server database. These applications are tightly integrated into the Windows operating system.

Visual Studio.NET

Sun and the other major competitors in the web server arena place strong reliance on Java as found in the J2EE APIs. In contrast, the .NET initiative will offer some degree of language independence by translating programs into an intermediate language that can be compiled to a native executable form for a particular system as needed. The .NET environment will provide a consistent interface to system services, called the Common Language Runtime (CLR), which is analogous to the Java Virtual Machine.

Visual Studio.NET will provide both high- and low-level programming interfaces. High-level interfaces will be able to create simple SOAP clients by working directly from published WSDL files in a very few programming steps. The low-level APIs rather resemble the way Apache SOAP currently creates client applications.

Visual C#.NET

I am sure that practically all Java programmers have heard about C#. This is Microsoft's new object-oriented language that bears an extraordinary resemblance to Java. The language is currently in the last stages of beta release and should be in a final release version by the time you read this.

Visual Basic.NET

To adapt Visual Basic to the object-oriented CLR, Microsoft had to make many changes. Experienced VB programmers may find the transition to VB.NET rather difficult, and a lot of legacy code will have to be rewritten. For example, to be consistent with the data types used in C#, there are changes in VB.NET data types. However, VB programmers will find that using SOAP services is quite easy due to the extensive support provided by the high-level APIs.

For Current Developer Information

A good starting point to locate current information on developer tools for .NET is the following site:

```
http://msdn.microsoft.com/library/default.asp
```

This page shows an expandable list on the left side. To locate information on the .NET My Services resources, expand the section labeled XML and Web Services:

```
XML and Web Services
    .NET My Services
```

For information specific to the SOAP client provided in the Windows XP operating system, follow this hierarchy:

```
Windows Development
    Windows XP
        Technical Articles
            Overview of SOAP client in Windows XP
```

SOAP Compatibility Problems

In spite of all of the efforts by the various XML-related W3C groups, there have been problems of incompatibility between Microsoft, Apache, and other SOAP implementations. A partial explanation is that the various standards involved, such as XML Schema, XML, and SOAP have evolved at different rates. Programmers have also made slightly different assumptions about the interpretation of the standards.

In an effort to locate the differences, an informal SOAPBuilders Interoperability Lab group tries to keep up with the latest versions. Specifications for the interoperability tests can be found at:

```
http://www.whitemesa.com/interop.htm
```

A site that summarizes the latest tests with respect to the compatibility of Apache SOAP and AXIS projects with other implementations is at:

```
http://www.apache.org/~rubys/ApacheClientInterop.html
```

Microsoft operates a site for testing interoperability at:

```
http://www.mssoapinterop.org/
```

Reported Compatibility Problem Areas

In this section, I discuss two of the most common problems programmers have reported when trying to get Microsoft and Apache SOAP implementations to communicate. Bear in mind that these problems may have been fixed in subsequent releases of either Microsoft or Apache toolkits.

Namespace Declaration Problem

This problem was reported on the Apache SOAP developer's mailing list. A Microsoft .NET server was found to return the wrong result when a namespace was defined as shown here:

```
<SOAP-ENV:Body>
  <ns1:test_AddThem
  xmlns:ns1="http://telemetrytech.net/VnocngWebService"
  SOAP-ENV:encodingStyle="http://schemas.xmlsoap.org/soap/encoding/">
  <FirstNum xsi:type="xsd:int">3</FirstNum>
  <SecondNum xsi:type="xsd:int">17</SecondNum>
  </ns1:test_AddThem>
</SOAP-ENV:Body>
```

However, the following SOAP message, with the ns1: removed, was processed correctly.

```
<SOAP-ENV:Body>
  <test_AddThem
   xmlns="http://telemetrytech.net/VnocngWebService"
   SOAP-ENV:encodingStyle="http://schemas.xmlsoap.org/soap/encoding/">
```

```
        <FirstNum xsi:type="xsd:int">3</FirstNum>
        <SecondNum xsi:type="xsd:int">17</SecondNum>
      </test_AddThem>
    </SOAP-ENV:Body>
```

Declaring Type Information

The problem most often experienced when trying to get Apache SOAP clients to talk to Microsoft SOAP services has to do with the specification of xsi:type values for parameters. As described in documentation at the Apache site, Apache SOAP expects the return value from an RPC request to include an xsi:type attribute, as shown in this example:

```
    <return xsi:type="xsd:date">1939-10-17</return>
```

When the return value does not have an xsi:type that the Apache client recognizes, the type parameter defaults to an empty String. As a rather ugly and limited work-around for this problem, you can have your client use a custom SOAPMappingRegistry object that maps one of the standard Apache serializers to the empty String type:

```
    SOAPMappingRegistry smr = new SOAPMappingRegistry ();
    DateSerializer dt = new DateSerializer ();
    smr.mapTypes (Constants.NS_URI_SOAP_ENC, new QName("", "Result"),
        null, null, dt);
```

This is reported to work correctly with Apache clients addressing Microsoft SOAP services.

The .NET Alternatives

Generally speaking, the competition for the .NET web services market emphasizes evolution of existing products based on standards such as XML, SOAP, UDDI, and WSDL. From a publicity and media point of view, this approach gets much less attention than .NET, but it builds on existing technology.

The OASIS (Organization for the Advancement of Structured Information Systems) consortium, which is supported by many computer industry leaders, has formed a Web Services Component Model (WSCM) Technical Committee to create web services presentation standards. The idea is to help promote a more consistent web service experience and avoid proprietary standards.

Note that OASIS also sponsors the ebXML (electronic business XML) specifications promoted by Sun. The ebXML working group decided to use SOAP for message transport, thus avoiding proliferation of XML messaging standards.

All of the organizations listed here have been very active in the standardization committees concerned with various aspects of XML, such as the XML Protocol group.

Sun Open Network Environment

For marketing purposes, Sun refers to Sun ONE (Open Network Environment). Given all of the work that Sun has put into the J2EE (Java 2 Enterprise Edition) and related APIs, it is not surprising that J2EE receives the main emphasis in Sun ONE. A good starting point to learn more about Sun ONE is:

    http://www.sun.com/sunone/

Naturally, Sun emphasizes the hardware- and operating system–independent standards of XML, WSDL, UDDI, and SOAP. Sun also emphasizes the strengths of the ebXML standard for business-to-business (B2B) communication and expects the real money to be found in B2B applications rather than individual users.

Sun marketing seems to be emphasizing tools for creating "services on demand," but the core technology remains the J2EE API. This is a good thing for independent developers because J2EE technology is widely supported on a variety of platforms.

HP Web Services

The HP Web Services Platform appears to be a rather standard approach for a Java-oriented system. It supports EJBs, SOAP, WSDL, and UDDI. However, a notable difference from other web service offerings is the use of the Apache Cocoon2 project for XML-based web site document management. If you are curious about this technology, visit:

    http://xml.apache.org/cocoon2/index.html

IBM Web Services

As a computer company, IBM has always been strong in hardware, software, and services. The pioneering Lotus Notes product pioneered many concepts of integrated messaging and data sharing in a corporate setting, so it is not surprising that IBM is active in similar areas on the Internet.

IBM has been heavily involved with Java as the ideal language for creating web services. The company has contributed core technology to the Apache organization XML efforts, including the base for SOAP. It has also been very active in creating the UDDI and WSDL standards.

IBM's approach to web services seems to emphasize integration into the existing product line, such as the MQSeries messaging service, and the Lotus product line. This will be accomplished with emphasis on the platform independence of Java and XML in an evolutionary rather than revolutionary fashion. A good starting point to investigate IBM's web service products is at:

    http://www-106.ibm.com/developerworks/webservices/

Oracle Dynamic Services

Given the extensive involvement of Oracle corporation researchers in developing XML, SOAP, WSDL, and UDDI standards, you can expect that Oracle's web services framework, entitled Oracle Dynamic Services, will make use of these technologies. You can read about XML and Java support in the Oracle9i product line at:

```
http://otn.oracle.com/products/dynamic_services/content.html
```

SOAP and Web Services

It appears that Microsoft's .NET initiative and all of its major competitors in the race to commercialize web services will be using XML and SOAP in conjunction with WSDL and UDDI. This widespread use of industry standards is certainly good news for software developers.

Hewlett Packard's approach is notable for the use of the XML-based Cocoon2 for content management. Aside from Microsoft, none of the proponents of web services seems to have put much effort into new approaches to content management. Microsoft recently (in mid-2001) bought a company that produces a content management product and has announced the availability of Content Management Server. It is unclear how this will be integrated with .NET.

Microsoft's .NET initiative is notable as the most extreme change from existing practice. It contrasts with the evolutionary approach of the other vendors. Microsoft's emphasis is also on income from hosting services, whereas Sun and HP want to sell the hardware and software to let you create services.

CHAPTER 11

SOAP and Database Access

- The Java Database Connectivity (JDBC) API

- Matching SQL and SOAP data types

- Finding a JDBC driver for your database

- Creating SQL statements

- Working with query results

- An example SOAP service using JDBC

M any SOAP-based web services will use connections to new or existing databases to provide essential services. These databases are typically of the relational type and use the well-established Structured Query Language (SQL) to formulate database commands. Java programmers are fortunate to have a well-designed application programming interface (API) that permits a standardized approach to dealing with SQL. In this chapter, I review some of the important factors a SOAP service designer must consider when dealing with this API.

Java and Databases

The Java Database Connectivity (JDBC) API is designed to give Java programmers a consistent set of classes and methods for access to a wide variety of databases. Commercial databases use a wide variety of file structures and algorithms, so creating a unified set of access methods is no trivial task. At the present state of development, the JDBC API offers access to the most commonly used functions of commercial relational databases. This is possible only because of a degree of convergence and standardization in the database management industry on relational database structure and the SQL for expressing database operations.

The SQL standard is defined by the ISO (International Organization for Standardization) and ANSI (American National Standards Institute). Major releases of the standard are known as SQL86, SQL89, SQL92, and SQL99. Just to confuse things, SQL99 is also known as SQL3. Due to the large number of features that were added to SQL92, it has three levels of feature conformance: entry-level, intermediate, and full. Most commercial products support the entry-level functionality and provide varying support for the higher levels.

Every SQL command is created by combining certain keywords from the fixed SQL command set with variable text from the problem domain. This results in a text representation that is readable by a human but also has an exact meaning to the database program. For example, the following statement defines a query to retrieve the values of the Text variable from a table named errsql for all entries where the isbn variable has a certain value. The SQL keywords are shown in uppercase by convention:

```
SELECT Text FROM errsql WHERE isbn = '1576102912'
```

A complete description of SQL commands is far beyond the scope of this chapter, particularly because there are many vendor-specific differences. A good recent reference is *Mastering SQL* by Martin Gruber (Sybex, 2000). Sybex also publishes a number of books that directly address the peculiarities of various commercial SQL implementations.

JDBC Versions

There are two major versions of JDBC: 1.0 and 2.0. JDBC 1.0 has been part of the Java standard library since JDK 1.1. JDBC 2.0, which arrived with the release of Java 2, supports all

JDBC 1.0 features and adds many improvements. The `java.sql` package contains the Java classes supporting the JDBC API at version 1.0 and most of the version 2.0 additions.

The `javax.sql` package is considered a standard extension and contains additional classes added for JDBC 2.0. It is not part of the Standard Edition but is considered an optional package. The 1.3 release of the Java Standard Edition added a new class, `SQLPermission`, to provide more fine-grained control over certain functions. Visit the following site to find the latest Sun material on JDBC:

```
http://java.sun.com/products/jdbc/
```

In this chapter, I will be using only the JDBC classes that come in versions 1.2 and 1.3 of the standard edition. The definitive guide to JDBC is *JDBC API Tutorial and Reference, Second Edition* by Seth White et al. (Addison-Wesley, 1999). This massive (1,060-page) book is the current official Sun guide to JDBC 2.0.

JDBC Data Types, SQL, and SOAP

In designing a Java SOAP application that works with SQL database, you must take into account the different data types that each component supports. On the SOAP side are the simple data types defined by the XML Schema, plus the capability of user-defined data types. As discussed in Chapter 5, "How SOAP Encodes Data," SOAP adopts all the types found in the "Data Types" section of the XML Schema specifications to be found at the following URL:

```
http://www.w3.org/TR/xmlschema-2/
```

On the JDBC and SQL side is a particular set of data types. The Java class `java.sql.Types` has a list of constants that are used in Java programs to indicate generic SQL data types. Unfortunately, the various SQL database vendors have, in many cases, created other data types or used different names in an attempt to differentiate their product and lock in users. The following is a quick survey of the relation of the most generally available SQL data types to Java and SOAP.

SQL Numeric Types

Here is a list of SQL numeric data types as defined in the SQL92 standard and as they are named in SQL statements when using the JDBC API. Terms in parentheses are alternative names you may see used in SQL statements.

INTEGER (INT)   A signed integer with unspecified precision. In practice, databases use at least a 32-bit integer, so it is usual to map INTEGER to Java's `int` primitive. Apache SOAP supports a 32-bit integer.

SMALLINT   A signed integer with implementation-specific size that uses less space than INTEGER. In practice, this is typically implemented as a 16-bit integer that maps to Java's `short` primitive and Apache SOAP's short type.

TINYINT   An unsigned 8-bit integer. Apparently, this is not supported widely at present in commercial databases. Because Java's and Apache's SOAP consider an 8-bit primitive as signed, the cautious programmer will map this to the short primitive.

NUMERIC   This is a signed decimal having precision that is set when the programmer creates a NUMERIC variable. A typical use would be as a currency value. Because of the arbitrary precision, the recommended Java mapping is the java.math.BigDecimal class. However, the 2.2 version of Apache SOAP does not provide a BigDecimal serializer, so you must either create one or use float or double.

DECIMAL   This is very similar to NUMERIC except that it may store a higher degree of precision using more decimal places. Obviously the double primitive would be best here.

REAL   A floating point number equivalent to Java's float primitive in some implementations and double in other implementations. Again, for SOAP, one should play it safe and use double.

DOUBLE PRECISION (DOUBLE)   A floating point number roughly equivalent to Java's double primitive. This is another place to use the double primitive.

SQL Binary Types

As the importance of multimedia data in Internet applications has increased, so has the interest in handling binary data in relational databases. You also find large chunks of text being stored in databases. Unfortunately, the size of files such as images can completely overwhelm the organization of other data types in usable database files. Therefore, really large chunks of binary data or text are handled by storing an indirect pointer to binary files in the database.

The data type for a large block of binary data may be referred to as a BLOB (Binary Large Object). JDBC 2.0 has introduced a Blob interface to provide access to this data type. The contents of a Blob may be retrieved by reading an input stream or as a byte array. Other JDBC binary types are as follows:

BINARY   In this type, the number of bytes is fixed when the variable is created; typically limited to 254 bytes.

VARBINARY   Similar to VARCHAR, an array of bytes with variable length up to some vendor-specific limit.

Long arrays   There is no SQL standard name, but JDBC uses the LONGVARBINARY name and translates as required to the particular database. The maximum size depends on the vendor.

As discussed in Chapter 5, SOAP can serialize byte arrays with hexBinary or base64Binary encoding. Really large byte arrays could create quite a memory management problem with the present Apache SOAP implementation because it marshals a complete message in memory before transmission. The Apache organization's AXIS project intends to address problems of efficiency and memory use.

SQL Character Types

The following character-storing SQL92 types can generally be treated as Java `String` objects or SOAP `xsd:string` encoding. An exception might be when LONGVARCHAR is used to store really large character sequences, in which case the JDBC `Clob` interface provides for reading the variable as a stream or a `String`.

CHAR (CHARACTER)   A character variable with a fixed length set by the database creator. Java `String` variables stored in a CHAR are padded with spaces or truncated to the fixed length. CHAR variables up to 254 characters in length are typically supported.

VARCHAR (CHARACTER VARYING)   Similar to CHAR except that `String` variables are not padded to the fixed length; typically limited to 254 characters or less.

LONGVARCHAR and CLOB   Similar to VARCHAR except that the text can be much longer. As with BLOB types, the database typically stores a pointer to a file containing the bulk text. This type could pose a real memory problem in Apache SOAP because the `rpcrouter` servlet marshals a complete message in memory as a `String`.

JDBC Drivers

To connect a Java program using the JDBC interface to a particular database, you need a chunk of software called a driver. The driver translates between the common JDBC method calls and the unique communication protocols used by a particular SQL database implementation.

Based on my observation of the messages in Java programming users groups, finding the right driver, getting it installed, and getting it running accounts for a very large portion of the problems that people have with JDBC.

All JDBC drivers fall into one of four types. You might be forced to decide which type to use based on the necessity of connecting with a particular database. If you are fortunate, you can choose according to your needs for efficiency. Most database vendors now supply information and driver software to assist you in connecting to their systems.

Type 1 Drivers

Type 1 drivers, illustrated in Figure 11.1, communicate with databases that have an ODBC (Open Database Connectivity) interface. This widespread industry standard interface is available on many commercial databases. Sun created JDBC-to-ODBC bridge software as part of the Java standard library. Each standard JDBC database operation is translated into an ODBC operation for submission to the database, and returned results go through another translation stage. Because the database's native interface may not exactly correspond to ODBC standards, another translation process might be necessary. Naturally, these extra translations take time, and not all JDBC operations can be supported this way.

FIGURE 11.1:

Connecting to a database with a type 1 driver

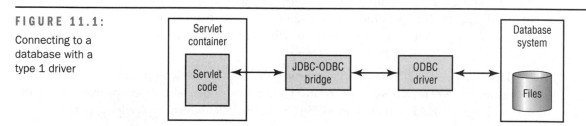

Regrettably, Sun's implementation of the JDBC-to-ODBC bridge driver is not really up to production standards. Even after years of development, some users report mysterious crashes when using it.

Type 2 Drivers

In this case, the JDBC driver interface is implemented in custom classes and native methods so that it can communicate directly with the database API. There is only one stage of translation from JDBC method calls to the database format and one stage of translation with returned data. However, because native code is involved, you may be giving up Java features such as garbage collection. A type 2 connection is illustrated in Figure 11.2.

FIGURE 11.2:

Connecting to a database with a type 2 driver

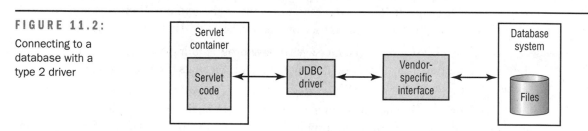

Type 3 Drivers

With type 3 drivers, an all-Java middle-tier application serves as an access point on the network for JDBC applications. This application can receive JDBC calls from clients and translate them to the required type 1 or type 2 access used by the actual database. This architecture is particularly suited to clients that are applets. A type 3 connection is illustrated in Figure 11.3.

FIGURE 11.3:

Connecting to a
database with a
type 3 driver

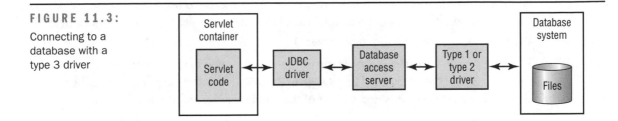

Type 4 Drivers

The type 4 driver provides an all-Java solution with a JDBC driver that can communicate with the database interface directly. This is the most efficient solution because it requires no translation steps and a minimum of network connections. Most commercial database makers now provide type 4 drivers. A type 4 connection is illustrated in Figure 11.4.

FIGURE 11.4:

Connecting to a
database with a
type 4 driver

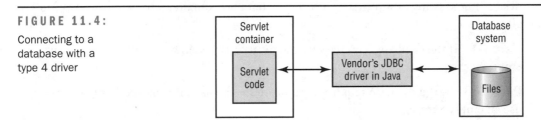

The Hypersonic Database software I will be using in the example provides a type 4 driver.

The *DriverManager* Class

The first step in establishing a connection with a database is registering the driver with static methods in the JDBC `java.sql.DriverManager` class. The static methods in this class provide for managing a set of drivers that may be established in a number of different ways:

By inspecting loaded classes   The `DriverManager` attempts to establish a database connection using all classes that have been loaded by your application that implement the `Driver` interface.

Drivers as system properties   Your system properties file may contain a list of fully qualified driver class names. The `DriverManager` looks for these properties when first initialized. The advantage of this approach is that it avoids the use of any specific class in program code.

By direct registration   Your code can create an instance of a driver and call the `Driver-Manager` `registerDriver` method.

Admittedly, the ability to tell the `DriverManager` which class to use looks pretty odd when you are accustomed to a more direct approach, but code such as the following does work:

```
Class.forName("org.hsqldb.jdbcDriver") ;
```

An alternative to `DriverManager` for getting database connections has been introduced in the most recent Sun JDBC releases. The `javax.sql.DataSource` interface is intended to be more flexible and powerful, but it is not yet part of the standard SDK and is not widely supported.

Database Connections

The basic requirement for any interaction with a specific database is an object implementing the `java.sql.Connection` interface. A `Connection` is typically obtained from the `DriverManager` using the `getConnection` method. There are three versions of this method; the most common takes three `String` objects, as follows:

URL This is a `String` that identifies the database according to the requirements of the driver. These strings always start with "jdbc:" but may contain a variety of information after that.

User ID If the database requires a user identity, it is passed here; otherwise, use an empty `String`.

Password If the database requires a password for the user, it is passed here; otherwise, use an empty `String`.

If the `DriverManager` can't create a `Connection` for any reason, an `SQLException` is thrown. Here is an example of obtaining a connection:

```
conn = DriverManager.getConnection("jdbc:hsqldb:hsql://localhost",
    "sa","");
```

Obtaining a `Connection` can be a relatively slow process, particularly if the database lives elsewhere on the network. Furthermore, a `Connection` can consume significant amounts of system resources, both on the database server and on the calling system. For that reason, special connection "pool" manager classes are frequently used.

A connection pool manager takes over the chore of obtaining a `Connection` and essentially loans `Connection` objects to applications. Being able to use an already open `Connection` typically improves the response time for database queries considerably.

There are a number of open source and/or free Java connection pool managers available on the Net. In addition, for the JDBC 2.0 release, Sun has defined standard connection pool management interfaces.

SQL Statements

Given that you have obtained a `Connection` object, the next step is to create an object representing a database operation, such as a query or database update. The following interfaces in the java.sql package are used:

Statement   The basic form of a SQL statement. When executing the statement, the SQL command is represented as a `String`.

PreparedStatement   A precompiled form of statement used when the basic structure of a statement is used repeatedly with different values plugged in. It can be considerably faster than `Statement`.

CallableStatement   An object implementing this interface can execute SQL stored procedures.

You obtain a `Statement` from a `Connection` with one of the following methods:

```
createStatement()
createStatement( int resultSetType, int resultSetConcurrency )
```

The `ResultSet` class contains constants that are used in the second form when you need to override the default values.

Some of the basic operations that can be performed with a `Statement` are:

executeQuery(String query)   This method returns a `ResultSet` object.

execute(String query)   This method returns a `boolean` value indicating success or failure. Multiple `ResultSet` objects may be held by the `Statement`.

executeUpdate(String cmd)   Executes a SQL command that modifies the database with an INSERT, DELETE, or UPDATE statement.

Working with Results

A successful query returns an object that implements the `ResultSet` interface. This object holds the retrieved data, which is the form of a set of rows of a table. It has a cursor that points at one of these rows. In a basic `ResultSet`, this cursor can make only a single pass through the table. New methods added in JDBC 2.0 make it possible to create a `ResultSet` that supports scrolling backward and forward through the table. This is done by specifying certain constants to the `createStatement` method.

The `ResultSet` interface specifies a large number of methods for creating Java objects or primitive values from the contents of the results table. Enumerating all of these methods is outside the scope of this chapter; for details, consult the `java.sql` package documentation. Here are some examples to give you an idea (`rslt` is a `ResultSet`):

```
String s = rslt.getString(1) ; // from the first column
boolean flag = rslt.getBoolean( 3) ;
Date d = rslt.getDate( n ) ; // where n is an index into rslt
```

Note that you can also get values by using the name of the variable in the column. In this usage, the case used for the name is ignored so you could use either of the following:

```
Date d = rslt.getDate( "start" );
Date d = rslt.getDate( "START" );
```

Due to methods added in JDBC 2.0, you can create a `ResultSet` in which the values in a row can be modified and used to update the database with the new values. This is much more convenient and faster than formulating a SQL statement to perform the update.

Using *ResultSetMetaData*

JDBC provides the `ResultSetMetaData` class to let you get information about the variables contained in a `ResultSet` object. This is information about the properties of the variable as seen by the database. For example, the following would set the `flag` variable `true` if column `n` contains a currency data type:

```
ResultSetMetaData rsmd = rslt.getMetaData();
boolean flag = rsmd.isCurrency( n );
```

An Example of SOAP and JDBC

Much of the SOAP server code presented here is very similar to what you have already seen. Also, I can't begin to exercise all aspects of JDBC in a single example—there are entire books on the subject. Therefore, the purpose of this example is to demonstrate certain unique points about JDBC programming for SOAP applications:

- Getting a driver
- Managing a connection
- Managing a query
- Adapting error handling to SOAP

The Hypersonic SQL Database

The database package I used for this example is a free, open-source Java implementation conforming to standard SQL92 syntax and JDBC interfaces. The package originated as Hypersonic SQL under the guidance of Thomas Mueller. It is now supported as the HSQLDB project using the facilities at the sourceforge site. Sourceforge is the world's largest open source development website, supporting thousands of projects in many languages, and is well worth a visit just to browse around. The version I used here is 1.61; you can download the latest Hypersonic SQL version from:

```
http://sourceforge.net/projects/hsqldb/
```

This is a very complete package, providing a number of different modes of operation, examples, and utilities. It also includes Javadoc format documentation. After downloading the zipped file, proceed as follows to install and test.

Unpack the contents into a new directory. In the demo subdirectory that will be created, you will find a run.bat file. Execute this as follows to run a short test of the installation:

```
run SelfTest
```

Starting the Hypersonic Server

The Hypersonic SQL system can be run in a variety of ways. Because most SOAP services will probably be contacting a server other than the web server, this example uses a stand-alone server. This server tries to read data from a properties file in the demo directory. Here is the content of the server.properties file as used in this example:

```
# properties file for hsqldb
port=9001
database=errata
silent=false
```

There is a convenient runServer batch file in the demo directory. Execute this file in a new MS-DOS prompt window. You should see something like the following status report. Specifying the silent parameter as false turns on simple reporting to this window.

```
F:\hsqldb1.61\demo>runServer
port    =9001
database=errata
silent  =false
Server 1.6 is running
Press [Ctrl]+[C] to abort
```

Creating the Example Database

For the purposes of this example, I have created a SQL database from an existing set of data on book errata that is normally in XML form. Since the conversion of the XML data to a SQL database is not germane to this chapter, the conversion program will not be reproduced here. However, it is on the CD-ROM, along with the following files to be used in creating the example database:

ecj2.xml   The example errata in XML format

BookErrata.dtd   The dtd file referred to in ecj2.xml

ErrataToSQL.class   The Java program

CreateExample.bat   The batch file to execute the Java program

After ensuring that your classpath includes the Sun JAXP parser jar files, open an MS-DOS console window in the directory containing these files and execute the batch file. You should see a series of reports as the parser finds various elements. In the window running the server, you should see lots of output reporting creation of the records.

Testing the Example Database

The Hypersonic SQL package includes a convenient application for testing various database functions. In an MS-DOS console window, change to the demo directory of the database installation and execute the runManager batch file. You should get a graphic interface window displayed with an initial dialog for getting a connection. Choose the HSQL Database Engine Server selection in the Type list. Don't change any of the other parameters, and click the OK button. When the dialog closes, you should see an entry for ERRSQL on the left-side display.

The database consists of a single table created by the following SQL statement:

```
CREATE CACHED TABLE errsql(SEQ INTEGER PRIMARY KEY
   isbn CHAR(12),Page CHAR(4),Printing INTEGER,
   Significance INTEGER, Author VARCHAR(10),Datemod CHAR(10),
   Text VARCHAR
```

The columns in this table are as follows:

SEQ   A record sequence number

isbn   The book ISBN number as a character array

Page   The page referred to—this can be Roman numerals, so a char representation is needed

Printing   Typically a number from 1 to 10

Significance   A value indicating significance of the error, ranging from 1 = high to 3 = minor

Author   The initials of the person last modifying the entry

Datemod   The date last modified

Text   The bulk text describing the error, typically including HTML formatting tags

This manager application is very convenient for testing database commands. However, now that correct installation has been verified, let's proceed to the SOAP service.

The *ErrataQuery* SOAP Service

The SOAP service that will access this database is contained in the ErrataQuery class. The constructor of the class establishes a Connection with the database, and the queryISBN method handles a SOAP RPC call to carry out a query. The Connection is used for one query and then discarded.

Obviously, this is very inefficient, and any production version of this service would use a connection pool and provide many more search functions. The purpose of this example is to illustrate the particular points I mentioned earlier, not to create a full application.

Listing 11.1 shows the ErrataQuery constructor, which is declared as throwing a SOAP-Exception. Failure to obtain a Connection object will cause a SQLException which is caught and used to create a SOAPException object because that is the kind of exception that the Apache SOAP RPCRouterServlet knows how to handle. Note that the failure to get a connection is a server failure so the SOAPException is created using the FAULT_CODE_SERVER constant.

The user ID and password parameters in the getConnection call are the default values for the Hypersonic SQL system.

Listing 11.1:   **Start of the *ErrataQuery* Source Code**

```
package com.lanw.soapsrvr ;

import java.sql.* ;
import java.util.* ;
import org.apache.soap.SOAPException ;
import org.apache.soap.Constants ;

public class ErrataQuery
{
  static String connectionURL =  "jdbc:hsqldb:hsql://localhost" ;
  static String driverClass = "org.hsqldb.jdbcDriver" ;
  static String tableName = "errsql" ;

  private Connection conn ;

  public ErrataQuery() throws SOAPException {
    try {
      Class.forName( driverClass ) ;
      // parameters are URL, User id, password
      conn = DriverManager.getConnection( connectionURL, "sa","");
      System.out.println("Got connection " );
    }catch(Exception e){
      throw new SOAPException(
          Constants.FAULT_CODE_SERVER, // standard fault
          "Database not available", // message
          e // cause
      );
    }
  }
}
```

The *queryISBN* Method

As shown in Listing 11.2, this method takes three parameters, a `String` holding the ISBN code, an `int` representing the significance of a particular errata entry, and an `int` representing the printing in which the error appeared. The first thing this method does is check for valid inputs. If the ISBN code is not supplied or is too short to be a valid value, a `SOAPException` indicating a client fault is thrown. Checking of the other parameters simply substitutes a valid value if the supplied value is out of range.

Note that, as with an `SQLException` thrown in the constructor, an exception thrown by the `executeQuery` method call gets turned into a `SOAPException` indicating a server fault.

Listing 11.2:   **The Method Used by the SOAP RPC Call**

```
public synchronized String[] queryISBN( String isbn,
  int significance, int printing ) throws SOAPException {
if( isbn == null || isbn.length() < 10 ){
    throw new SOAPException(
        Constants.FAULT_CODE_CLIENT, "Bad ISBN value" );
}
if( significance < 1 || significance > 3 ) {
    significance = 3 ;
}
if( printing < 1 || printing > 10 ){
    printing = 1 ;
}
ArrayList ret = new ArrayList() ;
try {
 Statement st = conn.createStatement();
 String query = "Select Text FROM " + tableName + " WHERE " +
    "isbn = '" + isbn + "' AND Significance <= " +
    significance + " AND Printing = " + printing ;
 ResultSet rslt = st.executeQuery( query );
 ResultSetMetaData rmd = rslt.getMetaData();
 while( rslt.next()){
   ret.add( rslt.getString(1));
   // note SQL column addressing convention starts with 1
 }
 st.close(); // good practice
 conn.close();
 conn = null ;
 return (String[])ret.toArray( new String[ ret.size() ] );
}catch(SQLException e){
    throw new SOAPException(
        Constants.FAULT_CODE_SERVER, "SQLexception", e );
}
}

public void finalize(){
  System.out.println("Finalize bean");
```

```
        try {
        if( conn != null ) conn.close();
        }catch(SQLException e){
        }
    }
}
```

It is important to note that a `Connection` object may hold significant resources on both the SQL server and the SOAP server side. Any JDBC operation must be careful to close any `Connection` object. As just shown, the `finalize` method in the `ErrataQuery` class closes the `Connection` object if for some reason it did not get closed in the normal course of operations.

Deploying *ErrataQuery*

Deploying the `ErrataQuery` class is similar to the previous examples, for instance, in Chapter 5. The class is placed in the `WEB-INF/classes` directory using the complete package name. In addition, the `hsqldb.jar` file must be placed in the `WEB-INF/lib` directory so that the Hypersonic SQL classes will be available.

Now let's look at the deployment descriptor used to deploy the `ErrataQuery` class in the Apache SOAP server. As shown in Listing 11.3, this is pretty simple because the `queryISBN` method returns a value, a `String` array, that is handled by the standard encoding methods.

Listing 11.3: **The Deployment Descriptor for the Service**

```
<isd:service xmlns:isd="http://xml.apache.org/xml-soap/deployment"
            id="urn:Errata">
  <isd:provider type="java"
    scope="Request"
    methods="queryISBN">
    <isd:java class="com.lanw.soapsrvr.ErrataQuery" static="false"/>
  </isd:provider>
  <isd:faultListener>org.apache.soap.server.DOMFaultListener
  </isd:faultListener>
</isd:service>
```

Now let's examine what happens when SOAP messages are sent to this service. I used the `UtilSnoop` utility to send messages under various conditions. A typical SOAP RPC request message is shown in Listing 11.4.

Listing 11.4: **The SOAP Request Used in the Example**

```
<?xml version='1.0' encoding='UTF-8'?>
<SOAP-ENV:Envelope
  xmlns:SOAP-ENV="http://schemas.xmlsoap.org/soap/envelope/"
  xmlns:xsi="http://www.w3.org/1999/XMLSchema-instance"
```

```
    xmlns:xsd="http://www.w3.org/1999/XMLSchema">
<SOAP-ENV:Body>
<ns1:queryISBN xmlns:ns1="urn:Errata"
    SOAP-ENV:encodingStyle="http://schemas.xmlsoap.org/soap/encoding/">
<isbn xsi:type="xsd:string" >1576102912</isbn>
<signif xsi:type="xsd:int" >1</signif>
<printing xsi:type="xsd:int" >1</printing>
</ns1:queryISBN>
</SOAP-ENV:Body>
</SOAP-ENV:Envelope>
```

An Example of Server Failure

In the first example, shown in Listing 11.5, the Hypersonic SQL server was not running when the request was sent. As expected, this resulted in a server fault, but note that Apache SOAP has added `BadTargetObjectURI` to the `faultcode` because instantiation of the Errata-Query object failed. The server has also modified the original message associated with the `SOAPException`, prefacing the message supplied with the text "Unable to resolve target object."

Listing 11.5:   **The Response with Server Failure**

```
<?xml version='1.0' encoding='UTF-8'?>
<SOAP-ENV:Envelope
    xmlns:SOAP-ENV="http://schemas.xmlsoap.org/soap/envelope/"
    xmlns:xsi="http://www.w3.org/1999/XMLSchema-instance"
    xmlns:xsd="http://www.w3.org/1999/XMLSchema">
<SOAP-ENV:Body>
<SOAP-ENV:Fault>
<faultcode>SOAP-ENV:Server.BadTargetObjectURI</faultcode>
<faultstring>Unable to resolve target object: Database not
      available</faultstring>
<faultactor>/soap/servlet/rpcrouter</faultactor>
<detail>
<stackTrace>[SOAPException: faultCode=SOAP-ENV:Server;
    msg=Database not available;
    targetException=java.lang.ClassNotFoundException:
    org.hsqldb.jdbcDriver]
 at com.lanw.soapsrvr.ErrataQuery.&lt;init&gt;(ErrataQuery.java:27)
 at java.lang.Class.newInstance0(Native Method)
 ........ many lines removed
</stackTrace>
</detail>
</SOAP-ENV:Fault>

</SOAP-ENV:Body>
</SOAP-ENV:Envelope>
```

The original message also contained many lines of stack trace that I have removed from this and the other example fault listings to save space.

An Example of Bad Data

Next let's look at the response to a request that contained a short string in the isbn tag. The result is shown in Listing 11.6. As expected, the fault code is of the "Client" type, but note that the server has not added any details to the code or the message.

Listing 11.6:   **The SOAP Response to Bad ISBN Data**

```xml
<?xml version='1.0' encoding='UTF-8'?>
<SOAP-ENV:Envelope
    xmlns:SOAP-ENV="http://schemas.xmlsoap.org/soap/envelope/"
    xmlns:xsi="http://www.w3.org/1999/XMLSchema-instance"
    xmlns:xsd="http://www.w3.org/1999/XMLSchema">
<SOAP-ENV:Body>
<SOAP-ENV:Fault>
<faultcode>SOAP-ENV:Client</faultcode>
<faultstring>Bad ISBN value</faultstring>
<faultactor>/soap/servlet/rpcrouter</faultactor>
<detail>
<stackTrace>[SOAPException: faultCode=SOAP-ENV:Client;
    msg=Bad ISBN value]
 at com.lanw.soapsrvr.ErrataQuery.queryISBN(ErrataQuery.java:38)
 at java.lang.reflect.Method.invoke(Native Method)
 at org.apache.soap.server.RPCRouter.invoke(RPCRouter.java:146)
....... many lines removed
</stackTrace>
</detail>
</SOAP-ENV:Fault>
</SOAP-ENV:Body>
</SOAP-ENV:Envelope>
```

Empty Result Example

Listing 11.7 shows the return when the isbn parameter specified a code for which no data was found. Note that the ns2:arrayType attribute shows xsd:string[0], indicating an empty array.

Listing 11.7:   **The Message Returned When No Data Was Found**

```xml
<?xml version='1.0' encoding='UTF-8'?>
<SOAP-ENV:Envelope
    xmlns:SOAP-ENV="http://schemas.xmlsoap.org/soap/envelope/"
    xmlns:xsi="http://www.w3.org/1999/XMLSchema-instance"
    xmlns:xsd="http://www.w3.org/1999/XMLSchema">
<SOAP-ENV:Body>
```

```
<ns1:queryISBNResponse xmlns:ns1="urn:Errata"
 SOAP-ENV:encodingStyle="http://schemas.xmlsoap.org/soap/encoding/">
<return xmlns:ns2="http://schemas.xmlsoap.org/soap/encoding/"
   xsi:type="ns2:Array" ns2:arrayType="xsd:string[0]">
</return>
</ns1:queryISBNResponse>
</SOAP-ENV:Body>
</SOAP-ENV:Envelope>
```

Successful Query Example

Finally, let's look at the response when some data was retrieved from the database. Listing 11.8 shows the initial and final parts of the SOAP message. The ns2:arrayType attribute shows xsd:string[19], indicating the array size. Each retrieved String is enclosed in an item tag, and the various formatting tags in the original data have been encoded.

Listing 11.8:   **The Response to a Query That Found Some Data**

```
<?xml version='1.0' encoding='UTF-8'?>
<SOAP-ENV:Envelope
   xmlns:SOAP-ENV="http://schemas.xmlsoap.org/soap/envelope/"
   xmlns:xsi="http://www.w3.org/1999/XMLSchema-instance"
   xmlns:xsd="http://www.w3.org/1999/XMLSchema">
<SOAP-ENV:Body>
<ns1:queryISBNResponse xmlns:ns1="urn:Errata"
 SOAP-ENV:encodingStyle="http://schemas.xmlsoap.org/soap/encoding/">
<return xmlns:ns2="http://schemas.xmlsoap.org/soap/encoding/"
   xsi:type="ns2:Array" ns2:arrayType="xsd:string[19]">
<item xsi:type="xsd:string">&lt;p&gt;&lt;b&gt;&lt;FONT
   COLOR=&quot;red&quot;&gt;On Cram Sheet
   &lt;sup&gt;&amp;lt;1&amp;gt;&amp;lt;2&amp;gt;&lt;/sup&gt;&lt;/font
   &gt;&lt;/b&gt;, Cram Sheet item 16 should state:&lt;br /&gt;Division
   ......... lines removed
</item>
   ......... lots of lines removed
</return>
</ns1:queryISBNResponse>

</SOAP-ENV:Body>
</SOAP-ENV:Envelope>
```

SOAP and JDBC

Due to the excellent support for databases provided by the JDBC API, it is easy to integrate just about any SQL database into a SOAP server. The hardest part is getting the right driver and getting it configured. After that, things get much simpler.

## CHAPTER 12

SOAP Goes Wireless

- Characteristics of current wireless devices

- SOAP's place in wireless connectivity

- Java 2 Micro Edition (J2ME) configurations and profiles

- Cool tools for wireless application development

- XML and SOAP packages for J2ME

- Examples on telephone and PalmPilot emulators

Recently, there's been an explosion of activity in the area of small but powerful electronic devices, such as cell phones and personal digital assistants with wireless Internet connection ability. It should be no surprise to learn that Java is very prominent as a development language to create applications on such devices and on the servers with which those devices interact.

Sun recognized Java's potential in this environment and has been pursuing the development of the Java 2 Micro Edition (J2ME) for several years. I am assuming that you may not be very familiar with J2ME and Java on small devices. The aim of this chapter is to provide the basic information required to develop for small devices, describe possible architectures for integrating SOAP into wireless applications, and demonstrate the use of Sun's J2ME Wireless Toolkit.

Architectures for SOAP with Wireless Devices

Before diving into the details of J2ME, it's appropriate to take a look at what is going on with wireless computing devices and think about where SOAP fits into that model. Consumers are confronted with a very wide range of wireless devices operating with a wide range of standards that are totally incompatible. I suppose this is inevitable at the start of a technological revolution, but it sure makes things hard for developers.

For example, the most successful wireless protocol in the world today appears to be the Short Message Service (SMS). A very compact way of sending short text messages, SMS lends itself to chatting and accounts for huge traffic in some environments.

One step above SMS in complexity is the Wireless Markup Language (WML), which provides a sort of simplified HTML for presentation of web pages on small devices.

Protocols such as SMS and WML render content supplied from a service according to some application protocol. In contrast, Java applications take over the display entirely, and each one is free to render the screen exactly according to the programmer's instructions. I feel that this is a very important distinction.

SOAP on the Client Device

Let's try to characterize present wireless devices in general. In comparison to the desktop or laptop computing most users are accustomed to, wireless devices tend to have the following:

Low memory   As a consequence of small size and low battery power, small devices have less memory for both data storage and program operation than desktop machines.

Slow processor   The limitations of battery power ensure that the computing power in a small device is less than that of a desktop system.

Slow communication   At present, communication rates are quite variable, depending on the protocol in use. This area may see vast improvement.

Intermittent connection   Your ability to get connected varies according to location and possible interference.

High-priced connections   This one is self-explanatory!

Implications of Low Memory

A typical mobile device user wants to have a lot of applications available. However, because of the low amount of storage capacity, applications that use a lot of space and return little functionality will be the first to be removed.

Applications that need access to large amounts of data will not keep that data on the mobile device but will use web services to give rapid access. This is starting to sound like Microsoft's .NET My Services as discussed in Chapter 10 ("SOAP and .NET"), isn't it?

Implications of a Slow Processor

Programmers have gotten used to the steady increase in processing speeds on the desktop to cover up inefficient algorithms. You must pay extra attention to efficiency and interface responsiveness when programming for small devices. For Java programmers, the standard precautions, such as avoiding excessive object creation and separating event response threads from intense computing threads, will pay off.

Implications of Slow Communication

At the present time, wireless communication is much slower than wired networks. In addition, wireless systems typically have to compete with cellular phone voice traffic. To compensate for the resulting reduced bandwidth, some systems limit the amount of data in a single transfer. For message protocols such as SOAP, which seems to get more excess baggage with every specification revision, this presents a significant problem. Message compression might help, but there you run into the slow processing speed problem. Simple protocols, such as the SMS (Short Message Service), have a definite advantage over SOAP here.

Implications of Intermittent Connection

As anybody who has used a cell phone knows, wireless communication is subject to fading, "dead zones," and interference. Therefore, any service must provide for storing messages until it can be verified that the complete message was received.

Implications of High-Priced Connections

Right now, wireless connectivity via cell phone networks can be pretty expensive. For example, certain Palm.net connection plans charge $0.20 per message kilobyte over a base amount.

Some of the SOAP message exchanges that appear in this book would end up costing a user over $1.00 on that schedule.

Connection costs are sure to come down, but this is unlikely in the near future due to several factors. For one thing, in Europe, at least, telecommunication companies paid out enormous amounts of cash to license radio spectrum space.

High connection price and slow speed argue for compact and efficient message structure for wireless applications. These are not exactly SOAP's strong points.

The Environment of Increasing Connectivity

The communication environment in which wireless devices may operate is changing rapidly. For example, wireless networking for home and office is becoming cheaper and cheaper. However, the current crop of wireless devices ignores that trend for the very good reason that you can't get subscription and service income from somebody who owns all the parts of a wireless communication system.

Ideally, the same device would communicate both with your own network when you are in range and with public networks when you are out of range. Also ideally, the interfaces and protocols would be the same for both situations.

Does SOAP Belong on Wireless Devices?

Taken together, all of these characteristics indicate that SOAP is not ideally suited for wireless devices. On the plus side is the system independence of SOAP and XML, which enables a wireless device to communicate with any SOAP service. On the minus side are the bulk and complexity of SOAP messages, leading to greater expense for routine use.

It seems to me that there is a lot to recommend a sort of personalized server system based on SOAP. You can see the beginnings of this sort of thing in websites that try to take the portal approach by providing personalization capabilities. Presently, portals put together various news resources based on your preferences, but they draw on limited resources.

I am suggesting that as WSDL and UDDI characterization of SOAP-based services becomes more widespread, it would be possible to put together a personalized portal combining data from any service on the entire web by using SOAP.

As an example of a current service operating this way, one ingenious site provides a service that sends SMS messages or other mobile phone events all over the world. Users communicate with the services using SOAP messages. The starting point to investigate this service is at:

```
http://www.salcentral.com/x/smsreg.asp
```

The Organization of J2ME

Creating an API to cover as many hardware configurations as possible has turned out to be rather difficult. J2ME has been through quite a long evolutionary process since the first dramatic release of Java-enabled PalmPilots at the 1999 JavaOne conference. However, a workable approach has been found, based on a layered approach.

Configurations and Profiles

To accommodate the wide range of small device capabilities, Sun has evolved a scheme of configurations and profiles. The capabilities for each have been ironed out in extensive negotiations with Sun's industry partners. Roughly speaking, a configuration defines a set of core classes usable by devices with similar capabilities.

Due to the rapidly evolving world of consumer electronics, this classification scheme will probably be modified. Up-to-date, detailed specifications for configurations and profiles can be downloaded from this website:

```
http://java.sun.com/j2me/
```

Configurations: CDC and CLDC

At present, two configurations are defined, Connected Device Configuration (CDC) and Connected Limited Device Configuration (CLDC). Most wireless devices, such as cell phones and PalmPilots, fall into the CLDC category, so I am going to concentrate on the characteristics of these devices.

Compared to J2SE (Java 2 Standard Edition), Java on a CLDC device has the following limitations, in roughly decreasing importance to programmers:

No floating point math   This means no `float` or `double` primitives.

No reflection   For example, you can't load a class by name.

No native methods   This means you cannot use native code to take advantage of the special capabilities of a device.

No user-defined class loader   All class loading is done by a standard virtual machine loader.

No ThreadGroups   A CLDC device must support threads but can't use `ThreadGroup` objects to organize them.

No Daemon Threads   There is no multiprocessing on CLDC devices; any application must have access to the entire capacity of the device. This means you can't have background processes.

No finalize methods   Only a simplified version of garbage collection is available.

Simplified security and byte code verification   As I will discuss under the "From Source Code to MIDlet" section, some security checking and verification of byte code is performed before an application is packaged instead of when it is loaded.

The CLDC specific classes of greatest interest for developers of wireless applications are those related to communication in the `javax.microedition.io` package. Because small devices have limited IO capabilities, the CLDC configuration of the `java.io` package is greatly limited, and `java.net` is not there at all. The `java.io` classes in the CLDC configuration support various kinds of byte-oriented and character-oriented streams.

The `javax.microedition.io` package consists mostly of interface definitions that create an abstract framework for creating connections. Exactly which protocols are supported is left to the implementers of a particular device, but HTTP is typically supported.

A device supporting the CDC configuration will support all of the classes that run on a CLDC configuration, plus many additional features. Generally speaking, neither the CLDC nor CDC specifies anything about user interaction—that is left up to profiles.

Profiles

A profile specification elaborates on a configuration and typically supplies user interface classes. The profile of interest here is the Mobile Information Device Profile (MIDP). A typical device that can use this profile is expected to have these characteristics:

- A display of at least 96 pixels wide by 54 high. This can be either monochrome or color.

- Input by either a touch screen, keypad, or keyboard.

- A wireless network connection (which can be intermittent).

- At least 128K of nonvolatile memory for Java, 8K of nonvolatile memory for data, and 32K of nonvolatile memory for runtime use.

A Java application running in the CLDC/MIDP environment is referred to as a midlet, by analogy with applets and servlets. There have been many upheavals in the design specifications for MIDP. The current Palm version, which was only released in October 2001, featured major changes from the experimental KVM that created so much excitement at the 1999 JavaOne convention.

Developing for J2ME

You are about to embark on a journey to new territory: cross platform development. This can get pretty tricky! Fortunately, however, the pioneers have created some tools and hints that will help. An excellent collection of useful Internet links can be found at:

```
http://www.geocities.com/lyttonhe/J2ME.html
```

To automate the complex steps involved in creating a midlet, as discussed in the next section, and to facilitate testing of midlets, Sun has put together the J2ME Wireless Toolkit. Among other utilities, this toolkit contains emulators for a Java-enabled mobile phone. You can download this toolkit from:

    http://java.sun.com/products/j2mewtoolkit/download.html

From Source Code to MIDlet

Applications running in the MID Profile are extensions of the `javax.microedition.midlet`
`.MIDlet` class called midlets. Here are the basic steps that have to be accomplished to get your midlet source code compiled and running in a J2ME environment:

1. **Compile** The `javac` compiler uses J2SE classes to run but has to refer to J2ME classes when your source refers to them. This cross-platform compilation capability is provided for with the `bootclasspath` command-line parameter. See your J2SE `tooldocs` documentation for details.

2. **Verify** In a normal Java application, the JVM performs various verification checks on class file byte code. This time-consuming process is particularly noticeable on devices with low processing power. To keep verification delays to a minimum, a "preverification" step checks and modifies the class files.

3. **Jar** All the class files your application needs have to be placed in a single jar file. Extra information about the application that is required by the J2ME environment must be placed in the manifest file contained in the jar. Many midlets that require the same library code can be placed in the same jar file.

4. **Application Descriptor** Additional descriptive information in the form of a "jad" file can be provided. The format is explained in the MIDP specification. This information is used for application management when installing and running the application and can also be used to hold configuration parameters. Certain parameters in the jad file must match those in the jar file manifest.

5. **Package** If the target device cannot download a jar file directly, a package conversion step may be required. For example, Palm devices require a file in the prc format.

6. **Transfer** Finally, the midlet package must be transferred to the device. For example, Palm devices have new applications installed during "desktop synchronization."

The J2ME Wireless Toolkit

The J2ME Wireless Toolkit provides an environment for creating J2ME applications that take care of many of the details involved. You can download the package from:

    http://java.sun.com/products/j2mewtoolkit/

At the present time, only a Windows version is available, and you must have a J2SE JDK version 1.3 or later already installed before installing the toolkit.

Installing the J2ME Wireless Toolkit

On executing the downloaded file, the main choice you will have to make is between using the toolkit stand-alone or integrated with Sun's Forte product. I am assuming that the Forte development environment is not that widely distributed so I will be discussing a stand-alone installation.

The drive you install on should have at least 40MB available, both for the toolkit and for the applications you will be developing. The toolkit utilities assume that all development will take place inside the toolkit directory structure. The main components installed under the main directory are as follows:

Executable files   Batch and EXE files for the utilities are in the bin subdirectory.

Documentation   PDF format files providing an overview of the tools and Javadoc format documentation of the J2ME classes are installed in the doc subdirectory.

Support files   Support files include the images used to emulate various Java capable devices (cell phones) and configuration files. These are in the lib subdirectory.

Examples   Example applications are provided in the apps subdirectory. By convention, your applications will also be placed in this directory.

Cross-Platform Developing Hints

If you are using command-line tools instead of the J2ME Wireless Toolkit, there are a lot of details you must provide for. For example, when using the javac compiler on a J2SE or J2EE system for the J2ME environment, you must specify the J2ME library using the bootclass-path command-line parameter.

Generally speaking, developing MIDP applications from the command line gets too complicated for batch files. Fortunately, the Apache organization has the perfect tool to help automate the process. The package is called ANT, essentially a Java-powered replacement for MAKE. ANT is available from:

```
http://jakarta.apache.org
```

SOAP in Small Places

A number of projects have been started to produce J2ME-compatible XML parsers compact enough for small memory systems. Here are two websites that explain well-developed projects:

```
http://www.extreme.indiana.edu/soap/xpp/
http://kxml.enhydra.org/
```

A recent search on Yahoo for "j2me xml" got thousands of hits, so you can see there is plenty of activity in the area.

The kXML Parser

In this section, I detail the use of a representative compact XML parser, the kXML parser from the Enhydra organization. The jar file that contains this library is only 32K in size—not the smallest, but quite compact. The primary website for the kXML project can be found at:

```
http://kxml.enhydra.org/
```

The download contains source code, Javadoc format documentation and samples. If you use this product, you should also examine the Enhydra Public License that governs its use.

Rather than go into the details of the kXML parser, the simplest thing to do is to show an example of the parser in action. For that purpose, I have modified one of the sample programs provided in the kXML package. This program creates an object in memory representing an XML document, but it uses classes that are simpler than those required to represent a full W3C DOM.

As shown in Listing 12.1, the main method takes a filename from the command line, creates a `FileReader` object, and hands it to the `parseReader` method of a new `KdomTest` object. After creating the document object, `parseReader` passes the root node to the `processNode` method that displays the entire contents. Note that these `Document` and `Element` classes are from the kXML library, not the JAXP library used in other examples in this book.

Listing 12.1:   **The Start of the *KdomTest* Program**

```
import java.io.*;

// modified from the kXML project KdomDemo example

import org.kxml.*;
import org.kxml.kdom.*;
import org.kxml.parser.*;

public class KdomTest {

  public static void main(String[] args) {
    try {
      KdomTest test = new KdomTest();
      Reader rd = new FileReader( args[0] );
      test.parseReader( rd );
      rd.close();
    }catch(Exception e ){
      e.printStackTrace( System.out );
    }
  }
```

```
// instance variables
org.kxml.kdom.Document doc ; //

public void parseReader( Reader rd ) {
  FileReader fin = null;
  try {
    XmlParser parser = new XmlParser( rd );
    doc = new Document();
    doc.parse(parser);
    Element root = doc.getRootElement();
    processNode(root, Xml.ELEMENT, "");
  } catch (Exception ex) {
    System.out.println("parseReader " + ex.getMessage());
    ex.printStackTrace(System.out);
  }
}
```

The processNode method shown in Listing 12.2 illustrates the kind of objects and methods available in the kXML library for XML processing. One of the main simplifications of this package is that all XML components other than Element are simply represented as String objects.

Listing 12.2: **The *processNode* Method Displays Information on One Node**

```
// Show type and content for this node
private void processNode(Object node, int type,
    String indent) {
  switch (type) {
    case Xml.ELEMENT:
      Element elem = (Element) node;
      String namespace = elem.getNamespace();
      String prefix = null;
      String name = elem.getName();
      int attributeCount = elem.getAttributeCount();
      int childCount = elem.getChildCount();
      System.out.println (indent + "Element name: '"+
        name + "'"
        + (Xml.NO_NAMESPACE.equals (namespace)
          ? " (no namespace)"
          : " namespace: '"+ namespace+ "'"));

      for (int i = 0; i < attributeCount; i++) {
        Attribute attrib = elem.getAttribute(i);
        System.out.println (indent +
          "- Attribute name: '"
          + attrib.getName()
          + "' value: '" + attrib.getValue() + "'");
      }
      for (int i = 0; i < childCount; i++) {
```

```
                  processNode(elem.getChild(i), elem.getType(i),
                      indent + ".");
              }
              break;
      // All other node types (other than Xml.ELEMENT) are
      // represented as Strings.
        case Xml.WHITESPACE:
          String space = (String) node;
          System.out.println (indent + "Whitespace length: "
                  +((String) node).length ());
          break;
        case Xml.TEXT:
          String text = (String) node;
          System.out.println (indent + "Text: '"+text+"'");
          break;
        case Xml.COMMENT:
          String comment = (String) node;
          System.out.print(indent + "Comment: '"
                  + comment +"'");
          break;
        case Xml.DOCTYPE:
          String doctype = (String) node;
          System.out.print(indent + "Doctype: '"
                  + doctype+"'");
          break;
        case Xml.PROCESSING_INSTRUCTION:
          String pi = (String) node;
          System.out.print(indent
                  + "Processing Instruction: '" + pi + "'");
          break;
        default:   // Should never happen
          System.out.println(indent + "Unknown node type: "
                  + type);
          break;
      }
    }
  }
}
```

As a demonstration of how this works, I ran the KdomTest program on the SOAP message shown in Chapter 5 ("How SOAP Encodes Data"), Listing 5.5. The first 30 lines of output are shown in Listing 12.3, with some long lines wrapped. Note that the kXML package tracks namespaces correctly and is thus suitable for processing SOAP messages. The Whitespace reports represent the end-of-line characters after an element.

Listing 12.3:   **Partial Result from Test Program**

```
Element name: 'Envelope' namespace:
    'http://schemas.xmlsoap.org/soap/envelope/'
.Whitespace length: 2
```

```
.Element name: 'Body' namespace:
    'http://schemas.xmlsoap.org/soap/envelope/'
..Whitespace length: 2
..Element name: 'getNthElementResponse' namespace:
    'urn:Exercise'
..- Attribute name: 'encodingStyle' value:
    'http://xml.apache.org/xml-soap/literalxml'
...Whitespace length: 2
...Element name: 'return' (no namespace)
....Whitespace length: 2
....Element name: 'Book' (no namespace)
....- Attribute name: 'isbn' value: '0-7821-2809-2'
.....Whitespace length: 6
.....Element name: 'Title' (no namespace)
......Text: 'Java Developer's Guide to Servlets and JSP'
.....Whitespace length: 6
.....Element name: 'Errata' (no namespace)
.....- Attribute name: 'code' value: 'jdgjsp'
.....Whitespace length: 6
.....Element name: 'Author' (no namespace)
......Text: 'Bill Brogden'
.....Whitespace length: 6
.....Element name: 'DatePublished' (no namespace)
.....- Attribute name: 'month' value: 'null'
.....- Attribute name: 'year' value: '2001'
.....Whitespace length: 6
.....Element name: 'Publisher' (no namespace)
......Text: 'Sybex'
.....Whitespace length: 6
.....Element name: 'Topic' (no namespace)
......Text: 'Java,servlets,JSP,XML,Tomcat,debugging,JDBC'
```

The kSOAP Classes

Enhydra has a compact SOAP message processor project that uses the kXML parser. You can find details on the kSOAP project at:

```
http://ksoap.enhydra.org/
```

The basic organization of the kSOAP classes naturally follows the components of a SOAP message, similar to the Apache SOAP project. The package comes with sample applications written for the J2ME MID Profile configuration.

In order to illustrate SOAP message handling with this configuration, I used the Stock-QuoteDemo midlet from the kSOAP samples. The source code for this midlet is shown in Listings 12.4 and 12.5.

The code shown in Listing 12.4 creates a form that accepts input of a stock ticker symbol. The details of interface programming for MIDP devices are beyond the scope of this book.

Listing 12.4: **The *StockQuoteDemo* from the Enhydra kSOAP Project**

```java
import javax.microedition.midlet.*;
import javax.microedition.lcdui.*;
import java.io.*;
import javax.microedition.io.*;

import org.ksoap.*;
import org.ksoap.transport.*;

public class StockQuoteDemo extends MIDlet implements
   CommandListener {
  Form mainForm = new Form ("StockQuotes");
  TextField symbolField = new TextField ("Symbol", "IBM",
     5, TextField.ANY);
  StringItem resultItem = new StringItem ("", "");
  Command getCommand = new Command ("Get", Command.SCREEN,
     1 ) ;

  public StockQuoteDemo () {
    mainForm.append (symbolField);
    mainForm.append (resultItem);
    mainForm.addCommand (getCommand);
    mainForm.setCommandListener (this);
  }

  public void startApp () {
    Display.getDisplay (this).setCurrent (mainForm);
  }

  public void pauseApp () { }

  public void destroyApp (boolean unconditional) { }
```

When a command event is generated, the method shown in Listing 12.5 is called. The symbol from the input field is built into a SOAP message that executes an RPC call on a web service at the xmethods.net site. The result returned is displayed as a String.

Listing 12.5: **The Method that Sends a SOAP Message**

```java
public void commandAction (Command c, Displayable d) {
  try {
    String symbol = symbolField.getString ();
    resultItem.setLabel (symbol);
    SoapObject rpc = new SoapObject
     ("urn:xmethods-delayed-quotes", "getQuote");

    rpc.addProperty ("symbol", symbol);
    resultItem.setText (""+new HttpTransport(
```

```
      "http://services.xmethods.net/soap",
      "urn:xmethods-delayed-quotes#getQuote").call (rpc));
  }
  catch (Exception e) {
    e.printStackTrace ();
    resultItem.setLabel ("Error:");
    resultItem.setText (e.toString ());
  }
}

  /** for me4se command line test */
  public static void main (String [] argv) {
    new StockQuoteDemo ().startApp ();
  }
}
```

Now that you have seen the code for a wireless SOAP application, let's look at how this code gets turned into a working application.

Creating the Project

The J2MEWTK imposes some restrictions on your development environment setup. It is best to let the KToolBar utility create the directories in the course of creating a new project. Start the utility by executing the ktoolbar.bat file in the bin directory of your J2MEWTK installation. Figure 12.1 shows the initial interface display.

FIGURE 12.1:

The *KToolBar* utility interface

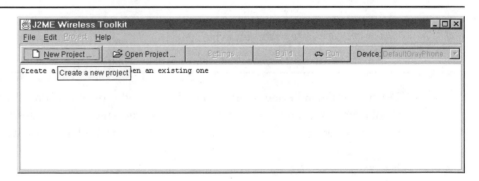

Now would be a good time to configure the preferences; from the Edit menu, select the Preferences option. The dialog lets you choose the phone emulator to be used, configure proxy information for your Internet connection, and select various debugging options. See the UsersGuide file that is included in the distribution for more details.

Clicking the New Project button brings up a dialog that requests a project name and the name of the midlet class. Use SoapStockDemo for the project and StockQuoteDemo for the class. The utility then creates a SoapStockDemo subdirectory in the apps directory.

Because all classes used in a midlet must be compiled, preverified, and packaged together, you can't simply include jar files for the kXML and kSOAP classes in the project. Instead, you must place all of the source code for these packages and the `SoapStockDemo.java` file from the kSOAP distribution under the `src` directory in a typical Java directory structure, as illustrated here:

```
J2MEWTK
    +-- bin  (batch and exe files)
    +-- apps  (project files)
        +-- SoapStockDemo
            +-- res
            +-- bin
            +-- classes
            +-- tmpclasses
            +-- src    (StockQuoteDemo.java here)
                +-- org
                    +-- kobjects (etc. - source code)
                    +-- ksoap
                    +-- kxml
```

With the project directory structure filled, you can select the Settings option to see the midlet descriptor parameters the toolkit has created for the project. Just leave these at the default values.

Compiling and Building

With the project source files in place, you can select the Build option from the toolbar. The utility will compile all of the classes, run the preverification utility, and finally create the jar and jad files. Assuming there are no compilation errors, you should get a display like that shown in Figure 12.2.

FIGURE 12.2:
Successful compila-
tion of the *SoapStock-
Demo* project

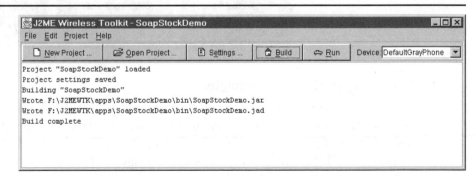

Executing in the Phone Emulator

It's time to run the utility that emulates a cell phone capable of an Internet connection. Ensure that your connection to the Internet is open and select the Run option from the toolbar. The emulator should appear and show something like the left phone in Figure 12.3.

Because the phone being emulated does not have a touch screen, you have to use the emulated controls. Click the center of the scrolling control directly below the emulated screen to run the demo.

You should get a display like the center phone in Figure 12.3. Now click the control right below the word "Get." If all goes well, you should get a result like the phone on the right in Figure 12.3.

FIGURE 12.3:

Three stages of emulating the *Soap-StockDemo*

Executing in the Palm Emulator

Sun has finally (October 2001) created an official release of a J2ME edition for the highly popular Palm operating system. You can download the MIDP for Palm OS version 1.0 FCS from this site:

        http://java.sun.com/products/midp4palm/index.html

This download does not include an emulator because Palm already has the well-supported Palm OS Emulator (POSE) emulator as a free developer tool. You can download this from:

        http://www.palmos.com/dev/tech/tools/emulator/

Setting up Java on a Palm

The Sun package provides a Java manager as a Palm application that provides full MIDP support for all Java midlets installed on a Palm. It is installed like any other application from the Palm desktop utility. The Java virtual machine and library support takes about 590K of your Palm's memory.

The Java manager shows up on your Palm screen as Java HQ. The first time you run it, you will be asked to accept Sun's license. With Java HQ controls you can set preferences for various aspects of the way midlets run on the Palm.

For development purposes, it is much easier to experiment using the POSE emulator. With the emulator running, you can load the Java manager prc file and save that POSE configuration. The following is great place to discuss problems with wireless development:

```
http://developer.java.sun.com/developer/products/wireless/
```

Converting the *SoapStockDemo*

All you have to do to get the midlet you created and ran in the Wireless Toolkit loaded onto a Palm is to convert the jar and jad files into the Palm prc format. This is done with the converter utility provided in the midp4palm download. This utility works from the command line, but it is easier to run with the GUI interface.

A batch file to execute the converter is in the converter subdirectory of your MIDP4Palm installation. However, the simplest thing to do is to open an MS-DOS prompt window, change to the converter subdirectory, and execute the following command line:

```
javaw -jar Converter.jar
```

You should get a window with instructions, as shown in Figure 12.4.

FIGURE 12.4:
Controls for the PRC
Converter utility

The PRC Converter Tool converts Java applications (**MIDlets**) into .prc files that can be installed onto Palm OS devices. MIDlets are composed of two parts: a .jad and .jar file.

Click on the 🗁 icon to find .jad/.jar files to convert to a .prc.

With the jar and jad files converted to a prc file, simply install the prc file on your Palm with the desktop utility or install it in the POSE emulator. Figure 12.5 shows the SoapStock-Demo running on the POSE emulator.

FIGURE 12.5:

The Palm emulator running the *Soap-StockDemo*

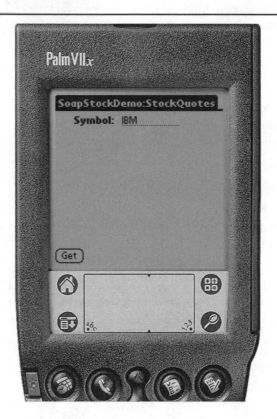

Java Is Ideal for Wireless

The use of Java on wireless devices such as cell phones and PDAs is increasing rapidly. It is feasible right now to implement SOAP services on wireless client devices.

Because of their display limitations, these devices must communicate with specialized web services, where Java is also the main technology in use. Naturally, SOAP will play a big part in these web services, but the extent to which wireless devices will actually communicate in SOAP messages as opposed to communicating with specialized web servers that use SOAP to assemble information is not yet clear.

CHAPTER 13

Situating SOAP in the Computing Landscape

- What is being done with SOAP right now

- The current situation with standards

- What is likely to be done with SOAP in the near future

- Technologies that compete with SOAP

With so much activity going on in the XML, SOAP, and web services arenas, it is kind of difficult to see any big picture emerging. In this final chapter, I will attempt to sketch out three landscapes: SOAP in the present, SOAP in the near future, and SOAP in a few years.

SOAP's Current Status

Right now, SOAP is not doing a whole lot of real work compared to the total volume of electronic messages. SOAP is all over the place in plans for the future, but in the short-term time frame (the first quarter of 2002), most services that companies expose over the Internet are still going to be based on the old standards of HTML pages, CGI processes, and e-mail.

I looked over the listings of 126 public SOAP service sites at www.xmethods.com and found that about one-third represented potentially useful services. Most of the rest were obviously more in the line of "proof of concept." Another interesting statistic from this list is that about one-quarter of the services were using a Microsoft SOAP tool, including .NET. Apache SOAP was the second most commonly used package, with Delphi not far behind. More than 30 different kinds of SOAP servers appear in that list.

As another measure of current activity, I took a look at this site, which tries to track development of SOAP implementations:

```
http://www.soapware.org/directory/4/implementations
```

In November 2001, there were 79 entries in the list of known SOAP server and client implementations. A variety of languages are represented in this list.

The Standards Framework

As you go up the hierarchy of complexity from basic XML to higher-level standardization, you find that many of the parts required for large-scale use of SOAP are not worked out well. Although many people are working with SOAP as defined in the SOAP 1.1 or 1.2 documentation, the XML Protocol group is still debating many essential points.

As discussed in Chapter 10, "SOAP and .NET," Microsoft feels that additional standards are needed to clarify and extend the existing SOAP specifications to make it really usable. The areas in which standards are proposed are as follows:

Routing   To define the use of the SOAP Header tag to control the path by which a message is passed from node to node.

Referral   To define how a SOAP intermediary can be allowed to dynamically alter the routing information.

Security   Standardization is needed in the areas of authentication, ensuring that SOAP messages have not been inappropriately altered, and encryption is needed to protect messages from snoopers.

Just to give you an idea of how many interrelated standardization efforts are underway, the current list of existing recommendations and active working groups at `www.w3.org` includes XML, XML Base, XML Encryption, XML Protocol, XML Query, XML Schema, XML Signature, XPath, XPointer, XSL, and XSLT.

It seems to me that lack of final standards in some of these areas is one of the factors preventing widespread use of SOAP at present. The large-scale frameworks, such as ebXML, for which SOAP is only a message format, still seem to be defining themselves. As far as I can tell, there is no major example application integrating SOAP into a larger framework.

Performance Problems

Many developers are worried about performance, in terms of the number of SOAP requests a service can handle per minute. Certainly, the Apache SOAP 2.2 package for SOAP messages over HTTP connections is no speed demon. This is not surprising, considering the fact that the package always parses a complete DOM. Given the number of XML elements that the DOM creates during parsing of a simple request, object creation, and subsequent garbage collection impose an irreducible processing load, no matter how simple the request.

The new vision of web services being promoted by Microsoft and others has large documents being moved about. If SOAP is to be the enabling technology for this, it must be with a version that does not require large documents in memory.

The Apache AXIS project represents a complete revision of the DOM approach, but because the project is still in an alpha state as of this writing, I can't say how much performance improvement will be achieved.

High-speed SOAP message processing programs are just now beginning to appear, typically incorporated into a web services product. It seems likely that we will be seeing a lot of competition for the title of fastest SOAP engine. However, without any recognized benchmark exercises, it will be hard to compare claims.

SOAP and Web Services

Microsoft would like you to think that SOAP with .NET is the real path to web services. People using Java for SOAP or Java for XML-RPC would naturally disagree. In reality, there seem to be many possible paths to web services. I think we should avoid defining web services too narrowly. Perhaps the best short definition would be "any service that can be described with WSDL."

The one thing that does appear certain is that XML is being used right now as the standard of choice for a variety of functions. XML has almost completely replaced a variety of systems for configuration of server applications—for example, in the web.xml files used by Java servlet engines to configure web applications. Content management, as in the Apache organization Cocoon2 project, is another area where XML seems to have a secure place.

The Future of Web Services

The magic words "web services" seem to mean a lot of different things to different people. In fact, many people suspect that web services will turn out to be another cycle of dotCOM mania like "portals" and selling furniture and groceries over the Web. Organizations that got scared by the dotCOM fallout will be reluctant to move quickly into integrating web services into their business plan.

Generally, industry pundits expect that communication inside corporate networks will be the real SOAP application market in the near future. Within a company, developers don't have to worry so much about operation with a wide variety of SOAP servers. Also, it is easier to identify the real customers and benefits inside an organization.

It seems likely that due to the availability of WSDL toolkits from multiple vendors, the average Java programmer may never have to write code that deals directly with a SOAP message. Instead, a utility will handle creating Java classes. For example, see Sun's JAXB project:

```
http://java.sun.com/xml/jaxb/index.html
```

The intent of this project is to create an architecture that provides an API and tools to automate mapping between XML documents and Java objects. It will generate classes to handle all the details of XML parsing and formatting, and it will even ensure that the constraints expressed in the XML schema are enforced.

Standardization Efforts

A number of standardization efforts related to XML, SOAP, and web services should be bearing fruit in the next few years. The XMLP working group should certainly be finished shortly after this book is published. However, there are many other standardization efforts related to the eventual form of web services currently underway.

For example, the OASIS (Organization for the Advancement of Structured Information Standards) group has recently formed a committee on the Web Services Component Model that expects to be working for one to two years. You can read further about this effort at:

```
http://www.oasis-open.org/committees/wscm/
```

One perhaps-unexpected obstacle to the wider use of web services with wireless devices is that they are restricted mainly to the United States. The variety of wireless standards for mobile phones has created obstacles to seamless communication with web services. In countries where only a single standard is used, the market is much better developed.

The Announced Web Server Projects

In the near future, the results of the initial releases of commercial systems with web service capability should emerge. Case studies on the application of .NET, Sun One, Oracle, IBM WebSphere, and HP's Web Services Platform should become available.

The Apache organization's major redesign, the AXIS project, will likely be replacing the Apache SOAP project as the platform of choice for Java programmers creating their own web servers in the near future.

XML Well Established

Everybody involved in trying to figure out exactly what "web services" is going to mean seem to at least agree that XML is the language of choice for describing and delivering whatever it is they are delivering. The JAXP XML package will be incorporated into the next release of Java. There is also some chance that the JDOM API will be an optional extension. The website for JDOM is at:

```
http://www.jdom.org
```

I am sure that every Java programmer will be glad to settle on some standardized APIs, because problems with parser incompatibility seem to be the cause of a large fraction of problems currently reported on SOAP user newsletters.

The Near Term Competitors for SOAP

It seems extremely unlikely to me that SOAP messaging will replace Java RMI API for object communication on closely coupled networks, especially because RMI is one of the core technologies for J2EE servers. RMI serialization of objects avoids many of the extra steps that are involved in SOAP serialization, so they will always be faster.

A strong competitor with SOAP in more loosely coupled but still all-Java systems is the Java Message Service (JMS). JMS has object-transmission capabilities and has the additional advantage of close integration with the latest J2EE through message-driven beans. However, as I demonstrated in Chapter 8, "SOAP Architecture Using Messages," SOAP messages can easily be transmitted via JMS, so perhaps SOAP and JMS will peacefully coexist.

Jini Project

Sun's vision of loosely coupled cooperating processes, as embodied in the Jini project, seems to be a valid competitor for SOAP messaging in all-Java systems. A primary advantage is that it can handle sending code as well as messages. Interfacing Jini systems to SOAP-based web services can easily be done and has lots of advantages.

Chapter 8 showed that JavaSpaces, as implemented in Sun's Jini project, can easily be used for SOAP messages. Perhaps we will see all-Java systems communicating with the outside world using SOAP messages simply because they can easily be turned into JavaSpaces messages.

CORBA

CORBA (Common Object Request Broker Architecture) is a system that permits RPC style communication between objects on different systems based on well accepted and understood standards. Before SOAP came along, CORBA was the dominant technology for this type of communication.

CORBA is widely considered to be a rather difficult technology to master. Furthermore, CORBA implementations vary considerably between vendor implementations. Thus SOAP has advantages of better standardization and simpler APIs.

The Object Management Group (OMG) has a technical committee working on specifications for mapping SOAP-formatted messages to CORBA syntax so that SOAP-based services will be able to talk to CORBA-based services directly. You can find the current status of this proposal at the OMG website:

```
http://www.omg.org
```

Because many companies have made major investments in CORBA systems, it seems likely that CORBA will not be replaced by SOAP anytime soon.

SOAP's Future

More than one or two years out, my crystal ball gets hazy. One of the biggest patches of fog has to do with Microsoft. The key to acceptance of Microsoft's My Services vision is likely to be the degree of public acceptance of Passport as a centralized repository/authentication site. A substantial income stream from Passport would tend to encourage more web services sharing the My Services API. This success would naturally encourage more developers to work with SOAP, WSDL, and UDDI.

Marketing pundits confidently predict that the rise of very low-cost wireless connectivity will bring about a world in which a typical person will have computing resources distributed from local appliances to the World Wide Web, all talking together and cooperating. When the cost per byte of message transmission becomes insignificant, SOAP messages may be the method of choice for communication between all of these different platforms.

Finally, I feel that in the future most Java developers using SOAP will not normally be composing SOAP messages by plugging together Java objects by hand. Instead, WSDL- and UDDI-related tools will take care of the details. However, developers will still need to know the details of how SOAP works in order to chase down bugs and develop specialized object serialization handling.

Appendix A

SOAP Resources

- XML standards and standards groups

- Web service standards and implementations

- Related Java APIs

- XML toolkits in Java

- Industry news sources

T his appendix provides pointers to SOAP-related documents, articles, code, and information on the Internet.

Standards

The World Wide Web Consortium (W3C) is the lead organization for standardizing high-level web communication protocols. The original SOAP proposal was submitted as a W3C Note on May 8, 2000. The original text can be found at:

    http://www.w3.org/TR/2000/Note-SOAP-20000508

XML Protocol Working Group

Rather than directly adopting SOAP as a standard, the W3C decided to create an XML Protocol Working Group to further develop SOAP under the XP acronym. The working group currently consists of 72 members representing 42 organizations. The basic organization is described on the XML Protocol Working Group home page at:

    http://www.w3.org/2000/xp/Group/

The initial aims of the group are described in the first draft requirements document at:

    http://www.w3.org/TR/2000/WD-xp-reqs-20001219/

The first significant document from this group was the December 11, 2000 Note titled "SOAP Messages with Attachments." It was the addition of the specification for attachments that prompted the ebXML (Electronic Business XML) group to adopt SOAP as a message transport format, so this is a significant document. It can be found at:

    http://www.w3.org/TR/2000/NOTE-SOAP-attachments-20001211

As of this writing, the current XP requirements document is a draft dated March 19, 2001. The latest version can be found at:

    http://www.w3.org/TR/xp-reqs/

The XML Protocol Working Group produced a Working Draft of a SOAP 1.2 specification, released July 9, 2001. This document contains significant changes from the SOAP 1.1 note. It can be found at:

    http://www.w3.org/TR/2001/WD-soap12-20010709/

Another document of interest is the XML Protocol Abstract Model. A Working Draft was released July 9, 2001, and the latest version can be found at:

    http://www.w3.org/TR/xmlp-am/

The conclusion one can draw from reading the XP group working documents is that they are gradually approaching a consensus, but a lot remains unsettled at this time.

XML Schema

After a long development period by the XML Schema Working Group (`http://www.w3.org/XML/Schema`), XML Schema was approved (May 2, 2001) as a W3C Recommendation. There are three documents available: "Schema Part 0: Primer," "Schema Part 1: Structures and XML," and "Schema Part 2: Data Types." These documents are to be found at these sites:

```
http://www.w3.org/TR/xmlschema-0/
http://www.w3.org/TR/xmlschema-1/
http://www.w3.org/TR/xmlschema-2/
```

This is admittedly heavy reading, and you may find some of the informal collections of schema information to be easier to cope with. The following site maintained by Robin Cover (who deserves the thanks of an entire industry for the effort) is very up-to-date:

```
http://www.oasis-open.org/cover/schemas.html
```

Other W3C Resources

This tabular summary of various XML-based protocols was originally created in March 2000, but it has been updated from time to time:

```
http://www.w3.org/2000/03/29-XML-protocol-matrix
```

XML Information Set and XML Base

The XML Information Set document provides a set of definitions that will probably end up in subsequent SOAP standards. Sometimes called the xml-infoset, the current document can be found here:

```
http://www.w3.org/TR/xml-infoset
```

Another definition that may find its way into SOAP is XML Base. Rather like the HTML Base tag, it defines the base for URIs in a SOAP document.

```
http://www.w3.org/TR/xmlbase/
```

Semantic Web Effort

The W3C has a long-term research project based on the idea of the "Semantic Web." The Semantic Web is a vision of a future Web in which data is identified and linked in such a way that it can be used both for the current functions of browsing by humans as well as for automation, integration, and reuse of data. Obviously, widespread use of the SOAP protocol would be a big help in achieving this goal.

A good place to start with the Semantic Web project is the charter for the coordination group at:

```
http://www.w3.org/2001/sw/CGcharter
```

Part of the Semantic Web project is frequently referred to as RDF (Resource Description Framework). Current status of this project is at:

```
http://www.w3.org/RDF/
```

Related Standards

There are a lot of other standardization efforts that are closely related to SOAP. To help you navigate in this maze, I have tried to find the most significant efforts.

Web Services Description Language (WSDL)

You can think of WSDL as the next step in the hierarchy of abstraction above SOAP. With the tools that are appearing, you may be able to define a simple web service in WSDL and have the SOAP processing code produced automatically.

Here is a collection of references for WSDL:

```
http://xml.coverpages.org/wsdl.html
```

A highly useful cross-indexed set of specification including WSDL is at:

```
http://www.zvon.org/xxl/WSDL1.1/Output/index.html
```

Universal Description, Discovery, and Integration (UDDI)

UDDI is intended to be the yellow pages equivalent for web services. You can think of it as the next stage of abstraction above WSDL. The standard is widely supported in the industry. The primary site for locating standards, APIs, and other documents can be found at:

```
http://www.uddi.org
```

Be sure to take a look at this:

```
http://www.uddi.org/bestpractices.html
```

UDDI sites, including test UDDI registry resources by the major web services players, are at:

```
http://www.ibm.com/services/uddi/
http://uddi.microsoft.com
```

The Internet Engineering Task Force (IETF)

This organization works on standards that are generally closer to hardware than things like the SOAP protocol:

```
http://www.ietf.org
```

For example, the following document discusses the use of SOAP with the BEEP (Blocks Extensible Exchange Protocol) protocol instead of HTTP:

```
http://search.ietf.org/internet-drafts/draft-etal-beep-soap-03.txt
```

Sun, OASIS, UN/CEFACT, and ebXML

OASIS (Organization for the Advancement of Structured Information Standards) is a non-profit, international consortium that creates interoperable industry specifications based on public standards such as XML and SGML, as well as others that are related to structured information processing. The ebXML (Electronic Business XML) standard is maintained by OASIS and UN/CEFACT (United Nations Centre for Trade Facilitation and Electronic Business). The main websites are at:

```
http://www.oasis-open.org
http://www.unece.org/cefact/
```

The ebXML standard can be found at:

```
http://www.ebxml.org/specs/index.htm
```

SOAP is recognized as the basis for a message service for ebXML messages.

Major backers of ebXML in addition to OASIS and UN/CEFACT include Sun and IBM. Microsoft barely recognizes its existence, preferring to push the BizTalk standard.

Sun's JAXM API

Sun has created Java APIs for XML Messaging (JAXM) as part of the ebXML development effort:

```
http://java.sun.com/xml/jaxm/index.html
```

JAXM supports SOAP 1.1 with attachments and is expected to become part of the Java standard extensions. Further development of this API is under the control of the Java Community Process; see the following for the current status:

```
http://jcp.org/jsr/detail/067.jsp
```

XML Toolkits

It seems like everybody has jumped into creating XML-related Java toolkits. In this section, I try to hit the high points.

Apache XML

The Apache organization has so many XML-related initiatives going that the best thing to do is to go to this site and browse:

```
http://xml.apache.org/
```

The Xerces parser and Xalan XSLT processor are particularly well regarded in the industry. All of these projects have source code available if you want to delve into the workings of XML processing.

Sun's JAXP Package

The intent of the JAXP API is to provide a uniform way to specify and get an instance of an XML parser with particular characteristics. Although it ships with DOM and SAX parsers from the Apache project, the idea is that any compatible parser could be plugged in without changing the application code. The primary site is at:

    http://java.sun.com/xml/jaxp.html

The 1.1 release meets SAX level 2 and DOM level 2 API requirements. Furthermore, it contains an XSLT processor. It is planned that JAXP will be part of the 1.4 release of the Java standard edition.

JDOM

JDOM was created in an attempt to provide an API for manipulation of XML that is closer to normal Java practice and easier to use than the W3C DOM approach. The primary website is at:

    http://www.jdom.org

Track the status of JDOM as a potential standard component of Java at:

    http://java.sun.com/aboutJava/communityprocess/jsr/jsr_102_jdom.html

Perl Language

Because Perl is oriented toward text processing, it is not surprising that the Perl programming community has developed modules for rapid processing of XML. A good starting point for using Perl with SOAP is at:

    http://www.soaplite.com

This version of the SOAP::Lite module collection supports most of the SOAP 1.1, SOAP 1.2, and SOAP Messages with Attachments specifications. For a quick introduction to using Perl for SOAP, go to:

    http://www.perl.com/pub/a/2001/01/soap.html

Integration with Oracle Database

Support for Java and XML is integrated in the Oracle 9i database:

    http://www.oracle.com/ip/deploy/database/9i/xmljava/index.html

Oracle also sells a web server based on Apache that supports SOAP:

    http://otn.oracle.com/products/ias/http/ohs-ds-v1022.html

General SOAP Articles

The following is an introductory-level article by Don Box; it assumes you are familiar with Microsoft COM and XML:

```
http://msdn.microsoft.com/msdnmag/issues/0300/soap/soap.asp
```

Here is one that assumes you are familiar with Visual Basic and XML (it may be a little out-of-date):

```
http://msdn.microsoft.com/msdnmag/issues/01/02/webcomp/webcomp.asp
```

Here is IBM's view of the rapidly changing world of web services and SOAP. This is the first of a continuing column and is full of good references.

```
http://www.ibm.com/developerworks/webservices/library/ws-ref1.html
```

Many SOAP FAQ (Frequently Asked Questions) sites have sprung up. Here are a few of them:

```
http://soap.manilasites.com
http://xml.apache.org/soap/faq/faq_chawke.html
http://www.develop.com/soap/
```

SOAP and Related Implementations

These organizations sell proprietary web services/application server toolkits that implement SOAP. In some cases, free downloads are available for developers. These systems are not necessarily Java based.

```
http://www.alphaworks.ibm.com/tech/wsde
```

```
http://www.systinet.com
```
 (includes UDDI and WSDI tools)

Here is a general entry point for Microsoft SOAP toolkits, and so on:

```
http://msdn.microsoft.com/soap/
```

The GLUE web services development system supports UDDI and WSDL and includes a high-speed XML parser:

```
http://www.themindelectric.com
```

An XML-based web content management system supporting SOAP is at:

```
http://frontier.userland.com
```

A SOAP client for Windows operating systems, originally developed for the PocketPC is at:

```
http://www.pocketsoap.com/pocketsoap/
```

The following organization sells web services platforms with full WSDL and UDDI support that can be integrated with popular Java IDEs:

```
http://www.systinet.com/products/index.html
```

UDDI Implementations

The following site discusses IBM's open source Java support for UDDI services:

`http://www.ibm.com/developerworks/webservices/library/ws-uddi4j.html`

Other Java UDDI implementations are combined in more complete web services development packages.

Interoperability Related Sites

Because SOAP is intended to be a universally acceptable XML message protocol, interoperability between the various implementations has been a major concern. Sites collecting recent interoperability test results and issues are at:

`http://www.apache.org/~rubys/ApacheClientInterop.html`
`http://www.xmethods.net/soapbuilders/interop.html`

The following site has a nice general discussion of interoperability problems and workarounds:

`http://www.perfectxml.com/articles/xml/soapguide.asp`

Web Services Development Using SOAP

Microsoft's early entry in the business to business server field is at:

`http://www.microsoft.com/biztalk/`

The GLUE package for web service development includes WSDL and UDDI facilities as well as utilities to expose any Java object for SOAP RPC:

`http://www.themindelectric.com`

XMLBus development framework for web services by IONA Technologies is at:

`http://www.xmlbus.com`

Hewlett-Packard's new Web Services Platform supports ebXML, WSDL, UDDI, and SOAP:

`http://h20008.www2.hp.com`

Industry News Sources

This site claims to be a vendor-neutral portal devoted to news and discussion of web services concepts, including SOAP, UDDI, .NET, Sun ONE, IBM, and ebXML:

`http://webservices.org`

Here is another site for general web services and SOAP information and resources including .NET, UDDI, Sun ONE, and HP:

`http://www.soaprpc.com`

The following site features an enormous number of resources on SOAP and web services in general:

```
http://www.webservices.org/
```

A general site for the Java/J2EE approach to web services is at:

```
http://theserverside.com/home/index.jsp
```

A site maintained by Dave Winer, one of the originators of XML-RPC and SOAP, is at:

```
http://soap.weblogs.com
```

Appendix B

SOAP Services Online

- Currency conversion service

- Text-to-speech service

- Geographic information service (GIS)

A large number of programmers are experimenting with SOAP and putting up example services. In this appendix, I look at three of them that I found listed at:

http://www.xmethods.net

These examples were chosen because they represent three types of web services that are likely to have commercial application. The currency conversion service makes use of the most recent figures for rapidly changing variables. The text-to-speech service is an example of applying a custom mathematical operation. The geographic information service (GIS) is an example of providing access to a complex database.

Currency Conversion Service

This is an example of a service that could become essential in many areas of electronic commerce. It has been created as a technology demonstration by Shinka Technologies. The service provides the current exchange rate for a variety of European currencies. The WSDL file shown in Listing B.1 describes the service. Note that some lines were broken arbitrarily to fit this page.

Listing B.1: **The WSDL File for the Currency Conversion Service**

```xml
<?xml version="1.0" encoding="UTF-8"?>
<definitions name="CurrencyConverter"
   targetNamespace="http://www.shinkatech.com/CurrencyConverter"
  xmlns:tns="http://www.shinkatech.com/CurrencyConverter"
  xmlns:soap="http://schemas.xmlsoap.org/wsdl/soap/"
  xmlns:SOAP-ENC="http://schemas.xmlsoap.org/soap/encoding/"
  xmlns:xsd="http://www.w3.org/2000/10/XMLSchema"
  xmlns:CurrencySchema="CurrencySchema"
  xmlns="http://schemas.xmlsoap.org/wsdl/">
<types>
  <schema xmlns="http://www.w3.org/2000/10/XMLSchema"
       targetNamespace="CurrencySchema">
  <simpleType name="CurrencySymbol" base="string">
   <enumeration value="ATS"/>
   <enumeration value="BEF"/>
   <enumeration value="DEM"/>
   <enumeration value="ESP"/>
   <enumeration value="FIM"/>
   <enumeration value="FRF"/>
   <enumeration value="GRD"/>
   <enumeration value="IEP"/>
   <enumeration value="ITL"/>
   <enumeration value="LUF"/>
   <enumeration value="NLG"/>
   <enumeration value="PTE"/>
```

```
    <enumeration value="EUR"/>
  </simpleType>
  <complexType name="ConvertMessage">
        <element name="currency" type="CurrencySymbol"/>
        <element name="amount" type="double"/>
        <element name="toCurrency" type="CurrencySymbol"/>
  </complexType>
  <complexType name="ExchangeRateList">
    <element name="ExchangeRate" type="ExchangeRate" minOccurs="0"
      maxOccurs="unbounded"/>
  </complexType>
  <complexType name="ExchangeRate">
    <element name="symbol" type="CurrencySymbol"/>
    <element name="rate" type="double"/>
    <element name="name" type="string"/>
  </complexType>
</schema>
</types>
<message name="getCurrenciesOutput">
    <part name="result" type="CurrencySchema:ExchangeRateList"/>
</message>
<message name="calculateExchangeRateInput">
    <part name="convert" type="CurrencySchema:ConvertMessage"/>
</message>
<message name="calculateExchangeRateOutput">
    <part name="amount" type="xsd:double"/>
</message>
<message name="void"/>
<portType name="CurrencyConverterPortType">
  <operation name="getCurrencies">
      <input message="tns:void"/>
      <output message="tns:getCurrenciesOutput"/>
  </operation>
  <operation name="calculateExchangeRate">
      <input message="tns:calculateExchangeRateInput"/>
      <output message="tns:calculateExchangeRateOutput"/>
  </operation>
</portType>
<binding name="CurrencyConverterSoapBinding"
    type="tns:CurrencyConverterPortType">
 <soap:binding style="rpc"
    transport="http://schemas.xmlsoap.org/soap/http"/>
 <operation name="getCurrencies">
   <soap:operation
     soapAction="http://www.shinkatech.com/CurrencyConverter/
     action/CurrencyConverter.getCurrencies"/>
   <input>
    <soap:body use="encoded"
  namespace="http://www.shinkatech.com/CurrencyConverter/message/"
  encodingStyle="http://schemas.xmlsoap.org/soap/encoding/"/>
   </input>
```

```
      <output>
          <soap:body use="encoded"
 namespace="http://www.shinkatech.com/CurrencyConverter/message/"
 encodingStyle="http://schemas.xmlsoap.org/soap/encoding/"/>
        </output>
      </operation>
      <operation name="calculateExchangeRate">
        <soap:operation
         soapAction="http://www.shinkatech.com/CurrencyConverter/
         action/CurrencyConverter.calculateExchangeRate"/>
        <input>
            <soap:body use="encoded"
   namespace="http://www.shinkatech.com/CurrencyConverter/message/"
   encodingStyle="http://schemas.xmlsoap.org/soap/encoding/"/>
        </input>
        <output>
          <soap:body use="encoded"
   namespace="http://www.shinkatech.com/CurrencyConverter/message/"
   encodingStyle="http://schemas.xmlsoap.org/soap/encoding/"/>
        </output>
      </operation>
    </binding>
    <service name="CurrencyConverter">
        <port name="CurrencyConverterPort0"
          binding="tns:CurrencyConverterSoapBinding">
          <soap:address location="http://212.99.131.154:7300/"/>
        </port>
    </service>
 </definitions>
```

Listing B.2 shows an example message to the `calculateExchangeRate` method requesting the rate for conversion of 100 deutsche marks to euros. This message is based on an example posted by Shinka Technologies at:

```
http://www.shinkatech.com/interop/Interop.phtml
```

Note that this request does not use schema designations of the variable types for the request parameters in the actual elements.

Listing B.2:   **A SOAP RPC to the Currency Converter Service**

```
POST / HTTP/1.1
Content-Type: text/xml
Host: localhost
SOAPAction: "http://www.shinkatech.com/CurrencyConverter/
     action/CurrencyConverter.calculateExchangeRate"
Content-Length: 538

<?xml version="1.0" encoding="UTF-8" standalone="no"?>
```

```
<SOAP-ENV:Envelope
  SOAP-ENV:encodingStyle="http://schemas.xmlsoap.org/soap/encoding/"
  xmlns:SOAP-ENV="http://schemas.xmlsoap.org/soap/envelope/">
<SOAP-ENV:Body>
  <m:calculateExchangeRate
    xmlns:m="http://www.shinkatech.com/CurrencyConverter/message/">
    <convert>
      <currency>DEM</currency>
      <amount>100</amount>
      <toCurrency>EUR</toCurrency>
    </convert>
  </m:calculateExchangeRate>
</SOAP-ENV:Body>
</SOAP-ENV:Envelope>
```

Listing B.3 shows the response to this request, with the single long line that was actually received from the service split to fit the page.

Listing B.3: **The Response Currency Conversion Message**

```
HTTP/1.1 200 OK
Server: Shinka-IS/1.2.102
Date: Mon Aug 20 16:30:15 CEST 2001
Content-Type: text/xml
Content-Length: 390
Connection: close

<?xml version="1.0" encoding="UTF-8" standalone="no"?>
<SOAP:Envelope
  xmlns:SOAP="http://schemas.xmlsoap.org/soap/envelope/"
SOAP:encodingStyle="http://schemas.xmlsoap.org/soap/encoding/">
<SOAP:Body>
<m:calculateExchangeRateResponse
 xmlns:m="http://www.shinkatech.com/CurrencyConverter/message/">
<amount>51.12918811962185</amount>
</m:calculateExchangeRateResponse>
</SOAP:Body>
</SOAP:Envelope>
```

Text to Speech Service

This service converts a text string to an encoded string representing a WAV file. The service is provided by ObjectSpace, Inc., a pioneer in distributed systems and creators of web service development tools. The general website for ObjectSpace is www.objectspace.com.

Listing B.4: **The Text to Speech Service WSDL**

```xml
<?xml version="1.0" encoding="UTF-8"?>
<definitions name="TTSService"
  targetNamespace="http://testvger.objectspace.com/TTSService"
  xmlns="http://schemas.xmlsoap.org/wsdl/"
  xmlns:soap="http://schemas.xmlsoap.org/wsdl/soap/"
  xmlns:tns="http://testvger.objectspace.com/TTSService"
    xmlns:xsd="http://www.w3.org/1999/XMLSchema">

<message
      name="IngetBase64WaveRequest">
  <part name="text"
      type="xsd:string"/>
  <part name="speed"
      type="xsd:float"/>
  <part name="pitch"
      type="xsd:float"/>
  <part name="volume"
    type="xsd:float"/>
</message>

<message
      name="OutgetBase64WaveResponse">
  <part name="Base64WaveString"
    type="xsd:string"/>
</message>

<message
      name="IngetBase64WaveRequest2">
  <part name="text"
    type="xsd:string"/>
</message>
<message
      name="OutgetBase64WaveResponse2">
  <part name="Base64WaveString"
    type="xsd:string"/>
</message>
<portType
      name="TTSService">
  <operation name="getBase64Wave">
    <input
        message="IngetBase64WaveRequest"/>
    <output
      message="OutgetBase64WaveResponse"/>
  </operation>
  <operation
        name="getBase64Wave">
    <input
        message="IngetBase64WaveRequest2"/>
    <output
      message="OutgetBase64WaveResponse2"/>
  </operation>
```

```
</portType>
<binding
    name="TTSServiceBinding" type="TTSService">
  <soap:binding
      style="rpc"
      transport="http://schemas.xmlsoap.org/soap/http"/>
  <operation
        name="getBase64Wave">
    <soap:operation
          soapAction="urn:TTSService"/>
    <input>
      <soap:body
        encodingStyle="http://schemas.xmlsoap.org/soap/encoding/"
        namespace="urn:TTSService"
        use="encoded"/>
    </input>
    <output>
      <soap:body
        encodingStyle="http://schemas.xmlsoap.org/soap/encoding/"
        namespace="urn:TTSService"
      use="encoded"/>
    </output>
  </operation>
  <operation
      name="getBase64Wave">
    <soap:operation
          soapAction="urn:TTSService"/>
    <input>
      <soap:body
      encodingStyle="http://schemas.xmlsoap.org/soap/encoding/"
      namespace="urn:TTSService"
      use="encoded"/>
    </input>
    <output>
      <soap:body
        encodingStyle="http://schemas.xmlsoap.org/soap/encoding/"
        namespace="urn:TTSService" use="encoded"/>
    </output>
  </operation>
</binding>

<service
      name="TTSService">
  <documentation>A Text-To-Speech Web Service</documentation>
  <port
      binding="TTSServiceBinding"
        name="TTSServicePort">
    <soap:address
location="http://testvger.objectspace.com/soap/servlet/rpcrouter"/>
  </port>
</service>
</definitions>
```

The SOAP request shown in Listing B.5 was based on the WSDL and dispatched to the service at:

```
http://testvger.objectspace.com/soap/servlet/rpcrouter
```

Listing B.5: **SOAP Request Sent to the TTSService**

```
POST /soap/servlet/rpcrouter HTTP/1.1
Content-Type: text/xml
Host: localhost
SOAPAction: ""
Content-Length: 352

<?xml version="1.0" encoding="UTF-8" standalone="no"?>
<SOAP-ENV:Envelope
 xmlns:SOAP-ENV="http://schemas.xmlsoap.org/soap/envelope/"
 xmlns:SOAP-ENC="http://schemas.xmlsoap.org/soap/encoding/"
  xmlns:xsi="http://www.w3.org/2001/XMLSchema-instance"
  xmlns:xsd="http://www.w3.org/2001/XMLSchema">
<SOAP-ENV:Body>
<urn:getBase64Wave xmlns:urn="urn:TTSService" use="encoded">
    <stra xsi:type="xsd:string">Greetings</stra>
</urn:getBase64Wave>
</SOAP-ENV:Body>
</SOAP-ENV:Envelope>
```

The reply was naturally rather long, so Listing B.6 has had most of the base 64–encoded speech string cut out. The continuous stream of encoded data was transmitted in 4096-character lines.

Listing B.6: **The Returned SOAP Message**

```
HTTP/1.1 200 ok
Date: Mon, 20 Aug 2001 20:08:20 GMT
Server: IBM_HTTP_Server/1.3.12.3 Apache/1.3.12 (Win32)
Set-Cookie: sesessionid=0KRZVLAMI3FFS13K3U14HUI;Path=/
Cache-Control: no-cache="set-cookie,set-cookie2"
Expires: Thu, 01 Dec 1994 16:00:00 GMT
Content-Length: 30816
Content-Type: text/xml; charset=utf-8
Content-Language: en

<?xml version='1.0' encoding='UTF-8'?>
<SOAP-ENV:Envelope xmlns:SOAP-
    ENV="http://schemas.xmlsoap.org/soap/envelope/"
    xmlns:xsi="http://www.w3.org/1999/XMLSchema-instance"
    xmlns:xsd="http://www.w3.org/1999/XMLSchema">
<SOAP-ENV:Body>
<ns1:getBase64WaveResponse xmlns:ns1="urn:TTSService" SOAP-ENV:
encodingStyle="http://schemas.xmlsoap.org/soap/encoding/">
```

```
<return
  xsi:type="xsd:string">UklGRtxYAABXQVZFZm1OIBQAAAABAAEAQB8AAIA+AAA
  CABAAAACsEmRhdGGOWAAAxABoABgA0P9s/0z/DP/s/rz+nP6c/pz+rP6s/sz+3
.. lots of base64 coding cut
</ns1:getBase64WaveResponse>

</SOAP-ENV:Body>
</SOAP-ENV:Envelope>
```

This particular example returned a type xsd:string, but other methods are defined as returning a byte[] and would thus follow the XML Schema base64 encoding.

Geographic Information Service

The GIS web service by Terra-Seek, Inc. puts a tremendous amount of geographic information online. Presently the coverage is restricted to the United States. Some of the functions that can be performed include:

- Find the nearest town or city to a latitude-longitude point

- Relate a town or city to a telephone area code

- Relate Global Positioning System (GPS) information to a neighborhood within a city

- Relate a zip code to a town or city

A starting point for locating more information about this service is at:

http://www.terraseek.com/home/gps.html

This service does not have a published WSDL. The example query shown in Listing B.7 requests the area code for Leander, Texas (a small town north of Austin).

Listing B.7:   A GIS Query for an Area Code for a City

```
POST /xmlrpc/soap_api.php HTTP/1.0
User-Agent: SOAPx4 v0.13492
Host: maui
Content-Type: text/xml
Content-Length: 732
SOAPAction: "soap-action"

<?xml version="1.0"?>
<SOAP-ENV:Envelope
 xmlns:SOAP-ENV="http://schemas.xmlsoap.org/soap/envelope/"
 xmlns:xsi="http://www.w3.org/1999/XMLSchema-instance"
 xmlns:xsd="http://www.w3.org/1999/XMLSchema"
 xmlns:SOAP-ENC="http://schemas.xmlsoap.org/soap/encoding/"
 xmlns:si="http://soapinterop.org/xsd"
 xmlns:ns6="http://testuri.org"
```

```
  SOAP-ENV:encodingStyle="http://schemas.xmlsoap.org/soap/encoding/">
<SOAP-ENV:Body>
<ns6:getAreaCode>
<return xsi:type="ns6:struct">
<city xsi:type="xsd:string">leander</city>
<state xsi:type="xsd:string">tx</state>
<zip xsi:type="xsd:string">78641</zip>
</return>
</ns6:getAreaCode>
</SOAP-ENV:Body>
</SOAP-ENV:Envelope>
```

The response is shown in Listing B.8. Note that the return schema type is an array of strings because some cities will have multiple area codes.

Listing B.8:   The Response to the Area Code Request

```
HTTP/1.1 200 OK
Date: Mon, 20 Aug 2001 02:23:45 GMT
Server: Apache/1.3.20 (Unix) PHP/4.0.6
X-Powered-By: PHP/4.0.6
Status: 200
Connection: Close
Content-Length: 603
Content-Type: text/xml; charset=UTF-8

<?xml version="1.0"?>
<SOAP-ENV:Envelope
 xmlns:SOAP-ENV="http://schemas.xmlsoap.org/soap/envelope/"
 xmlns:xsi="http://www.w3.org/1999/XMLSchema-instance"
 xmlns:xsd="http://www.w3.org/1999/XMLSchema"
 xmlns:SOAP-ENC="http://schemas.xmlsoap.org/soap/encoding/"
 xmlns:si="http://soapinterop.org/xsd"
 SOAP-ENV:encodingStyle="http://schemas.xmlsoap.org/soap/encoding/">
<SOAP-ENV:Body>
<getAreaCodeResponse>
<getAreaCode xsi:type="SOAP-ENC:Array"
    SOAP-ENC:arrayType="xsd:string[1]">
<item xsi:type="xsd:string">512</item>
</getAreaCode>
</getAreaCodeResponse>
</SOAP-ENV:Body>
</SOAP-ENV:Envelope>
```

Appendix C

Debugging SOAP
with UtilSnoop

- How to watch a client-server conversation

- Faking a SOAP client

- Debugging a SOAP client without a server

- How UtilSnoop works

One of the reasons SOAP applications are hard to debug is that a complete SOAP transaction involves so many steps. For example, with typical clients and the Apache SOAP servlets communicating with HTTP messages, you can't really tell what is passing back and forth.

The Apache SOAP 2.2 release provides the TcpTunnel and TcpTunnelGUI classes that can intercept the text of messages. However, several improvements occurred to me, resulting in the program described here.

Using *UtilSnoop*

The utility sits in the middle of a conversation between a SOAP client and server, capturing the client output and sending it on to the server and keeping a copy. Server output is treated the same way. This works because you can change the socket that a client sends to and make the utility appear to be the client as far as the server is concerned.

The complete source code is provided on the CD that accompanies this book and is also available for download from the following website:

    http://www.lanw.com/books/javasoap/

Any Java version from 1.2 on should work just fine with this code.

Rather than using command-line parameters, the program uses a setup file, so you start the utility from the command line like this:

    >java UtilSnoop

Setting Parameters

Parameters are loaded from File ➢ Load Properties. The program uses a standard java.util.Properties object to manage the settings. The properties file must set three parameters: the URL of the SOAP service or host, the port on which the host listens, and the port to which the client will send information.

Here is an example of a properties file that addresses the server as localhost:8080 and listens to the client on port 9000. In the present version, the client application and UtilSnoop are always assumed to be running on the same system, but this could be easily changed.

```
# UtilSnoop utility properties
#  snoop listens on clientport -
#  client addresses as localhost:clientport
#  snoop will connect to host:hostport
host=localhost
clientport=9000
hostport=8080
```

Snooping on Local Client-Server Conversation

This example assumes you have Apache SOAP installed, that you have tested the `addressbook` sample application and the `addressbook` service shows up on the list of deployed services.

1. From the Action menu, pick the Start Recording Both option.

2. Execute the `GetAddress` client with the port of 9000 instead of 8080 as in the following (all on one command line):

    ```
    java samples.addressbook.GetAddress
        http://localhost:9000/soap/servlet/rpcrouter "John B. Good"
    ```

3. You should see the client request appear in the top text area and, after a short delay, the server response in the bottom text area, as shown in Figure C.1. The client application will probably not process the response until you close the connection.

4. Choose Action ➤ Stop Recording. This closes both sockets, and the client should now process the results.

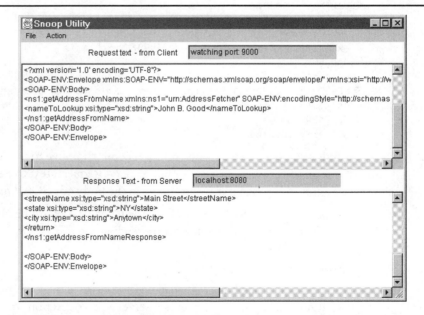

FIGURE C.1:

The UtilSnoop program capturing a client-server conversation

You can now save the request text and response text from the File menu, if desired.

Sending SOAP Messages from *UtilSnoop*

When testing server code, it is extremely convenient to work with the text of SOAP messages instead of having to change a client for every modification. `UtilSnoop` supports this by providing for editing and sending the text shown in the request text area. The following example sends a request to an experimental Internet SOAP service. The properties file for this example is as follows:

```
# UtilSnoop utility properties for Fortune service
host=www.lemurlabs.com
clientport=9000
hostport=80
```

The following SOAP message addresses the getAnyFortune method of the Fortune service at the lemurlabs website. This text is on the CD as the fortune.txt file in the utility directory. You can use normal cut and paste operations to edit text in the text area.

```
POST /rpcrouter HTTP/1.0
Host: localhost
Content-Type: text/xml; charset=utf-8
Content-Length: 420
SOAPAction: ""

<?xml version='1.0' encoding='UTF-8'?>
<SOAP-ENV:Envelope
    xmlns:SOAP-ENV="http://schemas.xmlsoap.org/soap/envelope/"
    xmlns:xsi="http://www.w3.org/1999/XMLSchema-instance"
    xmlns:xsd="http://www.w3.org/1999/XMLSchema">
<SOAP-ENV:Body>
<ns1:getAnyFortune xmlns:ns1="urn:lemurlabs-Fortune"
SOAP-ENV:encodingStyle="http://schemas.xmlsoap.org/soap/encoding/">
</ns1:getAnyFortune>
</SOAP-ENV:Body>
</SOAP-ENV:Envelope>
```

Naturally, you need to have your Internet connection live to do this. With this text pasted into the request text area, choose Action ➤ Send Request Text to Server. You should shortly see the response, a random fortune cookie in the body of a SOAP message.

Note that because SOAP servers check the Content-Length header, UtilSnoop patches the header with the correct byte count before sending the text.

Capturing Client Messages

The other function found in UtilSnoop lets you capture the content of a message from a client without actually sending it on to a server. Choose Action ➤ Capture Request. Now you can execute commands such as the following example using the addressbook sample:

```
java samples.addressbook.GetAddress
    http://localhost:9000/soap/servlet/rpcrouter "John B. Good"
```

The socket receiving text from the client remains open until you choose Action ➤ Stop Recording.

Limitations

The utility only records lines that are terminated with a line break, and all lines are recorded as Java `String` objects. Therefore, binary data transmissions will not be handled correctly. This does not present a problem with SOAP messages because binary data is transmitted in encoded form.

The *UtilSnoop* Code

The entire utility is done as one Java class to provide the GUI interface with inner classes to run the various threads. This makes for a rather large listing, so I have broken it up. Listing C.1 shows the import statements and major variables.

Listing C.1:   **The Start of the *UtilSnoop* Code**

```java
import java.awt.*;
import java.io.* ;
import java.util.* ;
import java.net.* ;

public class UtilSnoop extends java.awt.Frame implements java.lang.Runnable
{
  String version = "1.06 7/28/2001";
  String host = "localhost" ;
  int clientPort = 9000 ;
  int hostPort = 8080 ; // assume Tomcat
  String lineSep = System.getProperty("line.separator") ;
  Vector fromClient, fromServer ;
  boolean running = false ;

  PrintWriter toClient ;
  Socket clientSocket ;
  ServerSocket ssok ;

  PrintWriter toServer ;
  Socket serverSocket ;
```

Listing C.2 continues with some utility methods, including the method that sets configuration parameters from a Java `Properties` object.

Listing C.2:   ***UtilSnoop* Source Continued**

```java
  private void setWatchTF(){
    requestTF.setText("watching port: " + clientPort );
    responseTF.setText( host + ":" + hostPort );
  }
```

```
// set from properties file
private void setProp( Properties p ){
  try {
    String tmp = p.getProperty("host") ;
    if( tmp != null ) host = tmp ;
    tmp = p.getProperty("hostport");
    if( tmp != null ){
      hostPort = Integer.parseInt( tmp );
    }
    tmp = p.getProperty("clientport");
    if( tmp != null ){
      clientPort = Integer.parseInt( tmp );
    }
    requestTF.setText("watching port: " + clientPort );
  }catch( Exception e){
    System.out.println("Setting Propeties " + e );
  }
}
```

Listing C.3 shows the method executed to start recording both client and server transmissions. Three `Threads` are created and started in this method. Two provide for executing the `watchClient` and `watchServer` methods. The third executes the `UtilSnoop` run method.

Listing C.3: **The Method That Starts Recording Both Client and Server**

```
// start Threads for both client and server
void startMI_ActionPerformed(java.awt.event.ActionEvent event){
  // note: every start creates new Vectors and Threads
  stopMI.setEnabled(true); startMI.setEnabled(false );
  fromClient = new Vector();
  fromServer = new Vector();
  running = true ;
  Thread t1 = new Thread( new Runnable() {
    public void run(){
      while( running ){
        System.out.println("watchClient start");
        try{   watchClient();
          System.out.println("watchClient returns");
        }catch(Exception e1){
          System.out.println("watchClient " + e1 );
        }
      }
      System.out.println("exit watchClient Thread");
    } // end run method
  });
  t1.setPriority( Thread.MIN_PRIORITY );
  Thread t2 = new Thread( new Runnable() {
    public void run(){
      while( running ){
```

```
        System.out.println("watchServer start");
        try { watchServer();
           System.out.println("watchServer returns");
        }catch(Exception e2){
           System.out.println("watchServer " + e2 );
        }
      }
    }
    System.out.println("exit watchServer Thread");
  }
});
t2.setPriority( Thread.MIN_PRIORITY );
t1.start() ;
t2.start() ;
new Thread( this ).start();
disableWhileRunning( );
System.out.println("Start Action");
}
```

Listing C.4 shows the method executed when the Stop Recording option is selected. It sets the running variable to false and closes any open sockets. All threads waiting for socket input are interrupted.

Listing C.4:   **The Method That Stops Any Running Recording Threads**

```
// generalized stop
void stopMI_ActionPerformed( java.awt.event.ActionEvent event){
  running = false ;
  System.out.println("Stop Action");
  enableWhenStopped();
  try {
    if( serverSocket != null ){
      serverSocket.close();
      serverSocket = null;
    }
    if( clientSocket != null ){
      clientSocket.close();
      clientSocket = null ;
    }
    if( ssok != null ){
      ssok.close(); ssok = null ;
    }
  }catch(IOException e){
    e.printStackTrace( System.out );
  }
}
```

The run method shown in Listing C.5 simply watches for data captured from the client or server connections and displays it.

Listing C.5:   **The Method That Watches for Received Data and Moves It to the Display**

```java
// this Thread handles moving received text from both sides
// to the TextArea displays when recording client and server
public void run() {
  String tmp = null ;
  int errCt = 0 ;
  System.out.println("main run method starts");
  while( running ){
   try {
     if( fromClient.size() > 0 ){
       tmp = (String)fromClient.firstElement();
       toServer.print( tmp ); toServer.print("\r\n");
       toServer.flush();
       requestTA.append( tmp ); requestTA.append("\n");
       fromClient.removeElementAt(0);
     } // now look at fromServer
     if( fromServer.size() > 0 ){
       tmp = (String)fromServer.firstElement();
       toClient.print( tmp ); toClient.print("\r\n");
       toClient.flush();
       // System.out.println(":" + tmp );
       responseTA.append( tmp ); responseTA.append("\n");
       fromServer.removeElementAt(0);
     }
     Thread.sleep( 50 );
   }catch(Exception e){
      e.printStackTrace( System.out );
      if( ++errCt > 10 ) break ; ;
   }
  }
  System.out.println("main run stop");
}
```

Listing C.6 shows the methods that watch the client and server sockets when the Start Recording Both option is chosen.

Listing C.6:   **The Methods That Watch the Client and Server Sockets**

```java
void watchClient() throws IOException {
  if( ssok == null ){
    ssok = new ServerSocket( clientPort );
    requestTF.setText("watching port: " + clientPort );
  }
  clientSocket = ssok.accept();
  System.out.println("watchClient got socket");
  OutputStream os = clientSocket.getOutputStream();
  InputStream is = clientSocket.getInputStream();
  toClient = new PrintWriter( os );
  BufferedReader br = new BufferedReader(
```

```
              new InputStreamReader( is ));
    String tmp = br.readLine();
    while( running && tmp != null ){
      fromClient.addElement( tmp );
      tmp = br.readLine();
    }
    System.out.println("watchClient exit");
  }

  void watchServer() throws IOException {
    serverSocket = new Socket( host, hostPort );
    responseTF.setText( host + ":" + hostPort );
    OutputStream os = serverSocket.getOutputStream();
    toServer = new PrintWriter( os );
    InputStream is = serverSocket.getInputStream();
    BufferedReader bis = new BufferedReader(
            new InputStreamReader( is ) );
    System.out.println("watchServer got socket");
    String tmp = bis.readLine();
    while( running && tmp != null ){
      fromServer.addElement( tmp );
      tmp = bis.readLine();
    }
    System.out.println("watchServer exit");
  }
```

Listing C.7 shows the constructor. The GUI interface was built using the VisualCafé development environment, which inserts the special comments you see in several lines.

Listing C.7:   **The *UtilSnoop* Constructor**

```
public UtilSnoop()  {
  //{{INIT_CONTROLS
  setLayout(new GridLayout(2,1,0,0));
  setSize(600,400);
  setVisible(false);
  reqPanel.setLayout(new BorderLayout(0,0));
  add(reqPanel);
  reqPanel.setBounds(0,0,20,40);
  reqPanel.add("Center",requestTA);
  requestTA.setBounds(0,0,405,305);
  reqTopP.setLayout(new FlowLayout(FlowLayout.CENTER,5,5));
  reqPanel.add("North",reqTopP);
  reqTopP.setBounds(0,0,20,40);
  label1.setText("Request text  - from Client");
  reqTopP.add(label1);
  label1.setBounds(0,0,100,40);
  requestTF.setEditable(false);
  reqTopP.add(requestTF);
  requestTF.setBounds(0,0,100,40);
```

```
respPanel.setLayout(new BorderLayout(0,0));
add(respPanel);
respPanel.setBounds(0,0,20,40);
respTopP.setLayout(new FlowLayout(FlowLayout.CENTER,5,5));
respPanel.add("North",respTopP);
respTopP.setBounds(0,0,20,40);
label2.setText("Response Text - from Server");
respTopP.add(label2);
label2.setBounds(0,0,100,40);
responseTF.setEditable(false);
respTopP.add(responseTF);
responseTF.setBounds(0,0,100,40);
respPanel.add("Center",responseTA);
responseTA.setBounds(0,0,100,40);
setTitle("Snoop Utility");
//}}

//{{INIT_MENUS
menu1.setLabel("File");
menu1.add(loadPropMI);
loadPropMI.setLabel("Load Properties");
menu1.add(separatorMenuItem);
separatorMenuItem.setLabel("-");
menu1.add(saveReqMI);
saveReqMI.setLabel("Save Request Text");
menu1.add(saveRespMI);
saveRespMI.setLabel("Save Response Text");
menu1.add(menuItem2);
menuItem2.setEnabled(false);
menu1.add(exitMI);
exitMI.setLabel("Exit");
mainMenuBar.add(menu1);
menu2.setLabel("Action");
menu2.add(clearMI);
clearMI.setLabel("Clear All");
menu2.add(clearReqMI);
clearReqMI.setLabel("Clear Request");
menu2.add(clearRespMI);
clearRespMI.setLabel("Clear Response");
menu2.add(menuItem1);
menuItem1.setLabel("-");
menu2.add(startMI);
startMI.setLabel("Start Recording Both");
menu2.add(stopMI);
stopMI.setLabel("Stop Recording");
menu2.add(menuItem4);
menuItem4.setEnabled(false);
menu2.add(capReqMI);
capReqMI.setLabel("Capture Request");
menu2.add(sendReqMI);
sendReqMI.setLabel("Send Request Text to Server");
mainMenuBar.add(menu2);
```

```
//$$ mainMenuBar.move(0,312);
setMenuBar(mainMenuBar);
//}}

//{{REGISTER_LISTENERS
SymWindow aSymWindow = new SymWindow();
this.addWindowListener(aSymWindow);
SymAction lSymAction = new SymAction();
exitMI.addActionListener(lSymAction);
clearMI.addActionListener(lSymAction);
loadPropMI.addActionListener(lSymAction);
startMI.addActionListener(lSymAction);
stopMI.addActionListener(lSymAction);
clearReqMI.addActionListener(lSymAction);
clearRespMI.addActionListener(lSymAction);
saveReqMI.addActionListener(lSymAction);
saveRespMI.addActionListener(lSymAction);
sendReqMI.addActionListener(lSymAction);
capReqMI.addActionListener(lSymAction);
//}}
}
```

Listing C.8 shows more of the startup methods created by VisualCafé for the user interface.

Listing C.8:   **More of VisualCafé's Startup Code**

```
public UtilSnoop(String title) {
  this();
  setTitle(title);
}

public void setVisible(boolean b) {
  if(b){
    setLocation(50, 50);
  }
  super.setVisible(b);
}

static public void main(String args[]) {
  try {
      (new UtilSnoop()).setVisible(true);
  }  catch (Throwable t) {
    System.err.println(t);
    t.printStackTrace(System.err);
    //Ensure the application exits with an error condition.
    System.exit(1);
  }
}

public void addNotify() {
```

```
    // Record the size of the window prior to calling parents addNotify.
    Dimension d = getSize();
    super.addNotify();
    if (fComponentsAdjusted)return;
    // Adjust components according to the insets
    setSize(getInsets().left + getInsets().right + d.width,
        getInsets().top + getInsets().bottom + d.height);
    Component components[] = getComponents();
    for (int i = 0; i < components.length; i++)
    {
      Point p = components[i].getLocation();
      p.translate(getInsets().left, getInsets().top);
      components[i].setLocation(p);
    }
    fComponentsAdjusted = true;
  }

  // Used for addNotify check.
  boolean fComponentsAdjusted = false;
```

Listing C.9 continues the code created by VisualCafé to generate the user interface.

Listing C.9:   Declaring the AWT Components Used to Create the Interface

```
//{{DECLARE_CONTROLS
java.awt.Panel reqPanel = new java.awt.Panel();
java.awt.TextArea requestTA = new java.awt.TextArea();
java.awt.Panel reqTopP = new java.awt.Panel();
java.awt.Label label1 = new java.awt.Label();
java.awt.TextField requestTF = new java.awt.TextField(30);
java.awt.Panel respPanel = new java.awt.Panel();
java.awt.Panel respTopP = new java.awt.Panel();
java.awt.Label label2 = new java.awt.Label();
java.awt.TextField responseTF = new java.awt.TextField(30);
java.awt.TextArea responseTA = new java.awt.TextArea();
//}}

//{{DECLARE_MENUS
java.awt.MenuBar mainMenuBar = new java.awt.MenuBar();
java.awt.Menu menu1 = new java.awt.Menu();
java.awt.MenuItem loadPropMI = new java.awt.MenuItem();
java.awt.MenuItem separatorMenuItem = new java.awt.MenuItem();
java.awt.MenuItem saveReqMI = new java.awt.MenuItem();
java.awt.MenuItem saveRespMI = new java.awt.MenuItem();
java.awt.MenuItem menuItem2 = new java.awt.MenuItem("-");
java.awt.MenuItem exitMI = new java.awt.MenuItem();
java.awt.Menu menu2 = new java.awt.Menu();
java.awt.MenuItem clearMI = new java.awt.MenuItem();
java.awt.MenuItem clearReqMI = new java.awt.MenuItem();
java.awt.MenuItem clearRespMI = new java.awt.MenuItem();
```

```
java.awt.MenuItem menuItem1 = new java.awt.MenuItem();
java.awt.MenuItem startMI = new java.awt.MenuItem();
java.awt.MenuItem stopMI = new java.awt.MenuItem();
java.awt.MenuItem menuItem4 = new java.awt.MenuItem("-");
java.awt.MenuItem capReqMI = new java.awt.MenuItem();
java.awt.MenuItem sendReqMI = new java.awt.MenuItem();
//}}
```

The methods shown in Listing C.10 are used to disable and enable menu items according to the state of the program.

Listing C.10:   **Utility Code to Disable and Enable Menu Items**

```
MenuItem[] runners = {
  startMI, capReqMI, sendReqMI
};

private void disableWhileRunning(){
  for( int i = 0 ; i < runners.length ; i++ ){
    runners[i].setEnabled( false );
  }
  stopMI.setEnabled( true );
}
private void enableWhenStopped(){
  for( int i = 0 ; i < runners.length ; i++ ){
    runners[i].setEnabled( true );
  }
  stopMI.setEnabled( false );
}
```

Listing C.11 shows the inner classes used to create event listeners for window events and menu action events. These inner classes were also created by VisualCafé.

Listing C.11:   **The Inner Classes Implementing Event Listeners**

```
class SymWindow extends java.awt.event.WindowAdapter
{
  public void windowClosing(java.awt.event.WindowEvent event)
  {
    Object object = event.getSource();
    if (object == UtilSnoop.this)
      System.exit(0);
  }
}

class SymAction implements java.awt.event.ActionListener
{
  public void actionPerformed(java.awt.event.ActionEvent event)
```

```
{ Object obj = event.getSource();
  if (obj == exitMI)
    exitMI_ActionPerformed(event);
  if (obj == clearMI)
    clearMI_ActionPerformed(event);
  if (obj == loadPropMI)
    loadPropMI_ActionPerformed(event);
  if (obj == startMI)
    startMI_ActionPerformed(event);
  if (obj == stopMI)
    stopMI_ActionPerformed(event);
  if (obj == clearMI)
    clearMI_ActionPerformed(event);
  if (obj == clearReqMI)
    clearReqMI_ActionPerformed(event);
  if (obj == clearRespMI)
    clearRespMI_ActionPerformed(event);
  if (obj == saveReqMI)
    saveReqMI_ActionPerformed(event);
  if (obj == saveRespMI)
    saveRespMI_ActionPerformed(event);
  if (obj == sendReqMI)
    sendReqMI_ActionPerformed(event);
  if (obj == capReqMI)
    capReqMI_ActionPerformed(event);
  }
}
```

With Listing C.12, I start some of the methods implementing various menu actions.

Listing C.12:   Various Menu Action Methods

```
void exitMI_ActionPerformed(java.awt.event.ActionEvent event) {
  System.exit(0);
}

void clearMI_ActionPerformed(java.awt.event.ActionEvent event)
{ requestTA.setText("");
  responseTA.setText("");
}
void clearReqMI_ActionPerformed(java.awt.event.ActionEvent event)
{ requestTA.setText("");
}

void clearRespMI_ActionPerformed(java.awt.event.ActionEvent event)
{ responseTA.setText("");
}

void loadPropMI_ActionPerformed(java.awt.event.ActionEvent event)
{
```

```
FileDialog fd = new FileDialog(this,"Load Properties",
    FileDialog.LOAD );
fd.show();
String path = fd.getDirectory();
String fname = fd.getFile();
if( path == null || fname == null )return;
File f = new File( path, fname );
try{
  FileInputStream fis = new FileInputStream( f );
  Properties p = new Properties();
  p.load( fis );
  setProp( p );
}catch(IOException e){
  System.out.println( e.toString());
}
}
```

Listing C.13 shows the methods that carries out the Save Request Text or Save Response Text menu actions. Note that because the Java TextArea component uses only a \n character as a line separator, the text is output through the writeCRLF method.

Listing C.13:   The Methods to Save the Text in the Request or Response Text Area

```
void saveReqMI_ActionPerformed(java.awt.event.ActionEvent event)
{
  FileDialog fd = new FileDialog(this,"Save Request Text",
      FileDialog.SAVE );
  fd.show();
  String path = fd.getDirectory();
  String fname = fd.getFile();
  if( path == null || fname == null )return;
  File f = new File( path, fname );
  try{
    FileWriter fw = new FileWriter( f );
    String tmp = requestTA.getText();
    writeCRLF( tmp, fw );
    fw.close();
  }catch(IOException e){
    System.out.println("Save Request error " + e );
  }
}

void saveRespMI_ActionPerformed(java.awt.event.ActionEvent event)
{
  FileDialog fd = new FileDialog(this,"Save Response Text",
      FileDialog.SAVE );
  fd.show();
  String path = fd.getDirectory();
  String fname = fd.getFile();
```

```
    if( path == null || fname == null )return;
    File f = new File( path, fname );
    try{
      FileWriter fw = new FileWriter( f );
      String tmp = responseTA.getText();
      writeCRLF( tmp, fw );
      fw.close();
    }catch(IOException e){
      System.out.println("Save Response error " + e );
    }
  }

  // String with \n separators from a TextArea
  // - write it with proper separators to a file
  private void writeCRLF( String s, Writer w )throws IOException{
    int p = 0 ;
    int p2 = s.indexOf('\n', p ) ;
    int mx = s.length();
    while( p < mx ){
      if( p2 < 0 ){
        w.write( s, p,mx - p ); w.write(lineSep);
        break ;
      }
      w.write( s, p, p2 - p ); w.write(lineSep);
      p = p2 + 1 ; // pass the \n
      p2 = s.indexOf('\n', p ) ;
    }
    w.flush();
  }
```

Listing C.14 shows the method that takes the contents of the request text area, reformats it, and creates an inner class to execute the sendRequest method that sends it.

Listing C.14:   The Method That Carries Out the Send Request Text to Server Function

```
// connect to server and send request, capture response
// all in a separate Thread
void sendReqMI_ActionPerformed(java.awt.event.ActionEvent event)
{
  String tmp = requestTA.getText();
  if( tmp.length() == 0 ) return ;
  disableWhileRunning();
  requestTF.setText("Sending This Text");
  final String req = reformatReq( tmp ); // final for inner class
  requestTA.setText(req);
  running = true ;
  Thread t1 = new Thread( new Runnable() {
    public void run(){
    try {
      System.out.println("Start sendRequest");
```

```
      serverSocket = new Socket( host, hostPort );
      sendRequest( req,serverSocket );
  }catch(IOException e){
      System.out.println( "Send Request: " + e );
  }finally{
    enableWhenStopped();
    if( serverSocket != null ){
      try { serverSocket.close(); }catch(IOException ee){}
      serverSocket = null ;
    }
  }
  } // end run method
});
t1.setPriority(Thread.MIN_PRIORITY);
t1.start();
}
```

The `sendRequest` method shown in Listing C.15 sends the reformatted request text to the server and catches the response. Because each response line is caught, it is added to the response text area.

Listing C.15:   This Method Sends Text to the Server and Catches the Response

```
// writes full message to server, grabs response
// serverSocket will be closed by caller
private void sendRequest( String req, Socket serverSocket )
   throws IOException {
//  fromServer = new Vector();
  responseTF.setText( host + ":" + hostPort );
  OutputStream os = serverSocket.getOutputStream();
  os.write( req.getBytes() );
// System.out.print( req );
  InputStream is = serverSocket.getInputStream();
  BufferedReader bis = new BufferedReader(new InputStreamReader( is ) );
  System.out.println("Send Request reading");
  String tmp = bis.readLine();
  while( tmp != null ){
    System.out.print( tmp );
    responseTA.append( tmp );
    responseTA.append("\n");
    tmp = bis.readLine();
  }
  System.out.println("Send Request exit");
}
```

The `reformatReq` method shown in Listing C.16 is required because SOAP servers check the `Content-Length` header of a request against the actual received content byte count. The method assumes that the request text has correctly formatted headers followed by a blank line.

Listing C.16: **The Methods That Reformat Request Text**

```
/* reformat the request - separate into headers and body
   then compute content length of body and patch header */
private String reformatReq(String s) {
  BufferedReader br = new BufferedReader( new StringReader( s ));
  Vector headers = new Vector();
  StringBuffer body = new StringBuffer( s.length() );
  String tmp = null ;
  try {
    tmp = br.readLine();
    while( tmp != null && tmp.length() > 0 ){
      //till terminating blank line
      headers.addElement( tmp );
      tmp = br.readLine();
    }
    if( tmp == null ) {
      System.out.println(
          "Request text had no blank line after headers");
    }
    tmp = br.readLine();
  // blank line has been skipped, concatenate remainder with crlf
    while( tmp != null ){
      body.append( tmp ) ; body.append( "\r\n" );
      tmp = br.readLine();
    }
  }catch(IOException e){ // because of reader - impossible
  }
  int ct = body.length();
  String hdrs = patchHeaders( headers, ct );
  return hdrs + body.toString();
}

// locate the Content-Length: ### line and patch new count
private String patchHeaders( Vector headers, int ct ){
  StringBuffer head = new StringBuffer( 200 );
  for( int i = 0 ; i < headers.size(); i++ ){
    String tmp = ((String)headers.elementAt(i)).trim();
    if( tmp.startsWith("Content-Length") ){
      int p = tmp.lastIndexOf(' '); //
      tmp = tmp.substring(0,p+1) + Integer.toString( ct );
    }
    head.append( tmp ); head.append("\r\n");
  }
  head.append("\r\n");
  return head.toString();
}
```

Listing C.17 shows the method that creates a Thread to execute the captureClient method in response to a Capture Request menu action and the actual captureClient method.

Listing C.17:   **The Methods to Accomplish the Capture Request Function**

```java
void capReqMI_ActionPerformed(java.awt.event.ActionEvent event)
{
  System.out.println("Start client capture port: " + clientPort );
  disableWhileRunning();
  running = true ;
  Thread t1 = new Thread( new Runnable(){
    public void run(){
      try{ captureClient();
      } catch(Exception e){
          System.out.println("capReqMI " + e );
      }
    } // end run method
  });
  t1.setPriority( Thread.MIN_PRIORITY );
  t1.start();
}

void captureClient() throws IOException {
  if( ssok == null ){
    ssok = new ServerSocket( clientPort );
    requestTF.setText("watching port: " + clientPort );
  }
  clientSocket = ssok.accept();
  System.out.println("captureClient got socket");
  OutputStream os = clientSocket.getOutputStream();
  InputStream is = clientSocket.getInputStream();
  toClient = new PrintWriter( os );
  BufferedReader br = new BufferedReader( new InputStreamReader( is ));
  String tmp = br.readLine();
  while( running && tmp != null ){
    requestTA.append( tmp ); requestTA.append("\n");
    tmp = br.readLine();
  }
  running = false ;
  enableWhenStopped();
  System.out.println("captureClient exit");
}

}
```

Updates

Updates and improvements to the UtilSnoop class will be posted at the LANWrights website:

```
http://www.lanw.com/books/javasoap/
```

If you come up with any suggestions, please let me know at:

```
wbrogden@bga.com
```

APPENDIX D

SOAP Specifications

SOAP Version 1.2 Part 1: Messaging Framework

NOTE References to appendixes, author initials, and sections in this appendix are all related to this document, not other appendixes and sections of the book.

W3C Working Draft 2 October 2001

This version:

http://www.w3.org/TR/2001/WD-soap12-part1-20011002/

Latest version:

http://www.w3.org/TR/soap12-part1/

Previous versions:

http://www.w3.org/TR/2001/WD-soap12-20010709/

Editors:

Martin Gudgin, DevelopMentor
Marc Hadley, Sun Microsystems
Jean-Jacques Moreau, Canon
Henrik Frystyk Nielsen, Microsoft Corporation

Abstract

SOAP version 1.2 is a lightweight protocol for exchange of information in a decentralized, distributed environment. It is an XML-based protocol that consists of four parts: an envelope that defines a framework for describing what is in a message and how to process it, a transport binding framework for exchanging messages using an underlying protocol, a set of encoding rules for expressing instances of application-defined data types and a convention for representing remote procedure calls and responses. Part 1 (this document) describes the SOAP envelope and SOAP transport binding framework; Part 2 [1] describes the SOAP encoding rules, the SOAP RPC convention, and a concrete HTTP binding specification.

Status of This Document

NOTE This section describes the status of this document at the time of its publication. Other documents may supersede this document. The latest status of this document series is maintained at the W3C.

This is the second W3C Working Draft of the SOAP Version 1.2 specification for review by W3C members and other interested parties. It has been produced by the XML Protocol Working Group (WG), which is part of the XML Protocol Activity.

The specification has been split into two documents: SOAP Version 1.2, Part 1: Messaging Framework, which describes the SOAP envelope and the SOAP transport binding framework, and SOAP Version 1.2, Part 2: Adjuncts, which describes the SOAP encoding rules, the SOAP RPC convention, and a concrete HTTP binding specification.

For a detailed list of changes since the last publication of this document, refer to Appendix C, Part 1. A list of open issues against this document can be found at `http://www.w3.org/2000/xp/Group/xmlp-issues`.

Comments on this document should be sent to `xmlp-comments@w3.org` (public archive [11]). It is inappropriate to send discussion e-mails to this address.

Discussion of this document takes place on the `public xml-dist-app@w3.org` mailing list [12], per the e-mail communication rules in the XML Protocol Working Group Charter [13].

This is a public W3C Working Draft. It is a draft document and may be updated, replaced, or obsoleted by other documents at any time. It is inappropriate to use W3C Working Drafts as reference material or to cite them as other than "work in progress." A list of all W3C technical reports can be found at `http://www.w3.org/TR/`.

Table of Contents

1. Introduction

SOAP version 1.2 provides a simple and lightweight mechanism for exchanging structured and typed information between peers in a decentralized, distributed environment using XML. SOAP does not itself define any application semantics such as a programming model or implementation specific semantics; rather it defines a simple mechanism for expressing application semantics by providing a modular packaging model and encoding mechanisms for encoding application-defined data. This allows SOAP to be used in a large variety of systems ranging from messaging systems to remote procedure calls (RPC).

SOAP consists of four parts:

- The SOAP envelope (Section 4, *SOAP Envelope*) construct defines an overall framework for expressing what is in a message, who should deal with it, and whether it is optional or mandatory.

- The SOAP binding framework (Section 5, *SOAP Transport Binding Framework*) defines an abstract framework for exchanging SOAP envelopes between peers using an underlying protocol for transport. The SOAP HTTP binding [1] (SOAP in HTTP) defines a concrete instance of a binding to the HTTP protocol [2].

- The SOAP encoding rules [1] (Section 4, *SOAP Encoding*) defines a serialization mechanism that can be used to exchange instances of application-defined data types.

- The SOAP RPC representation [1] (Section 5, *SOAP for RPC*) defines a convention that can be used to represent remote procedure calls and responses.

These four parts are functionally orthogonal. In recognition of this, the envelope and the encoding rules are defined in different namespaces.

1.1   Design Goals

Two major design goals for SOAP are simplicity and extensibility. SOAP attempts to meet these goals by omitting features often found in messaging systems and distributed object systems such as:

- distributed garbage collection

- boxcarring or batching of messages

- objects-by-reference (which requires distributed garbage collection)

- activation (which requires objects-by-reference)

1.2   Notational Conventions

The keywords "MUST", "MUST NOT", "REQUIRED", "SHALL", "SHALL NOT", "SHOULD", "SHOULD NOT", "RECOMMENDED", "MAY", and "OPTIONAL" in this document are to be interpreted as described in [3].

The namespace prefixes "env" and "enc" used in the prose sections of this document are associated with the SOAP namespace names "http://www.w3.org/2001/09/soap-envelope" and "http://www.w3.org/2001/09/soap-encoding", respectively.

The namespace prefixes "xs" and "xsi" used in the prose sections of this document are associated with the namespace names "http://www.w3.org/2001/XMLSchema" and "http://www.w3.org/2001/XMLSchema-instance", respectively, both of which are defined in the XML Schemas specification [4] [5].

Note that the choice of any namespace prefix is arbitrary and not semantically significant.

Namespace URIs of the general form "http://example.org/..." and "http://example.com/..." represent an application-dependent or context-dependent URI [6].

This specification uses the augmented Backus-Naur Form (BNF) as described in [2].

1.3   Example of SOAP Message

The following example shows a simple notification message expressed in SOAP. The message contains the header block `alertcontrol` and the body block `alert`, which are both application defined and not defined by SOAP. The header block contains the parameters `priority` and `expires`, which may be of use to intermediaries as well as the ultimate destination of the message. The body block contains the actual notification message to be delivered.

Example: **SOAP message containing a header block and a body block**

```
<env:Envelope xmlns:env="http://www.w3.org/2001/09/soap-envelope">
 <env:Header>
  <n:alertcontrol xmlns:n="http://example.org/alertcontrol">
   <n:priority>1</n:priority>
   <n:expires>2001-06-22T14:00:00-05:00</n:expires>
  </n:alertcontrol>
 </env:Header>
 <env:Body>
  <m:alert xmlns:m="http://example.org/alert">
   <m:msg>Pick up Mary at school at 2pm</m:msg>
  </m:alert>
 </env:Body>
</env:Envelope>
```

1.4 SOAP Terminology

1.4.1 Protocol Concepts

SOAP   The formal set of conventions governing the format and processing rules of a SOAP message and basic control of interaction between SOAP nodes generating and accepting SOAP messages for the purpose of exchanging information along a SOAP message path.

SOAP binding   The formal set of rules for carrying a SOAP message within or on top of another protocol (underlying protocol) for the purpose of transmission. Example SOAP bindings include carrying a SOAP message within an HTTP message, or on top of TCP.

SOAP node   A SOAP node processes a SOAP message according to the formal set of conventions defined by SOAP. The SOAP node is responsible for enforcing the rules that govern the exchange of SOAP messages and accesses the services provided by the underlying protocols through SOAP bindings. Non-compliance with SOAP conventions can cause a SOAP node to generate a SOAP fault (see also "SOAP receiver" and "SOAP sender").

1.4.2 Data Encapsulation Concepts

SOAP message   A SOAP message is the basic unit of communication between peer SOAP nodes.

SOAP envelope   The outermost syntactic construct or structure of a SOAP message defined by SOAP within which all other syntactic elements of the message are enclosed.

SOAP block   A syntactic construct or structure used to delimit data that logically constitutes a single computational unit as seen by a SOAP node. The type of a SOAP block is identified by the fully qualified name of the outer element for the block, which consists of the namespace URI and the local name. A block encapsulated within the SOAP header is called a header block and a block encapsulated within a SOAP body is called a body block.

SOAP header   A collection of zero or more SOAP blocks, which may be targeted at any SOAP receiver within the SOAP message path.

SOAP body   A collection of zero or more SOAP blocks targeted at the ultimate SOAP receiver within the SOAP message path.

SOAP fault   A special SOAP block, which contains fault information generated by a SOAP node.

The following diagram illustrates how a SOAP message is composed.

General composition
of a SOAP message

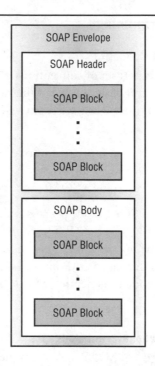

1.4.3   Message Sender and Receiver Concepts

SOAP sender   A SOAP sender is a SOAP node that transmits a SOAP message.

SOAP receiver   A SOAP receiver is a SOAP node that accepts a SOAP message.

SOAP message path   The set of SOAP senders and SOAP receivers through which a single SOAP message passes. This includes the initial SOAP sender, zero or more SOAP intermediaries, and the ultimate SOAP receiver.

Initial SOAP sender   The SOAP sender that originates a SOAP message as the starting point of a SOAP message path.

SOAP intermediary   A SOAP intermediary is both a SOAP receiver and a SOAP sender, targetable from within a SOAP message. It processes a defined set of blocks in a SOAP message along a SOAP message path. It acts in order to forward the SOAP message towards the ultimate SOAP receiver.

Ultimate SOAP receiver   The SOAP receiver that the initial sender specifies as the final destination of the SOAP message within a SOAP message path. A SOAP message may not reach the ultimate recipient because of a SOAP fault generated by a SOAP node along the SOAP message path.

2. SOAP Message Exchange Model

SOAP messages are fundamentally one-way transmissions from a SOAP sender to a SOAP receiver; however, SOAP messages are often combined to implement patterns such as request/response.

SOAP implementations can be optimized to exploit the unique characteristics of particular network systems. For example, the HTTP binding described in [1] (*Using SOAP in HTTP*) provides for SOAP response messages to be delivered as HTTP responses, using the same connection as the inbound request.

2.1 SOAP Nodes

A SOAP node can be the initial SOAP sender, the ultimate SOAP receiver, or a SOAP intermediary, in which case it is both a SOAP sender and a SOAP receiver. SOAP does not provide a routing mechanism, however; SOAP does recognize that a SOAP sender originates a SOAP message which is sent to an ultimate SOAP receiver, via zero or more SOAP intermediaries.

A SOAP node receiving a SOAP message MUST perform processing, generate SOAP faults, SOAP responses, and if appropriate, send additional SOAP messages, as provided by the remainder of this specification.

2.2 SOAP Actors and SOAP Nodes

In processing a SOAP message, a SOAP node is said to act in the role of one or more SOAP actors, each of which is identified by a URI known as the SOAP actor name. Each SOAP node MUST act in the role of the special SOAP actor named "http://www.w3.org/2001/ 09/soap-envelope/actor/next", and can additionally assume the roles of zero or more other SOAP actors. A SOAP node can establish itself as the ultimate SOAP receiver by acting in the (additional) role of the anonymous SOAP actor. The roles assumed MUST be invariant during the processing of an individual SOAP message; because this specification deals only with the processing of individual SOAP messages, no statement is made regarding the possibility that a given piece of software might or might not act in varying roles when processing more than one SOAP message.

SOAP nodes MUST NOT act in the role of the special SOAP actor named "http://www.w3.org/2001/09/soap-envelope/actor/none" (see also 4.2.2, *SOAP actor Attribute*).

While the purpose of a SOAP actor name is to identify a SOAP node, there are no routing or message exchange semantics associated with the SOAP actor name. For example, SOAP actors MAY be named with a URI useable to route SOAP messages to an appropriate SOAP node. Conversely, it is also appropriate to use SOAP actor roles with names that are related more indirectly to message routing (e.g., "http://example.org/banking/anyAccountMgr") or which are unrelated to routing (e.g., a URI meant to identify "all cache management software"; such a header might be used, for example, to carry an indication to any concerned software that the containing SOAP message is idempotent, and can safely be cached and replayed).

2.3   Targeting SOAP Header Blocks

SOAP header blocks carry optional *attribute information items* with a local name of `actor` and a namespace name of *http://www.w3.org/2001/09/soap-envelope* (see 4.2.2, *SOAP* `actor` *Attribute*) that are used to target them to the appropriate SOAP node(s). SOAP header blocks with no such *attribute information item* and the SOAP body are implicitly targeted at the anonymous SOAP actor, implying that they are to be processed by the ultimate SOAP receiver. The specification refers to the (implicit or explicit) value of the SOAP `actor` attribute as the SOAP actor for the corresponding SOAP block (either a SOAP header block or a SOAP body block).

A SOAP block is said to be targeted to a SOAP node if the SOAP `actor` (if present) on the block matches (see [7]) a role played by the SOAP node, or in the case of a SOAP block with no `actor` *attribute information item* (including SOAP body blocks), if the SOAP node has assumed the role of the anonymous SOAP actor.

2.4   Understanding SOAP Headers

It is likely that specifications for a wide variety of header functions will be developed over time, and that each SOAP node MAY include the software necessary to implement one or more such extensions. A SOAP header block is said to be understood by a SOAP node if the software at that SOAP node has been written to fully conform to and implement the semantics conveyed by the combination of local name and namespace name of the outermost *element information item* of that block.

SOAP header blocks carry optional *attribute information items* with a local name of `must-Understand` and a namespace name of *http://www.w3.org/2001/09/soap-envelope* (see 4.2.3, *SOAP* `mustUnderstand` *Attribute*). When the value of such an *attribute information item* is "true", the SOAP block is said to be mandatory. For such SOAP blocks, the targeted SOAP node MUST: either process the SOAP block according to the semantics conveyed by the combination of local name and namespace name of the outermost *element information item* of that block; or not process the SOAP message at all, and fail (see 4.4, *SOAP Fault*).

2.5   Processing SOAP Messages

This section sets out the rules by which SOAP messages are processed. Unless otherwise stated, processing must be semantically equivalent to performing the following steps separately, and in the order given. Note, however, that nothing in this specification should be taken to prevent the use of optimistic concurrency, roll back, or other techniques that might provide increased flexibility in processing order as long as all SOAP messages, SOAP faults and application-level side effects are equivalent to those that would be obtained by direct implementation of the following rules.

1. Generate a single SOAP MustUnderstand fault (see 4.4.2, *MustUnderstand Faults*) if one or more SOAP blocks targeted at the SOAP node are mandatory and are not understood by that node. If such a fault is generated, any further processing MUST NOT be done.

2. Process SOAP blocks targeted at the SOAP node, generating SOAP faults (see 4.4, *SOAP Fault*) if necessary. A SOAP node MUST process SOAP blocks identified as mandatory. A SOAP node MAY process or ignore SOAP blocks not so identified. In all cases where a SOAP block is processed, the SOAP node must understand the SOAP block and must do such processing in a manner fully conformant with the specification for that SOAP block. Faults, if any, must also conform to the specification for the processed SOAP block. It is possible that the processing of particular SOAP block would control or determine the order of processing for other SOAP blocks. For example, one could create a SOAP header block to force processing of other SOAP header blocks in lexical order. In the absence of such a SOAP block, the order of processing is at the discretion of the SOAP node. SOAP nodes can make reference to any information in the SOAP envelope when processing a SOAP block. For example, a caching function can cache the entire SOAP message, if desired.

If the SOAP node is a SOAP intermediary, the SOAP message pattern and results of processing (e.g., no fault generated) MAY require that the SOAP message be sent further along the SOAP message path. Such relayed SOAP messages MUST contain all SOAP header blocks and the SOAP body blocks from the original SOAP message, in the original order, except that SOAP header blocks targeted at the SOAP intermediary MUST be removed (such SOAP blocks are removed regardless of whether they were processed or ignored). Additional SOAP header blocks MAY be inserted at any point in the SOAP message, and such inserted SOAP header blocks MAY be indistinguishable from one or more just removed (effectively leaving them in place, but emphasizing the need to reinterpret at each SOAP node along the SOAP message path).

3. Relation to XML

All SOAP messages have an XML Information Set [10].

NOTE   Editorial note: JJM—20010918: The following paragraph is related to the versioning model described in 4.1.2 and the transition appendix. It has been suggested to remove the duplication with Section 4.1.2 so that the relevant information is presented only once.

A SOAP node MUST ensure that all *element information items* and *attribute information items* in messages that it generates are correctly namespace qualified. A SOAP node MUST be able to process SOAP namespace information in messages that it receives. It MUST discard messages that have incorrect namespace information (see 4.4, *SOAP Fault*).

This document defines the following namespaces [7]:

- The SOAP envelope has the namespace identifier "http://www.w3.org/2001/09/soap-envelope".

- The SOAP MustUnderstand fault has the namespace identifier "http://www.w3.org/2001/09/soap-faults".

- The SOAP Upgrade element has the namespace identifier "http://www.w3.org/2001/09/soap-upgrade".

Schema documents for these namespaces can be found by dereferencing the namespace identifiers. These schemas are normative.

A SOAP message MUST NOT contain a Document Type Declaration. A SOAP message MUST NOT contain *processing instruction information items* [8].

SOAP uses unqualified *attribute information items* with a local name of id and a type of *ID* in the *http://www.w3.org/2001/XMLSchema* namespace to specify the unique identifier of an encoded element.

SOAP uses unqualified *attribute information items* with a local name of href and a type of *anyURI* in the *http://www.w3.org/2001/XMLSchema* namespace to specify a reference to such a value, in a manner conforming to the XML Specification [8], XML Schema Specification [5], and XML Linking Language Specification [9].

A SOAP message MUST NOT impose any XML schema processing (assessment and validation) requirement on the part of any receiving SOAP node. Therefore, SOAP REQUIRES that all *attribute information items*, whether specified in this specification or whether they belong to a foreign namespace, be carried in the serialized SOAP envelope.

4. SOAP Envelope

NOTE   Editorial note: JJM—20010918: Trailers have been removed from this Working Draft, and will also be omitted from the next version of this specification unless significant evidence for the contrary is provided.

A SOAP message has an XML Infoset that consists of a *document information item* with exactly one child, which is an *element information item* as described below.

The document *element information item* has:

- A local name of `Envelope`
- A namespace name of *http://www.w3.org/2001/09/soap-envelope*
- Zero or more namespace qualified *attribute information items*
- One or two *element information item* children in order as follows:

    1. An optional `Header` *element information item*, see 4.2, *SOAP Header*.

    2. A mandatory `Body` *element information item*, see 4.3, *SOAP Body*.

4.1   Envelope Encoding and Versioning

4.1.1   SOAP *encodingStyle* Attribute

SOAP defines an `encodingStyle` *attribute information item* which can be used to indicate the encoding rules used to serialize a SOAP message.

The `encodingStyle` *attribute information item* has:

- A local name of `encodingStyle`
- A namespace name of *http://www.w3.org/2001/09/soap-envelope*

NOTE   Editorial note: MJG—20010802: The following sentence conflicts with the definition of the Body.

It may appear on any *element information item* in the SOAP message. Its scope is that of its owner *element information item* and that *element information item's* descendants, unless a descendant itself owns such an *attribute information item*.

The `encodingStyle` *attribute information item* is a whitespace-delimited list where each item in the list is of type *anyURI* in the namespace *http://www.w3.org/2001/XMLSchema*. Each item in the list identifies a set of serialization rules that can be used to deserialize the SOAP message. The sets of rules should be listed in the order most specific to least specific.

Example: **Example values for the *encodingStyle* attribute**

```
encodingStyle="http://www.w3.org/2001/09/soap-encoding"
encodingStyle="http://example.org/encoding/restricted
   http://example.org/encoding/"
encodingStyle=""
```

The serialization rules defined by SOAP (see [1] Section 4, *SOAP Encoding*) are identified by the URI "http://www.w3.org/2001/09/soap-encoding". SOAP messages using this particular serialization SHOULD indicate this using the SOAP `encodingStyle` *attribute information item*. In addition, all URIs syntactically beginning with "http://www.w3.org/2001/09/soap-encoding" indicate conformance with the SOAP encoding rules defined in [1] (Section 4, *SOAP Encoding*), though with potentially tighter rules added.

A value of the zero-length URI ("") explicitly indicates that no claims are made for the encoding style of contained elements. This can be used to turn off any claims from containing elements.

4.1.2   Envelope Versioning Model

SOAP does not define a traditional versioning model based on major and minor version numbers. If a SOAP message is received by a SOAP 1.2 node in which the document *element information item* does NOT have a local name of `Envelope` and a namespace name of *http://www.w3.org/2001/09/soap-envelope*, the SOAP node MUST treat this as a version error and generate a VersionMismatch SOAP fault (see 4.4, *SOAP Fault*). A SOAP VersionMismatch fault message MUST use the SOAP/1.1 envelope namespace "http://schemas.xmlsoap.org/soap/envelope/" (see Appendix A, *Version Transition From SOAP/1.1 to SOAP Version 1.2*).

4.2   SOAP Header

SOAP provides a flexible mechanism for extending a SOAP message in a decentralized and modular way without prior knowledge between the communicating parties. Typical examples of extensions that can be implemented as SOAP header blocks are authentication, transaction management, payment, etc.

The `Header` *element information item* has:

- A local name of `Header`
- A namespace name of *http://www.w3.org/2001/09/soap-envelope*
- Zero or more namespace qualified *attribute information item* children
- Zero or more namespace qualified *element information item* children

All child *element information items* of the SOAP Header are called SOAP header blocks.

Each SOAP header block *element information item*:

- MUST be namespace qualified
- MAY have an `encodingStyle` *attribute information item*
- MAY have an `actor` *attribute information item*
- MAY have a `mustUnderstand` *attribute information item*

4.2.1   Use of Header Attributes

The SOAP header block *attribute information items* defined in this section determine how a SOAP receiver should process an incoming SOAP message, as described in Section 2, *SOAP Message Exchange Model*.

A SOAP sender generating a SOAP message SHOULD only use the SOAP header block *attribute information items* on child *element information items* of the SOAP Header *element information item*.

A SOAP receiver MUST ignore all SOAP header block *attribute information items* that are applied to other descendant *element information items* of the SOAP Header *element information item*.

Example: **Example header with a single header block**

```
<env:Header xmlns:env="http://www.w3.org/2001/09/soap-envelope" >
  <t:Transaction xmlns:t="http://example.org/2001/06/tx" env:mustUnderstand="1" >
    5
  </t:Transaction>
</env:Header>
```

SOAP header block *attribute information items* MUST appear in the SOAP message itself in order to be effective; default values which may be specified in an XML Schema or other description language do not affect SOAP processing (see Section 3, *Relation to XML*).

4.2.2   SOAP *actor* Attribute

As described in Section 2, *SOAP Message Exchange Model*, not all parts of a SOAP message may be intended for the ultimate SOAP receiver. SOAP defines an actor *attribute information item* that can be used to indicate the SOAP node at which a particular SOAP header block is targeted.

The actor *attribute information item* has the following Infoset properties:

- A local name of actor
- A namespace name of *http://www.w3.org/2001/09/soap-envelope*
- A specified property with a value of true

The type of the actor *attribute information item* is *anyURI* in the namespace *http://www.w3.org/2001/XMLSchema*. The value of the actor *attribute information item* is a URI that names a role that a SOAP node may assume.

At a SOAP receiver, the special URI "http://www.w3.org/2001/09/soap-envelope/actor/next" indicates that the SOAP header block is targeted at the current SOAP node. This is similar to the hop-by-hop scope model represented by the Connection header field in HTTP. Blocks marked with this special actor URI are subject to the same processing rules, outlined in Section 2, *SOAP Message Exchange Model*, as user-defined URIs.

At a SOAP receiver, the special URI "http://www.w3.org/2001/09/soap-envelope/actor/none" indicates that the SOAP header block is not targeted at any SOAP node. This allows data which is common to several blocks to be referenced from them, without being processed.

Omitting the SOAP `actor` *attribute information item* implicitly targets the SOAP header block at the ultimate SOAP receiver.

4.2.3   SOAP *mustUnderstand* Attribute

As described in 2.4, *Understanding SOAP Headers*, the SOAP `mustUnderstand` *attribute information item* is used to indicate whether the processing of a SOAP header block is mandatory or optional at the target SOAP node.

The `mustUnderstand` *attribute information item* has the following Infoset properties:

- A local name of `mustUnderstand`
- A namespace name of *http://www.w3.org/2001/09/soap-envelope*
- A specified property with a value of true

The type of the `mustUnderstand` *attribute information item* is boolean in the namespace *http://www.w3.org/2001/XMLSchema*. Omitting this attribute information item is defined as being semantically equivalent to including it with a value of "false".

The SOAP `mustUnderstand` *attribute information item* allows for robust evolution of SOAP itself, of related services such as security mechanisms, and of applications using SOAP. SOAP blocks tagged with a SOAP `mustUnderstand` *attribute information item* with a value of "true" MUST be presumed to somehow modify the semantics of their parent or peer *element information items*. Tagging SOAP blocks in this manner assures that this change in semantics will not be silently (and, presumably, erroneously) ignored by those who may not fully understand it. Specific rules for processing header blocks with `mustUnderstand` *attribute information items* are provided in 2.4, *Understanding SOAP Headers* and 2.5, *Processing SOAP Messages*.

The SOAP `mustUnderstand` *attribute information item* is useful for detecting situations in which a SOAP block targeted at a node is not understood (see 2.4, *Understanding SOAP Headers*) by that node; it is not intended as a mechanism for detecting errors in routing, misidentification of nodes, failure of a node to serve in its intended role(s), etc., any of which may result in a failure to even attempt processing of a given header block. For that reason, this specification does not require any fault to be generated based on the presence or value of the `mustUnderstand` *attribute information item* on a header block not targeted to the processing node. Processors SHOULD NOT generate such faults, and this specification includes no standard representation for such a fault. This rule applies to the endpoint as well as to intermediaries; it is not, in general, an error for a mustUnderstand header block targeted to a node other than the endpoint to reach the endpoint without having been processed.

NOTE   SOAP extensions can be defined for indicating the order in which processing is to occur, and for generating faults when a header entry is not processed in the appropriate order. Specifically, it is possible to create SOAP header blocks, which are themselves targeted to the endpoint (or intermediaries), have a mustUnderstand *attribute information item* with a value of "true", and which have as their semantic a requirement to generate some particular fault if other headers have inadvertently survived past the intended point in the message path message (presumably due to a failure to reach the intended processing node earlier in the path). Such extensions MAY depend on the presence or value of the mustUnderstand *attribute information item* in the surviving headers when determining whether an error has occurred.

4.3   SOAP Body

The SOAP Body *element information item* provides a simple mechanism for exchanging mandatory information intended for the ultimate SOAP receiver of a SOAP message. Example uses of SOAP Body include marshalling RPC calls and error reporting.

The Body *element information item* has:

- A local name of Body
- A namespace name of *http://www.w3.org/2001/09/soap-envelope*
- Zero or more *element information item* children

NOTE   Editorial note: MJG—20010802: The description of Body does not allow additional attributes.

All child *element information items* of the SOAP Body *element information item* are called SOAP body blocks.

Each SOAP body block *element information item*:

- MAY be namespace qualified
- MAY have an encodingStyle *attribute information item*

SOAP defines one particular SOAP body block, the SOAP fault, which is used for reporting errors (see 4.4, *SOAP Fault*).

4.3.1   Relationship between SOAP Header and Body

While both SOAP Header and SOAP Body are defined as independent *element information items*, they are in fact related. The relationship between a SOAP body block and a SOAP header block is as follows: a SOAP body block is semantically equivalent to a SOAP header block targeted at the default actor and with a SOAP mustUnderstand *attribute information item* with a value of true. The default actor is indicated by omitting the actor *attribute information item* (see 4.2.2, *SOAP actor Attribute*).

4.4   SOAP Fault

The SOAP Fault *element information item* is used to carry error and/or status information within a SOAP message. If present, the SOAP Fault MUST appear as a SOAP body block and MUST NOT appear more than once within a SOAP Body.

The Fault *element information item* has:

- A local name of Fault
- A namespace name of *http://www.w3.org/2001/09/soap-envelope*
- Two or more child *element information items* in order as follows:
    1. A mandatory faultcode *element information item* as described below
    2. A mandatory faultstring *element information item* as described below
    3. An optional faultactor *element information item* as described below
    4. An optional detail *element information item* as described below

The faultcode *element information item* has:

- A local name of faultcode
- A namespace name which is empty

The type of the faultcode *element information item* is *QName* in the *http://www.w3.org/2001/XMLSchema* namespace. It is intended for use by software to provide an algorithmic mechanism for identifying the fault. SOAP defines a small set of SOAP fault codes covering basic SOAP faults (see 4.4.1, *SOAP Fault Codes*).

The faultstring *element information item* has:

- A local name of faultstring
- A namespace name which is empty

The type of the faultstring *element information item* is *string* in the *http://www.w3.org/2001/XMLSchema* namespace. It is intended to provide a human readable explanation of the fault and is not intended for algorithmic processing. This *element information item* is similar to the 'Reason-Phrase' defined by HTTP [2] and SHOULD provide at least some information explaining the nature of the fault.

The `faultactor` *element information item* has:

- A local name of `faultactor`
- A namespace name which is empty

The type of the `faultactor` *element information item* is *anyURI* in the *http://www.w3.org/ 2001/XMLSchema* namespace. It is intended to provide information about which SOAP node on the SOAP message path caused the fault to happen (see Section 2, *SOAP Message Exchange Model*). It is similar to the SOAP `actor` *attribute information item* (see 4.2.2, *SOAP actor Attribute*) but instead of indicating the target of a SOAP header block, it indicates the source of the fault. The value of the `faultactor` *element information item* identifies the source of the fault. SOAP nodes that do not act as the ultimate SOAP receiver MUST include this *element information item* The ultimate SOAP receiver MAY include this *element information item* to indicate explicitly that it generated the fault.

The `detail` *element information item* has:

- A local name of `detail`
- A namespace name which is empty
- Zero or more *attribute information items*
- Zero or more child *element information items*

The `detail` *element information item* is intended for carrying application-specific error information related to the SOAP `Body`. It MUST be present when the contents of the SOAP `Body` could not be processed successfully . It MUST NOT be used to carry error information about any SOAP header blocks. Detailed error information for SOAP header blocks MUST be carried within the SOAP header blocks themselves.

The absence of the `detail` *element information item* indicates that a SOAP `Fault` is not related to the processing of the SOAP `Body`. This can be used to find out whether the SOAP `Body` was at least partially processed by the ultimate SOAP receiver before the fault occurred, or not.

All child *element information items* of the `detail` *element information item* are called detail entries.

Each such *element information item*:

- MAY be namespace qualified
- MAY have an `encodingStyle` *attribute information item*

The SOAP `encodingStyle` *attribute information item* is used to indicate the encoding style used for the detail entries (see 4.1.1, *SOAP encodingStyle Attribute*).

4.4.1 SOAP Fault Codes

The SOAP `faultcode` values defined in this section MUST be used as values for the SOAP `faultcode` *element information item* when describing faults defined by SOAP 1.2, Part 1 (this document). The namespace identifier for these SOAP `faultcode` values is "http://www.w3.org/2001/09/soap-envelope". Use of this namespace is recommended (but not required) in the specification of methods defined outside of the present specification.

SOAP `faultcode` values are defined in an extensible manner that allows for new SOAP `faultcode` values to be defined while maintaining backwards compatibility with existing SOAP `faultcode` values. The mechanism used is very similar to the 1*xx*, 2*xx*, 3*xx*, etc. basic status classes defined in HTTP (see [2], Section 10). However, instead of integers, they are defined as XML-qualified names [7]. The character "." (dot) is used as a separator of SOAP `faultcode` values, indicating that what is to the left of the dot is a more generic fault code value than the value to the right. This is illustrated in the following example.

Example: Sample authentication fault code

```
Client.Authentication
```

The `faultcode` values defined by SOAP are listed in the following table.

Name	Meaning
VersionMismatch	The processing party found an invalid namespace for the SOAP `Envelope` *element information item* (see 4.1.2, *Envelope Versioning Model*).
MustUnderstand	An immediate child *element information item* of the SOAP `Header` *element information item* that was either not understood or not obeyed by the processing party contained a SOAP `mustUnderstand` *attribute information item* with a value of "true" (see 4.2.3, *SOAP `mustUnderstand` Attribute*).
DataEncodingUnknown	A header or body block targeted at the current SOAP node is scoped (see 4.1.1, *SOAP `encodingStyle` Attribute*) with a data encoding that the current node does not support.
Client	The Client class of errors indicates that the message was incorrectly formed or did not contain the appropriate information in order to succeed. For example, the message could lack the proper authentication or payment information. It is generally an indication that the message should not be resent without change. See also 4.4, *SOAP Fault*, for a description of the SOAP fault `detail` sub-element.
Server	The Server class of errors indicates that the message could not be processed for reasons not directly attributable to the contents of the message itself but rather to the processing of the message. For example, processing could include communicating with an upstream SOAP node, which did not respond. The message may succeed at a later point in time. See also 4.4, *SOAP Fault*, for a description of the SOAP fault `detail` sub-element.

4.4.2   MustUnderstand Faults

When a SOAP node generates a MustUnderstand fault, it SHOULD provide, in the generated fault message, header blocks as described below which detail the qualified names (QNames, per the XML Schema Data Types specification [5]) of the particular header block(s) which were not understood.

Each such header block *element information item* has:

- A local name of `Misunderstood`
- A namespace name of *http://www.w3.org/2001/09/soap-faults*
- A qname *attribute information item* as described below

The qname *attribute information item* has the following Infoset properties:

- A local name of qname
- A namespace name which is empty
- A specified property with a value of true

The type of the qname *attribute information item* is *QName* in the *http://www.w3.org/2001/XMLSchema* namespace. Its value is the QName of a header block which the faulting node failed to understand.

Consider the following message:

Example: **SOAP envelope that will cause a SOAP MustUnderstand fault if *Extension1* or *Extension2* are not understood**

```
<env:Envelope xmlns:env='http://www.w3.org/2001/09/soap-envelope'>
  <env:Header>
    <abc:Extension1 xmlns:abc='http://example.org/2001/06/ext'
                    env:mustUnderstand='1' />
    <def:Extension2 xmlns:def='http://example.com/stuff'
                    env:mustUnderstand='1' />
  </env:Header>
  <env:Body>
  . . .
  </env:Body>
</env:Envelope>
```

The above message would result in the fault message shown below if the recipient of the initial message does not understand the two header elements abc:Extension1 and def:Extension2.

Example: **SOAP fault generated as a result of not understanding *Extension1* and *Extension2***

```
<env:Envelope xmlns:env='http://www.w3.org/2001/09/soap-envelope'
    xmlns:f='http://www.w3.org/2001/09/soap-faults' >
```

```
<env:Header>
  <f:Misunderstood qname='abc:Extension1'
 xmlns:abc='http://example.org/2001/06/ext' />
  <f:Misunderstood qname='def:Extension2'
 xmlns:def='http://example.com/stuff' />
</env:Header>
<env:Body>
  <env:Fault>
    <faultcode>env:MustUnderstand</faultcode>
    <faultstring>One or more mandatory headers not understood</faultstring>
  </env:Fault>
</env:Body>
</env:Envelope>
```

Note that when serializing the qname *attribute information item*, there must be an in-scope namespace declaration for the namespace name of the misunderstood header and the value of the *attribute information item* must use the prefix of such a namespace declaration.

Note also that there is no guarantee that each MustUnderstand error contains ALL misunderstood header QNames. SOAP nodes MAY generate a fault after the first header block that causes an error containing details about that single header block only; alternatively, SOAP nodes MAY generate a combined fault detailing all of the MustUnderstand problems at once.

5. SOAP Transport Binding Framework

> **NOTE** Editorial note: JJM—20010920: This section will, in due time, contain a complete description of the SOAP Transport Binding Framework. This framework will describe what logical operations are necessary to use a new or existing transport to transfer SOAP messages from an initial SOAP sender to an ultimate SOAP recipient. The HTTP binding provided in the second part of this specification will then be rewritten to use the terminology and concepts defined in this section. Currently, this section contains a fraction of the text that will be available in the final version.

5.1 Binding to Application-Specific Protocols

Some underlying protocols may be designed for a particular purpose or application profile. SOAP bindings to such protocols MAY use the same endpoint identification (e.g., TCP port number) as the underlying protocol, in order to reuse the existing infrastructure associated that protocol.

However, the use of well-known ports by SOAP may incur additional, unintended handling by intermediaries and underlying implementations. For example, HTTP is commonly thought of as a 'Web browsing' protocol, and network administrators may place certain restrictions upon its use, or may interpose services such as filtering, content modification, routing, etc. Often, these services are interposed using port number as a heuristic.

As a result, binding definitions for underlying protocols with well-known default ports or application profiles SHOULD document potential (harmful?) interactions with commonly deployed infrastructure at those default ports or in-conformance with default application profiles. Binding definitions SHOULD also illustrate the use of the binding on a non-default port as a means of avoiding unintended interaction with such services.

5.2 Security Considerations

NOTE   Editorial note: MJG—20010926: This section will in a future revision provide some guidelines for the security considerations that should be taken into account when using the binding framework defined in this document.

6. References

6.1 Normative References

1. W3C Working Draft "SOAP Version 1.2 Part 2: Adjuncts", Martin Gudgin, Marc Hadley, Jean-Jacques Moreau, Henrik Frystyk Nielsen, 2 October 2001. (See `http://www.w3.org/TR/2001/WD-soap12-part2-20011002/`.)

2. IETF "RFC 2616: Hypertext Transfer Protocol—HTTP/1.1", R. Fielding, J. Gettys, J. C. Mogul, H. Frystyk, T. Berners-Lee, January 1997. (See `http://www.ietf.org/rfc/rfc2616.txt`.)

3. IETF "RFC 2119: Key words for use in RFCs to Indicate Requirement Levels", S. Bradner, March 1997. (See `http://www.ietf.org/rfc/rfc2119.txt`.)

4. W3C Recommendation "XML Schema Part 1: Structures", Henry S. Thompson, David Beech, Murray Maloney, Noah Mendelsohn, 2 May 2001. (See `http://www.w3.org/TR/2001/REC-xmlschema-1-20010502/`.)

5. W3C Recommendation "XML Schema Part 2: Data Types", Paul V. Biron, Ashok Malhotra, 2 May 2001. (See `http://www.w3.org/TR/2001/REC-xmlschema-2-20010502/`.)

6. IETF "RFC 2396: Uniform Resource Identifiers (URI): Generic Syntax", T. Berners-Lee, R. Fielding, L. Masinter, August 1998. (See `http://www.ietf.org/rfc/rfc2396.txt`.)

7. W3C Recommendation "Namespaces in XML", Tim Bray, Dave Hollander, Andrew Layman, 14 January 1999. (See `http://www.w3.org/TR/1999/REC-xml-names-19990114/`.)

8. W3C Recommendation "Extensible Markup Language (XML) 1.0 (Second Edition)", Tim Bray, Jean Paoli, C. M. Sperberg-McQueen, Eve Maler, 6 October 2000. (See `http://www.w3.org/TR/2000/REC-xml-20001006`.)

9. W3C Proposed Recommendation "XML Linking Language (XLink) Version 1.0", Steve DeRose, Eve Maler, David Orchard, 20 December 2000. (See `http://www.w3.org/ TR/2000/PR-xlink-20001220/`.)

10. W3C Proposed Recommendation "XML Information Set", John Cowan, Richard Tobin, 10 August 2001. (See `http://www.w3.org/TR/2001/PR-xml-infoset-20010810/`.)

6.2   Informative References

11. XML Protocol Comments Archive. (See `http://lists.w3.org/Archives/Public/ xmlp-comments/`.)

12. XML Protocol Discussion Archive. (See `http://lists.w3.org/Archives/Public/ xml-dist-app/`.)

13. XML Protocol Charter. (See `http://www.w3.org/2000/09/XML-Protocol-Charter`.)

14. W3C Note "Simple Object Access Protocol (SOAP) 1.1", Don Box, David Ehnebuske, Gopal Kakivaya, Andrew Layman, Noah Mendelsohn, Henrik Nielsen, Satish Thatte, Dave Winer, 8 May 2000. (See `http://www.w3.org/TR/SOAP/`.)

Appendix A: Version Transition From SOAP/1.1 to SOAP Version 1.2

NOTE   Editorial note—20010806: The scope of the mechanism provided in this section is for transition between SOAP/1.1 and SOAP version 1.2. The Working Group is considering providing a more general transition mechanism that can apply to any version. Such a general mechanism may or may not be the mechanism provided here, depending on whether it is deemed applicable.

The SOAP/1.1 specification [14] says the following on versioning in Section 4.1.2:

> "*SOAP does not define a traditional versioning model based on major and minor version numbers. A SOAP message MUST have an* Envelope *element associated with the "http://schemas .xmlsoap.org/soap/envelope/" namespace. If a message is received by a SOAP application in which the SOAP* Envelope *element is associated with a different namespace, the application MUST treat this as a version error and discard the message. If the message is received through a request/response protocol such as HTTP, the application MUST respond with a SOAP Version-Mismatch faultcode message (see Section 4.4) using the SOAP "http://schemas.xmlsoap.org/ soap/envelope/" namespace*".

That is, rather than a versioning model based on short names (typically version numbers), SOAP uses a declarative extension model which allows a sender to include the desired features within the SOAP envelope construct. SOAP says nothing about the granularity of extensions nor how extensions may or may not affect the basic SOAP processing model. It is entirely up to extension designers, be it either in a central or a decentralized manner, to determine which features become SOAP extensions.

The SOAP extensibility model is based on the following three basic assumptions:

1. SOAP versioning is directed only at the SOAP envelope. It explicitly does not address versioning of blocks, encodings, protocol bindings, or otherwise.

2. A SOAP node must determine whether it supports the version of a SOAP message on a per-message basis. In the following, "support" means understanding the semantics of the envelope version identified by the QName of the Envelope element information item:

   - A SOAP node receiving an envelope that it doesn't support must not attempt to process the message according to any other processing rules regardless of other up- or down-stream SOAP nodes.

   - A SOAP node may provide support for multiple envelope versions. However, when processing a message, a SOAP node must use the semantics defined by the version of that message.

3. It is essential that the envelope remains stable over time and that new features are added using the SOAP extensibility mechanism. Changing the envelope inherently affects interoperability, adds complexity, and requires central control of extensions—all of which directly conflicts with the SOAP requirements.

The rules for dealing with the possible SOAP/1.1 and SOAP Version 1.2 interactions are as follows:

1. Because of the SOAP/1.1 rules, a compliant SOAP/1.1 node receiving a SOAP Version 1.2 message will generate a VersionMismatch SOAP fault using an envelope qualified by the "http://schemas.xmlsoap.org/soap/envelope/" namespace identifier.

2. A SOAP Version 1.2 node receiving a SOAP/1.1 message may either process the message as SOAP/1.1 or generate a SOAP VersionMismatch fault using the "http://schemas .xmlsoap.org/soap/envelope/" namespace identifier. As part of the SOAP VersionMismatch fault, a SOAP Version 1.2 node should include the list of envelope versions that it supports using the SOAP upgrade extension identified by the "http://www.w3.org/2001/09/soap-upgrade" identifier.

The upgrade extension contains an ordered list of namespace identifiers of SOAP envelopes that the SOAP node supports in the order most to least preferred. Following is an example of a VersionMismatch fault generated by a SOAP Version 1.2 node including the SOAP upgrade extension:

Example: **VersionMismatch fault generated by a SOAP Version 1.2 node, and including a SOAP upgrade extension**

```
<env:Envelope xmlns:env="http://schemas.xmlsoap.org/soap/envelope/">
  <env:Header>
    <V:Upgrade xmlns:V="http://www.w3.org/2001/09/soap-upgrade">
      <envelope qname="ns1:Envelope" xmlns:ns1="http://www.w3.org/2001/09/
        soap-envelope"/>
    </V:Upgrade>
  </env:Header>
  <env:Body>
    <env:Fault>
      <faultcode>env:VersionMismatch</faultcode>
      <faultstring>Version Mismatch</faultstring>
    </env:Fault>
  </env:Body>
</env:Envelope>
```

Note that existing SOAP/1.1 nodes are not likely to indicate which envelope versions they support. If nothing is indicated, then this means that SOAP/1.1 is the only supported envelope.

Appendix B: Acknowledgments (Non-Normative)

This document is the work of the W3C XML Protocol Working Group.

Members of the Working Group are (at the time of writing, and by alphabetical order): Yasser al Safadi (Philips Research), Vidur Apparao (Netscape), Don Box (DevelopMentor), Charles Campbell (Informix Software), Michael Champion (Software AG), Dave Cleary (webMethods), Ugo Corda (Xerox), Paul Cotton (Microsoft Corporation), Ron Daniel (Interwoven), Glen Daniels (Allaire), Doug Davis (IBM), Ray Denenberg (Library of Congress), Paul Denning (MITRE Corporation), Frank DeRose (TIBCO Software, Inc.), James Falek (TIBCO Software, Inc.), David Fallside (IBM), Chris Ferris (Sun Microsystems), Daniela Florescu (Propel), Dietmar Gaertner (Software AG), Rich Greenfield (Library of Congress), Martin Gudgin (DevelopMentor), Hugo Haas (W3C), Marc Hadley (Sun Microsystems), Mark Hale (Interwoven), Randy Hall (Intel), Gerd Hoelzing (SAP AG), Oisin Hurley (IONA Technologies), Yin-Leng Husband (Compaq), John Ibbotson (IBM), Ryuji Inoue (Matsushita Electric Industrial Co., Ltd.), Scott Isaacson (Novell, Inc.), Kazunori Iwasa (Fujitsu Software Corporation), Murali Janakiraman (Rogue Wave), Mario Jeckle (Daimler-Chrysler Research and Technology), Eric Jenkins (Engenia Software), Mark

Jones (AT&T), Anish Karmarkar (Oracle), Jeffrey Kay (Engenia Software), Richard Koo (Vitria Technology, Inc.), Jacek Kopecky (IDOOX s.r.o.), Yves Lafon (W3C), Tony Lee (Vitria Technology, Inc.), Michah Lerner (AT&T), Henry Lowe (OMG), Richard Martin (Active Data Exchange), Noah Mendelsohn (Lotus Development), Jeff Mischinsky (Oracle), Nilo Mitra (Ericsson Research Canada), Jean-Jacques Moreau (Canon), Highland Mary Mountain (Intel), Masahiko Narita (Fujitsu Software Corporation), Mark Needleman (Data Research Associates), Eric Newcomer (IONA Technologies), Henrik Frystyk Nielsen (Microsoft Corporation), Mark Nottingham (Akamai Technologies), David Orchard (BEA Systems), Kevin Perkins (Compaq), Jags Ramnaryan (BEA Systems), Andreas Riegg (Daimler-Chrysler Research and Technology), Herve Ruellan (Canon), Marwan Sabbouh (MITRE Corporation), Shane Sesta (Active Data Exchange), Miroslav Simek (IDOOX s.r.o.), Simeon Simeonov (Allaire), Nick Smilonich (Unisys), Soumitro Tagore (Informix Software), Lynne Thompson (Unisys), Patrick Thompson (Rogue Wave), Asir Vedamuthu (webMethods) Ray Whitmer (Netscape), Volker Wiechers (SAP AG), Stuart Williams (Hewlett-Packard), Amr Yassin (Philips Research) and Jin Yu (Martsoft Corporation).

Previous members were: Eric Fedok (Active Data Exchange), Susan Yee (Active Data Exchange), Dan Frantz (BEA Systems), Alex Ceponkus (Bowstreet), James Tauber (Bowstreet), Rekha Nagarajan (Calico Commerce), Mary Holstege (Calico Commerce), Krishna Sankar (Cisco Systems), David Burdett (Commerce One), Murray Maloney (Commerce One), Jay Kasi (Commerce One), Yan Xu (DataChannel), Brian Eisenberg (DataChannel), Mike Dierken (DataChannel), Michael Freeman (Engenia Software), Bjoern Heckel (Epicentric), Dean Moses (Epicentric), Julian Kumar (Epicentric), Miles Chaston (Epicentric), Alan Kropp (Epicentric), Scott Golubock (Epicentric), Michael Freeman (Engenia Software), Jim Hughes (Fujitsu Ltd.), Dick Brooks (Group 8760), David Ezell (Hewlett Packard), Fransisco Cubera (IBM), David Orchard (Jamcracker), Alex Milowski (Lexica), Steve Hole (MessagingDirect Ltd.), John-Paul Sicotte (MessagingDirect Ltd.), Vilhelm Rosenqvist (NCR), Lew Shannon (NCR), Art Nevarez (Novell, Inc.), David Clay (Oracle), Jim Trezzo (Oracle), David Cleary (Progress Software), Andrew Eisenberg (Progress Software), Peter Lecuyer (Progress Software), Ed Mooney (Sun Microsystems), Mark Baker (Sun Microsystems), Anne Thomas Manes (Sun Microsystems), George Scott (Tradia, Inc.), Erin Hoffmann (Tradia, Inc.), Conleth O'Connell (Vignette), Waqar Sadiq (Vitria Technology, Inc.), Randy Waldrop (WebMethods), Bill Anderson (Xerox), Tom Breuel (Xerox), Matthew MacKenzie (XMLGlobal Technologies), David Webber (XMLGlobal Technologies), John Evdemon (XMLSolutions) and Kevin Mitchell (XMLSolutions).

The people who have contributed to discussions on xml-dist-app@w3.org are also gratefully acknowledged.

Appendix C: Part 1 Change Log (Non-Normative)

C.1   SOAP Specification Changes

Date	Author	Description
20010926	MJG	Updated member list.
20010926	MJG	Removed extra double quotes around certain URLs.
20010921	MJG	Changed `targetNamespace` attribute of faults schema to `http://www.w3.org/2001/09/soap-faults`.
20010921	MJG	Changed `targetNamespace` attribute of upgrade schema to `http://www.w3.org/2001/09/soap-upgrade`.
20010921	MJG	Changed `targetNamespace` attribute of envelope schema to `http://www.w3.org/2001/09/soap-envelope`.
20010921	MJG	Modified content model of Envelope complex type in envelope schema to disallow content after the Body element.
20010920	JJM	Included MarkN's text regarding issues 11 and 13 as amended by Stuart in the specification and expand the ednote appropriately.
20010920	JJM	Changed the namespace of the envelope to `http://www.w3.org/2001/09/`....
20010918	JJM	Incorporated several editorial comments from Stuart Williams.
20010918	JJM	Removed reference to trailer from the "SOAP Envelope" section.
20010914	JJM	Fixed issues 124, 126, 127, 128, and 132.
20010914	JJM	Used the rewrite from Mark Nottingham for section "SOAPAction attribute."
20010914	JJM	Incorporated text from Mark Nottingham clarifying the role of none blocks.
20010914	JJM	Referenced the XML InfoSet Proposed Recommendation instead of the Candidate Recommendation.
20010911	JJM	Changed XML Information Set into a normative reference. Changed XML Protocol Comments Archive, Discussion Archive, and Charter into non-normative references. Removed "as illustrated above" from Section 2. Added missing parentheses in Sections 2.5 and 4.1.1.
20010905	MJH	Wordsmithed abstract and introduction to better reflect split into Parts 1 and 2. Rationalized list of references so only cited works appear. Removed encoding schema changes. Added bibref entries for cross-references to Part 2, fixed links so they target the HTML, instead of XML version of the doc.
20010831	JJM	Added a close paragraph tag before starting a new olist or ulist.
20010831	JJM	Properly declared the language for the spec, so that we can generate valid HTML.

continued on next page

Date	Author	Description
20010830	MJG	Added an element declaration for a Fault element of type Fault to the envelope schema.
20010830	JJM	Removed terminology not relevant for Part 1.
20010830	JJM	Moved some introductory examples to Part 2.
20010830	JJM	Moved SOAP example appendix to part 2.
20010830	JJM	Added a paragraph to Section 1 pointing to Part 2 for encoding, rpc, and http binding.
20010829	JJM	Added a placeholder for the forthcoming Transport Binding Framework section.
20010829	JJM	Updated the spec's title.
20010829	JJM	Replaced specref with xspecref for references to Part 2 items.
20010829	JJM	Added bibliography entry for SOAP 1.2, Part 2.
20010829	JJM	Removed former Sections 5, 6, 7, and 8.
20010829	JJM	Did split the spec into two parts.
20010829	JJM	Referred to the proper DTD and stylesheet.
20010829	JJM	Updated the list of WG members: one person per line in the XML file, for easier updating.
20010816	MJH	Replaced a mustUnderstand="1" with mustUnderstand="true". Slight rewording in mu description.
20010810	MJH	Merged in RPC fault rules text from Jacek. Added new Data-EncodingUnknown fault code to SOAP Fault Codes section. Added editorial notes about introduction of new fault code namespace for RPC.
20010809	MJH	Merged in "mustHappen" descriptive text from Glen and Noah.
20010809	MJH	Fixed language around "default" values of attributes.
20010809	MJH	Removed HTTP extension framework, added editorial note to describe why.
20010808	MJH	Added Infoset "specified" property text from Chris.
20010808	MJH	Removed assumption 4 from version transition appendix.
20010808	MJH	Added reference to SOAP 1.1 specification to references section, removed SOAP 1.1 author list from acknowledgments section.
20010807	MJH	Converted specification from HTML to XML conforming to W3C XMLSpec DTD. Numerous resulting formatting changes.
20010720	MJG	Applied Infoset terminology to Sections 1, 2, 3 and 4.
20010629	MJG	Amended description of routing and intermediaries in Section 2.1.
20010629	JJM	Changed "latest version" URI to end with soap12.
20010629	JJM	Remove "previous version" URI.
20010629	JJM	Removed "Editor copy" in <title>.
20010629	JJM	Removed "Editor copy" in the title.

continued on next page

Date	Author	Description
20010629	JJM	Added "Previous version" to either point to SOAP/1.1, or explicitly mentioned there was no prior draft.
20010629	JJM	Pre-filed publication URIs.
20010629	JJM	Incorporated David's suggested changes for the examples in Sections 4.1.1 to 4.4.2.
20010629	JJM	Fixed some remaining typos.
20010629	MJH	Fixed a couple of typos.
20010628	MJG	Made various formatting, spelling, and grammatical fixes.
20010628	MJG	Moved soap:encodingStyle from soap:Envelope to children of soap:Header/soap:Body in examples 1, 2, 47, 48, 49, and 50.
20010628	MJG	Changed text in Section 2.1 from 'it is both a SOAP sender or a SOAP receiver' to 'it is both a SOAP sender and a SOAP receiver'.
20010628	MJG	Fixed caption on example 24.
20010628	MJH	Fixed a couple of capitalization errors where the letter "A" appeared as a capital in the middle of a sentence.
20010628	MJH	Updated Figure 1, removed ednote to do so.
20010622	HFN	Removed the introductory text in terminology section 1.4.3 as it talks about model stuff that is covered in Section 2. It was left over from original glossary, which also explained the SOAP model.
20010622	HFN	Moved the definition of block to encapsulation section in terminology.
20010622	HFN	Removed introductory section in 1.4.1 as this overlaps with the model description in Section 2 and doesn't belong in a terminology section.
20010622	HFN	Removed reference to "Web Characterization Terminology & Definitions Sheet" in terminology section as this is not an active WD.
20010622	HFN	Added revised glossary.
20010622	HFN	Added example 0 to Section 1.3 and slightly modified text for examples 1 and 2 to make it clear that HTTP is used as a protocol binding.
20010622	MJG	Added `http://example.com/`... to list of application/context specific URIs in Section 1.2.
20010622	MJG	Updated examples in Section 4.1.1 to be `encodingStyle` attributes rather than just the values of attributes.
20010622	MJG	Added table.norm, td.normitem and td.normtext styles to stylesheet. Used said styles for table of fault code values in Section 4.4.1.
20010622	MJG	In Appendix C, changed upgrade element to Upgrade and env to envelope. Made envelope unqualified. Updated schema document to match.

continued on next page

Date	Author	Description
20010622	MJG	Moved MisunderstoodHeader from envelope schema into separate faults schema. Removed entry in envelope schema change table in Appendix D.2 that referred to addition of said element. Modified example in Section 4.4.2 to match. Added reference to schema document to Section 4.4.2.
20010622	MJH	Added binding as a component of SOAP in introduction. Fixed a couple of typos and updated a couple of example captions.
20010622	MJG	Made BNF in Section 6.1.1 into a table.
20010622	MJG	Made BNFs in Section 5.1, clause 8 into tables. Added associated 'bnf' style for `table` and `td` elements to stylesheet.
20010622	MJG	Amended text regarding namespace prefix mappings in Section 1.2.
20010622	MJG	Added link to schema for the *http://www.w3.org/2001/06/soap-upgrade* namespace to Appendix C. Updated associated ednote.
20010622	MJG	Added reference numbers for XML Schema Recommendation to text prior to schema change tables in Appendix D.2 and linked said numbers to local references in this document.
20010622	MJG	Reordered entries in schema change classification table in Appendix D.2.
20010622	MJG	Changed type of `mustUnderstand` and `root` attributes to standard boolean and updated schema change tables in Appendix D.2 accordingly.
20010622	JJM	Manually numbered all the examples (53 in total!).
20010622	JJM	Added caption text to all the examples.
20010622	JJM	Replaced remaining occurrences of SOAP/1.2 with SOAP Version 1.2 (including <title>).
20010621	HFN	Added ednote to Sections 4.2.2 and 4.2.3 so that we know they have to be incorporated with Section 2.
20010621	HFN	Added version transition Appendix C.
20010621	HFN	Applied new styles to examples.
20010621	HFN	Changed term "transport" to "underlying protocol".
20010621	HFN	Changed example URNs to URLs of the style `http://example.org/....`
20010621	MJH	Updated the Acknowledgments section.
20010621	JJM	Added new stylesheet definitions (from XML Schema) for examples, and used them for examples 1 and 2.
20010621	JJM	Incorporated David Fallside's comments on status and intro sections.
20010620	HFN	Changed the status section.
20010620	HFN	Changed title to SOAP Version 1.2 and used that first time in abstract and in body.

continued on next page

Date	Author	Description
20010620	HFN	Removed question from Section 2.4 as this is an issue and is to be listed in the issues list.
20010620	HFN	Moved change log to appendix.
20010615	JJM	Renamed default actor to anonymous actor for now (to be consistent).
20010615	JJM	Fixed typos in Section 2.
20010614	JJM	Updated Section 2 to adopt the terminology used elsewhere in the spec.
20010613	MJH	Updated mustUnderstand fault text with additions from Martin Gudgin.
20010613	MJH	Added schema changes appendix from Martin Gudgin.
20010613	MJH	Added mustUnderstand fault text from Glen Daniels.
20010612	MJH	Fixed document <title>.
20010612	MJH	Moved terminology subsection from message exchange model section to introduction section.
20010612	MJH	Fixed capitalization errors by replacing "...A SOAP..." with "...a SOAP..." where appropriate.
20010612	MJH	Removed trailing "/" from encoding namespace URI.
20010612	MJH	Fixed links under namespace URIs to point to W3C space instead of schemas.xmlsoap.org.
20010612	MJH	Removed some odd additional links with text of "/" pointing to the encoding schema following the text of the encoding namespace URI in several places.
20010611	MJH	Incorporated new text for Section 2.
20010611	JJM	Changed remaining namespaces, in particular next.
20010609	JJM	Changed the spec name from XMLP/SOAP to SOAP.
20010609	JJM	Changed the version number from 1.1 to 1.2.
20010609	JJM	Changed the namespaces from `http://schemas.xmlsoap.org/soap/` to `http://www.w3.org/2001/06/soap-`.
20010609	JJM	Replaced the remaining XS and XE prefixes to env and enc, respectively.
20010601	MJH	Updated the examples in Section 1, Section 6, and Appendix A with text suggested by Martin Gudgin to comply with XML Schema Recommendation.
20010601	JJM	Updated the examples in Sections 4 and 5 with text suggested by Martin Gudgin, to comply with XML Schema Recommendation.
20010531	HFN	Removed Appendixes C and D and added links to live issues list and separate schema files.
20010531	MJH	Added this change log and updated schemas in Appendix C to comply with XML Schema Recommendation.

C.2 XML Schema Changes

The envelope schema has been updated to be compliant with the XML Schema Recommendation [4] [5]. The table below shows the categories of change.

Class	Meaning
Addition	New constructs have been added to the schema.
Clarification	The meaning of the schema has been changed to more accurately match the specification.
Deletion	Constructs have been removed from the schema.
Name	The schema has been changed due to a data type name change in the XML Schema specification.
Namespace	A namespace name has been changed.
Semantic	The meaning of the schema has been changed.
Style	Style changes have been made to the schema.
Syntax	The syntax of the schema has been updated due to changes in the XML Schema specification.

The table below lists the changes to the envelope schema.

Class	Description
Namespace	Updated to use the *http://www.w3.org/2001/XMLSchema* namespace.
Namespace	Value of `targetNamespace` attribute changed to *http://www.w3.org/2001/06/soap-envelope*.
Clarification	Changed element and attribute wildcards in Envelope complex type to namespace="##other".
Clarification	Changed element and attribute wildcards in Header complex type to namespace="##other".
Clarification	Added explicit namespace="##any" to element and attribute wildcards in Body complex type.
Clarification	Added explicit namespace="##any" to element and attribute wildcards in detail complex type.
Clarification	Added an element wildcard with namespace="##other" to the Fault complex type.
Name	Changed item type of `encodingStyle` from uri-reference to anyURI.
Name	Changed type of `actor` attribute from uri-reference to anyURI.
Name	Changed type of `faultactor` attribute from uri-reference to anyURI.
Semantic	Added processContents="lax" to all element and attribute wildcards.

continued on next page

Class	Description
Semantic	Changed type of the `mustUnderstand` attribute from restriction of boolean that only allowed 0 or 1 as lexical values to the standard boolean in the *http://www.w3.org/2001/XMLSchema* namespace. The lexical forms 0, 1, false, true are now allowed.
Style	Where possible, comments have been changed into annotations.
Syntax	Changed all occurrences of maxOccurs="*" to maxOccurs="unbounded".
Syntax	Added <xs:sequence> to all complex type definitions derived implicitly from the ur-type.
Syntax	Added <xs:sequence> to all named model group definitions.

In addition, several changes occurred in the names of data types in the XML Schema specification and some data types were removed. The following table lists those changes.

Data Type	Class	Description
timeDuration	Renamed	New name is duration.
timeInstant	Renamed	New name is dateTime.
recurringDuration	Removed	The recurringDuration data type no longer exists.
recurringInstant	Removed	The recurringInstant data type no longer exists.
binary	Removed	The binary data type has been replaced by the hexBinary and base64Binary data types.
month	Renamed	New name is gYearMonth.
timePeriod	Removed	The timePeriod data type no longer exists.
year	Renamed	New name is gYear.
century	Removed	The century data type no longer exists.
recurringDate	Renamed	New name is gMonthDay.
recurringDay	Renamed	New name is gDay.

SOAP Version 1.2 Part 2: Adjuncts

W3C Working Draft 2 October 2001

This version:

   http://www.w3.org/TR/2001/WD-soap12-part2-20011002/

Latest version:

   http://www.w3.org/TR/soap12-part2/

Previous versions:

`http://www.w3.org/TR/2001/WD-soap12-20010709/`

Editors:

Martin Gudgin, DevelopMentor
Marc Hadley, Sun Microsystems
Jean-Jacques Moreau, Canon
Henrik Frystyk Nielsen, Microsoft Corporation

Abstract

SOAP version 1.2 is a lightweight protocol for exchange of information in a decentralized, distributed environment. It is an XML-based protocol that consists of four parts: an envelope that defines a framework for describing what is in a message and how to process it, a transport binding framework for exchanging messages using an underlying protocol, a set of encoding rules for expressing instances of application-defined data types, and a convention for representing remote procedure calls and responses. Part 2 (this document) describes the RPC convention and encoding rules along with a concrete HTTP binding specification; the SOAP envelope and transport binding framework are described in Part 1 [1].

Status of This Document

NOTE This section describes the status of this document at the time of its publication. Other documents may supersede this document. The latest status of this document series is maintained at the W3C.

This is the second W3C Working Draft of the SOAP Version 1.2 specification for review by W3C members and other interested parties. It has been produced by the XML Protocol Working Group (WG), which is part of the XML Protocol Activity.

The specification has been split into two documents: SOAP Version 1.2, Part 1: Messaging Framework, which describes the SOAP envelope and the SOAP transport binding framework, and SOAP Version 1.2, Part 2: Adjuncts, which describes the SOAP encoding rules, the SOAP RPC convention and a concrete HTTP binding specification.

For a detailed list of changes since the last publication of this document, refer to Appendix C, Part 2, *Change Log*. A list of open issues against this document can be found at `http://www.w3 .org/2000/xp/Group/xmlp-issues`.

Comments on this document should be sent to xmlp-comments@w3.org (public archive [12]). It is inappropriate to send discussion e-mails to this address.

Discussion of this document takes place on the public xml-dist-app@w3.org mailing list [13], per the e-mail communication rules in the XML Protocol Working Group Charter [14].

This is a public W3C Working Draft. It is a draft document and may be updated, replaced, or obsoleted by other documents at any time. It is inappropriate to use W3C Working Drafts as reference material or to cite them as other than "work in progress". A list of all W3C technical reports can be found at http://www.w3.org/TR/.

Table of Contents

1. Introduction

SOAP version 1.2 provides a simple and lightweight mechanism for exchanging structured and typed information between peers in a decentralized, distributed environment using XML. SOAP does not itself define any application semantics such as a programming model or implementation-specific semantics; rather it defines a simple mechanism for expressing application semantics by providing a modular packaging model and encoding mechanisms for encoding application-defined data. This allows SOAP to be used in a large variety of systems ranging from messaging systems to remote procedure calls (RPC).

SOAP consists of four parts:

- The SOAP envelope [1] (Section 4, *SOAP Envelope*) construct defines an overall framework for expressing what is in a message, who should deal with it, and whether it is optional or mandatory.

- The SOAP binding framework [1] (Section 5, *SOAP Transport Binding Framework*) defines an abstract framework for exchanging SOAP envelopes between peers using an underlying protocol for transport. The SOAP HTTP binding (Section 6, *Using SOAP in HTTP*) defines a concrete instance of a binding to the HTTP protocol [2].

- The SOAP encoding rules (Section 4, *SOAP Encoding*) define a serialization mechanism that can be used to exchange instances of application-defined data types.

- The SOAP RPC representation (Section 5, *Using SOAP for RPC*) defines a convention that can be used to represent remote procedure calls and responses.

These four parts are functionally orthogonal. In recognition of this, the envelope and the encoding rules are defined in different namespaces.

1.1   Notational Conventions

The keywords "MUST", "MUST NOT", "REQUIRED", "SHALL", "SHALL NOT", "SHOULD", "SHOULD NOT", "RECOMMENDED", "MAY", and "OPTIONAL" in this document are to be interpreted as described in [3].

The namespace prefixes "env" and "enc" used in the prose sections of this document are associated with the SOAP namespace names "http://www.w3.org/2001/09/soap-envelope" and "http://www.w3.org/2001/09/soap-encoding", respectively.

The namespace prefixes "xs" and "xsi" used in the prose sections of this document are associated with the namespace names "http://www.w3.org/2001/XMLSchema" and "http://www.w3.org/2001/XMLSchema-instance", respectively, both of which are defined in the XML Schemas specification [4] [5].

Note that the choice of any namespace prefix is arbitrary and not semantically significant.

Namespace URIs of the general form "http://example.org/..." and "http://example.com/..." represent an application-dependent or context-dependent URI [6].

This specification uses the augmented Backus-Naur Form (BNF) as described in [2].

1.2 Examples of SOAP Messages

SOAP messages may be bound to different underlying protocols and used in a variety of message exchange patterns. The following two examples show SOAP used in connection with HTTP as the underlying protocol taking advantage of the request/response mechanism provided by HTTP (Section 6, *Using SOAP in HTTP*).

The following example shows a sample SOAP/HTTP request. The SOAP/HTTP request contains a block called GetLastTradePrice which takes a single parameter, the ticker symbol for a stock. Note that the GetLastTradePrice element is not defined by SOAP itself. The service's response to this request contains a single parameter, the price of the stock. The SOAP Envelope element is the top element of the XML document representing the SOAP message. XML namespaces are used to disambiguate SOAP identifiers from application-specific identifiers.

Example: **Sample SOAP Message embedded in an HTTP Request**

```
POST /StockQuote HTTP/1.1
Host: www.example.org
Content-Type: text/xml; charset="utf-8"
Content-Length: nnnn
SOAPAction: "http://example.org/2001/06/quotes"

<env:Envelope xmlns:env="http://www.w3.org/2001/09/soap-envelope">
 <env:Body>
  <m:GetLastTradePrice
        env:encodingStyle="http://www.w3.org/2001/09/soap-encoding"
        xmlns:m="http://example.org/2001/06/quotes">
    <symbol>DIS</symbol>
  </m:GetLastTradePrice>
 </env:Body>
</env:Envelope>
```

The following example shows the SOAP message sent by the StockQuote service in response to the request shown in the preceeding example.

Example: **Sample SOAP Message embedded in an HTTP Response**

```
HTTP/1.1 200 OK
Content-Type: text/xml; charset="utf-8"
Content-Length: nnnn
```

```
<env:Envelope xmlns:env="http://www.w3.org/2001/09/soap-envelope" >
 <env:Body>
  <m:GetLastTradePriceResponse
        env:encodingStyle="http://www.w3.org/2001/09/soap-encoding"
        xmlns:m="http://example.org/2001/06/quotes">
   <Price>34.5</Price>
  </m:GetLastTradePriceResponse>
 </env:Body>
</env:Envelope>
```

More examples are available in Appendix A, *SOAP Envelope Examples*.

1.3   SOAP Terminology

1.3.1   Data Encoding Concepts

SOAP data model   A set of abstract constructs that can be used to describe common data types and link relationships in data.

SOAP data encoding   The syntactic representation of data described by the SOAP data model within one or more SOAP blocks in a SOAP message.

2. Relation to XML

All SOAP messages have an XML Information Set [10].

A SOAP node MUST ensure that all *element information items* and *attribute information items* in messages that it generates are correctly namespace qualified. A SOAP node MUST be able to process SOAP namespace information in messages that it receives. It MUST discard messages that have incorrect namespace information (see [1] 4.4, *SOAP Fault*)

This document defines the following namespaces [7]:

- The SOAP serialisation has the namespace identifier "http://www.w3.org/2001/09/soap-encoding".

- The RPC result element has the namespace identifier "http://www.w3.org/2001/09/soap-rpc".

A schema document for these namespaces can be found by dereferencing the relevant namespace identifier.

A SOAP message MUST NOT contain a Document Type Declaration. A SOAP message MUST NOT contain *processing instruction information items* [8].

SOAP uses unqualified *attribute information items* with a local name of id and a type of *ID* in the *http://www.w3.org/2001/XMLSchema* namespace to specify the unique identifier of an encoded element. SOAP uses unqualified *attribute information items* with a local name of href and a type of *anyURI* in the *http://www.w3.org/2001/XMLSchema* namespace to specify a reference to such a value, in a manner conforming to the XML Specification [8], XML Schema Specification [5], and XML Linking Language Specification [9].

A SOAP message MUST NOT impose any XML schema processing (assessment and validation) requirement on the part of any receiving SOAP node. Therefore, SOAP REQUIRES that all *attribute information items*, whether specified in this specification or whether they belong to a foreign namespace, be carried in the serialized SOAP envelope.

3. The SOAP Data Model

NOTE   Editorial note: JJM—20010914: Section 4 currently defines a data model in the form of a directed graph. Elements of the data model include struct, array, and id/href. In addition to the data model, Section 4 includes a particular encoding of that model without clearly separating the two. The WG would like to clarify the relationship between the data model and the particular encoding by saying that the SOAP encoding is one of several potential encodings of the SOAP data model. This section is the placeholder for the description of the SOAP data model (see also Section 3.5 in the XML Protocol WG Draft Requirements).

4. SOAP Encoding

NOTE   Editorial note: JJM—20010920: The Working Group is aware that the following section does not use the XML Infoset terminology used elsewhere in this specification, and most notably in Part 1. The WG expects to rewrite this section using the XML Infoset terminology at a later date.

The SOAP encoding style is based on a simple type system that is a generalization of the common features found in type systems in programming languages, databases and semi-structured data. A type either is a simple (scalar) type or is a compound type constructed as a composite of several parts, each with a type. This is described in more detail below.

This section defines rules for serialization of a graph of typed objects. It operates on two levels. First, given a schema in any notation consistent with the type system described, a schema for an XML grammar may be constructed. Second, given a type-system schema and a particular graph of values conforming to that schema, an XML instance may be constructed. In reverse, given an XML instance produced in accordance with these rules, and given also the original schema, a copy of the original value graph may be constructed.

The data serialized according to the rules defined in this section MAY contain references to data outside the serialization. When present, these references MUST be Uniform Resource Identifiers (see [6]).

The namespace identifier for the elements and attributes defined in this section is "http://www.w3.org/2001/09/soap-encoding". The encoding samples shown assume all namespace declarations are at a higher element level.

Use of the data model and encoding style described in this section is encouraged but not required; other data models and encodings can be used in conjunction with SOAP (see [1] 4.1.1, *SOAP* `encodingStyle` *Attribute*).

4.1 Rules for Encoding Types in XML

XML allows very flexible encoding of data. SOAP defines a narrower set of rules for encoding. This section defines the encoding rules at a high level, and the next section describes the encoding rules for specific types when they require more detail. The encodings described in this section can be used in conjunction with the mapping of RPC calls and responses specified in Section 5, *Using SOAP for RPC*.

To describe encoding, the following terminology is used:

1. A "value" is a string, the name of a measurement (number, date, enumeration, etc.) or a composite of several such primitive values. All values are of specific types.

2. A "simple value" is one without named parts. Examples of simple values are particular strings, integers, enumerated values, etc.

3. A "compound value" is an aggregate of relations to other values. Examples of compound values are particular purchase orders, stock reports, street addresses, etc.

4. Within a compound value, each related value is potentially distinguished by a role name, ordinal, or both. This is called its "accessor." Examples of compound values include particular purchase orders, stock reports, etc. Arrays are also compound values. It is possible to have compound values with several accessors each named the same, as for example, RDF does.

5. An "array" is a compound value in which ordinal position serves as the only distinction among member values.

6. A "struct" is a compound value in which accessor name is the only distinction among member values, and no accessor has the same name as any other.

7. A "simple type" is a class of simple values. Examples of simple types are the classes called "string," "integer," enumeration classes, etc.

8. A "compound type" is a class of compound values. An example of a compound type is the class of purchase order values sharing the same accessors (shipTo, totalCost, etc.), though with potentially different values (and perhaps further constrained by limits on certain values).

9. Within a compound type, if an accessor has a name that is distinct within that type but is not distinct with respect to other types, that is, the name plus the type together are needed to make a unique identification, the name is called "locally scoped." If, however, the name is based in part on a Uniform Resource Identifier, directly or indirectly, such that the name alone is sufficient to uniquely identify the accessor irrespective of the type within which it appears, the name is called "universally scoped."

10. Given the information in the schema relative to which a graph of values is serialized, it is possible to determine that some values can only be related by a single instance of an accessor. For others, it is not possible to make this determination. If only one accessor can reference it, a value is considered "single-reference". If referenced by more than one, actually or potentially, it is "multi-reference." Note that it is possible for a certain value to be considered "single-reference" relative to one schema and "multi-reference" relative to another.

11. Syntactically, an element may be "independent" or "embedded." An independent element is any element appearing at the top level of a serialization. All others are embedded elements.

Although it is possible to use the xsi:type attribute such that a graph of values is self-describing both in its structure and the types of its values, the serialization rules permit that the types of values MAY be determinate only by reference to a schema. Such schemas MAY be in the notation described by "XML Schema Part 1: Structures" [4] and "XML Schema Part 2: Data Types" [5] or MAY be in any other notation. Note also that, while the serialization rules apply to compound types other than arrays and structs, many schemas will contain only struct and array types.

The rules for serialization are as follows:

1. All values are represented as element content. A multi-reference value MUST be represented as the content of an independent element. A single-reference value SHOULD NOT be (but MAY be).

2. For each element containing a value, the type of the value MUST be represented by at least one of the following conditions: (a) the containing element instance contains an xsi:type attribute, (b) the containing element instance is itself contained within an element containing a (possibly defaulted) enc:arrayType attribute or (c) or the name of the element bears a definite relation to the type, that type then determinable from a schema.

3. A simple value is represented as character data, that is, without any subelements. Every simple value must have a type that is either listed in the XML Schemas Specification, Part 2 [5] or whose source type is listed therein (see also 4.2, *Simple Types*).

4. A Compound Value is encoded as a sequence of elements, each accessor represented by an embedded element whose name corresponds to the name of the accessor. Accessors whose names are local to their containing types have unqualified element names; all others have qualified names (see also 4.4, *Compound Types*).

5. A multi-reference simple or compound value is encoded as an independent element containing a local, unqualified attribute named id and of type "ID" per the XML Specification [8]. Each accessor to this value is an empty element having a local, unqualified attribute named href and of type "uri-reference", per the XML Schema Specification [5], with a href attribute value of a URI fragment identifier referencing the corresponding independent element.

6. Strings and byte arrays are represented as multi-reference simple types, but special rules allow them to be represented efficiently for common cases (see also 4.2.1, *Strings* and 4.2.3, *Array of Bytes*). An accessor to a string or byte-array value MAY have an attribute named id and of type "ID", per the XML Specification [8]. If so, all other accessors to the same value are encoded as empty elements having a local, unqualified attribute named href and of type "uri-reference", per the XML Schema Specification [5], with a href attribute value of a URI fragment identifier referencing the single element containing the value.

7. It is permissible to encode several references to a value as though these were references to several distinct values, but only when from context it is known that the meaning of the XML instance is unaltered.

8. Arrays are compound values (see also 4.4.2, *Arrays*). SOAP arrays are defined as having a type of "enc:Array" or a type derived there from. SOAP arrays have one or more dimensions (rank) whose members are distinguished by ordinal position. An array value is represented as a series of elements reflecting the array, with members appearing in ascending ordinal sequence. For multi-dimensional arrays, the dimension on the right side varies most rapidly. Each member element is named as an independent element (see rule 2/>). SOAP arrays can be single-reference or multi-reference values, and consequently may be represented as the content of either an embedded or independent element. SOAP arrays MUST contain a enc:arrayType attribute whose value specifies the type of the contained elements as well as the dimension(s) of the array. The value of the enc:arrayType attribute is defined as follows:

Value of *enc:arrayType*

[1]	arrayTypeValue	=	atype asize
[2]	atype	=	QName *(rank)
[3]	rank	=	"[" *(",") "]"
[4]	asize	=	"[" #length "]"
[5]	length	=	1*DIGIT

The "atype" construct is the type name of the contained elements expressed as a QName as would appear in the type attribute of an XML Schema element declaration and acts as a type constraint (meaning that all values of contained elements are asserted to conform to the indicated type; that is, the type cited in enc:arrayType must be the type or a super-type of every array member). In the case of arrays of arrays or "jagged arrays", the type component is encoded as the "innermost" type name followed by a rank construct for each level of nested arrays starting from 1. Multi-dimensional arrays are encoded using a comma for each dimension starting from 1.

The "asize" construct contains a comma-separated list of zero, one, or more integers indicating the lengths of each dimension of the array. A value of zero integers indicates that no particular quantity is asserted but that the size may be determined by inspection of the actual members.

For example, an array with 5 members of type array of integers would have an arrayType-Value value of "int[][5]", of which the atype value is "int[]" and the asize value is "[5]". Likewise, an array with 3 members of type two-dimensional arrays of integers would have an arrayTypeValue value of "int[,][3]", of which the atype value is "int[,]" and the asize value is "[3]".

A SOAP array member MAY contain a enc:offset attribute indicating the offset position of that item in the enclosing array. This can be used to indicate the offset position of a partially represented array (see 4.4.2.1, *PartiallyTransmitted Arrays*). Likewise, an array member MAY contain a enc:position attribute indicating the position of that item in the enclosing array. This can be used to describe members of sparse arrays (see 4.4.2.2, *SparseArrays*). The value of the enc:offset and the enc:position attribute is defined as follows:

Value of *enc:offset* and *enc:position*

```
[6]    arrayPoint       =        "[" #length "]"
```

with offsets and positions based at 0.

9. A NULL value or a default value MAY be represented by omission of the accessor element. A NULL value MAY also be indicated by an accessor element containing the attribute xsi:nil with value "1 or true" or possibly other application-dependent attributes and values.

Note that rule 2 allows independent elements and also elements representing the members of arrays to have names which are not identical to the type of the contained value.

4.2   Simple Types

For simple types, SOAP adopts all the types found in the section "Built-in Data Types" of the "XML Schema Part 2: Data Types" Specification [5], both the value and lexical spaces. Examples include:

Type	Example
int	58502
float	314159265358979E+1
negativeInteger	–32768
string	Louis "Satchmo" Armstrong

The data types declared in the XML Schema specification may be used directly in element schemas. Types derived from these may also be used. For example, for the following schema:

Example: **Schema with simple types**

```
<!- schema document ->
<xs:schema xmlns:xs="http://www.w3.org/2001/XMLSchema" >

  <xs:element name="age" type="xs:int" />
  <xs:element name="height" type="xs:float" />
  <xs:element name="displacement" type="xs:negativeInteger" />
  <xs:element name="color" >
    <xs:simpleType base="xsd:string">
      <xs:restriction base="xs:string">
        <xs:enumeration value="Green"/>
        <xs:enumeration value="Blue"/>
      </xs:restriction>
    </xs:simpleType>
  </xs:element>

</xs:schema>
```

the following elements would be valid instances:

Example: **Message fragment corresponding to the preceding schema**

```
<!- Example instance elements ->
<age>45</age>
<height>5.9</height>
<displacement>-450</displacement>
<color>Blue</color>
```

All simple values MUST be encoded as the content of elements whose type is either defined in "XML Schema Part 2: Data Types" Specification [5], or is based on a type found there by using the mechanisms provided in the XML Schema specification.

If a simple value is encoded as an independent element or member of a heterogenous array, it is convenient to have an element declaration corresponding to the data type. Because the "XML Schema Part 2: Data Types" Specification [5] includes type definitions but does not include corresponding element declarations, the enc schema and namespace declares an element for every simple data type. These MAY be used.

Example: **Using elements declared in SOAP encoding schema**

```
<enc:int xmlns:enc="http://www.w3.org/2001/09/soap-encoding"
    id="int1">45</enc:int>
```

4.2.1   Strings

The data type "string" is defined in "XML Schema Part 2: Data Types" Specification [5]. Note that this is not identical to the type called "string" in many database or programming languages, and in particular may forbid some characters those languages would permit. (Those values must be represented by using some data type other than xsd:string.)

A string MAY be encoded as a single-reference or a multi-reference value.

The containing element of the string value MAY have an id attribute. Additional accessor elements MAY then have matching href attributes.

For example, two accessors to the same string could appear, as follows:

Example: **Two accessors for the same string**

```
<greeting id="String-0">Hello</greeting>
<salutation href="#String-0"/>
```

However, if the fact that both accessors reference the same instance of the string (or subtype of string) is immaterial, they may be encoded as two single-reference values as follows:

Example: **Two accessors for the same string**

```
<greeting>Hello</greeting>
<salutation>Hello</salutation>
```

Schema fragments for these examples could appear similar to the following:

Example: **Schema for preceding example**

```
<xs:schema xmlns:xs="http://www.w3.org/2001/XMLSchema"
           xmlns:enc="http://www.w3.org/2001/09/soap-encoding" >

  <xs:import namespace="http://www.w3.org/2001/09/soap-encoding" />

  <xs:element name="greeting" type="enc:string" />
  <xs:element name="salutation" type="enc:string" />

</xs:schema>
```

In this example, the type enc:string is used as the element's type as a convenient way to declare an element whose data type is "xsd:string" and which also allows id and href attributes. See the SOAP Encoding schema for the exact definition. Schemas MAY use these declarations from the SOAP Encoding schema but are not required to.

4.2.2   Enumerations

The "XML Schema Part 2: Data Types" Specification [5] defines a mechanism called "enumeration." The SOAP data model adopts this mechanism directly. However, because programming and other languages often define enumeration somewhat differently, the specification further describes how a value that is a member of an enumerated list of possible values is to be encoded. Specifically, it is encoded as the name of the value.

"Enumeration" as a concept indicates a set of distinct names. A specific enumeration is a specific list of distinct values appropriate to the base type. For example, the set of color names ("Green", "Blue", "Brown") could be defined as an enumeration based on the string built-in type. The values ("1", "3", "5") are a possible enumeration based on integer, and so on. "XML Schema Part 2: Data Types" [5] supports enumerations for all of the simple types except for boolean. The language of "XML Schema Part 1: Structures" Specification [4] can be used to define enumeration types. If a schema is generated from another notation in which no specific base type is applicable, use "string". In the following schema example, "EyeColor" is defined as a string with the possible values of "Green", "Blue", or "Brown" enumerated, and instance data is shown accordingly.

Example: **Schema with enumeration**

```
<xs:schema xmlns:xs="http://www.w3.org/2001/XMLSchema"
                 xmlns:tns="http://example.org/2001/06/samples"
                 targetNamespace="http://example.org/2001/06/samples" >
```

```
<xs:element name="EyeColor" type="tns:EyeColor" />
<xs:simpleType name="EyeColor" >
  <xs:restriction base="xs:string" >
    <xs:enumeration value="Green" />
    <xs:enumeration value="Blue" />
    <xs:enumeration value="Brown" />
  </xs:restriction>
</xs:simpleType>

</xs:schema>
```

Example: **Message fragment corresponding to the preceding schema**

```
<p:EyeColor xmlns:p="http://example.org/2001/06/samples" >Brown</p:EyeColor>
```

4.2.3 Array of Bytes

An array of bytes MAY be encoded as a single-reference or a multi-reference value. The rules for an array of bytes are similar to those for a string.

In particular, the containing element of the array of bytes value MAY have an `id` attribute. Additional accessor elements MAY then have matching `href` attributes.

The recommended representation of an opaque array of bytes is the 'base64' encoding defined in XML Schemas [4] [5], which uses the base64 encoding algorithm defined in MIME [15]. However, the line length restrictions that normally apply to base64 data in MIME do not apply in SOAP. A "enc:base64" subtype is supplied for use with SOAP.

Example: **Image with base64 encoding**

```
<picture xmlns:xsi="http://www.w3.org/2001/XMLSchema-instance"
         xmlns:enc="http://www.w3.org/2001/09/soap-encoding"
         xsi:type="enc:base64" >
  aG93IG5vDyBicm73biBjb3cNCg==
</picture>
```

4.3 Polymorphic Accessor

Many languages allow accessors that can polymorphically access values of several types, each type being available at run time. A polymorphic accessor instance MUST contain an `xsi:type` attribute that describes the type of the actual value.

For example, a polymorphic accessor named "cost" with a value of type "xsd:float" would be encoded as follows.

Example: **Polymorphic accessor**

```
<cost xmlns:xsi="http://www.w3.org/2001/XMLSchema-instance"
      xmlns:xs="http://www.w3.org/2001/XMLSchema"
            xsi:type="xs:float">29.95</cost>
```

as contrasted with a cost accessor whose value's type is invariant, as follows:

Example: **Accessor whose value type is invariant**

```
<cost>29.95</cost>
```

4.4 Compound Types

SOAP defines types corresponding to the following structural patterns often found in programming languages:

Struct   A "struct" is a compound value in which accessor name is the only distinction among member values, and no accessor has the same name as any other.

Array   An "array" is a compound value in which ordinal position serves as the only distinction among member values.

SOAP also permits serialization of data that is neither a Struct nor an Array, for example, data such as is found in a Directed-Labeled-Graph Data Model in which a single node has many distinct accessors, some of which occur more than once. SOAP serialization does not require that the underlying data model make an ordering distinction among accessors, but if such an order exists, the accessors MUST be encoded in that sequence.

4.4.1 Compound Values and References to Values

The members of a Compound Value are encoded as accessor elements. When accessors are distinguished by their name (as, for example, in a struct), the accessor name is used as the element name. Accessors whose names are local to their containing types have unqualified element names; all others have qualified names.

The following is an example of a struct of type "Book":

Example: **Book structure**

```
<e:Book xmlns:e="http://example.org/2001/06/books" >
   <author>Henry Ford</author>
   <preface>Prefactory text</preface>
   <intro>This is a book.</intro>
</e:Book>
```

and this is a schema fragment describing the above structure:

Example: **Schema for Book structure**

```
<xs:element name="Book"
            xmlns:xs='http://www.w3.org/2001/XMLSchema' >
  <xs:complexType>
    <xs:sequence>
      <xs:element name="author" type="xs:string" />
      <xs:element name="preface" type="xs:string" />
      <xs:element name="intro" type="xs:string" />
    </xs:sequence>
  </xs:complexType>
</xs:element>
```

Below is an example of a type with both simple and complex members. It shows two levels of referencing. Note that the href attribute of the Author accessor element is a reference to the value whose id attribute matches. A similar construction appears for the Address accessor element.

Example: **Book with multi-reference addresses**

```
<e:Book xmlns:e="http://example.org/2001/06/books" >
  <title>My Life and Work</title>
  <author href="#Person-1"/>
</e:Book>
<e:Person xmlns:e="http://example.org/2001/06/books"
          id="Person-1" >
  <name>Henry Ford</name>
  <address href="#Address-2"/>
</e:Person>
<e:Address xmlns:e="http://example.org/2001/06/books"
           id="Address-2" >
  <email>mailto:henryford@hotmail.com</email>
  <web>http://www.henryford.com</web>
</e:Address>
```

The form above is appropriate when the "Person" value and the "Address" value are multi-reference. If these were instead both single-reference, they SHOULD be embedded, as follows:

Example: **Book with single-reference addresses**

```
<e:Book xmlns:e="http://example.org/2001/06/books" >
  <title>My Life and Work</title>
  <author>
    <name>Henry Ford</name>
    <address>
```

```
        <email>mailto:henryford@hotmail.com</email>
        <web>http://www.henryford.com</web>
      </address>
    </author>
  </e:Book>
```

If instead there existed a restriction that no two persons can have the same address in a given instance and that an address can be either a Street-address or an Electronic-address, a Book with two authors would be encoded as follows:

Example: **Book with two authors having different addresses**

```
<e:Book xmlns:e="http://example.org/2001/06/books" >
   <title>My Life and Work</title>
   <firstauthor href="#Person-1"/>
   <secondauthor href="#Person-2"/>
</e:Book>
<e:Person xmlns:e="http://example.org/2001/06/books"
          xmlns:xsi="http://www.w3.org/2001/XMLSchema-instance"
          id="Person-1" >
   <name>Henry Ford</name>
   <address xsi:type="e:ElectronicAddressType">
       <email>mailto:henryford@hotmail.com</email>
       <web>http://www.henryford.com</web>
   </address>
</e:Person>
<e:Person xmlns:e="http://example.org/2001/06/books"
          xmlns:xsi="http://www.w3.org/2001/XMLSchema-instance"
          id="Person-2">
   <name>Samuel Crowther</name>
   <address xsi:type="e:StreetAddressType">
       <street>Martin Luther King Rd</street>
       <city>Raleigh</city>
       <state>North Carolina</state>
   </address>
</e:Person>
```

Serializations can contain references to values not in the same resource:

Example: **Book with external references**

```
<e:Book xmlns:e="http://example.org/2001/06/books" >
   <title>Paradise Lost</title>
   <firstAuthor href="http://www.dartmouth.edu/~milton/" />
</e:Book>
```

and this is a schema fragment describing the above structures:

Example: **Schema for preceding example**

```
<xs:schema xmlns:xs="http://www.w3.org/2001/XMLSchema"
           xmlns:tns="http://example.org/2001/06/books"
                  targetNamespace="http://example.org/2001/06/books" >

  <xs:element name="Book" type="tns:BookType" />
  <xs:complexType name="BookType" >
    <xs:annotation>
        <xs:documentation>
          <info>
        Either the following group must occur or else the
        href attribute must appear, but not both.
              </info>
          </xs:documentation>
      </xs:annotation>
      <xs:sequence minOccurs="0" maxOccurs="1" >
        <xs:element name="title" type="xs:string" />
        <xs:element name="firstAuthor" type="tns:PersonType" />
        <xs:element name="secondAuthor" type="tns:PersonType" />
      </xs:sequence>
      <xs:attribute name="href" type="xs:anyURI" />
      <xs:attribute name="id" type="xs:ID" />
      <xs:anyAttribute namespace="##other" />
  </xs:complexType>

  <xs:element name="Person" type="tns:PersonType" />
  <xs:complexType name="PersonType" >
    <xs:annotation>
        <xs:documentation>
          <info>
        Either the following group must occur or else the
        href attribute must appear, but not both.
              </info>
          </xs:documentation>
          </xs:annotation>
      <xs:sequence minOccurs="0" maxOccurs="1" >
        <xs:element name="name" type="xs:string" />
        <xs:element name="address" type="tns:AddressType" />
      </xs:sequence>
      <xs:attribute name="href" type="xs:anyURI" />
      <xs:attribute name="id" type="xs:ID" />
      <xs:anyAttribute namespace="##other" />
  </xs:complexType>

  <xs:element name="Address" base="tns:AddressType" />
  <xs:complexType name="AddressType" abstract="true" >
    <xs:annotation>
        <xs:documentation>
```

```
        <info>
    Either one of the following sequences must occur or
            else the href attribute must appear, but not both.
            </info>
        </xs:documentation>
      </xs:annotation>
  <xs:choice>
        <xs:sequence minOccurs="0" maxOccurs="1" >
          <xs:element name="email" type="xs:string" />
            <xs:element name="web" type="xs:anyURI" />
        </xs:sequence>
        <xs:sequence minOccurs='0' maxOccurs='1' >
      <xs:element name="street" type="xs:string" />
      <xs:element name="city" type="xs:string" />
      <xs:element name="state" type="xs:string"/>
        </xs:sequence>
      </xs:choice>
  <xs:attribute name="href" type="xs:anyURI"/>
  <xs:attribute name="id" type="xs:ID"/>
  <xs:anyAttribute namespace="##other"/>
</xs:complexType>

<xs:complexType name="StreetAddressType">
  <xs:annotation>
      <xs:documentation>
        <info>
    Either the second sequence in the following group
            must occur or else the href attribute must appear,
            but not both.
            </info>
        </xs:documentation>
      </xs:annotation>
      <xs:complexContent>
        <xs:restriction base="tns:AddressType" >
          <xs:sequence>
            <xs:sequence minOccurs="0" maxOccurs="0" >
              <xs:element name="email" type="xs:string" />
                <xs:element name="web" type="xs:anyURI" />
            </xs:sequence>
          <xs:sequence minOccurs="0" maxOccurs="1">
            <xs:element name="street" type="xs:string" />
            <xs:element name="city" type="xs:string" />
            <xs:element name="state" type="xs:string"/>
          </xs:sequence>
            </xs:sequence>
      <xs:attribute name="href" type="xs:anyURI"/>
      <xs:attribute name="id" type="xs:ID"/>
      <xs:anyAttribute namespace="##other"/>
        </xs:restriction>
      </xs:complexContent>
</xs:complexType>
```

```
<xs:complexType name="ElectronicAddressType">
  <xs:annotation>
      <xs:documentation>
        <info>
      Either the first sequence in the following group
            must occur or else the href attribute must appear,
            but not both.
            </info>
      </xs:documentation>
    </xs:annotation>
    <xs:complexContent>
      <xs:restriction base="tns:AddressType" >
        <xs:sequence>
        <xs:sequence minOccurs="0" maxOccurs="1">
          <xs:element name="email" type="xs:string" />
          <xs:element name="web" type="xs:anyURI" />
        </xs:sequence>
              <xs:sequence minOccurs="0" maxOccurs="0">
          <xs:element name="street" type="xs:string" />
          <xs:element name="city" type="xs:string" />
          <xs:element name="state" type="xs:string"/>
        </xs:sequence>
            </xs:sequence>
        <xs:attribute name="href" type="xs:anyURI"/>
      <xs:attribute name="id" type="xs:ID"/>
      <xs:anyAttribute namespace="##other"/>
      </xs:restriction>
    </xs:complexContent>
  </xs:complexType>

</xs:schema>
```

4.4.2 Arrays

SOAP arrays are defined as having a type of enc:Array or a derived type having that type in its derivation hierarchy (see also rule 8 in 4.1, *Rules for Encoding Types in XML*). Such derived types would be restrictions of the enc:Array type and could be used to represent, for example, arrays limited to integers or arrays of some user-defined enumeration. Arrays are represented as element values, with no specific constraint on the name of the containing element (just as values generally do not constrain the name of their containing element). The elements which make up the array can themselves can be of any type, including nested arrays.

The representation of the value of an array is an ordered sequence of elements constituting the items of the array. Within an array value, element names are not significant for distinguishing accessors. Elements may have any name. In practice, elements will frequently be named so that their declaration in a schema suggests or determines their type. As with compound types generally, if the value of an item in the array is a single-reference value, the item contains its value. Otherwise, the item references its value via an href attribute.

The following example is a schema fragment and an array containing integer array members:

Example: **Schema declaring an array of integers**

```
<xs:schema xmlns:xs="http://www.w3.org/2001/XMLSchema"
           xmlns:enc="http://www.w3.org/2001/09/soap-encoding" >
  <xs:import namespace="http://www.w3.org/2001/09/soap-encoding" />
  <xs:element name="myFavoriteNumbers" type="enc:Array" />
</xs:schema>
```

Example: **Array conforming to the preceding schema**

```
<myFavoriteNumbers xmlns:xs="http://www.w3.org/2001/XMLSchema"
                   xmlns:enc="http://www.w3.org/2001/09/soap-encoding"
                   enc:arrayType="xs:int[2]" >
  <number>3</number>
  <number>4</number>
</myFavoriteNumbers>
```

In the preceding example, the array myFavoriteNumbers contains several members, each of which is a value of type xs:int. This can be determined by inspection of the enc:arrayType attribute. Note that the enc:Array type allows both unqualified element names and qualified element names from any namespace. These convey no type information, so when used they must either have an xsi:type attribute or the containing element must have a enc:arrayType attribute. Naturally, types derived from enc:Array may declare local elements, with type information.

As previously noted, the enc schema contains declarations of elements with names corresponding to each simple type in the "XML Schema Part 2: Data Types" Specification [5]. It also contains a declaration for Array. They are used in the following example:

Example: **Using the *enc:Array* element**

```
<enc:Array xmlns:enc="http://www.w3.org/2001/09/soap-encoding"
           xmlns:xs="http://www.w3.org/2001/XMLSchema"
           enc:ArrayType="xs:int[2]" >
  <enc:int>3</enc:int>
  <enc:int>4</enc:int>
</enc:Array>
```

Arrays can contain instances of any subtype of the specified arrayType. That is, the members may be of any type that is substitutable for the type specified in the arrayType attribute, according to whatever substitutability rules are expressed in the schema. So, for example, an array of integers can contain any type derived from integer (for example, "int" or any user-defined derivation of integer). Similarly, an array of "address" might contain a restricted or extended type such as "internationalAddress". Because the supplied enc:Array type admits members of any type, arbitrary mixtures of types can be contained unless specifically limited by use of the arrayType attribute.

Types of member elements can be specified using the xsi:type attribute in the instance, or by declarations in the schema of the member elements, as the following two arrays demonstrate, respectively:

Example: **Array with elements of varying types**

```
<enc:Array xmlns:enc="http://www.w3.org/2001/09/soap-encoding"
           xmlns:xs="http://www.w3.org/2001/XMLSchema"
                xmlns:xsi="http://www.w3.org/2001/XMLSchema-instance"
           enc:arrayType="xs:anyType[4]">
    <thing xsi:type="xs:int">12345</thing>
    <thing xsi:type="xs:decimal">6.789</thing>
    <thing xsi:type="xs:string">
        Of Mans First Disobedience, and the Fruit
        Of that Forbidden Tree, whose mortal tast
        Brought Death into the World, and all our woe,
    </thing>
    <thing xsi:type="xs:anyURI">
        http://www.dartmouth.edu/~milton/reading_room/
    </thing>
</enc:Array>
```

Example: **Array with elements of varying types**

```
<enc:Array xmlns:xs="http://www.w3.org/2001/XMLSchema"
           xmlns:enc="http://www.w3.org/2001/09/soap-encoding"
           enc:arrayType="xs:anyType[4]" >
    <enc:int>12345</enc:int>
    <enc:decimal>6.789</enc:decimal>
    <enc:string>
        Of Mans First Disobedience, and the Fruit
        Of that Forbidden Tree, whose mortal tast
        Brought Death into the World, and all our woe,
    </enc:string>
    <enc:anyURI>
        http://www.dartmouth.edu/~milton/reading_room/
    </enc:anyURI >
</enc:Array>
```

Array values may be structs or other compound values. For example, an array of "xyz:Order" structs:

Example: **Arrays containing structs and other compound values**

```
<enc:Array xmlns:enc="http://www.w3.org/2001/09/soap-encoding"
           xmlns:xyz="http://example.org/2001/06/Orders"
           enc:arrayType="xyz:Order[2]">
    <Order>
        <Product>Apple</Product>
        <Price>1.56</Price>
    </Order>
    <Order>
        <Product>Peach</Product>
        <Price>1.48</Price>
    </Order>
</enc:Array>
```

Arrays may have other arrays as member values. The following is an example of an array of two arrays, each of which is an array of strings.

Example: **Array containing other arrays**

```
<enc:Array xmlns:xs="http://www.w3.org/2001/XMLSchema"
           xmlns:enc="http://www.w3.org/2001/09/soap-encoding"
           enc:arrayType="xs:string[][2]" >
    <item href="#array-1"/>
    <item href="#array-2"/>
</enc:Array>
<enc:Array xmlns:xs="http://www.w3.org/2001/XMLSchema"
           xmlns:enc="http://www.w3.org/2001/09/soap-encoding"
           id="array-1"
           enc:arrayType="xs:string[3]">
    <item>r1c1</item>
    <item>r1c2</item>
    <item>r1c3</item>
</enc:Array>
<enc:Array xmlns:xs="http://www.w3.org/2001/XMLSchema"
           xmlns:enc="http://www.w3.org/2001/09/soap-encoding"
           id="array-2"
           enc:arrayType="xs:string[2]">
    <item>r2c1</item>
    <item>r2c2</item>
</enc:Array>
```

The element containing an array value does not need to be named "enc:Array". It may have any name, provided that the type of the element is either enc:Array or is derived from enc:Array by restriction. For example, the following is a fragment of a schema and a conforming instance array:

Example: **Schema for an array**

```
<xs:schema xmlns:xs="http://www.w3.org/2001/XMLSchema"
           xmlns:enc="http://www.w3.org/2001/09/soap-encoding"
           xmlns:tns="http://example.org/2001/06/numbers"
           targetNamespace="http://example.org/2001/06/numbers" >

  <xs:simpleType name="phoneNumberType" >
    <xs:restriction base="xs:string" />
  </xs:simpleType>

  <xs:element name="ArrayOfPhoneNumbers" type="tns:ArrayOfPhoneNumbersType" />

  <xs:complexType name="ArrayOfPhoneNumbersType" >
    <xs:complexContent>
      <xs:restriction base="enc:Array" >
          <xs:sequence>
          <xs:element name="phoneNumber" type="tns:phoneNumberType"
            maxOccurs="unbounded" />
          </xs:sequence>
        <xs:attributeGroup ref="enc:arrayAttributes" />
        <xs:attributeGroup ref="enc:commonAttributes" />
      </xs:restriction>
    </xs:complexContent>
  </xs:complexType>

</xs:schema>
Example: Array conforming to the preceding schema
<abc:ArrayOfPhoneNumbers xmlns:abc="http://example.org/2001/06/numbers"
                         xmlns:enc="http://www.w3.org/2001/09/soap-encoding"
                         enc:arrayType="abc:phoneNumberType[2]" >
  <phoneNumber>206-555-1212</phoneNumber>
  <phoneNumber>1-888-123-4567</phoneNumber>
</abc:ArrayOfPhoneNumbers>
```

Arrays may be multi-dimensional. In this case, more than one size will appear within the asize part of the arrayType attribute:

Example: **Multi-dimensional array**

```
<enc:Array xmlns:xs="http://www.w3.org/2001/XMLSchema"
           xmlns:enc="http://www.w3.org/2001/09/soap-encoding"
           enc:arrayType="xs:string[2,3]" >
  <item>r1c1</item>
  <item>r1c2</item>
  <item>r1c3</item>
```

```
        <item>r2c1</item>
        <item>r2c2</item>
        <item>r2c3</item>
    </enc:Array>
```

While the examples above have shown arrays encoded as independent elements, array values MAY also appear embedded and SHOULD do so when they are known to be single-reference.

The following is an example of a schema fragment and an array of phone numbers embedded in a struct of type "Person" and accessed through the accessor "phoneNumbers":

Example: **Schema fragment for array of phone numbers embedded in a struct**

```
<xs:schema xmlns:xs="http://www.w3.org/2001/XMLSchema"
           xmlns:enc="http://www.w3.org/2001/09/soap-encoding"
           xmlns:tns="http://example.org/2001/06/numbers"
                targetNamespace="http://example.org/2001/06/numbers" >

    <xs:import namespace="http://www.w3.org/2001/09/soap-encoding" />

    <xs:simpleType name="phoneNumberType" >
        <xs:restriction base="xs:string" />
    </xs:simpleType>


    <xs:element name="ArrayOfPhoneNumbers" type="tns:ArrayOfPhoneNumbersType" />

    <xs:complexType name="ArrayOfPhoneNumbersType" >
        <xs:complexContent>
            <xs:restriction base="enc:Array" >
                <xs:sequence>
                <xs:element name="phoneNumber" type="tns:phoneNumberType"
                    maxOccurs="unbounded" />
                </xs:sequence>
            <xs:attributeGroup ref="enc:arrayAttributes" />
            <xs:attributeGroup ref="enc:commonAttributes" />
            </xs:restriction>
        </xs:complexContent>
    </xs:complexType>

    <xs:element name="Person">
        <xs:complexType>
            <xs:sequence>
            <xs:element name="name" type="xs:string" />
            <xs:element name="phoneNumbers" type="tns:ArrayOfPhoneNumbersType" />
            </xs:sequence>
        </xs:complexType>
    </xs:element>

</xs:schema>
```

> **Example:**   **Array of phone numbers embedded in a struct conforming to the preceding schema**

```
<def:Person xmlns:def="http://example.org/2001/06/numbers"
            xmlns:enc="http://www.w3.org/2001/09/soap-encoding" >
    <name>John Hancock</name>
    <phoneNumbers enc:arrayType="def:phoneNumber[2]">
        <phoneNumber>206-555-1212</phoneNumber>
        <phoneNumber>1-888-123-4567</phoneNumber>
    </phoneNumbers>
</def:Person>
```

Here is another example of a single-reference array value encoded as an embedded element whose containing element name is the accessor name:

> **Example:**   **Single-reference array encoded as an embedded element**

```
<xyz:PurchaseOrder xmlns:xyz="http://example.org/2001/06/Orders" >
    <CustomerName>Henry Ford</CustomerName>
    <ShipTo>
        <Street>5th Ave</Street>
        <City>New York</City>
        <State>NY</State>
        <Zip>10010</Zip>
    </ShipTo>
    <PurchaseLineItems xmlns:enc="http://www.w3.org/2001/09/soap-encoding"
                       enc:arrayType="xyz:Order[2]">
        <Order>
            <Product>Apple</Product>
            <Price>1.56</Price>
        </Order>
        <Order>
            <Product>Peach</Product>
            <Price>1.48</Price>
        </Order>
    </PurchaseLineItems>
</xyz:PurchaseOrder>
```

4.4.2.1   PartiallyTransmitted Arrays

SOAP provides support for partially transmitted arrays, known as "varying" arrays in some contexts [5]. A partially transmitted array indicates in an `enc:offset` attribute the zero-origin offset of the first element transmitted. If omitted, the offset is taken as zero.

The following is an example of an array of size five that transmits only the third and fourth element counting from zero.

Example: **Array of size five that transmits only the third and fourth element**

```
<enc:Array xmlns:enc="http://www.w3.org/2001/09/soap-encoding"
           xmlns:xs="http://www.w3.org/2001/XMLSchema"
           enc:arrayType="xs:string[6]"
           enc:offset="[3]" >
  <item>The fourth element</item>
  <item>The fifth element</item>
</enc:Array>
```

4.4.2.2   SparseArrays

SOAP provides support for sparse arrays. Each element representing a member value contains a enc:position attribute that indicates its position within the array. The following is an example of a sparse array of two-dimensional arrays of strings. The size is 4 but only position 2 is used:

Example: **Sparse array**

```
<enc:Array xmlns:enc="http://www.w3.org/2001/09/soap-encoding"
           xmlns:xs="http://www.w3.org/2001/XMLSchema"
           enc:arrayType="xs:string[,][4]" >
  <enc:Array href="#array-1" enc:position="[2]" />
</enc:Array>
<enc:Array id="array-1"
           enc:arrayType="xs:string[10,10]" >
  <item enc:position="[2,2]">Third row, third col</item>
  <item enc:position="[7,2]">Eighth row, third col</item>
</enc:Array>
If the only reference to "array-1" occurs in the enclosing array, this example
could also have been encoded as follows:
Example: Alternative serialisation
<enc:Array xmlns:enc="http://www.w3.org/2001/09/soap-encoding"
           xmlns:xs="http://www.w3.org/2001/XMLSchema"
           enc:arrayType="xs:string[,][4]" >
  <enc:Array enc:position="[2]" enc:arrayType="xs:string[10,10]" >
  <item enc:position="[2,2]">Third row, third col</item>
    <item enc:position="[7,2]">Eighth row, third col</item>
  </enc:Array>
</enc:Array>
```

4.4.3   Generic Compound Types

The encoding rules just cited are not limited to those cases where the accessor names are known in advance. If accessor names are known only by inspection of the immediate values to be encoded, the same rules apply, namely that the accessor is encoded as an element whose name matches the name of the accessor, and the accessor either contains or references its value. Accessors containing values whose types cannot be determined in advance MUST always contain an appropriate xsi:type attribute giving the type of the value.

Similarly, the rules cited are sufficient to allow serialization of compound types having a mixture of accessors distinguished by name and accessors distinguished by both name and ordinal position (that is, having some accessors repeated). This does not require that any schema actually contain such types, but rather says that if a type-model schema does have such types, a corresponding XML syntactic schema and instance may be generated.

Example: **Generic compound types**

```
<xyz:PurchaseOrder xmlns:xyz="http://example.org/2001/06/Orders" >
   <CustomerName>Henry Ford</CustomerName>
   <ShipTo>
      <Street>5th Ave</Street>
      <City>New York</City>
      <State>NY</State>
      <Zip>10010</Zip>
   </ShipTo>
   <PurchaseLineItems>
      <Order>
         <Product>Apple</Product>
         <Price>1.56</Price>
      </Order>
      <Order>
         <Product>Peach</Product>
         <Price>1.48</Price>
      </Order>
   </PurchaseLineItems>
</xyz:PurchaseOrder>
```

Similarly, it is valid to serialize a compound value that structurally resembles an array but is not of type (or subtype) enc:Array. For example:

Example: **Compound value**

```
<PurchaseLineItems>
    <Order>
        <Product>Apple</Product>
        <Price>1.56</Price>
    </Order>
    <Order>
        <Product>Peach</Product>
        <Price>1.48</Price>
    </Order>
</PurchaseLineItems>
```

4.5   Default Values

An omitted accessor element implies either a default value or that no value is known. The specifics depend on the accessor, method, and its context. For example, an omitted accessor typically implies a Null value for polymorphic accessors (with the exact meaning of Null accessor-dependent). Likewise, an omitted Boolean accessor typically implies either a False value or that no value is known, and an omitted numeric accessor typically implies either that the value is zero or that no value is known.

4.6   SOAP *root* Attribute

The SOAP root attribute can be used to label serialization roots that are not true roots of an object graph so that the object graph can be deserialized. The attribute can have one of two values, either "true" or "false". True roots of an object graph have the implied attribute value of "true". Serialization roots that are not true roots can be labeled as serialization roots with an attribute value of "true". An element can explicitly be labeled as not being a serialization root with a value of "false".

The SOAP root attribute MAY appear on any subelement within the SOAP Header and SOAP Body elements. The attribute does not have a default value.

The SOAP root attribute information item is of type boolean from the namespace "http://www.w3.org/2001/XMLSchema".

5. Using SOAP for RPC

NOTE   Editorial note: JJM—20010920: The Working Group is aware that the following section does not use the XML Infoset terminology used elsewhere in this specification, and most notably in Part 1. The WG expects to rewrite this section using the XML Infoset terminology at a later date.

One of the design goals of SOAP is to encapsulate remote procedure call functionality using the extensibility and flexibility of XML. This section defines a uniform representation of RPC invocations and responses.

Although it is anticipated that this representation is likely to be used in combination with the encoding style defined in Section 4, *SOAP Encoding*, other representations are possible. The SOAP encodingStyle attribute (see [1] 4.1.1, *SOAP encodingStyle Attribute*) can be used to indicate the encoding style of the RPC invocation and/or the response using the representation described in this section.

Using SOAP for RPC is orthogonal to the SOAP protocol binding (see Section 6, *Using SOAP in HTTP*). In the case of using HTTP as the protocol binding, an RPC invocation maps naturally to an HTTP request and an RPC response maps to an HTTP response. However, using SOAP for RPC is not limited to the HTTP protocol binding.

To invoke an RPC, the following information is needed:

- The URI of the target SOAP node
- A procedure or method name
- An optional procedure or method signature
- The parameters to the procedure or method
- Optional header data

SOAP relies on the protocol binding to provide a mechanism for carrying the URI. For example, for HTTP, the request URI indicates the resource that the invocation is being made against. Other than it be a valid URI, SOAP places no restriction on the form of an address (see RFC 2396 [6] for more information on URIs).

5.1 RPC and SOAP Body

RPC invocations and responses are both carried in the SOAP Body element (see [1] 4.3, *SOAP Body*) using the following representation:

- An RPC invocation is modeled as a struct.
- The invocation is viewed as a single struct containing an accessor for each [in] or [in/out] parameter. The struct is both named and typed identically to the procedure or method name.
- Each [in] or [in/out] parameter is viewed as an accessor, with a name corresponding to the name of the parameter and type corresponding to the type of the parameter. These appear in the same order as in the procedure or method signature.
- An RPC response is modeled as a struct.
- The response is viewed as a single struct containing an accessor for the return value and each [out] or [in/out] parameter. The return value accessor SHOULD be first, followed by the accessors for the parameters which SHOULD be in the same order as they appear in the procedure or method signature.
- Each parameter accessor has a name corresponding to the name of the parameter and type corresponding to the type of the parameter. The name of the return value accessor is "result" and it is namespace-qualified with the namespace identifier "http://www.w3.org/2001/09/soap-rpc". The return value accessor MUST be present if the return value of the procedure is non-void. The return value accessor MUST NOT be present if the return value of the procedure is void.
- Invocation faults are handled according to the rules in 5.3, *RPC Faults*. If a protocol binding adds additional rules for fault expression, those MUST also be followed.

As noted above, RPC invocation and response structs can be encoded according to the rules in Section 4, *SOAP Encoding,* or other encodings can be specified using the `encodingStyle` attribute (see [1] 4.1.1, *SOAP encodingStyle Attribute*).

Applications MAY process invocations with missing parameters but also MAY return a fault.

Because a result indicates success and a fault indicates failure, it is an error for an RPC response to contain both a result and a fault.

5.2   RPC and SOAP Header

Additional information relevant to the encoding of an RPC invocation but not part of the formal procedure or method signature MAY be expressed in the RPC encoding. If so, it MUST be expressed as a header block.

An example of the use of a header block is the passing of a transaction ID along with a message. Since the transaction ID is not part of the signature and is typically held in an infrastructure component rather than application code, there is no direct way to pass the necessary information with the invocation. By adding a header block with a fixed name, the transaction manager on the receiving side can extract the transaction ID and use it without affecting the coding of remote procedure calls.

5.3   RPC Faults

The RPC representation introduces additional SOAP fault codes to those described in [1] 4.4.1, *SOAP Fault Codes.* The namespace identifier for these SOAP `faultcode` *element information item* values is "http://www.w3.org/2001/09/soap-rpc" and the namespace prefix `rpc:` is used in this section to indicate association with this namespace.

Errors arising during RPC invocations are reported according to the following rules (in decreasing order of precedence):

1. A `soap-env:Server` fault SHOULD be generated when the server cannot handle the message because of some temporary condition, e.g., when it is out of memory.

2. A `soap-env:DataEncodingUnknown` fault SHOULD be generated when the arguments are encoded in a data encoding unknown to the server.

3. An `rpc:ProcedureNotPresent` fault MUST be generated when the server cannot find the procedure specified.

4. An `rpc:BadArguments` fault MUST be generated when the server cannot parse the arguments or when there is a mismatch between what the server expects and what the client has sent.

5. Other faults arising in an extension or from the application SHOULD be generated as described in [1] 4.4, *SOAP Fault.*

In all cases, the values of the `detail` and `faultstring` *element information items* are implementation defined. They MAY be specified by some external document.

6. Using SOAP in HTTP

This section describes how to use SOAP within HTTP. Binding SOAP to HTTP provides the advantage of being able to use the formalism and decentralized flexibility of SOAP with the rich feature set of HTTP. Carrying SOAP in HTTP does not mean that SOAP overrides existing semantics of HTTP but rather that SOAP over HTTP inherits HTTP semantics.

SOAP naturally follows the HTTP request/response message model by providing a SOAP request message in a HTTP request and SOAP response message in a HTTP response. Note, however, that SOAP intermediaries are NOT the same as HTTP intermediaries. That is, an HTTP intermediary addressed with the HTTP Connection header field cannot be expected to inspect or process the SOAP entity body carried in the HTTP request.

HTTP applications MUST use the media type "text/xml" according to RFC 2376 [11] when including SOAP messages in HTTP exchanges.

6.1 SOAP HTTP Request

Although SOAP might be used in combination with a variety of HTTP request methods, this binding only defines SOAP within HTTP POST requests (see Section 5, *Using SOAP for RPC*, for how to use SOAP for RPC).

6.1.1 The SOAPAction HTTP Header Field

NOTE Editorial note: JJM—20010821: SOAPAction is an optional feature of SOAP. The Working Group is considering a formal definition of the general characteristics of such "optional features" for inclusion in a future revision of this specification. At such time, the above description of SOAPAction would be revised, if necessary, to make clear its status as such a feature.

Some SOAP Receivers using this binding might need certain information to be readily available within the underlying protocol. This binding uses the SOAPAction HTTP request header field to supply this information.

SOAP Action HTTP Header

```
[7]     soapaction        =    "SOAPAction" ":" <"> URI-reference <">
[8]     URI-reference     =    <as defined in RFC2396>
```

The value of this request header field can be any URI reference, including absolute URIs and relative URIs, in which case it is interpreted relative to the Request-URI.

SOAPAction's presence in this binding's request messages is OPTIONAL. SOAP Receivers MAY use it as a hint to optimise processing, but SHOULD NOT require its presence in order to operate.

> **NOTE** Editorial note: JJM—20010818: A specific HTTP Status Code (427 proposed) shall be registered with IANA for the purpose of providing a means by which a SOAP Receiver can indicate to a SOAP client that the SOAPAction Header Field is required.

If a SOAP Receiver does require SOAPAction's presence in order to operate, it MUST respond to requests which either contain an unrecognized SOAPAction header value or do not contain a SOAPAction header with a 427 "SOAPAction Required" HTTP response status code. Such response messages MAY contain a 'Required-SOAPAction' HTTP response header field, whose value is the URI which can be used in the SOAPAction request header field to re-submit the request.

Required SOAP Action HTTP Header

```
[9]    req-soapaction    =    "required-SOAPAction" ":" <"> URI-reference <">
```

Support for SOAPAction is OPTIONAL in implementations. Implementations SHOULD NOT generate or require SOAPAction UNLESS they have a particular purpose for doing so (e.g., a SOAP Receivers specifies its use).

6.2 SOAP HTTP Response

SOAP over HTTP follows the semantics of the HTTP Status codes for communicating status information in HTTP. For example, a *2xx* status code indicates that the client's request including the SOAP component was successfully received, understood, and accepted, etc.

If an error occurs while processing the request, the SOAP HTTP server MUST issue an HTTP 500 "Internal Server Error" response and include a SOAP message in the response containing a SOAP fault (see [1] 4.4, *SOAP Fault*) indicating the SOAP processing error.

6.3 The HTTP Extension Framework

> **NOTE** Editorial note: MJH—20010809: Due to its status as an experimental RFC [17], all normative references to the HTTP extension framework [16] have been removed from this specification. Unless feedback to the contrary is received, the remains of this subsection, including this note, will be removed from the next working draft.

6.4 Security Considerations

NOTE   Editorial note: MJG—20010926: This section will in a future revision provide some guidelines for the security considerations that should be taken into account when using the HTTP binding defined in this document.

6.5 SOAP HTTP Examples

Example: **SOAP HTTP request using POST**

```
POST /StockQuote HTTP/1.1
Content-Type: text/xml; charset="utf-8"
Content-Length: nnnn
SOAPAction: "http://www.example.org/abc#MyMessage"

<env:Envelope xmlns:env="http://www.w3.org/2001/09/soap-envelope" >
 . . .
</env:Envelope>
```

Example: **SOAP HTTP response to preceding request**

```
HTTP/1.1 200 OK
Content-Type: text/xml; charset="utf-8"
Content-Length: nnnn

<env:Envelope xmlns:env="http://www.w3.org/2001/09/soap-envelope" >
 . . .
</env:Envelope>
```

7. References

7.1 Normative References

1. W3C Working Draft "SOAP Version 1.2 Part 1: Messaging Framework", Martin Gudgin, Marc Hadley, Jean-Jacques Moreau, Henrik Frystyk Nielsen, 2 October 2001. (See http://www.w3.org/TR/2001/WD-soap12-part1-20011002/.)

2. IETF "RFC 2616: Hypertext Transfer Protocol—HTTP/1.1", R. Fielding, J. Gettys, J. C. Mogul, H. Frystyk, T. Berners-Lee, January 1997. (See http://www.ietf.org/rfc/rfc2616.txt.)

3. IETF "RFC 2119: Key words for use in RFCs to Indicate Requirement Levels", S. Bradner, March 1997. (See http://www.ietf.org/rfc/rfc2119.txt.)

4. W3C Recommendation "XML Schema Part 1: Structures", Henry S. Thompson, David Beech, Murray Maloney, Noah Mendelsohn, 2 May 2001. (See `http://www.w3.org/TR/2001/REC-xmlschema-1-20010502/`.)

5. W3C Recommendation "XML Schema Part 2: Data Types", Paul V. Biron, Ashok Malhotra, 2 May 2001. (See `http://www.w3.org/TR/2001/REC-xmlschema-2-20010502/`.)

6. IETF "RFC 2396: Uniform Resource Identifiers (URI): Generic Syntax", T. Berners-Lee, R. Fielding, L. Masinter, August 1998. (See `http://www.ietf.org/rfc/rfc2396.txt`.)

7. W3C Recommendation "Namespaces in XML", Tim Bray, Dave Hollander, Andrew Layman, 14 January 1999. (See `http://www.w3.org/TR/1999/REC-xml-names-19990114/`.)

8. W3C Recommendation "Extensible Markup Language (XML) 1.0 (Second Edition)", Tim Bray, Jean Paoli, C. M. Sperberg-McQueen, Eve Maler, 6 October 2000. (See `http://www.w3.org/TR/2000/REC-xml-20001006`.)

9. W3C Proposed Recommendation "XML Linking Language (XLink) Version 1.0", Steve DeRose, Eve Maler, David Orchard, 20 December 2000. (See `http://www.w3.org/TR/2000/PR-xlink-20001220/`.)

10. W3C Proposed Recommendation "XML Information Set", John Cowan, Richard Tobin, 10 August 2001. (See `http://www.w3.org/TR/2001/PR-xml-infoset-20010810/`.)

11. IETF "RFC 2376: XML Media Types", E. Whitehead, M. Murata, July 1998. (See `http://www.ietf.org/rfc/rfc2376.txt`.)

7.2 Informative References

12. XML Protocol Comments Archive. (See `http://lists.w3.org/Archives/Public/xmlp-comments/`.)

13. XML Protocol Discussion Archive. (See `http://lists.w3.org/Archives/Public/xml-dist-app/`.)

14. XML Protocol Charter. (See `http://www.w3.org/2000/09/XML-Protocol-Charter`.)

15. IETF "RFC2045: Multipurpose Internet Mail Extensions (MIME) Part One: Format of Internet Message Bodies", N. Freed, N. Borenstein, November 1996. (See `http://www.ietf.org/rfc/rfc2045.txt`.)

16. IETF "RFC 2774: An HTTP Extension Framework", H. Nielsen, P. Leach, S. Lawrence, February 2000. (See `http://www.ietf.org/rfc/rfc2774.txt`.)

17. IETF "RFC 2026: The Internet Standards Process—Revision 3", Section 4.2.3, S. Bradner, October 1996. (See `http://www.ietf.org/rfc/rfc2026.txt`.)

Appendix A: SOAP Envelope Examples (Non-Normative)

A.1   Sample Encoding of Call Requests

Example: **SOAP message using SOAP encoding in HTTP POST with a mandatory header**

```
POST /StockQuote HTTP/1.1
Host: www.example.org
Content-Type: text/xml; charset="utf-8"
Content-Length: nnnn
SOAPAction: "http://example.org/2001/06/quotes"

<env:Envelope
  xmlns:env="http://www.w3.org/2001/09/soap-envelope" >
  <env:Header>
      <t:Transaction
          xmlns:t="http://example.org/2001/06/tx"
          env:encodingStyle="http://www.w3.org/2001/09/soap-encoding"
          env:mustUnderstand="1" >
              5
      </t:Transaction>
  </env:Header>
  <env:Body >
      <m:GetLastTradePrice
          env:encodingStyle="http://www.w3.org/2001/09/soap-encoding"
          xmlns:m="http://example.org/2001/06/quotes" >
          <m:symbol>DEF</m:symbol>
      </m:GetLastTradePrice>
  </env:Body>
</env:Envelope>
```

Example: **SOAP message using SOAP encoding in HTTP POST with multiple request parameters**

```
POST /StockQuote HTTP/1.1
Host: www.example.org
Content-Type: text/xml; charset="utf-8"
Content-Length: nnnn
SOAPAction: "http://example.org/2001/06/quotes"

<env:Envelope xmlns:env="http://www.w3.org/2001/09/soap-envelope" >
  <env:Body>
      <m:GetLastTradePriceDetailed
          env:encodingStyle="http://www.w3.org/2001/09/soap-encoding"
          xmlns:m="http://example.org/2001/06/quotes" >
          <Symbol>DEF</Symbol>
          <Company>DEF Corp</Company>
          <Price>34.1</Price>
      </m:GetLastTradePriceDetailed>
  </env:Body>
</env:Envelope>
```

A.2 Sample Encoding of Response

Example: SOAP message using SOAP encoding in HTTP response including a mandatory header

```
HTTP/1.1 200 OK
Content-Type: text/xml; charset="utf-8"
Content-Length: nnnn

<env:Envelope xmlns:env="http://www.w3.org/2001/09/soap-envelope" >
   <env:Header>
      <t:Transaction xmlns:t="http://example.org/2001/06/tx"
                     xmlns:xsi="http://www.w3.org/2001/XMLSchema-instance"
                     xmlns:xs="http://www.w3.org/2001/XMLSchema"
                     xsi:type="xs:int"
                     env:encodingStyle="http://www.w3.org/2001/09/
                        soap-encoding"
                     env:mustUnderstand="1" >
            5
      </t:Transaction>
   </env:Header>
   <env:Body>
      <m:GetLastTradePriceResponse
            env:encodingStyle="http://www.w3.org/2001/09/soap-encoding"
            xmlns:m="http://example.org/2001/06/quotes" >
         <Price>34.5</Price>
      </m:GetLastTradePriceResponse>
   </env:Body>
</env:Envelope>
```

Example: Similar to previous example but using a struct for the body and ommitting the mandatory header

```
HTTP/1.1 200 OK
Content-Type: text/xml; charset="utf-8"
Content-Length: nnnn

<env:Envelope xmlns:env="http://www.w3.org/2001/09/soap-envelope" >
   <env:Body>
      <m:GetLastTradePriceResponse
            env:encodingStyle="http://www.w3.org/2001/09/soap-encoding"
            xmlns:m="http://example.org/2001/06/quotes" >
         <PriceAndVolume>
            <LastTradePrice>34.5</LastTradePrice>
            <DayVolume>10000</DayVolume>
         </PriceAndVolume>
      </m:GetLastTradePriceResponse>
   </env:Body>
</env:Envelope>
```

Example: **Must understand fault in HTTP response**

```
HTTP/1.1 500 Internal Server Error
Content-Type: text/xml; charset="utf-8"
Content-Length: nnnn

<env:Envelope xmlns:env="http://www.w3.org/2001/09/soap-envelope">
   <env:Body>
      <env:Fault>
         <faultcode>env:MustUnderstand</faultcode>
         <faultstring>SOAP Must Understand Error</faultstring>
      </env:Fault>
   </env:Body>
</env:Envelope>
```

Example: **SOAP fault, resulting from failure to handle the SOAP body, in HTTP response**

```
HTTP/1.1 500 Internal Server Error
Content-Type: text/xml; charset="utf-8"
Content-Length: nnnn

<env:Envelope xmlns:env="http://www.w3.org/2001/09/soap-envelope" >
  <env:Body>
    <env:Fault>
      <faultcode>env:Server</faultcode>
      <faultstring>Server Error</faultstring>
      <detail>
        <e:myfaultdetails xmlns:e="http://example.org/2001/06/faults" >
          <message>My application didn't work</message>
          <errorcode>1001</errorcode>
        </e:myfaultdetails>
      </detail>
    </env:Fault>
  </env:Body>
</env:Envelope>
```

Appendix B: Acknowledgments (Non-Normative)

This document is the work of the W3C XML Protocol Working Group.

Members of the Working Group are (at the time of writing, and by alphabetical order): Yasser al Safadi (Philips Research), Vidur Apparao (Netscape), Don Box (DevelopMentor), Charles Campbell (Informix Software), Michael Champion (Software AG), Dave Cleary (webMethods), Ugo Corda (Xerox), Paul Cotton (Microsoft Corporation), Ron Daniel (Interwoven), Glen Daniels (Allaire), Doug Davis (IBM), Ray Denenberg (Library of Congress), Paul Denning (MITRE Corporation), Frank DeRose (TIBCO Software, Inc.), James

Falek (TIBCO Software, Inc.), David Fallside (IBM), Chris Ferris (Sun Microsystems), Daniela Florescu (Propel), Dietmar Gaertner (Software AG), Rich Greenfield (Library of Congress), Martin Gudgin (DevelopMentor), Hugo Haas (W3C), Marc Hadley (Sun Microsystems), Mark Hale (Interwoven), Randy Hall (Intel), Gerd Hoelzing (SAP AG), Oisin Hurley (IONA Technologies), Yin-Leng Husband (Compaq), John Ibbotson (IBM), Ryuji Inoue (Matsushita Electric Industrial Co., Ltd.), Scott Isaacson (Novell, Inc.), Kazunori Iwasa (Fujitsu Software Corporation), Murali Janakiraman (Rogue Wave), Mario Jeckle (Daimler-Chrysler Research and Technology), Eric Jenkins (Engenia Software), Mark Jones (AT&T), Anish Karmarkar (Oracle), Jeffrey Kay (Engenia Software), Richard Koo (Vitria Technology, Inc.), Jacek Kopecky (IDOOX s.r.o.), Yves Lafon (W3C), Tony Lee (Vitria Technology, Inc.), Michah Lerner (AT&T), Henry Lowe (OMG), Richard Martin (Active Data Exchange), Noah Mendelsohn (Lotus Development), Jeff Mischinsky (Oracle), Nilo Mitra (Ericsson Research Canada), Jean-Jacques Moreau (Canon), Highland Mary Mountain (Intel), Masahiko Narita (Fujitsu Software Corporation), Mark Needleman (Data Research Associates), Eric Newcomer (IONA Technologies), Henrik Frystyk Nielsen (Microsoft Corporation), Mark Nottingham (Akamai Technologies), David Orchard (BEA Systems), Kevin Perkins (Compaq), Jags Ramnaryan (BEA Systems), Andreas Riegg (Daimler-Chrysler Research and Technology), Herve Ruellan (Canon), Marwan Sabbouh (MITRE Corporation), Shane Sesta (Active Data Exchange), Miroslav Simek (IDOOX s.r.o.), Simeon Simeonov (Allaire), Nick Smilonich (Unisys), Soumitro Tagore (Informix Software), Lynne Thompson (Unisys), Patrick Thompson (Rogue Wave), Asir Vedamuthu (webMethods) Ray Whitmer (Netscape), Volker Wiechers (SAP AG), Stuart Williams (Hewlett-Packard), Amr Yassin (Philips Research) and Jin Yu (Martsoft Corporation).

Previous members were: Eric Fedok (Active Data Exchange), Susan Yee (Active Data Exchange), Dan Frantz (BEA Systems), Alex Ceponkus (Bowstreet), James Tauber (Bowstreet), Rekha Nagarajan (Calico Commerce), Mary Holstege (Calico Commerce), Krishna Sankar (Cisco Systems), David Burdett (Commerce One), Murray Maloney (Commerce One), Jay Kasi (Commerce One), Yan Xu (DataChannel), Brian Eisenberg (DataChannel), Mike Dierken (DataChannel), Michael Freeman (Engenia Software), Bjoern Heckel (Epicentric), Dean Moses (Epicentric), Julian Kumar (Epicentric), Miles Chaston (Epicentric), Alan Kropp (Epicentric), Scott Golubock (Epicentric), Michael Freeman (Engenia Software), Jim Hughes (Fujitsu Limited), Dick Brooks (Group 8760), David Ezell (Hewlett Packard), Fransisco Cubera (IBM), David Orchard (Jamcracker), Alex Milowski (Lexica), Steve Hole (MessagingDirect Ltd.), John-Paul Sicotte (MessagingDirect Ltd.), Vilhelm Rosenqvist (NCR), Lew Shannon (NCR), Art Nevarez (Novell, Inc.), David Clay (Oracle), Jim Trezzo (Oracle), David Cleary (Progress Software), Andrew Eisenberg (Progress Software), Peter Lecuyer (Progress Software), Ed Mooney (Sun Microsystems), Mark Baker (Sun Microsystems), Anne Thomas Manes (Sun Microsystems), George Scott (Tradia, Inc.), Erin

Hoffmann (Tradia, Inc.), Conleth O'Connell (Vignette), Waqar Sadiq (Vitria Technology, Inc.), Randy Waldrop (WebMethods), Bill Anderson (Xerox), Tom Breuel (Xerox), Matthew MacKenzie (XMLGlobal Technologies), David Webber (XMLGlobal Technologies), John Evdemon (XMLSolutions) and Kevin Mitchell (XMLSolutions).

The people who have contributed to discussions on xml-dist-app@w3.org are also gratefully acknowledged.

Appendix C: Part 2 Change Log (Non-Normative)

C.1   SOAP Specification Changes

Date	Author	Description
20010926	MJG	Updated member list.
20010926	MJG	Updated ednote in Section 6.4.
20010926	MJG	Changed rpc namespace to `http://www.w3.org/2001/09/soap-rpc`.
20010921	MJG	Added rpc namespace to list in Section 2.
20010921	MJG	Added new schema for rpc result element as described in Section 5.1.
20010921	MJG	Amended Section 5.1 to incorporate description of rpc result element.
20010921	MJG	Changed `targetNamespace` attribute of encoding schema to `http://www.w3.org/2001/09/soap-encoding`.
20010921	JJM	Used text proposed by Noah for ednote on SOAPAction.
20010920	JJM	Make the wording clarification regarding issue 45 (decreasing order of precedence).
20010920	JJM	Removed current security section; added new security subsection to HTTP binding section, with a temporary ednote, until we get text from Henrik and Chris.
20010920	JJM	Change the namespace of the envelope to `http://www.w3.org/2001/09/....`
20010920	JJM	Add an editorial note about why some sections are not written in terms of Infoset.
20010920	JJM	Add ednote from Jacek regarding SOAPAction.
20010918	JJM	Added ednote to the "SOAPAction" section indicating that a HTTP status code needs to be obtained from IANA.
20010918	JJM	Removed last `electrocommerce.org` URL from examples.

continued on next page

Date	Author	Description
20010914	JJM	Added text from Henrik to beef-up the "Data Model" section place-holder text.
	JJM	Back to "Adjuncts" again.
20010914	JJM	Fixed issues 124, 126, 127, 128, and 132.
20010914	JJM	Fixed typos and indentation.
20010914	JJM	Referenced the XML InfoSet Proposed Recommendation instead of the Candidate Recommendation.
20010911	JJM	Changed XML Information Set into a normative reference. Changed XML Protocol Comments Archive, Discussion Archive and Charter into non-normative references. Added a reference to RFC 2396 in Section 4, 3rd paragraph.
20010905	MJH	Wordsmithed abstract and introduction to better reflect split into Parts 1 and 2. Rationalized list of references so only cited works appear. Removed envelope schema changes. Added bibref entries for cross references to Part 1, fixed links so they target the HTML instead of XML version of the doc.
20010831	JJM	Added a close paragraph tag before starting a new olist or ulist.
20010831	JJM	Properly declared the language for the spec, so that we can generate valid HTML.
20010831	JJM	Added text from Hugo to emphasize the fact that the SOAP root attribute is of type XMLSchema boolean.
20010830	MJG	Copied "Relation to XML" section from Part 1.
20010830	MJG	Removed Design Goals section (design goals listed relevant to Part 1, not Part 2).
20010830	JJM	Removed terminology not relevant to Part 2.
20010830	JJM	Added SOAP examples from Part 1, introductory sections.
20010830	JJM	Added SOAP example appendix from Part 1.
20010830	JJM	Added a paragraph to Section 1 pointing to Part 2 for encoding, rpc and http binding.
20010830	JJM	Added a paragraph at the beginning of Section 3 to cover serializations containing references to data outside the serialization, as per 20010829 teleconference.
20010830	JJM	Remove 2nd sentence, bullet 5, RPC faults section, as per 20010829 teleconference.
20010830	JJM	Remove 2nd sentence, bullet 1, RPC faults section, as per 20010822 teleconference.
20010829	JJM	Added a placeholder for the forthcoming Data Model section.
20010829	JJM	Removed the Envelope Example section, already present in Part 1.
20010829	JJM	Updated the spec's title.

continued on next page

Date	Author	Description
20010829	JJM	Replaced specref with xspecref for references to Part 1 items.
20010829	JJM	Added bibliography entry for SOAP 1.2, Part 1.
20010829	JJM	Removed former Sections 1, 2, 3, and 4, and the SOAP versioning appendix. Moved the RPC section before the HTTP binding section, as per the 20010815 teleconference call.
20010829	JJM	Did split the spec into two parts.
20010829	JJM	Referred to the proper DTD and stylesheet.
20010829	JJM	Updated the list of WG members: one person per line in the XML file, for easier updating.
20010816	MJH	Replaced a mustUnderstand="1" with mustUnderstand="true". Slight rewording in mu description.
20010810	MJH	Merged in RPC fault rules text from Jacek. Added new Data-EncodingUnknown fault code to SOAP Fault Codes section. Added editorial notes about introduction of new fault code namespace for RPC.
20010809	MJH	Merged in "mustHappen" descriptive text from Glen and Noah.
20010809	MJH	Fixed language around "default" values of attributes.
20010809	MJH	Removed HTTP extension framework, added editorial note to describe why.
20010808	MJH	Added Infoset "specified" property text from Chris.
20010808	MJH	Removed assumption 4 from version transition appendix.
20010808	MJH	Added reference to SOAP 1.1 specification to references section, removed SOAP 1.1 author list from acknowledgments section.
20010807	MJH	Converted specification from HTML to XML conforming to W3C XMLSpec DTD. Numerous resulting formatting changes.
20010720	MJG	Applied Infoset terminology to Sections 1, 2, 3, and 4.
20010629	MJG	Amended description of routing and intermediaries in Section 2.1.
20010629	JJM	Changed "latest version" URI to end with soap12.
20010629	JJM	Removed "previous version" URI.
20010629	JJM	Removed "Editor copy" in <title>.
20010629	JJM	Removed "Editor copy" in the title.
20010629	JJM	Added "Previous version" to either point to SOAP/1.1, or explicitly mention there was no prior draft.
20010629	JJM	Pre-filed publication URIs.
20010629	JJM	Incorporated David's suggested changes for the examples in Sections 4.1.1 to 4.4.2.
20010629	JJM	Fixed some remaining typos.
20010629	MJH	Fixed a couple of typos.

continued on next page

Date	Author	Description
20010628	MJG	Made various formatting, spelling, and grammatical fixes.
20010628	MJG	Moved soap:encodingStyle from soap:Envelope to children of soap:Header/soap:Body in examples 1, 2, 47, 48, 49, and 50.
20010628	MJG	Changed text in Section 2.1 from 'it is both a SOAP sender or a SOAP receiver' to 'it is both a SOAP sender and a SOAP receiver'.
20010628	MJG	Fixed caption on example 24.
20010628	MJH	Fixed a couple of capitalization errors where the letter "A" appeared as a capital in the middle of a sentence.
20010628	MJH	Updated Figure 1, removed ednote to do so.
20010622	HFN	Removed the introductory text in terminology section 1.4.3 as it talks about model stuff that is covered in Section 2. It was left over from original glossary which also explained the SOAP model.
20010622	HFN	Moved the definition of block to encapsulation section in terminology.
20010622	HFN	Removed introductory section in 1.4.1 as this overlaps with the model description in Section 2 and doesn't belong in a terminology section.
20010622	HFN	Removed reference to "Web Characterization Terminology & Definitions Sheet" in terminology section as this is not an active WD.
20010622	HFN	Added revised glossary.
20010622	HFN	Added example 0 to Section 1.3 and slightly modified text for examples 1 and 2 to make it clear that HTTP is used as a protocol binding.
20010622	MJG	Added `http://example.com/...` to list of application/context specific URIs in Section 1.2.
20010622	MJG	Updated examples in Section 4.1.1 to be `encodingStyle` attributes rather than just the values of attributes.
20010622	MJG	Added table.norm, td.normitem, and td.normtext styles to stylesheet. Used said styles for table of fault code values in Section 4.4.1.
20010622	MJG	In Appendix C, changed upgrade element to Upgrade and env to envelope. Made envelope unqualified. Updated schema document to match.
20010622	MJG	Moved MisunderstoodHeader from envelope schema into separate faults schema. Removed entry in envelope schema change table in Appendix D.2 that referred to addition of said element. Modified example in Section 4.4.2 to match. Added reference to schema document to Section 4.4.2.
20010622	MJH	Added binding as a component of SOAP in introduction. Fixed a couple of typos and updated a couple of example captions.
20010622	MJG	Made BNF in Section 6.1.1 into a table.

continued on next page

Date	Author	Description
20010622	MJG	Made BNFs in Section 5.1, clause 8 into tables. Added associated 'bnf' style for `table` and `td` elements to stylesheet.
20010622	MJG	Amended text regarding namespace prefix mappings in Section 1.2.
20010622	MJG	Added link to schema for the *http://www.w3.org/2001/06/soap-upgrade* namespace to Appendix C. Updated associated ednote.
20010622	MJG	Added reference numbers for XML Schema Recommendation to text prior to schema change tables in Appendix D.2 and linked said numbers to local references in this document.
20010622	MJG	Reordered entries in schema change classification table in Appendix D.2.
20010622	MJG	Changed type of `mustUnderstand` and `root` attributes to standard boolean and updated schema change tables in Appendix D.2 accordingly.
20010622	JJM	Manually numbered all the examples (53 in total!).
20010622	JJM	Added caption text to all the examples.
20010622	JJM	Replaced remaining occurrences of SOAP/1.2 with SOAP Version 1.2 (including <title>).
20010621	HFN	Added ednote to Sections 4.2.2 and 4.2.3 so that we know they have to be incorporated with Section 2.
20010621	HFN	Added version transition Appendix C.
20010621	HFN	Applied new styles to examples.
20010621	HFN	Changed term "transport" to "underlying protocol".
20010621	HFN	Changed example URNs to URLs of the style `http://example.org/....`
20010621	MJH	Updated the Acknowledgments section.
20010621	JJM	Added new stylesheet definitions (from XML Schema) for examples, and used them for examples 1 and 2.
20010621	JJM	Incorporated David Fallside's comments on Status and Intro sections.
20010620	HFN	Changed the status section.
20010620	HFN	Changed title to SOAP Version 1.2 and used that first time in abstract and in body.
20010620	HFN	Removed question from Section 2.4 as this is an issue and is to be listed in the issues list.
20010620	HFN	Moved change log to appendix.
20010615	JJM	Renamed default actor to anonymous actor for now (to be consistent).
20010615	JJM	Fixed typos in Section 2.

continued on next page

Date	Author	Description
20010614	JJM	Updated Section 2 to adopt the terminology used elsewhere in the spec.
20010613	MJH	Updated mustUnderstand fault text with additions from Martin Gudgin.
20010613	MJH	Added schema changes appendix from Martin Gudgin.
20010613	MJH	Added mustUnderstand fault text from Glen Daniels.
20010612	MJH	Fixed document <title>.
20010612	MJH	Moved terminology subsection from message exchange model section to introduction section.
20010612	MJH	Fixed capitalization errors by replacing "...A SOAP..." with "...a SOAP..." where appropriate.
20010612	MJH	Removed trailing "/" from encoding namespace URI.
20010612	MJH	Fixed links under namespace URIs to point to W3C space instead of schemas.xmlsoap.org.
20010612	MJH	Removed some odd additional links with text of "/" pointing to the encoding schema following the text of the encoding namespace URI in several places.
20010611	MJH	Incorporated new text for Section 2.
20010611	JJM	Changed remaining namespaces, in particular next.
20010609	JJM	Changed the spec name from XMLP/SOAP to SOAP.
20010609	JJM	Changed the version number from 1.1 to 1.2.
20010609	JJM	Changed the namespaces from `http://schemas.xmlsoap.org/soap/` to `http://www.w3.org/2001/06/soap-`.
20010609	JJM	Replaced the remaining XS and XE prefixes to env and enc, respectively.
20010601	MJH	Updated the examples in Sections 1 and 6 and Appendix A with text suggested by Martin Gudgin to comply with XML Schema Recommendation.
20010601	JJM	Updated the examples in Sections 4 and 5 with text suggested by Martin Gudgin, to comply with XML Schema Recommendation.
20010531	HFN	Removed Appendixes C and D, and added links to live issues list and separate schema files.
20010531	MJH	Added this change log and updated schemas in Appendix C to comply with XML Schema Recommendation.

C.2 XML Schema Changes

The encoding schema has been updated to be compliant with the XML Schema Recommendation [4] [5]. The table below shows the categories of change.

Class	Meaning
Addition	New constructs have been added to the schema.
Clarification	The meaning of the schema has been changed to more accurately match the specification.
Deletion	Constructs have been removed from the schema.
Name	The schema has been changed due to a data type name change in the XML Schema specification.
Namespace	A namespace name has been changed.
Semantic	The meaning of the schema has been changed.
Style	Style changes have been made to the schema.
Syntax	The syntax of the schema has been updated due to changes in the XML Schema specification.

The table below lists the changes to the encoding schema.

Class	Description
Namespace	Updated to use the *http://www.w3.org/2001/XMLSchema* namespace.
Namespace	Value of `targetNamespace` attribute changed to *http://www.w3.org/2001/06/soap-encoding*.
Semantic	Changed type of the `root` attribute from restriction of boolean that only allowed 0 or 1 as lexical values to the standard boolean in the *http://www.w3.org/2001/XMLSchema* namespace. The lexical forms 0, 1, false, true are now allowed.
Addition	Added processContents="lax" to all element and attribute wildcards.
Syntax	Changed base64 simple type to be a vacuous restriction of the base64Binary type in the *http://www.w3.org/2001/XMLSchema* namespace.
Syntax	Updated all complex type definitions with simple base types to new syntax.
Syntax	Added <xs:sequence> to all complex type definitions derived implicitly from the ur-type.
Syntax	Added <xs:sequence> to all named model group definitions.
Deletion	Removed the timeDuration data type.
Addition	Added duration data type derived by extension from the duration data type in the *http://www.w3.org/2001/XMLSchema* namespace.
Deletion	Removed the timeInstant data type.
Addition	Added dateTime data type derived by extension from the dateTime data type in the *http://www.w3.org/2001/XMLSchema* namespace.
Addition	Added gYearMonth data type derived by extension from the gYearMonth data type in the *http://www.w3.org/2001/XMLSchema* namespace.

continued on next page

Class	Description
Addition	Added gYear data type derived by extension from the gYear data type in the *http://www.w3.org/2001/XMLSchema* namespace.
Addition	Added gMonthDay data type derived by extension from the gMonthDay data type in the *http://www.w3.org/2001/XMLSchema* namespace.
Addition	Added gDay data type derived by extension from the gDay data type in the *http://www.w3.org/2001/XMLSchema* namespace.
Addition	Added gDay data type derived by extension from the gDay data type in the *http://www.w3.org/2001/XMLSchema* namespace.
Deletion	Removed the binary data type.
Addition	Added hexBinary data type derived by extension from the hexBinary data type in the *http://www.w3.org/2001/XMLSchema* namespace.
Addition	Added base64Binary data type derived by extension from the base64Binary data type in the *http://www.w3.org/2001/XMLSchema* namespace.
Deletion	Removed the uriReference data type.
Addition	Added anyURI data type derived by extension from the anyURI data type in the *http://www.w3.org/2001/XMLSchema* namespace.
Addition	Added normalizedString data type derived by extension from the normalized-String data type in the *http://www.w3.org/2001/XMLSchema* namespace.
Addition	Added token data type derived by extension from the token data type in the *http://www.w3.org/2001/XMLSchema* namespace.
Clarification	Added explicit namespace="##any" to all element and attribute wildcards which did not previously have an explicit namespace attribute.
Style	Where possible, comments have been changed into annotations.

Glossary

100% Pure Java   The designation for classes and applications that comply with Sun's criteria for total independence from the underlying operating system.

abstract   A Java keyword describing classes or methods that define a runtime behavior but that don't provide a complete implementation. You can't create an object from an `abstract` class, but an object created from a class extending the `abstract` class can be referred to with the `abstract` class name.

abstract pathname   The internal path designation inside a `File` object that is independent of the underlying operating system.

Abstract Window Toolkit (AWT)   The package of Java interfaces, classes, exceptions, and errors that create a Java GUI using the GUI components of the underlying platform. The AWT is simpler than the "swing" GUI package.

accessibility   The `javax.accessibility` package stipulates interfaces that provide ease-of-use Java application features for users with disabilities.

Active Server Pages (ASP)   Microsoft's technology for embedding Visual Basic or VBScript code inside HTML pages to create dynamic web pages.

adapter   Design pattern for converting or adapting one class interface to another. For example, there are classes in the `java.awt.event` package that support the creation of event listeners.

Adjustable **(interface)**   Java interface (`java.awt.Adjustable`) that stipulates methods for handling changeable control, such as a scrollbar.

algorithm   A problem-solving operation that proceeds one step at a time to accomplish a specific program task.

alpha   The typical designation given a program or application that is undergoing initial (internal) testing before being released for testing outside the company that developed it. *See also* beta.

American Standard Code for Information Interchange (ASCII)   The ubiquitous computer industry standard for encoding text and control characters.

anonymous **(class)**   Unnamed Java local class declared and instantiated in a single statement.

Apache eXtensible Interaction System (AXIS)   The next generation implementation of SOAP classes from the Apache organization. It is expected to be considerably faster and handle large messages than SOAP 2.2.

API   *See* application programming interface.

applet   A Java program that operates within a Java Virtual Machine (JVM), supplied by the user's web browser. You can think of the browser as providing an applet container that lets it run on the client machine more or less independently of the underlying operating system.

application   A Java program that runs on a client machine and that can access all the client system's resources. *See also* applet.

application programming interface (API)   Calling conventions or instruction set used by an application to access operating system and library services.

Application Service Provider (ASP)   An Internet server that provides more than simple web pages.

Application Services   Sun's classification of a collection of interface improvements that are included in the Java Foundation Classes (JFC).

argument   Java method call data item that can designate a Java primitive or object.

ArithmeticException   Java runtime exception that indicates an exceptional arithmetic condition has occurred, typically due to integer non-floating-point division by zero.

array   Group of data items that share the same type, in which a 32-bit integer index addresses each data item uniquely.

Arrays (class)   Java class (`java.util.Arrays`) that includes `static` methods for operations on primitives, arrays, and object references.

ASCII   *See* American Standard Code for Information Interchange.

ASP   *See* Active Server Pages; *see* Application Service Provider.

assignable   Relationship between an object reference and a reference variable when both are the same type or the variable is an ancestor of the object reference in the class hierarchy.

assignment   Java operators that assign a value to a variable, for example, = and +=.

atomic   A program step that cannot be interrupted by another `Thread` is said to be atomic. All Java assignment operations with 32-bit variables are atomic, but 64-bit variable (long and double) operations are not.

attribute   In XML, a name-value pair within the start tag of an element.

automatic (local) variable   Variable declared inside a method to which memory is automatically allocated when the method is called.

AWT   *See* Abstract Window Toolkit (sometimes called the Annoying Window Toolkit by frustrated programmers).

AXIS   *See* Apache eXtensible Interaction System.

bean   *See* Java bean.

beta   The typical designation given a program or application that is under development and is released for testing outside the company that developed it; usually the step just prior to commercial release. *See also* alpha.

bitwise   An operator that works on individual bits; an operator that manipulates Java integer primitive types on an individual-bit basis.

block   A section of Java code that is contained within matching { and } characters.

break   A Java keyword governing two programmatic actions. Used alone, it prompts continuation of program execution after the present code block; used with a statement label, it prompts continuation of program execution after the code block tagged by that label. *See also* continue.

byte   An 8-bit Java integer-type primitive that is treated as a signed integer.

Byte (class)   The Java wrapper class for values of 8-bit byte primitives.

bytecode   Java Virtual Machine (JVM) instruction in platform-independent format, such as that used with Java applets.

CAB (cabinet)   Microsoft's format for compressed class and other resource files and for distributing installation files.

case-insensitive   Programming language naming convention that does not distinguish between upper- and lowercase letters.

case-sensitive   Programming language naming convention that distinguishes between upper- and lowercase letters; in other words, "Text" and "text" are read differently. Java is case-sensitive.

cast   Reserved word (not presently used); syntax for changing Java expression type, for example, casting an `int` value to a long value.

catch   Java keyword that declares a specific exception type and creates a block of code or clause that executes when that exception contained in code with a `try` statement is thrown.

CGI   *See* Common Gateway Interface.

char   Java integer primitive variable that represents Unicode characters as 16-bit unsigned integers.

Character (class)   The Java wrapper class for `char` values.

character data   The text contents of an element or attribute.

checked exceptions   Java programmatic exceptions that require explicit handling code.

child   In context of object-oriented programming, any object that inherits from and obtains information from another object; a Java class that inherits from another class (parent or superclass).

class   In general context of object oriented programming, a method for grouping objects that share some characteristic or characteristics; all Java classes descend from the `Object` class.

Class (class)   The Java class (`java.lang.Class`) class that indicates the runtime type of any object.

class file   The outcome of compiling a Java class.

class method   Java method declared `static` and attached to an entire class, rather than to objects in the class.

class modifiers   Java keywords (`public`, `abstract`, and `final`) that establish class properties or characteristics.

class variable   A variable (`static`) that belongs to a Java class rather than to a class instance of the class.

ClassCastException   An exception that is thrown whenever the JVM identifies an attempt to cast an object reference to an incompatible type.

clone method   Java method in the `Object` class that can generate a copy of an object.

Collection (interface)   Java interface (`java.util.Collection`) that defines basic behavior for Collections API objects.

Collections API   Java 2 set of classes and interfaces that provide a number of methods for handling collections of objects.

Collections (class)   Java class (`java.util.Collections`) containing `static` methods applicable to collections.

Color (class)   Java class (`java.awt.Color`) that encompasses red, green, and blue intensities of screen color.

Common Gateway Interface (CGI)   The conventions governing communication between web servers and auxiliary programs, such as search engines. This was the first technology that supported dynamic interaction between users (via browsers) and web servers.

Comparator (interface)   Java interface (`java.util.Comparator`) that provides the means of access between custom classes and `Arrays` class sorting and searching methods.

completeness   Java term denoting whether a class behavior is fully developed or requires further development by subclasses.

Component (class)   Java abstract class (`java.awt.Component`) that is the parent of all screen components in the AWT graphics package except those related to menus.

constraints   Java object that is passed to a layout manager that implements the `LayoutManager2` interface and that defines the way in which a component is handled.

constructor   Special kind of member function called on the creation of a class instance using `new`; initializes the object. Java classes can declare none, one, or many constructor methods.

constructor chaining   A Java constructor that calls another constructor, according to a specific set of Java-enforced rules.

container   In Sun's terminology, the environment a Java applet, servlet, or EJB operates in is a specialized container that is required to provide specific services.

Container (class)   The Java class (`java.awt.Container`) that is the ancestor for all AWT GUI objects that contain and manage interface components.

contentPane   In Swing primary container classes, such as `JFrame`, the container to which all interface components are added.

continue   Java keyword used in two contexts: inside a looping construct, it causes continuation of execution with the next innermost loop activity; when used with a statement label, it moves control to the next labeled loop. *See also* break.

controller   In the Model-View-Controller design pattern, the controller provides functions or services for communicating user input to the model and view(s).

conversion   Used in a Java expression, conversion changes the expression type.

cookie   A small chunk of text data stored by a web browser as a consequence of visiting a website. This data is returned to the web server on subsequent visits to the site and may be used to identify a user.

crimson   The project name for an XML parser provided in the JAXP package in the crimson.jar file.

daemon Thread   Daemon is a UNIX term for programs that operate in the background and handle requests for network services. Java Threads can be tagged daemon by the set-Daemon method as a way of distinguishing them from user threads, and they are generally JVM utilities, such as the garbage collection Thread. A Java application stops when the only Threads left running are daemon Threads.

data binding object   A Java object with accessor and mutator methods that affect the underlying data store.

deadlock   Situation in which two or more Java Threads need the same resource and consequently come to a stop.

decorator   Java design pattern in which an attached object adds functions to a core class.

decrement   Operator (--) attached to a primitive numeric variable and that subtracts one from the variable.

deep copy   Programming term for a method of cloning objects that copies both the object and all objects to which that object refers. The clone method in the Object class is not a deep copy.

delegate   Object that handles a component's look and feel (Swing convention) or that combines view and controller functions (Model-View-Controller design pattern).

delegation (model)   Java 1.1 event model in which event-generating components transfer event handling to specific event listeners.

deprecated   JDK (Java Developers' Kit) term that indicates a method whose use is no longer recommended.

deserialize   To reconstruct a Java object stored by serialization, usually by use of ObjectInputStream.

destructor   C++ method that cleans up for a user-defined object type, reclaiming designated memory and other resources. Java uses automatic garbage collection rather than destructors. *See also* finalize.

directives   In JavaServer Pages, directives are tags that define general policies or conditions for a page or part of a page.

Distributed Computing   In general, an architecture in which programs running on different physical computers cooperate to solve a problem by communicating over a network.

DLL   *See* dynamic link library.

doclet   Java program developed with classes in sun.tools.javadoc for customizing javadoc output.

Document Object Model (DOM)   An approach to processing an XML document in which the entire document is stored in memory as a parsed hierarchy of elements. Also, in web browsers, the hierarchical structure of the HTML document.

document type declaration   A structure within an XML document that points to or contains markup declarations that describe a class of XML documents.

Document Type Definition (DTD) The markup declarations that describe a class of XML documents.

DOM *See* Document Object Model.

***double* (double precision)** Java 64-bit floating-point primitive type.

***Double* (class)** Java wrapper class for `double` primitive values.

DTD *See* Document Type Definition.

dynamic link library (DLL) Executable packages or modules that a programmer can bring into memory and link to as needed by an application.

dynamic method lookup The manner in which the JVM (Java Virtual Machine) locates and calls the appropriate method at runtime based on an object's actual (rather than reference) type.

editable A property of `TextArea` and `TextField` components that is true if the contents can be changed by a user.

element An XML structural construct consisting of a start tag, an end tag and information between the tags (contents).

enabling events Java method (`enableEvents`) in `java.awt.Component` called to enable creation of user interface events. The exact events enabled are determined by an event mask.

encapsulation Term used in object-oriented programming for enclosing information and behavior within an object, hiding its structure and implementation from other objects. Encapsulation allows programmers to modify the way the object's internal functions without affecting any other code using the object.

entity An XML structural construct that associates character data or well-formed XML with a name. An entity can be referred to using an *entity reference*.

entity reference An XML structural construct that is used to refer to an entity. An entity reference is delimited by an ampersand and a semicolon.

***Enumeration* (interface)** Java 1.0 interface (`java.util.Enumeration`) that stipulates the manner in which a collection generates a series of the collection's elements, using `nextElement` and `hasMoreElements` methods. Sun intends that `Enumeration` be replaced by the Java 2 `Iterator` interface, but `Enumeration` is still widely used.

equals Java method that compares two object references and returns `true` when the objects' content is identical. The `Object` class default `equals` method returns `true` when both reference the same object.

***Error* (class)** Java class (`java.lang.Error`) that is the parent class of all Java error classes and a subclass of `Throwable`. Errors are typically conditions that a program cannot recover from, such as running out of memory.

escape sequence A character string for encoding a character that is not a normal keyboard character or would cause trouble for the Java compiler.

event listener Java object that is registered with a particular control associated with user activity and that is notified when a specific event takes place.

event mask   A java.awt.Component class feature that dictates the types of GUI events the object generates.

Exception (class)   Java class (java.lang .Exception) that is the parent class of all Java exceptions and a subclass of Throwable. Exceptions generally signal conditions that the program may be able to recover from.

extends   Java keyword used to define a new class that indicates the base class from which the new class will inherit.

Extensible Markup Language (XML)   A simplified form of SGML that is the standard for creating custom markup languages. Its purpose is to permit the tags in a document to exactly describe the contents.

Extensible Stylesheet Language (XSL)   A specification for transforming and presenting documents created with XML.

field   Java variable that defines a particular class characteristic.

File (class)   Java class (java.io.File) that manages file and directory pathnames instead of actual data files.

file separator   Character that indicates the division of path and file name components.

filter (file I/O sense)   Package of interfaces (java.io) that specify filtering methods for input and output streams and file names.

filter (image sense)   The Java java.awt.image package provides so-called filter classes for transforming image information.

Filter (Java servlet sense)   An interface introduced with the servlet 2.3 API used to create objects that modify a servlet request or response.

final   Java keyword that stipulates that a class cannot have subclasses. Applied to a member method, this stipulates that the method cannot be overridden by subclasses. Applied to a member variable, it stipulates the variable is a constant whose value cannot be changed once it is set.

finalize   Object method executed by the Java garbage collection process when the memory that object occupies is to be reclaimed. Typically used to ensure that system resources are recovered when an object is discarded.

finally   Java keyword for attaching a code block that always has to be executed to a try block.

float   Java 32-bit floating-point primitive type.

Float (class)   Java wrapper class for float primitive values.

form   A structure used in HTML pages to create elements that can accept user input and transmit it to a web server using CGI conventions.

garbage collection   JVM (Java Virtual Machine) process of locating and recovering memory that is allocated to objects the program can no longer use.

GIF   *See* Graphics Interchange Format.

graphical user interface (GUI)   A computer user interface that uses graphical elements, windows, and a pointing device; Mac OS, Windows, and X11 are examples of GUIs; supported by JVM.

Graphics Java class (`java.awt.Graphics`) that supplies the context for drawing components and screen images.

graphics context Hardware-specific information used by an operating system in allowing applications to draw on a graphics device, such as the computer screen.

Graphics Interchange Format (GIF) Ubiquitous HTML-compressed graphics file format (.gif file extension) for inline graphic elements. Unisys owns the format's patent. *See also* Joint Photographic Experts Group (JPEG).

Graphics2D **(class)** Java 2 class (`java.awt.Graphics2D`) that extends `Graphics`.

GUI *See* graphical user interface.

Hailstorm The code name used during development for Microsoft's web services program that became My Services.

hashcode In computing context, a characteristic number derived from a data item's contents that allows a program or application to locate the item quickly by operating on the number.

hashCode The method in every Java object that generates an `int` primitive hashcode value characteristic of the object.

Hashtable **(class)** Java class (`java.util.Hashtable`) object that stores Object references denoted by "key" objects using the key's hashcode.

heavyweight components Java GUI interface components that use a corresponding operating system peer, in contrast to "lightweight" components in the "Swing" GUI toolkit.

hex (hexadecimal) Mathematical base 16 system used in computer programming that uses alphanumeric characters 0 through 9 and *A* through *F* or *a* through *f*.

hidden variable In an HTML form, a hidden variable holds information that cannot be seen or modified by the user but that will be transmitted to the web server.

hierarchical Logical arrangement of elements, also called a tree structure, in which every element with the exception of the root object has parents and might or might not have child objects (children). Examples of this structure can be found in the Java class library, XML documents, and computer file systems.

HTML *See* HyperText Markup Language.

HttpServlet **(class)** The base class in the `javax.servlet.http` package extended by servlets that need to respond to GET and POST operations.

HyperText Markup Language (HTML) The document markup language used to create web pages and standardized by the W3C.

Hypertext Transfer Protocol (HTTP) The set of rules (protocols) based on TCP/IP that provides the foundation for communication between web clients and servers.

IDE *See* Integrated Development Environment.

identifier Name given an item in a Java program or application.

IEEE *See* Institute of Electrical and Electronics Engineers.

Image **(class)**   Java abstract class (`java.awt`
`.Image`) that defines how graphics representation information is held.

implements   Java keyword in class declarations that precedes a list of one or more interfaces for which the class supplies methods.

implicit variables   In a JavaServer Page, these variables are always created.

import   Java source code file statement that informs the Java compiler as to which package holds classes used in the code.

increment   Operator (++) attached to a primitive numeric variable that adds one to that variable to which it is attached.

IndexOutOfBoundsException   Java exception thrown when an attempt is made to address a nonexistent array element; `ArrayIndexOutOfBoundsException` and `StringIndexOutOfBoundsException` are subclasses of `IndexOutOfBoundsException`.

inheritance   In object-oriented programming, relationship among hierarchically arranged objects by which some objects (children) are granted attributes of another object (parent).

init **(applet method)**   By convention, a method that belongs to a Java applet's initial class and that is called by a web browser's JVM after the applet object is created but before it is displayed.

init **(servlet method)**   A method that belongs to a Java servlet class and that is called by the servlet engine after the servlet object is created but before it services any user requests.

initialize; initialization   Setting a variable's starting value.

inner class   Nested class or interface with access to all member fields and methods of the class in which it is nested, including any declared `private`.

InputStream **(class)**   Java abstract base class (`java.io.InputStream`) for various Java classes that read data as a byte stream.

Insets **(class)**   Java class (`java.awt.Insets`) used in graphic interfaces containing an object that delineates border widths on all sides of a container.

instance   An object created from a specific class is said to be an instance of that class.

instance fields   The set of distinct member variables for each class instance.

instance methods   Member methods that are executable only through a reference to a class instance.

instance variable   Java variable that is part of a class instance instead of the class itself (class or `static` variable).

instanceof   Logical operator used to determine the type of a reference in an expression.

Institute of Electrical and Electronics Engineers (IEEE)   Professional organization that develops computer hardware and software standards, as well as standards for the electronics industry.

int   Java 32-bit integer primitive type that is always treated as a signed integer.

Integer **(class)**   Java wrapper class for `int` values.

Integrated Development Environment (IDE) Application development system that incorporates in one package programming tools, such as a source code editor, compiler, debugger, and project tracking functions.

interface Similar to a Java class definition, but provides only method declarations, not implementations. A Java class is free to implement as many interfaces as needed.

International Organization for Standardization (ISO) Group comprised of national standards organizations from 89 countries that establishes international standards for telecommunications and technology.

interrupt Java Thread class instance method; if Thread is in sleep or wait state, calling interrupt wakes the Thread and generates InterruptedException; otherwise, the interrupted flag is set.

interrupted **(Thread private variable)** Java flag set to true when a Thread is interrupted.

interrupted **(Thread static method)** Java static method that a running Thread uses to determine whether it has been interrupted.

InterruptedException Exception that can be generated when a Thread that is sleeping or waiting is interrupted. The Thread cannot continue with what it was doing but must instead handle the exception.

IOException **(class)** Java class (java.io .Exception) that is the parent class of all exceptions related to I/O processes, e.g., opening and reading a file.

isInterrupted Java Thread class instance method by which a Thread can be queried to determine whether or not it has been interrupted.

ISO *See* International Organization for Standardization.

Iterator **(interface)** Java interface (java.util .Iterator) intended to replace Enumeration as the preferred method of examining elements in a collection.

J2EE *See* Java 2 Enterprise Edition.

J2ME *See* Java 2 Micro Edition.

J2SE *See* Java 2 Standard Edition.

JAR (Java ARchive) File format similar to Zip for collecting multiple resources (such as class files and Java class libraries) in a single file.

Java 2 Enterprise Edition (J2EE) The largest of Sun's collection of Java utilities and libraries, designed for creation of Internet applications.

Java 2 Micro Edition (J2ME) Sun's collection of Java utilities and libraries that have been reduced in size and complexity to fit small computing environments such as mobile phones and PalmPilots.

Java 2 Standard Edition (J2SE) Sun's collection of Java utilities and libraries designed to fit most developer's needs.

Java 2D Group of Java classes that provide a number of advanced graphics methods.

Java API for XML Parsing (JAXP) Sun's API that provides a standardized way to specify operations on XML documents. This API is intended to be independent of the actual parser used.

Java bean Reusable software component written for a specific function or use and that meets the JavaBeans standard for getting and setting instance variable values.

Java Communications API Group of Java classes and operating system–specific code that supports direct interaction with serial and parallel I/O ports.

Java Database Connectivity (JDBC) The collection of Java classes in the java.sql package that enables Java programs to connect to SQL-style databases.

Java Development Kit (JDK) Java package of development tools, utilities, a class library, and documentation that is downloadable from the java.sun.com website.

Java Foundation Classes (JFC) Sun's name for the collection of five Java toolkits (Swing, Java 2D, Accessibility, Drag and Drop, and Application Services) for creating advanced GUIs in Java 2.

Java Mail Sun's API for Java applications accessing electronic mail functions, currently in version 1.2.

Java Message Service (JMS) Sun's message-oriented middleware API usable for both point-to-point and publish/subscribe message applications.

Java Native Interface (JNI) Java interface (API) that gives programmers access to a host system's language and determines Java's interaction with native code modules.

Java Runtime Environment (JRE) A collection of programs and libraries for a particular operating system that enables execution of Java programs but doesn't include the compiler or classes used in the compiler.

Java Virtual Machine (JVM) Nonphysical (virtual) computer that is part of the Java runtime environment and interprets Java bytecodes, providing the foundation for the cross-platform features of Java programs.

JavaBeans Java programming standard for components that comply with a standard interface.

JavaBeans Activation Framework (JAF) A standard extension to Java that permits flexible creation of Java objects.

javac Java application that starts the compiler.

javadoc Java utility that allows automatic documentation by processing source code and producing reference pages in HTML format.

JavaScript Web page scripting language developed by Netscape (originally called LiveScript) that controls the way in which web pages appear in browsers. Provides limited support for embedded Java applets.

JavaServer Pages (JSP) The Java API that allows a programmer to combine HTML and Java code in a single document to create a dynamic web page. A JSP page is converted into a servlet automatically.

JavaSpaces An advanced system for communication in distributed applications based on storage and retrieval of Java objects based on the object contents.

JAXP *See* Java API for XML Parsing.

JComponent (class)   Java class (`javax.swing.Jcomponent`) that is base class for the Swing visual components.

JDBC   *See* Java Database Connectivity.

JDK   *See* Java Development Kit.

JFC   *See* Java Foundation Classes.

JIT   *See* Just In Time.

join   Thread class instance method for coordinating Threads.

Joint Photographic Experts Group (JPEG)   Compressed graphics file format (.jpg file extension) supported by JVM and often found in web pages. *See also* Graphics Interchange Format (GIF).

JMS   *See* Java Message Service.

JNI   *See* Java Native Interface.

JPEG   *See* Joint Photographic Experts Group.

JRE   *See* Java Runtime Environment.

JSP   See JavaServer Pages.

jspDestroy (JSP method)   A method that is always called just before a web server removes JSP code from memory.

jspInit (JSP method)   A method that is always created in a JSP page and is always called before a user request is processed.

jspService (JSP method)   A method that is always created in a JSP page to process a user's HTTP request.

Just In Time (JIT)   Technology that speeds up the execution of Java programs by dynamically replacing the Java bytecode with machine language on-the-fly as methods are called.

JVM   *See* Java Virtual Machine.

label   An identifier followed by a colon appended to a Java statement; used only with `break` and `continue` statements.

layout manager   An object for controlling screen component position and size within a `java.awt.Container` object.

lightweight components   Java interface components that lack an operating system peer and for which the JVM carries out all screen drawing and event processing.

List (interface)   Java interface (`java.util.List`) that supplies an ordered collection of object references.

listener   Java 1.1 event model object registered with a generating component that is informed about a particular class of events.

local class   Java inner class defined within a member method that can access all class members and all local `final` variables.

local variable   *See* automatic variable.

lock   The equivalent of a variable associated with every object that controls access to the object by threads. Locks can be manipulated only by the JVM in the process of synchronizing access to the object.

long   Java 64-bit integer primitive type; always treated as signed integer. *See also* `double` (double precision).

Long (class)   Java wrapper class for `long` values.

low-level event   Java events that are close to operating system raw events; for example, mouse movements.

main (application method)   Java `static` method required by a Java application's initial class and that is executed by the JVM after loading the class to start the application.

manifest   File in all JAR files that provides supplementary information about other files in the JAR (such as digital signatures and encryption information). Manifest information is accessed via the `java.util.jar.Manifest` class.

Map (interface)   Java interface (`java.util.Map`) that requires the class implementing it to associate unique key objects with value objects. Classes implementing `Map` include `Hashtable` and `SortedMap`.

marshalling   In distributed computing techniques, the process of assembling objects and variables for transmission to a remote process.

maximumSize   Parameter that applies to graphic interface objects descended from `Jcomponent`; set with `setMaximumSize` method.

MAX_PRIORITY   Java `Thread` class constant.

member   Java variables, methods, and inner classes declared as part of a class are called members of the class.

member class   Java inner class not declared as `static`, nor within a member method.

Message Oriented Middleware (MOM)   An application that exists to transmit application messages over networks.

method   Java class function that is named and for which specific input parameters and return types are declared.

method signature   Combination of name and parameters that distinguishes one method from others.

MIME   *See* Multipurpose Internet Mail Extensions.

MIN_PRIORITY   Java `Thread` class constant.

model   In the Model-View-Controller design pattern, the Java object that contains data.

Model 1   Refers to a JSP application architecture in which the JSP code does both the primary decision making and formatting. In Model-View-Controller terminology, the JSP page is both controller and view, whereas JavaBean objects handle the model function.

Model 2   Refers to a JSP application architecture in which the primary decision making is handled by a servlet which delegates display to JSP pages using a RequestDispatcher. In Model-View-Controller terminology, the controller is a servlet, whereas JSP handles only the view.

Model-View-Controller (MVC)   Design pattern in which data is held by the `model` object and displayed by the `view` object, and a `controller` object informs both model and view objects of user input.

modulus (modulo)   Java operator (%), used with either integer or floating-point types, that divides the left operand by the right operand and returns the result.

monitor   JVM mechanism that uses object locks in controlling Thread access to objects.

multiple inheritance   In object-oriented programming, inheriting variables and methods from more than one class. Java does not provide for multiple inheritance.

Multipurpose Internet Mail Extensions (MIME) A standard way of denoting content type in a resource; originated for use with e-mail but now widely used in network applications, including SOAP.

multitasking   Process by which an operating system runs or appears to be running more than one program simultaneously.

multithreading   Characteristic of a runtime environment that executes multiple independent paths (threads) within a program, allowing each thread access to the entire program's main memory and resources.

MVC   *See* Model-View-Controller.

namespace   1. Complete set of class and method names and other program items that the Java compiler tracks to identify an item uniquely. 2. A way to resolve naming conflicts between elements from different vocabularies in an XML document.

NaN   *See* Not a Number.

***narrowing conversion* (primitives)**   Java process of converting one primitive type to another primitive type that might lose information; for example, the conversion of int to byte eliminates extra bits.

***narrowing conversion* (reference type)**   Java process of converting a reference type to a subclass, for example, a conversion from Object to String.

NEGATIVE_INFINITY   Java constant defined in the Float and Double classes that results from the floating-point division of a negative floating-point primitive by zero.

nested top-level inner class or interface   Java inner class that's declared static and handled in the same way as any other Java outer class.

new   Java keyword indicating the creation of a new object or array.

NORM_PRIORITY   Java Thread class constant.

Not a Number (NaN)   Java special floating-point constant that denotes results of arithmetical operations, such as taking the square root of a negative number, that don't have a correct numerical representation; defined in the Float and Double classes.

notify   Java Object class method that causes a Thread on the object's wait list to become runnable; Thread does not run until allowed to do so by the JVM scheduling mechanism.

notifyAll   Similar to notify but causes all Threads on the object's wait list to become runnable.

null   Java special literal value that is used for the value of an uninitialized reference variable.

object   A class instance.

***Observable* (class)**   Java class (`java.util`
`.Observable`) that supplies basic methods or
procedures for adding and notifying objects that
implement the `Observer` interface; in `Observer`-
`Observable` design pattern, object whose change
in state is of interest to an `Observer`.

***Observer* (interface)**   Java interface (`java`
`.util.Observer`) that designates the `update`
method used by `Observable` objects in notifying
`Observer` objects.

***OutputStream* (class)**   Java `abstract` base class
(`java.io.OutputStream`) for classes that write
data as a stream of bytes.

overloading   A Java class containing multiple
methods with the same name but different parameter lists; called *overloading the method name.*

overriding   A subclass method supercedes (overrides) a superclass method with the same return
type and signature as a method.

package   Collection of associated Java classes and
interfaces organized into distinct namespaces.

parent   In a hierarchical system, any class that is
the ancestor of another class.

path separator   Character that separates paths in a
list, as in the Windows environment variable
PATH. The `File` class supplies the `pathSeparator`
`String` appropriate to a given environment.

peer   An operating system GUI object that corresponds to some Java AWT object.

pixel (picture element)   Smallest visible addressable unit on a monitor or other output device
and used in Java to define size and location of
screen and image operations.

pointer   A C programming language mechanism that provides indirect access to objects and
variables; not available in Java.

polymorphic   An object's capacity to have multiple identities, based on the object's interfaces,
inheritance, and overloaded methods.

port address   On computer networks based on
TCP/IP, the socket identifier at a given network
address for which a program or a service looks.

POSITIVE_INFINITY   Java constant defined in
the `Float` and `Double` classes that results from
floating-point division of a positive floating-
point primitive by zero.

primary container   A `Swing` object that has an
operating system peer and that can support an
independent window.

primitive   Java types (`boolean`, `char`, `byte`,
`short`, `int`, `long`, `float`, and `double`) that are
stored and accessed directly in binary form.

priority   Value from 1 to 10 that is assigned to
`Threads` and that the JVM uses in determining
which `Thread` is to run next.

private   Java keyword used to tag variables and
methods that can be accessed only by methods
declared within the same class.

promotion   Compiler process that uses widening
conversion of a number to a type a particular
operation requires.

protected   Keyword used to tag variables and
methods that can be accessed only by methods
of classes in the same package or by methods of
classes for which that class is the superclass.

protocol   Rules that govern a transaction or data transmission between devices.

public   Java keyword for modifying visibility of classes and members, making them accessible by all objects, regardless of package boundaries.

random access   The ability of a programmer to move a file pointer to any point in a file and begin reading or writing at that point.

***Reader* (class)**   Java `abstract` base class (`java.io.Reader`) for classes that read data as a stream of 16-bit Unicode characters.

reference   In Java, the process handled by the JVM by which a programmer works a "pointer" to an object (object reference) rather than directly with an object's physical memory address.

reference variable   All Java variables with the exception of primitives.

Reflection API   Java API comprised of classes that enable a program to ascertain the constructors, methods, and variables available in any class, as well as the interface the class implements.

Remote Method Invocation (RMI)   Java communications standard for distributed computing that allows a Java program to execute a method on an object that resides on another system or JVM as if it were a local object. RMI is a core technology for J2EE-based servers.

remote procedure call (RPC)   The general term for executing a method on an application that resides on another system by means of some communication protocol.

resume   Java `Thread` instance method (deprecated) that allows continuation of a suspended `Thread`.

RMI   *See* Remote Method Invocation.

RPC   *See* remote procedure call.

root   The one item or object from which all others descend in a hierarchical system.

Runnable   Java interface (`java.lang.Runnable`) that defines the `Threads run` method.

RuntimeException   Java class (`java.lang .RuntimeException`) that is the parent class of every exception that doesn't require declaration in a method `throws` clause.

SAX   *See* Simplified API for XML.

schema   A formal specification of the structure of an XML document.

scope   The identifier attribute that controls the identifier's accessibility to other parts of a program.

semantic event   An event that includes additional logic; contrasted with low-level event.

serialize   To convert a Java primitive value or object into a byte stream or character stream that is formatted in a way that allows reconstruction of the primitive value or object on the other end of a communication link.

server   Network computer that supplies resources and services to client computers.

servlet   Java program that runs in a servlet container on a web server and processes network requests (typically http requests).

servlet container   The environment in which a servlet runs. The servlet API defines a number of services that a servlet container must provide.

session   In servlet and JSP applications, a session maintains information about a user during the course of interaction with an application.

Set (interface)   Java interface (java.util.Set) that is an extension of the Collection interface that holds object references and that is restricted so as to prevent duplication of references; hence, every reference is unique.

SGML   *See* Standard Generalized Markup Language.

shallow copy   Copy produced by the clone method in the Object class that copies only the values of reference variables.

short   Java 16-bit integer primitive variable type; always treated as signed integer.

Short (class)   Java wrapper class for short values.

sign bit   Most significant bit in the Java byte, short, int, and long primitives, which, when turned on, causes a number to be interpreted as negative.

signature   Java method's name along with the type and order of parameters in its argument list.

Simple Object Access Protocol (SOAP)   A standard way to transmit messages over networks using XML-formatted documents. The words "Object Access" are there to indicate that SOAP lends itself to object-oriented programming, typically in remote procedure calls (RPCs).

Simplified API for XML (SAX)   An approach to processing XML documents in which the parser identifies and parses elements as it encounters them in a single pass through the document. The user of SAX must provide methods to process the parsed elements.

singleton   Design pattern that allows the creation of only one instance of a class; a static class method controls access to the instance.

sleep   Java static method of the Thread class, which when called, causes the calling Thread to sleep for a specified number of milliseconds.

SOAP   *See* Simple Object Access Protocol.

socket   On computer networks, the combination of a computer address and a port number that provides a unique channel of communications.

Socket (class)   Java class object (java.net .Socket) representing a single network socket connection; can supply an InputStream and OutputStream for communication.

SortedSet (interface)   Java interface, an extension of Set, which maintains references in a sorting order determined by the compareTo method.

SQL   *See* Structured Query Language.

stack trace   Formatted text output that can provide the history of a Thread's execution of a method that throws an exception or results in an error.

Standard Generalized Markup Language (SGML)   A standard for annotating text documents with tags that expresses the structure of the document and how the content should be treated. SGML served as the basis for HTML and XML.

static Java method or variable tag that indicates the variable or method belongs to a class, rather than to a class instance.

static fields Member fields of a Java class attached to the class itself, as opposed to fields attached to class instances.

static methods Member methods of a Java class that execute in the environment of the class rather than a particular class instance.

stop Java `Thread` instance method (deprecated) that causes a `ThreadDeath` exception and brings a `Thread` to an abrupt halt, often with unpredictable and unwanted results.

stream A sequence (stream) of bytes that can be read only in sequence from start to finish.

Structured Query Language (SQL) A standard for creating and accessing the contents of relational databases via text statements.

subclass Class that extends (indirectly or directly) another class; all Java classes (except `Object`) are subclasses of the `Object` class.

super Java keyword that refers to parent class variables, methods, or constructors.

superclass In Java class hierarchy, ancestor of a class; the immediate ancestor is the direct superclass. *See also* `extends`, parent.

suspend Java `Thread` instance method (deprecated) that stops a `Thread` until the `resume` method is called.

Swing Set of advanced Java interface components that are improvements on original AWT components; standard extensions for Java 2.

synchronized Java keyword that activates a method's or code block's monitor mechanism.

syntax Explicit rules for constructing code statements, including particular values and the order or placement of symbols.

System (Class) Java class (`java.lang.System`) composed of `static` methods and variables that the JVM initializes when a program starts.

tag In markup languages such as HTML, XML, and JSP pages, a tag is a special character sequence that is not part of the document text but defines additional information.

taglib In JSP technology, a programmer can define his own library of special-purpose Java functions identified by tags. A special `taglib` directive tells JSP to use a particular library.

TCP/IP *See* Transmission Control Protocol/Internet Protocol.

Thread (class) Java class (`java.lang.Thread`) that encloses a single thread of control in the JVM and defines its behavior.

ThreadDeath Special type of error that brings a `Thread` to a stop.

ThreadGroup (class) Java class (`java.lang.ThreadGroup`), the objects of which are used by the JVM to define a set of `Thread` objects and to govern operations on the set.

throw A Java statement that causes normal statement processing to halt and starts processing of an exception; must be associated with a `Throwable` object.

***Throwable* (class)**   Java class (`java.lang`
`.Throwable`) that is the parent class of every
Java exception and error class.

throws   Java keyword that is employed in
method declarations to introduce a list of the
exceptions that method can throw.

timestamp   Java `long` primitive variable that
holds the system time for an event's occurrence.

toString   Method possessed by all Java reference types that the compiler uses to evaluate
statements that include `String` objects and the `+`
operator.

**Transmission Control Protocol/Internet Protocol
(TCP/IP)**   Suite of communications protocols
developed to support mixed network environments, such as the Internet.

try   Java statement that constructs a code block
in which an exception can occur; must be followed by at least one associated `catch` clause
and/or a `finally` clause.

type   A Java object's class or interface. In
object-oriented programming in general, an
object's interface is sometimes considered separately from its implementation, resulting in a
further division into class and type.

UDDI   *See* Universal Description, Discovery,
and Integration.

UDP   *See* User Datagram Protocol.

UML   *See* Unified Modeling Language.

unary   Java operators, such as `++`, that affect one
operand.

unchecked exceptions   Exceptions descending
from `RuntimeException` for which the compiler
doesn't require a programmer to provide
explicit handling code.

Unicode   International ANSI 16-bit standard
for the representation of alphabets (includes
over 65,000 characters, including graphics). Java
uses the 2.0 version of Unicode (`http://www`
`.unicode.org`).

Unified Modeling Language (UML)   A standard
notation for drawing object-oriented designs.

Uniform Resource Identifier   The generic set of
all names and addresses that refer to resources.

Uniform Resource Locator   The set of URI
schemes that contains explicit instructions on
how to access a resource on the Internet.

**Universal Description, Discovery, and Integration
(UDDI)**   The proposed standard for a registry
and API used in locating services on the web
(`www.uddi.org`).

URI   *See* Uniform Resource Identifier.

URL   *See* Uniform Resource Locator.

***URL* (class)**   Java class (`java.net.URL`) that rep-
resents a Uniform Resource Locator for a web
server.

User Datagram Protocol (UDP)   A connectionless
packet communication protocol (alternative to
TCP/IP) for simple communication among
programs; considered unreliable because a
packet can be lost completely.

user Thread   Any Java `Thread` that has not been
tagged as a daemon.

Valid XML XML that conforms to the vocabulary specified in a DTD or schema.

variable shadowing Java variables in the same scope that can prevent direct access to other variables that have the same identifier.

***Vector* (class)** Java class (`java.util.Vector`) object that comprises extensible array of `Object` references.

view Java command that creates a specific model data display in the Model-View-Controller design pattern.

viewport Logical window in which part of the Java `JViewPort` view object is viewable.

visibility Level of access a Java class grants to other Java classes.

W3C *See* World Wide Web Consortium.

wait Java `Object` class method that, when called by a `Thread`, releases the `Thread`'s lock on the object, causes the `Thread` to become inactive, and places the `Thread` on the object's wait list.

wait list List of Java `Threads` that are attached to a particular object and waiting for notification, also known as a wait set.

wait set *See* wait list.

Web application A collection of servlets, JSP pages, HTML files, image files, and other resources that exist in a structured hierarchy of directories on a server.

Web Application Resource (WAR) A collection of all files needed to create a web application in a single file using the Zip compression algorithm. Specified in the servlet 2.2 API.

Web Services Descriptive Language (WSDL) The proposed XML-based system for describing a network service in detail sufficient to permit automated creation of a client to use the service.

well-formed XML XML markup that meets the requirements of the W3C Recommendation for XML 1.0.

widening conversions Primitive types conversions that do not lose magnitude information or reference types conversions from a subclass to a class located higher in the class hierarchy.

Wireless Markup Language (WML) A simplified variant of HTML designed for small wireless device displays.

World Wide Web Consortium (W3C) The organization that creates standards for the web (`www.w3.org`).

wrapper classes Java classes that correspond to each of the primitive types, providing related utility functions.

***Writer* (class)** Java `abstract` base class (`java.io.Writer`) of classes that writes data as a stream of 16-bit characters.

WSDL *See* Web Services Descriptive Language.

XML *See* Extensible Markup Language.

XMLP Title of the XML Protocol project at the W3C that has taken over development of SOAP standards.

XSL *See* Extensible Stylesheet Language.

Index

Note to the Reader: Throughout this index **bolded** page references indicate main discussion of a topic and definitions. *Italicized* references indicate illustrations.

The quotation on the bottom of the front cover is taken from the forty-seventh chapter of Lao Tzu's Tao Te Ching, the classic work of Taoist philosophy. These particular verses are from the translation by D. C. Lau (copyright 1963) and communicate the larger vision of the sage who has attained wisdom.

It is traditionally held that Lao Tzu lived in the fifth century B.C. in China, but it is unclear whether he was actually a historical figure. The concepts embodied in the Tao Te Ching influenced religious thinking in the Far East, including Zen Buddhism in Japan. Many in the West, however, have wrongly understood the Tao Te Ching to be primarily a mystical work; in fact, much of the advice in the book is grounded in a practical moral philosophy governing personal conduct.